T0301640

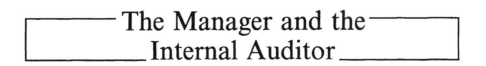

The Manager and the Internal Auditor

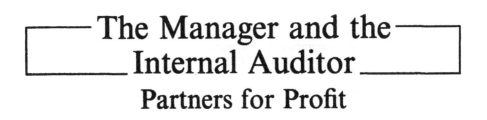

The Manager and the Internal Auditor
Partners for Profit

Lawrence B. Sawyer and Gerald Vinten

John Wiley and Sons
Chichester · New York · Brisbane · Toronto · Singapore

Copyright © 1979 by Lawrence B. Sawyer
Copyright © 1996 by Lawrence B. Sawyer and Gerald Vinten
Published 1996 by John Wiley & Sons Ltd,
                    Baffins Lane, Chichester,
                    West Sussex PO19 1UD, England

                    National   01243 779777
                    International   (+44) 1243 779777

Other Wiley Editorial Offices

John Wiley & Sons, Inc., 605 Third Avenue,
New York, NY 10158-0012, USA

Jacaranda Wiley Ltd, 33 Park Road, Milton,
Queensland 4064, Australia

John Wiley & Sons (Canada) Ltd, 22 Worcester Road,
Rexdale, Ontario M9W 1L1, Canada

John Wiley & Sons (Asia) Pte Ltd, 2 Clementi Loop #02-01
Jin Xing Distripark, Singapore 0512

Library of Congress Cataloging-in-Publication Data

Sawyer, Lawrence B.
   The manager and the internal auditor : partners for profit / by
   Lawrence B. Sawyer and Gerald Vinten
       p. cm.
   Rev. ed. of: The manager and the modern internal auditor
   / Lawrence B. Sawyer. 1979.
   Includes bibliographical references and index.
   ISBN 0-471-96117-5 (cloth)
   1. Management. 2. Auditing, Internal. I. Sawyer, Lawrence B.
   II. Sawyer, Lawrence B. Manager and the modern internal auditor.
   III. Title.
   HD38.V52   1995
   658.4—dc20   95–31232
                                                                  CIP

British Library Cataloguing in Publication Data

A catalogue record for this book is available from the British Library

ISBN 0-471-96117-5

Typeset in 10/12pt Times by Vision Typesetting, Manchester

Printed and Bound by Antony Rowe Ltd, Eastbourne

Contents

Preface

The first edition of this book was published under the title *The Manager and the Modern Internal Auditor* by AMACOM in 1979. Since then both scientific management and professional internal auditing have undergone changes and expansions. This edition seeks to provide a more current look at both vocations, pointing out those aspects that are new, but retaining the basic philosophies that still persist. The book has been substantially revised and updated, with four chapters being entirely new

Internal auditors and managers have the same objective: the well-being and effectiveness of their organizations. To help achieve their objective, a special relationship must be created and maintained between them: a professional relationship. It must be one that is no different from that which exists between a lawyer and client.

The lawyer evaluates the client's problems, provides guidance and instruction, and recommends a course of action, but does not make decisions for the client. Internal auditors function in the same way. They must carry out responsibilities so that the manager will look upon them as counselor and problem-solving partner, not as adversary or an object of fear and distrust. And they must maintain that relationship despite the fact that, as internal auditors, they may ultimately report what they find to levels above the manager.

The lawyer who is not thoroughly acquainted with the client's business and its goals, functions, and operations cannot provide an able, professional service. And internal auditors who do not understand the functions, responsibilities, theories, and practices of management cannot ably assist and counsel managers.

One of the purposes of this book, therefore, is to explore the profession of management so as to show internal auditors how to enlarge their service to their organizations by expanding their own approach to internal auditing. The internal auditor will find that an understanding of management principles and good business practice will help further the highest aspiration: to be a part of executive management much as the organization's legal counsel is.

Identifying unsatisfactory conditions and making recommendations for improvement represent only two aspects of internal auditing. There are others. They include counseling those whose activities the auditors evaluate. And to carry out that responsibility, internal auditors must have thorough indoctrination in what management is all about. They must therefore have a working knowledge of the nature of management, the skills of management, and the process of management.

Both internal auditing and management are relatively young professions. Their flowering emerged in this century, which puts them in the budding stage, as professions go. And they are parallel functions. Indeed, they are symbiotic—relying on each other for life support of effectiveness. It is time that they understand each other.

This book also seeks to acquaint managers with internal auditors and to cement a partnership that can become an effective, productive working relationship in all kinds of organizations. There is a need to broadcast the essential nature of that relationship; for when it flourishes in an organization, both the individual managers and their people stand to gain.

Managers can gain through objective analyses of operations of all kinds, through professional appraisals of control systems and performance, through recommendations that are designed to improve operations and enhance profits, and through suggestions for establishing policies, installing procedures or tightening controls to reduce the possibility of errors, deviations from instructions, or intentional wrongdoing. Chiefly, they stand to gain through counsel on good business practices, the adherence to proven principles of management, and in the formulation of control self-assessments.

Moreover, there is useful information here for managers of small departments or small companies. The precepts directed toward internal auditors apply equally to such managers, who should be able to do for themselves what the internal auditor does for the managers of larger organizations.

This book brings together material on the principles of management that has been developed by respected writers and researchers. The focus has been on the relations between managers and internal auditors. But we have also sought to construct this book as a simply stated summary of management growth and principles for the following readers:

- All people concerned with management, as a brief indoctrination to or refresher course in the principles of management.
- Executive managers, to show what a topflight internal audit team can do for them and for subordinate managers.
- Audit committees of boards of directors, to show how objective information can be obtained about internal and operating controls and how those controls are functioning.
- Operating managers, to show that internal auditors can be a help and not a

carping hindrance.

- Working internal auditors, to show how the principles of management can be applied to their day-to-day jobs and to lay out a new dimension to their approach to internal auditing.
- Students of business administration, to show the inviting potentialities of the new and rewarding profession of internal auditing.
- Teachers of business administration, to point out hitherto little-known aspects of what many of them have regarded as merely a verification process.
- Candidates for the Certified Internal Auditing examination, and national equivalents such as the UK and Eire's MIIA (Member of the Institute of Internal Auditors). Management is prominent in new syllabuses.

The book is divided into three parts.

The first deals with the nature of internal auditing and of management. It is concerned with the development of internal auditing from the early beginnings, when internal auditors were employed chiefly to detect errors and fraud, up to the present management-oriented approach. It looks into the growth of management and at some of the people who developed the science of management. Finally, it explores management and management theories and shows how internal auditors deal with the various models of managers.

The second part of the book deals with the skills of management. It speaks of how managers and internal auditors deal with people and emphasizes the patterns of behavior that occur at all levels of an enterprise. It is concerned with decision making and problem solving; how managers make decisions and how internal auditors can help them by making sure they are supplied with the information they need for rational decision making. It deals with communications and the results of poor communication. It has to do with measuring and evaluating performance and the forms of measurement available to managers and internal auditors. Finally, it explores the scientific methods available to both managers and internal auditors to carry out their jobs with greater precision.

The third and last part deals with the process of management: planning, organizing, directing and controlling. It relates the process to both management and internal auditing. In Chapter 15, Controlling, it explores a new relationship that is forming: that between the internal auditor and the board of directors. Each part contains copious illustrations of areas of application, and the use of the index will enable a comprehensive picture to be built up of all major areas of an organization's operations and strategy, and the internal audit contribution thereto.

Beyond the initial chapters, chapters are divided into two parts. The first part deals with the principles of management. The second part deals with internal auditors' involvement with those principles—how they are providing assistance to management in those fields, and the opportunities to expand that assistance.

Dr Lawrence B Sawyer CIA, JD
Professor Gerald Vinten FIIA, LLD

PART I
Trends in Internal Auditing and Professional Management

1
Meeting a Management Need

In days past most managers obtained their data personally. They observed how their people performed, how their systems functioned and how their facilities operated. In today's expanding universe, managers, particularly senior managers, rarely have the time, the inclination, or the ability to gather those facts themselves.

Managers must turn to others. As they turn, they earnestly hope that the suppliers of data are competent, reliable, and utterly trustworthy, dedicated to assisting managers and bettering the enterprise. Fully meeting these criteria is a new breed of employees: modern internal auditors. They are a far cry from the stereotyped, green-eyeshaded accountants whose prime function was to assure the chief accountant that figures added up accurately and that nobody had sticky fingers in the till. Instead, the new breed is concerned with the broad spectrum of problems that face management, because modern internal auditors are an extension of management.

Internal auditors are professionals. They are often certified and have advanced degrees and they are oriented more toward principles of management than toward principles of accounting. Their *Standards for the Professional Practice of Internal Auditors* proclaim their objectives as being "to assist members of the organization in the effective discharge of their responsibilities."(1) Those members of the organization run the gamut from middle managers through senior officers to board members.

Professional internal auditors are equipped, and are generally given the authority, to evaluate any activity in the organization, both financial and operational. Virtually nothing is immune from their review. The purpose of these evaluations, according to the *Standards*, is to furnish managers with analyses, appraisals, recommendations, counsel, and information.

What enhances the usefulness of the evaluations is the utter faith that managers and board members can have in the integrity and usefulness of the information furnished. To that end, The Institute of Internal Auditors Code of Ethics provides that:

- "Internal Auditors shall have an obligation to exercise honesty, objectivity, and diligence in the performance of their duties and responsibilities."
- "Internal Auditors, in holding the trust of their employers, shall exhibit loyalty in all matters pertaining to the affairs of the employer or to whomever they may be rendering a service."(2)

Internal audit literature is rich with illustrations of the benefits managers have gained from internal audit valuations. Here are some explanations and examples, under the headings of the purposes set forth in the *Standards.*

ANALYSES AND APPRAISALS

Internal auditors, like professional accountants, are expert at breaking down any totality to determine its components and values. In addition, internal auditors can analyze an activity or a condition to determine its true nature. They can discover or uncover qualities, causes, effects, motives, or possibilities. All these provide managers with the bases for judgment and action. Here are two examples:

1. A company negotiated a leasehold agreement with a contractor who was to rent the completed building to the company. The rental payments were to be based on the contractor/landlord's total construction costs. Upon completion of the building, the landlord set forth the rentals to be paid and submitted a schedule of construction costs as evidence. Internal auditors analyzed the schedule and found that $1.8 million in planning and development costs did not meet the definition of "construction costs." The internal auditors presented their analyses to the company's managers and attorneys, and the result was a reduction in rentals that totaled close to $1 million.(3)

2. An internal auditor's company was to receive a percentage of certain liquid products captured by an operator's plant. The company engineer had negotiated the contract with the operator. The engineer used a computer model to determine the processing percentage. He assured the internal auditor of the propriety and reliability of the computer model, adding airily that the internal auditor was not an engineer and could not appraise the correctness of the percentages of the products the company received. Not to be deterred, the internal auditor analyzed the model, made a number of comparisons, and found some puzzling inadequacies. Pressing on, the internal auditor found that the samples used in the model were neither sufficient nor representative. Also, neither the engineer nor the operator could produce supporting data for the samples used. The net result of the internal auditor's appraisal was a refund of $1,000,000.(4)

RECOMMENDATIONS

Internal auditors help managers by reporting weaknesses in control and performance and in recommending improvements. Also, they have an obligation to pursue a continuing defect until it is corrected. This can make for unhappy relationships. Few people love critics or their recommendations for change. As Machiavelli observed:

> "It must be considered that there is nothing more difficult to carry out, nor more doubtful of success, nor more dangerous to handle, than to initiate a new order of things. For the reformers have enemies who profit by the old order, and only lukewarm defenders in all those who would profit by the new order."(5)

Nevertheless, needs must when the devil drives. For objectives must be met no matter what obstacles intervene, and if corrective action is needed for the betterment of the organization, it must be taken. Yet the methods of the old-fashioned internal auditor may do more harm than good. Even in a company which regards its internal auditors highly, those auditors who issue orders for change will receive little support and see even less corrective action. This is particularly true when the defects are of no great significance and where the recommendations are made abrasively. One corporate president had this to say about corrective action:

> "I run a high-tech company. One of my main concerns is attracting the right kind of management talent into my organization and keeping these people happy. I support my internal auditors and want them to do their job. But I don't appreciate it when they upset my managers unnecessarily."(6)

Professional internal auditors are fully aware of these traps and barriers. They make recommendations, it is true, but they know when to make them and how to make them. They do not wait until the audit report first presents the managers with the findings and the recommendations. They do not imply in their reports that the auditee/manager was guilty of a crime if there was none.

They do not seek to show senior managers how much wiser they are than the operating managers. On the contrary, they seek to make the manager look good, not bad, in the absence of pure ineptitude or wrongdoing. They discuss findings and recommendations during the course of the field work. They seek to come to an accommodation on the action to be taken. Then, in the audit report, after agreement has been reached, they give credit to the operating manager for having conceived and taken the corrective action.

Here are two examples of reporting a recommendation in a matter that required some organizational changes—a fertile ground for confrontation and rejection. The problem the internal auditors found was the loss of considerable income because of improper credit evaluations of customers. The basic cause was that the credit manager reported to the Vice President of Sales instead of to the Director of Financial Operations. The first example makes use of the "Thou shalt" method of presenting a recommendation:

> *We recommend that the credit manager be transferred from the office of the Vice President of Sales to the office of the Director of Financial Operations.*

Credit and sales have inconsistent goals. As a result, credit evaluations were often not objective, and losses therefrom totaled $XX XXX.

Now observe how the very same finding is dealt with by giving the credit for corrective action to the people responsible for the activity and showing corrective action as an accomplished fact instead of an ultimatum from the internal auditors:

Losses from sales to poor credit risks totaled $XXXXX in the last year.
Under the existing form of organization, the credit manager reports directly to the Vice President of Sales. As a result, credit evaluations of customers were not always objective, since credit and sales have different purposes. We discussed the matter with all concerned, and before our audit was completed an agreement was reached to transfer the credit manager to the Office of the Director of Financial Operations.

The first approach raises hackles and hostile confrontation that might involve the Chief Executive Officer. The second approach implies a problem-solving partnership where corrective action was amicably accomplished and the CEO had naught to do but nod agreeably. This is the kind of internal auditing which helps all managers from auditee to CEO.

COUNSEL

The newest form of assistance that professional internal auditors provide is to counsel managers and boards of directors on the solution of business problems. The assistance can take many different forms:

- It can provide a subtle education to managers on the principles of management.
- It can help managers in decision making by providing objective views on highly technical matters.
- It can evaluate ongoing programs to assess their potential success or to point out problems in meeting goals.

The list is almost endless, but a discussion of the three matters just enumerated will indicate the kind of counsel that can be invaluable to managers in an enterprise.

Principles of Management

Almost invariably the fundamental cause of every deficiency finding that internal auditors unearth is rooted in the violation of some basic principle of management. The finding itself may be corrected, but it will sprout again if the operating manager has learned nothing about the true cause. So it is the function of the professional internal auditor not only to correct the instant problem, but to improve the manager's ability to manage. Here is one example:

An audit of a storeroom in the Engineering Division disclosed a host of defects. Quantities of items in bins did not agree with those on the records. Many bins were unlabeled. Many items were overstocked; others were not available because they had not been ordered in time. Delicate items were stored improperly, causing extensive damage or loss. The list of defects went on and on.

True, the auditors discussed their findings with the operating manager as the audit proceeded, and corrective action was taken promptly. But they knew the problems would recur if some of the basic management practices were not improved. They therefore suggested to the manager that he perform a self-evaluation periodically instead of waiting for the internal auditors to do the evaluation for him. They recommended that he prepare check lists of proper storage procedures and have his three supervisors use them to make periodic tests of the stored supplies. They were to carry out the tests formally, recording their findings and correcting what needed improvement. Then they were to submit the completed lists to the manager for his review and approval. When the manager realized the obvious benefits to be obtained he adopted the plan enthusiastically.

The internal auditors followed up the corrective action about four months later. They found a vast improvement in storeroom practices and were able to write a highly complimentary audit report on their findings. The internal auditors had improved a system. They had educated a manager in hands-on supervision and self-evaluation. But above all, they had made a friend and helped the organization.

Decisions on Technical Matters

Business and government are getting more and more complicated. Decisions are often based on computer models and abstruse methods of quantification. Faced with decisions that call for such methodology, some senior managers may not be equipped to determine the reasonableness or the propriety of the models or the mathematics. It is then that they may turn to their professional internal auditors who are trained in such matters. Here is an actual example:

A budget manager had presented to a Vice President of Finance a new method of estimating overhead rates based on a computer model employing multiple regression analysis. The proponent of the new method presented it as being more accurate and a great deal less expensive and time-consuming than the old manual method.

But the Vice President was familiar and comfortable with the manual method; the new method was beyond his comprehension. There he was, on the horns of a dilemma, reluctant to approve something he did not fully understand, and just as reluctant to reject what might be revolutionary in estimating overhead rates. In desperation he called on the internal auditors.

The auditors found a comparable model in *Statistical Inference—Volume Three of the Mathematics for Management Series*.(7) It too used a computer and multiple regression analysis and it showed the complete input and results of the study. So the auditors cranked into the computer the input from the *Management Series* book, using the budget manager's program. In a few minutes the computer spewed out the results, but these did not agree with those of the budget manager. As a result, the budget manager was persuaded to go back to the drawing board. Sure enough he found a flaw in the programmed instructions. The flaw was corrected, and again the auditors cranked in the information. This time the results shown in the *Management Series* book and those of the budget manager agreed completely. Based on the audit findings and the auditors' counsel, the Vice President felt comfortable in accepting the new approach to estimating overhead rates.

Program Evaluation

Program evaluation is a relatively new technique which internal auditors perform but which is quite different from normal audit examinations. Yet it can be invaluable to senior managers and to their decision-making ability.

Auditing usually looks back over what was performed or over what systems were used. Program evaluation uses systematic research methods to assess policy or program design. The United States General Accounting Office has taken giant strides in the practice of program evaluation. It performs three kinds of evaluations for Congress:(8)

- Assessing a policy or program still in the design phase (e.g., informing congress whether enough evidence is available to support a particular policy on AIDS or a program for homeless people). In the private sector, the program might include the evaluation of a proposed acquisition and the form of management used there.
- Measuring program or policy implementation (e.g., identifying the quality of medical care given Medicaid patients or the initial results of efforts by states to establish enterprise zones). In the private sector, teams of internal auditors and technical consultants were assigned to follow the progress of producing two airplanes from the time the first parts and assemblies were put together to the time the aircraft were delivered to the customers.
- Establishing the actual effects achieved by a policy or program (e.g., determining the impact of "back-to-basics" education reforms on student performance or the effects of sewage treatment plants on water pollution). In the private sector, it could be the savings attributable to a data processing application as compared to what its proponents promised senior management.

Auditing is a process of objectively obtaining and evaluating evidence regarding assertions about economic and operating actions and events to ascertain the degree of correspondence between those assertions and established criteria. Program evaluation focuses more often on measuring what has occurred, estimating what could have happened without the program or policy, and comparing the two to determine program effects. These evaluations make use of scientific methods and models, often with assistance from experts borrowed from nonauditing fields—experts like mathematicians, engineers, and social scientists.

As an example of the differences between the two techniques, consider the question of whether students' performance had improved under a new program. An auditing approach compares what is with what should be. That is, if performance criteria call for a score of 8 and actual student performance was only 5, the review yields a result of -3 for the program. An evaluation approach works differently. The actual student performance was a score of 5; but without the program at all, the expected performance would be only 1. The actual achievement is then a +4. Much depends on what management or the government wants or needs.

Not only are results different under the two methods; practice is also different. For example:

- Auditing objectives must be pinned down specifically. Program evaluation seeks to determine what would have happened without the program.
- Auditing is aimed at determining specific deficits. Program evaluation is more generalized, looking for cause and effect.
- Auditing uses case studies and surveys. Program evaluation uses not only these but also experimental design and its variations, as well as such techniques as time series analyses.
- Auditing employs evidence that comes from authoritative sources and makes considerable use of documentation. Program evaluation relies heavily on structured interviews and questionnaires.
- Auditing tends to record data in a linear way. Program evaluation groups data to facilitate analysis and to permit eventual reuse of the data.
- Auditing tends to focus on individual cases, searching for critical events or discrepancies, although it may use statistical techniques when attacking large populations. Program evaluation often generates estimates of events or conditions based on principles of statistical probability.

As time goes on and professional internal auditors become more comfortable with operations research methods and with the integration of other disciplines in their audit teams, program evaluation will come into greater use. It can then serve its true purpose of making management more effective, more responsive to events, and more accountable.

INFORMATION

The lifeblood of an organization is information. The arterial channels leading to the organization's brains must carry information that is timely, reliable, and useful. Be the recipients operating managers, senior managers, or board members, they cannot perform their jobs effectively without the right kind of information. Internal auditors are in a position to supply facts, figures, and observations to people at all levels. The recipient need but ask, for the professional internal auditor is a gold mine of data which can be presented to meet any manager's or board member's needs. What follows is a brief summary of some of the information that can be supplied to these decision makers.

Operating Managers

The information supplied to operating managers usually conveys the results of audit reviews. If the auditee/managers are receptive they can obtain informal or formal briefings as the audit proceeds—briefings on both satisfactory and unsatisfactory controls and performance.

Accordingly, managers are in a position to discuss problems and their potential solutions, making use of the internal auditor's experience in similar situations.

At the conclusion of the field work, managers can receive an overview of what the audit disclosed together with an indication of what the final, formal audit report will contain. So the report need hold no surprises. Also, in many organizations reports are balanced, giving a recital of both the good and the bad. In that way, operating managers may be content that the report that reaches their superiors is not always a reciting of evils. They know that they will be given a pat on the back for jobs well done. As an example, here is an actual audit opinion which certainly made that manager's day:

> Based on the results of our review, we formed the opinion that adequate controls had been provided over the activities of the Procurement Services Department. We also formed the opinion that the controls were working effectively and efficiently. We considered this department to be highly effective in accomplishing its assigned mission. We believe this can be attributed to motivated and knowledgeable supervision and key personnel; good communication and feedback between management and subordinates; thorough on-the-job training of the individual employee, reinforced by a rotation assignment policy; up-to-date comprehensive job instructions; constant vigilance on the part of supervision and alternates to monitor workload schedules and performance and to minimize errors; good rapport and loyalty between the manager and the group supervisors; and the participation of the manager and her supervisors in arriving at management decisions.

Where the results of the audit warrant—supported by confirmation from peripheral organizations, as insurance—such statements of opinion can do much to create the desired problem-solving partnership between auditor and auditee. Such rapport will influence the auditees to see the audit as a joint venture in which management problems are aired, reviewed, and sought to be corrected.

Senior Management

Internal auditors in many organizations are the Chief Executive Officer's follow-up system and designated sceptic. They can be a source of comfort because they have learned what the CEO wants and needs and they can be a fountainhead of completely reliable information.

The CEO relies on the internal auditors to ask the same questions that the CEO would ask. For example: Is this department or activity doing what management expects? Is this system delivering the required productivity and efficiency? Is the total organization more effective because of these departments, activities, or systems? Is there a better way of doing this particular thing? Is the CEO told promptly of actual or potential problems? Or is the CEO being misled about the true nature of things? What is the enterprise's rate of success in achieving its desired growth and its fiscal goals?

CEOs make their decisions on the basis of reports. Hence, they must be able to trust them. The professional internal auditor will generally have a list of all top-level reports on which the CEO relies. These are allocated to programmed audits and reviewed along with other auditable matters. In reviewing those reports the professional will evaluate them to determine whether they are understandable, reliable, relevant, timely, consistent, and comparable. Internal auditors will seek to determine not only whether the reports can be relied upon but also whether they are needed at all.

Internal auditors can be helpful to senior management in a myriad of ways. Here are some, selected at random:

- They can be useful in reviewing risk management. In one instance an auditor observed that insurance policies were being bid by the same three insurance companies over a long period. He suggested to senior management that other insurance companies be asked to bid; as a result millions were saved.(9)
- In this age of almost complete reliance on the computer, the CEO would most certainly look to the internal auditors to review contingency plans to help recover from computer disasters.
- Internal auditors can provide continuing information on the health of the organization. One form is the executive summary attached to audit reports. These are one-page summaries of what the auditors reviewed; general opinions about what they examined, putting both findings and opinions in perspective; and a summary of the most serious defects along with what is being done or proposed to correct them. Another form of information on the health of the organization is the periodic activity report which points up the audits made, summaries of audit opinions, audit findings still open, and an overview of how well the organization is being administered.

What stands out in all these matters is the fact that the CEO can rely on the internal auditors to tell the truth, the relevant truth, and the significant truth at all times.

The Board Audit Committee

One chairman of a board of directors said:

"The relationship between the board of directors and the internal auditor is among the most crucial in today's business world . . . You have heard it said that it's lonely at the top. It is. We often find ourselves isolated from daily operations. That is why we turn to our internal auditors."(10)

In the United States, the Securities and Exchange Commission in 1972 endorsed the establishment by all publicly held companies of audit committees composed of outside directors. Canada had made moves slightly earlier. There is no legal requirement for audit committees in the United Kingdom, with a preference for voluntary action. However, there are influential voices raised in favor of the audit committee. These include the Institute of Directors, the Bank of England, the Stock Exchange, the Confederation of British Industry, the Institute of Management, and a specially constituted group, PRO NED, which stands for Promotion of Non-Executive Directors, and was started in 1982.(11) Audit committees are increasingly common in larger organizations in the UK, and during the 1980s this came to include the public sector and by the 1990s charities joined the trend.(12) The Cadbury Committee, referred to elsewhere, has been a major impetus in furthering the use of the audit committee, and other instruments of corporate governance, and the Cadbury model is now being assumed in many other countries. The US President's Blue Ribbon Commission on Defense Management (Packard Commission) in 1986, and the Commission on Fraudulent Financial Reporting (Treadway Commission) in 1987, proposed that audit committees assume broadly expanded oversight responsibilities, as did its sequel in 1991.(13)

Beleaguered board members, subject to legal action for failing to carry out their responsibilities, desperately reach out for reliable information. Here is some of the information internal auditors can provide audit committees:

- Potential law suits against the enterprise.
- The reliability and integrity of the management information system.
- Compliance with standards of conduct within the organization and appraisal of the controls designed to bring to light the possibility of intentional wrongdoing, errors and omissions, inefficiency, waste, ineffectiveness and conflicts of interest.
- The variances between capital budgets and actual costs and whether approved capital expenditures produced the results expected.
- Determination on whether audited entities are meeting their objectives and goals.
- Company background data. Properly designed, summaries of internal audit reports can provide information on the functioning of the enterprise.
- The fraud, thefts, and defalcation attempted against the enterprise; how they were disposed of; what were the losses; what litigation has taken place; and which of the operating areas are most vulnerable to loss, misappropriation of assets, misstatements of financial conditions and the like.
- The internal auditors' opinion of the external auditors.

CONCLUSION

Professional internal auditors assume a key role in assisting all members of management and the board in accomplishing their assigned duties. At each level, operating managers, senior managers, and board members have a need for vital information to help in the decision-making process. Today's internal auditors can supply that information. Of special significance is the reliance that can be placed on it and on the auditors' competence to evaluate the most complex matters.

Internal auditors can offer management comfort unavailable from any other people in the enterprise. Instead of enduring the old-style tick and turn, toter and tester, managers can welcome professional internal auditors as problem-solving partners of the top management team.

The next chapter considers the internal auditor as management assistant, and how the auditor aspires to meet the reality rather than the mythology of the managerial situation.

REFERENCES

(1) *Standards for the Professional Practice of Internal Auditors* (Altamonte Springs, Florida: The Institute of Internal Auditors, 1978), Introduction, p. 1.
(2) *The Institute of Internal Auditors Code of Ethics* (Altamonte Springs, Florida: The Institute of Internal Auditors 1988.
(3) "The Round Table," *The Internal Auditor*, April, 1990, p. 75.
(4) "The Round Table," February 1990, p. 6..
(5) Nicolo Machiavelli, *The Prince*, Luigi Ricci (New York: Random House, 1940), p. 21.
(6) Gil Courtemanche, *Audit Management and Supervision* (New York: John Wiley and Sons, (1989), p. 98.
(7) C.H. Springer, R.E. Herlihy, R.T. Mall, R.I. Beggs, *Statistical Inference—Volume Three of the Mathematics for Management Series* (Homewood, Illinois: Richard D. Irwin, Inc., 1966), p. 39ff.
(8) Eleanor Chelimsky, "Expanding GAO's Capabilities in Program Evaluation, *The GAO Journal*, Winter/Spring 1990, p. 43.
(9) W.C. Westmoreland, "Contributing to the Bottom Line," *The Internal Auditor,* April, 1987, p. 55.
(10) J.D. Williams, "The Board of Directors" Reliance on the Internal Auditor," *The Internal Auditor*, August 1988, p. 31.
(11) A.D. Chambers, G.M. Selim and G. Vinten, "Internal Auditing," Commercial Clearing House, Chicago, and Pitman, London, 1987 pp. 277–290.
(12) G. Vinten and C. Lee, "Audit Committees and Corporate Control," *Managerial Auditing Journal* Vol. 8 No. 3, 1993, pp. 11–24.
(13) Committee of Sponsoring Organizations of the Treadway Commission, "Internal Control–Integrated Framework," 1991, 1211 Avenue of the Americas, 6th floor, New York, N.Y. 10036–8775.

2
The Internal Auditor: Management Assistant

The introduction to the Standards for the Professional Practice of Internal Auditing makes it clear that audit is a service to the organization.(1) This represented a change from the preceding Statement of Responsibilities which spoke of a service to management.(2) For this reason the Statement had to be amended to bring it into alignment with the Standards. Since, however, the introduction also states that the members of the organization to be assisted by internal auditing include those in management and the board of directors, the service to management is by no means neglected, and is likely to represent the larger portion of the auditor's activity. The Statements on Internal Audit Practice–Public Sector of the Chartered Institute of Public Finance and Accountancy propose that audit provides a service to all levels of management.(3) The Auditing Guideline *Guidance for Internal Auditors* which replaced it makes the extension to the organization by stating that:

"Internal audit is an independent appraisal function established by the management of an organization for the review of the internal control system as a service to the organization."(4)

The Government Internal Audit Manual defines audit as a service to management.(5) The needs of managers have increasingly been presented to internal auditors, and this development reaches its peak in the present text which is exclusively devoted to this theme. Brink and Witt have given increasing emphasis to this aspect in the successive editions of their text, devoting an early chapter to "Understanding Management Needs" (Chapter 3), and considering that service to management remains the controlling mission of the internal auditor.(6)

In order to assist managers it is necessary to have a reasonable notion as to what a manager is and does. One of the reasons for the lack of implementation of audit recommendations, not to mention the hostility engendered by the audit process, is that auditors fail to appreciate the exact nature of the managerial role and tasks. It is also true that managers, apart from being the object of audit reports, also become the subject. Leo Herbert has discussed this aspect of the audit process.(7) Whether as object or subject of the audit report it is equally important to understand the management process from the inside.

Mintzberg bases his conclusions on a synthesis of his own and others' research.(8) His own study involved five American Chief Executive Officers of middle-to-large-sized organizations—a consulting firm, a technology company, a hospital, a consumer goods company and a school system. For one intensive week he observed each executive, recording aspects of every piece of mail, incoming and outgoing, and of every verbal contact. The other studies included executives maintaining detailed diary logs of activities; an "anthropological" approach with the researcher moving freely within a company, collecting whatever appeared to be significant; studies of the American presidency, foremen and hospital top executives, and a study of street gang leaders which showed surprising similarities to the characteristics of corporate managers.

Striking similarities emerged as to the true nature of managerial activity. This was very different from what many managers imagine they do. They normally express their role as being to plan, organize, co-ordinate and control. These four words have dominated thinking about management ever since the French industrialist Henri Fayol introduced them in 1916. Yet this classical view of management activity was found to be both unhelpful and misleading. This finding is profoundly disturbing. It is disturbing generally since it suggests that management information systems may have been wrongly designed for an image of management need that is a figment of the imagination. Similarly, management education and other support services to managers may have been ill-conceived. It is disturbing specifically to the auditor, as one form of support service, since it suggests that auditors may have been providing a service to management that is either unwanted or even counterproductive. This is especially the case since the major internal audit texts, Brink and Witt, Sawyer, and Chambers, all mention the classical view as their primary management orientation.(6)(9)(10) It is interesting that the new editions of these texts—Sawyer and Sumners, and Chambers, Selim and Vinten—present a much more rounded view of the range of management theory.(11),(12) Not only that, but the very first Statement on Internal Auditing Standards, published by the Institute of Internal Auditors in December 1983 and concerned with "Control: Concepts and Responsibilities," commits the Internal Auditing Standards to the classical view by its constant and repetitive harping on the terms "planning, organizing and directing." Without the SIAS the standards were neutral as between the different schools of management theory, but now the dice are heavily loaded. A City University MSc dissertation by Nick Sibley provides a full and trenchant critique of the SIAS.(13)

It is time to examine the myths and facts about the manager's job and to see whether audit practice needs to be modified to align itself with the facts rather than the folklore.

- *Folklore 1:* The manager is a reflective, systematic planner.
- *Fact 1:* Managers work at an unrelenting pace, their activities are characterized by brevity, variety and discontinuity, and they are strongly oriented to action and dislike reflective activities.

The evidence on this was overwhelming. A diary study of 160 British middle and top managers found that they worked for half an hour or more without interruption only about once every two days. Of the activities of the five chief executives in Mintzberg's research, half lasted less than nine minutes, and only 10% exceeded one hour. A study of 56 American foremen discovered an average of 583 activities per eight-hour shift, that is one every 48 seconds. The manager, then, is a real-time responder who prefers live to delayed action.

- *Folklore 2:* The effective manager has no regular duties to perform.
- *Fact 2:* In addition to handling exceptions, managerial work involves performing a number of regular duties, including ritual and ceremony, negotiations and processing of soft information that links the organization with its environment.

These duties include presenting gold watches, seeing visitors so that everyone else can get on with their work, and passing on "soft" information, only available to them because of their status, to their subordinates.

- *Folklore 3:* Senior managers need aggregated information, which a formal management system best provides.
- *Fact 3:* Managers strongly favor the verbal media—telephone calls and meetings.

Managers ignore much of what comes to them as part of a budgetary or management information system. Mail was considered a burden to be dispensed with, one chief executive working through 142 pieces in just three hours. Only 13% was of specific and immediate use. Only two out of 40 routine reports received over a five-week period received an immediate response. "Soft" information, such as gossip, hearsay and speculation, was preferred, since these provided timely and useful information on customers, competitors and other matters that could be translated into rapid action.

Managers write down little of what they hear, and their heads are the computerized databank on which the organization runs. They are therefore reluctant to delegate since they would need to spend so much time briefing subordinates that they prefer to undertake tasks themselves.

- *Folklore 4:* Management is, or is quickly becoming, a science and a profession.

- Fact 4: The managers' programmes—to schedule time, process information, make decisions and so on—remain locked deep inside their brains.

Management is too unsystematic to make it a science, and its knowledge base is too uncertain to call it a profession.

AUDIT IMPLICATIONS

It is plain that these research results overthrow many of the cosy working assumptions of the auditor. It explains why auditors and their reports may be greeted with nonchalance if not downright hostility. If a discursive audit report is not perceived as being of immediate relevance to a manager then it will not be one of the "two out of 40" reports to be given red carpet treatment. In an operating division of one organization, audit reports were popularly known as "books." Since managers have no time to devote to reading them they were welcomed with the exasperated irony of "Oh no, here comes another book!" In addition managers do not have the same control orientation as does the auditor, and may see auditors as an obstruction to the pursuit of their proper duties.

Even more worrying is that, far from helping, the auditor may add to the considerable pressure and stress that managers frequently experience. An audit report that is difficult for a manager to deal with may lead to both quantitative and qualitative work overload. Quantitative overload means having "too much to do," and occurs if an audit report recommends management action that is cumbersome or difficult to implement, or involves a manager in protracted negotiations, such as with trade unions. Qualitative overload refers to work that is "too difficult." Audit reports have an unfortunate reputation in some quarters for mentioning everything that is wrong with no helpful suggestions as to any recommended courses of action, on the mistaken basis that to recommend anything undermines audit objectivity when the area is reviewed in the future. Alternatively, reports may be full of audit or accountancy jargon that managers find difficult to understand.

The British Health Education Authority has not yet issued a poster bearing the slogan "Audit may ruin a manager's health," and audit reports do not need to carry a Government health warning! The effect of overload in most systems, whether mechanical or human, is breakdown. Overload is strongly linked to cigarette smoking, which is an important risk factor with coronary heart disease. It is also significantly related to a number of symptoms or indicators of stress: escapist drinking, absenteeism from work, low motivation to work, lowered self-esteem, and an absence of positive suggestions to employers. In medical terms there result abnormal electro-cardiographic readings, raised diastolic blood pressure, increased serum cholesterol levels, and abnormal pulse rates—all associated with coronary heart disease and other medical conditions. Unhelpful criticism is identified in the research as adding to work pressure. Cooper and Payne's symposium on the subject suggests that "it is important to try and encourage organisations to be sensitive to the needs of their managers and begin to audit managerial distress."(14)

SIAS 1—A SERIOUS DISTORTION?

The first Statement on Internal Auditing Standards (Control: Concepts and Responsibilities) makes much of the classical view of management, with planning, organizing and directing appearing as the central activities of the manager. The question is whether, in the light of Mintzberg's research, this represents a serious distortion. There can be no doubt of the need for planning, organizing, directing and control within organizations. The distortion arises if it is considered that managerial activity can be neatly compartmentalized in these three or four divisions, and that this is all the auditor needs to understand about a manager to offer help and assistance. In reality these three or four activities often overlap, and are somehow in the midst of the manager's frenetic life, rather than being easily separately identifiable.

There are some managers who are more inclined than others to adopt this planning, organization, directing and controlling orientation. This may be a matter of personal inclination, or connected with the post of the manager. Thus the corporate planning manager or the production controller or director of finance are likely to be more so oriented than the head of research and development or the marketing manager. There will also be a difference of viewpoint according to the level of management hierarchy occupied, with top management and the board of directors being the most preoccupied with these issues. However it is the supreme role and justification of internal audit that it seeks to ensure that this emphasis is not completely buried within the organization, and that somehow it emerges out of the disparate concerns of the organization's management. The Statement is therefore not necessarily a distortion, but it does need to be footnoted and read in the light of Mintzberg's research.

The Standards do offer some help, for they put constant emphasis on the co-operative and reciprocal partnership relationship between internal auditor and manager. Section 300.01 places the scope of audit work and activities within a general framework of management and board of directors approval. Section 300 concludes by emphasizing the primary responsibility of management for objectives, goals, and systems, but internal auditors assist by examining for the appropriateness of underlying assumptions, information, and suitable controls. In this close relationship management has ample opportunity to state if internal audit reports do not meet their requirements, and to bring influence to bear on the director of internal audit.

Section 400 goes into considerable detail to ensure that audits are well planned, expertly carried out, suitably communicated, and duly followed up. Thus under planning there is communication with all who need to know (410.4) and an on-site survey during which auditee comments are invited (410.5). Communication involves discussing conclusions and recommendations at appropriate levels of management before issuing final written reports (430.2), and incorporation of the auditees' views (430.6), and at the follow-up phase management and the board "sign off" audit reports on which they do not wish to take corrective action. The second Statement on Internal Auditing Standards (Communicating Results) also goes out of its way to suggest a product—the audit report—which will provide maximum benefit to the manager. Section 430.5 also makes the positive suggestion that satisfactory performance should be acknowledged, and the SIAS briefly elaborates on this.

Under section 430 and the SIAS advice is given that the report should be objective, clear, concise, constructive and timely (430.3). The SIAS defines concise as being to the point and avoiding unnecessary detail, thus expressing thoughts completely in the fewest possible words. It is also possible that an executive summary, or an index, could assist a manager to find a path through a longer report.

It is therefore concluded that audit reports do benefit managers. Since internal audit is rarely mandatory, its continued existence must be a token of its continuing usefulness. Auditors may fall into using the stereotype sometimes, but then auditors are charged to ensure that planning, organizing, directing and controlling are present within the organization in appropriate mix and balance. The Standards give considerable assistance, and if followed there should be no reason why the Mintzberg type manager should not experience assistance and reports relevant to the role which such a manager occupies.

CONCLUSION

Auditors whose sole orientation in assisting management is that of classical management thinking will only be of limited help. Indeed, exclusive emphasis on "planning, organizing, directing and controlling" may have dysfunctional consequences not only for the organization but for the health of the individual managers. Auditors need to become aware of all the ramifications of the management role. Only then will they truly fulfil the brief set for them in the Standards for the Professional Practice of Internal Auditing.

The next chapter considers how internal audit has developed over its history to meet the needs of managers, including dealing with wrongdoing.

REFERENCES

(1) Institute of Internal Auditors, *Standards for the Professional Practice of Internal Auditing*, 1979.

(2) Institute of Internal Auditors, *Statement of Responsibilities*, 1976, revised 1981.

(3) Chartered Institute of Public Finance & Accountancy, *Statements on Internal Audit Practice—Public Sector*, 1979.

(4) Auditing Practices Board, *Guidance for Internal Auditors, Auditing Guideline*, London, 1990.

(5) Her Majesty's Treasury, *Government Internal Audit Manual*, Her Majesty's Stationery Office, London, 1988.

(6) V. Z. Brink and H. Witt *Modern Internal Auditing*, 4th ed., Institute of Internal Auditors, 1982.

(7) L. Herbert, *Auditing the Performance of Management*, Lifetime Learning Publications, 1979.

(8) H. Mintzberg, "The Manager's Job: Folklore and Fact: *Harvard Business Review*, July–August, 1975, pp. 49–61.

(9) L. B. Sawyer, *The Practice of Modern Internal Auditing*, Institute of Internal Auditors, 1973.

(10) A. D. Chambers, *Internal Auditing*, Pitman, 1981.

(11) L. B. Sawyer, G. E. Sumners, "Sawyer's Internal Auditing," *The Practice of Modern Internal Auditing*, 2nd ed., Institute of Internal Auditors, 1988.

(12) A. D. Chambers, G. M. Selim, and G. Vinten, *Internal Auditing*, 2nd ed., Pitman, 1987.

(13) N. J. Sibley, "Auditing Managers," unpublished MSc dissertation, City University Business School, 1988.

(14) C. L. Cooper and R. Payne, (eds.), *Stress at Work*, Wiley, Chichester, 1978.

3
The Development of Modern Internal Auditing

ORIGINS

Modern internal auditing is a distinctive discipline. It is not the clone or sibling of public accounting or of the auditing of financial records or statements. It stands alone as an evolving profession, dedicated to assisting management in all matters which concern the enterprise.

This was not always so. It took a long time for internal auditing to achieve its present professional status. The broad field of auditing—both internal and external—is rooted in antiquity. According to early Mesopotamian records reaching back to 3600BC, scribes used to prepare summaries of financial transactions. These were separate from the lists of amounts handled and which others had prepared.(1)

Tiny marks, dots, and circles indicated the painstaking comparison of one record with another—marks that have survived the centuries and that auditors still use to tick off their verification of records. Thus there were born two control devices still used around the world: division of duties; provision for the review of another's work.

The Greeks, and the Romans after them, had an abiding regard for rigid control over finances. Their records give evidence of such controls as the authorization of transactions and the auditing of records. The suspicious Greeks preferred slaves to freemen as accountants. Their reasons had a brutal logic: they reckoned that a slave under torture could be relied upon to be more trustworthy than a freeman under oath.

With the development of paper and pen, transactions became easier to record and review. During the Roman empire, officials known as "quaestors" were assigned to examine the accounts of provincial governors. Later, toward the end of the Dark Ages, rulers wanted assurance that they would receive all revenues due. So they provided for the records of amounts due and received. Audits of these amounts were first made by barons and justices. Later they were made by specially appointed officials. Even Columbus, in 1492, was accompanied to America by an auditor representing Queen Isabella.

GROWTH

The auditing function, as we know it now, started during the Industrial Revolution. Many commercial and industrial organizations employed expert accountants to examine and certify the validity of their accounts. Auditing spread.

In the United States, the Comptroller General, head of the General Accounting Office, audits federal accounts and operations. He is responsible to the Congress and is independent of the executive branches he reviews. Most states and municipalities conduct audits through comptrollers' offices. Many others make use of independent accounting firms.

The General Accounting Office auditors have long performed so-called comprehensive audits in which they examine government operations for efficiency and economy and review program results for effectiveness. A number of city and state audit teams are following their lead. The Canadians have their Canadian Comprehensive Auditing Foundation, based in Ottawa, with an impact on both public and private sectors.

In most European countries there are government branches responsible for the review and appraisal of public accounts. In France it is the "cour des comptes". In Germany it is the "Rechnungshof des deutschen Reiches." In the British Isles the Exchequer and Audit Act of 1866 gave authority to the Crown to appoint a Comptroller and Auditor General to examine the accounts of the various government departments.

The concern throughout the ages, still widespread today, has been with matters financial. The term "internal auditor" has been equated with "accountant." Although as experts in accountancy internal auditors are strong and important adjuncts to management in reviewing financial records, they do not reach their true potential in that role. They have other and more significant things to do in order to serve managers fully. That, as we have seen in Chapter 1, is because managers have additional needs that must be met, and those needs gave rise to modern internal auditors.

DEFINITIONS

How do we define this new role for auditors? Many attempts have been made to encapsulate the meaning of this new profession. We shall quote three of them.

The first is the definition included in the *Standards for the Professional Practice of Internal Auditing.* While adequate for an introduction to the *Standards,* it is something less than sufficiently descriptive of the profession:

1. Internal auditing is an independent appraisal function established within an organization to examine and evaluate its activities as a service to the organization.(2)

The second definition advanced by Mautz, Tiessen, and Colson—all professors of accounting—evolved as a result of their excellent survey of internal auditing and internal auditors. It highlights risks to the enterprise and seems to reflect the accounting orientation of the authors, since it deals much more with controls than with performance:

2. Internal auditing, which is ultimately responsible to the owners of the enterprise, is a service to senior management and other enterprise interests that includes (i) monitoring management controls; (ii) anticipating, identifying, and assessing risks to enterprise assets and activities; (iii) investigating actual and potential lapses of control and incidents of risk; and (iv) making recommendations for improvement of control, the response to risk, and the attainment of enterprise objectives.(3)

Our third definition seeks to focus on the broad scope and objectives of internal auditing and to encapsulate its comprehensive approach:

3. Internal auditing is a systematic, objective appraisal by internal auditors of the diverse operations and controls within an organization to determine whether (i) financial and operating information is accurate and reliable, (ii) risks to the enterprise are identified and minimized, (iii) external regulations and acceptable internal policies and procedures are followed, (iv) satisfactory standards are met, (v) resources are used efficiently and economically, and (vi) the organization's objectives are effectively achieved—all for the purpose of assisting members of the organization in the effective discharge of their responsibilities.(4)

THE PROBLEM-SOLVING PARTNERSHIP

Under the third definition, most internal auditors see the objective of their profession as being to form a partnership with management. The function of the partnership is to solve problems, to prevent difficulties from happening, and to correct those that do happen. Managers see to it that things get done, despite all obstacles. Modern internal auditors help managers do their jobs effectively, efficiently, and economically.

This partnership will work only if managers understand what modern internal auditing has to offer. This calls for legitimacy on the part of internal auditors and for internal auditors who have achieved professional status. It also calls for managers to know how modern internal auditors have developed from accounting-oriented verifiers of things past to evaluators who can audit anything under the sun . . . have evolved from carping critics to working partners with management. Here is an actual example of how that partnership can work:

Three engineers in a large manufacturing company had been assigned by the company's chief executive officer to answer some questions about a research and development function within the company—questions designed to search out capability, productivity, the prudent deployment of resources, and the value of the R&D work done. The engineers turned to the internal auditors, seeking a partnership in a field—internal auditing—with which they were unfamiliar. The internal auditors pointed out that any measurements require standards to measure against. So the first step was to compile standards of excellence for the R&D activity. The engineers identified some 40 to 50 standards by which such activities could be measured—standards closely related to management principles—including such matters as these:

- The objectives and goals for the development standards should be reduced to writing and should be clearly understood by those doing the work. (Planning)
- The technological requirement for the R&D work should be identified, and personnel responsible for the work should have the requisite knowledge and skills in their technologies. (Organizing)
- A free interchange of information should be permitted among the technical people that would look toward the improvement of work and the greater contribution to cost reductions and profit enhancement. (Directing)
- R&D managers should be provided with adequate systems of financial control designed to assist them in accomplishing their goals and missions within allocated budgets. (Controlling)

Having established their standards, the audit team of internal auditors and engineers met with the director of R&D and asked for his views on the list of criteria developed. The list was accepted as satisfactory. The audit team then asked the director to engage in a partnership with the audit team whereby both auditors and R&D managers could constitute themselves as a sort of committee of the whole to carry out the audit objectives. The director agreed. The auditors then developed a questionnaire, based on the standards, which would be answered by R&D managers. The questions were keyed to principles of management. Some examples of the questions and the answers elicited, were as follows:

Planning:
Q. What are the objectives and goals of the R&D division?
A. Our objectives are to design new products, to develop new uses for existing products, and to improve products in use. Our goal for the next year is to design two new, patentable products.
Organizing
Q. What are the basic technologies required for development work within the R&D division? What special skills and knowledge should individuals have to be assigned to R&D work in each of these technologies?
A. See the attached job descriptions for positions in the research and development groups.
Directing
Q. What action is taken to encourage open and frank exchanges of information and to motivate creative thinking?

A. "Rap" sessions are held on research and development projects, and in each of them the participants are encouraged to participate and contribute ideas. See copy of minutes for session held 13 FebruaryXX. See also agenda for next session.

Controlling

Q. What forms of feedback are used to help managers see that goals are accomplished within allocated budgets? Who is responsible for deciding on the size of the budget, and what input is used to help make the decisions?

A. Managers prepare status reports at key milestones. They also make recommendations for specific action to recover from unfavourable trends. See copy of report dated 27 February XX. The executive committee sets budgets based on proposals identifying budget elements. See copy of budget proposal for last year.

At an agreed-upon day, the R&D director gave the audit team the answers to the questionnaires. The results exceeded the most optimistic expectations. All the questions were answered with specificity. Documents supported and validated many of the responses. The participation was complete and wholehearted. Of course, some of the questions could not be answered because of inadequate procedures or practices; in that case the R&D people said that they would take appropriate corrective action. The R&D managers welcomed the opportunity for a structured, well-planned self-analysis of their operations. They agreed that the audit had a cleansing, fine-tuning effect.

This example shows internal auditing as a problem-solving partnership in the most effective sense.

LEGITIMACY

It is doubtful that managers would accept internal auditors into a problem-solving partnership unless they had a high regard for the background and capability of the partner. An aura of professionalism has a great effect on the acceptance of a partner's ideas and recommendations. It is well, therefore, for managers to be aware of the propriety of the internal auditor's claim to legitimacy. To that end, let us explore the growth of internal auditing and its right to be taken seriously in its bid to be partners of managers. Here are some of the changes in internal auditing in the past 50 years which show its transformation from a clerical or accounting function to one that bespeaks professionalism.(5)

The Institute of Internal Auditors

The IIA is the professional organization for internal auditors around the world. It was founded in 1941 by about 40 internal auditors. It has grown since then to a membership exceeding 53 000, with members in over 100 chapters around the world.

Among its other functions, the Institute provides for professional publications, interchange of information in local and international meetings and conferences, and seminars on all facets of internal auditing. It deals with kindred organizations and has testified in appropriate cases before the American Congress. Also, it has been given consultative status by the United Nations. It maintains a large staff of professional and clerical personnel in Altamonte Springs, Florida.

Statement of Responsibilities

In 1947, the Institute published its first *Statement of Responsibilities for the Internal Auditor*. It was a bold step forward for that time, because it dared to show the internal auditor's concern for "matters of an operating nature." Yet the emphasis was still on "accounting and financial" matters. In later *Statements,* the scope of internal audit responsibility was expanded by replacing "accounting, financial, and other operations" by the single word "operations." This denoted the comprehensive nature of internal auditing. Appendix A contains the entire text of the latest *Statement.*

Code of Ethics

In 1968, The Institute published its first *Code of Ethics*. It outlines criteria of professional behaviour and expects members of The Institute to maintain standards of competence, morality, and dignity.

The *Code* recognizes that ethics are an important consideration in the practice of modern internal auditing, and it charges members to exercise honesty, objectivity, diligence, and loyalty to employers; to avoid conflicts of interest and not to accept fees and gifts without the knowledge of senior management; to treat information gained as confidential; to factually support their opinions; to reveal all material facts known to them; and to seek self improvement (see Appendix B).

The Certification Program

The Institute approved a certification program in 1972 and gave its first examination in 1974. It moved internal auditing up another rung on the ladder that reached for professionalism, because one of the attributes of a profession is a credible and exacting course of study and provision for the examination and certification of candidates.

The certification program brought legitimacy to internal auditing that many years of practice could not. It gave to certified internal auditors participation in a recognized profession, higher levels of professional training, recognition by peers, better acceptance in the job market, and the personal satisfaction in passing a demanding examination.

Some comments of those who passed the examination are revealing. For example:

> "So much internal auditing is related to management principles . . . that the Certified Internal Auditor (CIA) is more real world than the Certified Public Accountant (CPA). The management portion of the examination and the lessons learned in preparing for it can readily be applied to the job."

"Qualifications for the CIA are more germane to management interests that the CPA is, and internal audit experience in a first-class department is of more value to management than Big-8 public experience."(6)

Clearly, if an executive seeking to start an internal auditing department, or a director of internal auditing seeking to add to the staff, has no other objective criteria to go by, the designation of Certified Internal Auditor is a powerful inducement to hire the candidate possessing it. That designation is an objective evaluation that no other qualification could equal. Also, the designation is portable; the examination is now being translated into French and Spanish. In 1980 the United Kingdom introduced its own qualification and examinations, but close relations are maintained with the US. The United Kingdom Institute is the largest outside the US, and is pivotal within the context of the European Union.(7,8) More and more universities are adopting courses in internal auditing which are designed to prepare students for the Certified Internal Auditor examination, or national equivalents.

The Standards

The Institute approved the *Standards for the Professional Practice of Internal Auditing* in 1978. Along with the certification program it was one of the most significant changes in the history of internal auditing. What for years was a catch-as-catch can practice emerged as a distinctive profession. It provided rules and criteria that are recognized throughout the world. Many internal auditing departments use it as a guide in establishing departmental policies and procedures as well as statements of function and responsibility (see Appendix C).

The *Standards* establish a yardstick for internal audit operations that permit consistent measurement of audit performance, and these criteria apply throughout all entities and auditing departments. They are a unifying force for internal auditing worldwide.

The *Standards* can be a two-edged sword. True, they add unity, better quality, recognition, and credibility to this new profession. At the same time, however, they will underscore the fact that internal auditors are responsible for their own actions. They may be called upon for greater accountability to their organizations and to society as a whole. A more sobering thought is that they may increase the liability of those who fail to follow the *Standards* in their practice.

THE APPROACH TO WRONGDOING

The concept of a problem-solving partnership does not imply that the modern internal auditor must be a perennial "nice guy" who is all sweetness and light no matter what the circumstances. The partnership—in the presence of wrongdoing at the operating levels—must extend upward to senior management. Executives bear the primary responsibility for the stewardship of the organization's resources.

Internal auditors should employ openness and candor in their regular assignments. That approach is beneficial for the auditors' clients, their audit objectives, and themselves but, as the lawyers say, "Fraud vitiates everything." To engage in a problem-solving partnership with a villain is ludicrous on its face. When wrongdoing is found, internal auditors must be part of the team that identifies it and roots it out.

Still, internal auditors do not bear and cannot be charged with the unlimited responsibility for the prevention and detection of fraud in their organizations. What they are responsible for is due professional care. And according to the *Standards* (280.01, 02), ". . . internal auditors should be alert to the possibility of intentional wrongdoing, errors and omissions, inefficiency, waste, ineffectiveness, and conflicts of interest. They should also be alert to those conditions and activities where irregularities are most likely to occur. In addition, they should identify inadequate controls and recommend improvements to promote compliance with acceptable procedures and practices.' But the *Standards* go on to say that "Due care implies reasonable care and competence, not infallibility or extraordinary performance." This is supported by the professional guidelines and legal decisions relating to the responsibilities of the external auditor for fraud detection.

It follows, then, that the internal auditors' prime responsibility with respect to irregularities is to identify the risks to the enterprise and the controls needed to minimize those risks. Thus, their training and background must equip them to identify the risk indicators and the most efficient and economical controls needed to prevent wrongdoing. That is much more cost effective and efficient than waiting for wrongdoing to occur and then tracking down the wrongdoer.

At the same time, internal auditors are responsible for carrying through to a conclusion and tracking down any serious problem or potential problem that comes or is brought to their attention and that is within the purview of their responsibilities. Some internal auditing departments—banks are a prime example—have trained investigators on their staffs. In those cases the department takes full responsibility for investigations and interrogations of suspects. In other organizations, and these are probably in the majority, the security department is separate from the internal auditing department. In those organizations, when they become aware of illegal or potentially illegal activities, internal auditors should promptly bring the matter to the attention of the trained security investigators.

Thereafter, the internal auditors may work together with the investigators to develop whatever evidence and information may be needed to bring the case to a conclusion. They are trained and experienced in analyzing accounting records and other documents. They can become invaluable problem-solving partners with the security investigators. However, unless internal auditors are trained investigators, they must be aware of the dangers implicit in investigations and interrogations. They may find themselves open to charges of defamation of character, false arrest, false imprisonment, libel, slander, or malicious prosecution.(9)

Internal auditors have learned that the commission of fraud is usually found when there is an intent to steal, the opportunity to steal, and the ability to carry it off. So what an organization must do is reduce temptation and opportunity and increase the certainty of detection. Internal auditors best carry out their responsibilities if they recommend controls designed to achieve those ends. Executive management, therefore, should provide them with the authority to pass on the control systems and to have the right to review and approve intentional overrides of the systems at any level of the enterprise. In some organizations it is top management policy for all such overrides to be approved in advance and in writing by the Controller and the Director of Internal Auditing before any manager or executive may override an established control.

CONTROLLED ERRORS

As we have seen, internal auditors cannot be held responsible for detecting fraud as a part of their regular audit program. Yet, modern internal auditors can test a system's ability to detect and reject errors or improprieties. The technique used is what has been variously referred to as "created," "planted," or "controlled" errors or as "custom-made frauds." The procedure provides for the introduction of false or fictitious transactions into a manual system to determine whether the system or the people running it will detect and reject the spurious transactions. Such a technique is used regularly in testing computer systems: test decks containing fictitious transactions are used as input to test the computer's ability to flash "Tilt!" when the erroneous transaction is encountered.

Few people object to created errors in testing computer systems. But there is considerable opposition to using the technique when people are involved. The objections can be summed up as follows:

1. The organization may lay itself open to charges of entrapment.
2. Some managers or supervisors may take it upon themselves to use the practice surreptitiously to their own advantage. If detected, they can declare innocently that they were only "testing the system."
3. It would be impossible to keep the practice secret, and honest people might be alienated.
4. The internal auditor's reputation for fairness would be damaged.

On the other hand, there are those who support the practice, giving the following arguments:

1. The doctrine of entrapment does not apply. Entrapment is neither a crime nor a civil wrong; it is a defense that a defendant can raise in a criminal trial. The

defense must prove that government officers or agents (not private individuals) conceived the entire crime and then *persuaded the defendant to commit it.* The defense would not apply when the purpose of the test was to evaluate a system's ability to detect and reject erroneous transactions with no intent to prosecute criminally.

2. Properly administered, the controlled testing program could not be used with impunity by unscrupulous operating managers or supervisors. The rules for the program would have to be strict. Each test would have to be approved in writing by at least three members of top management. Any controlled test not so approved would be as improper as any other deviation from prescribed policies and procedures.

3. There is no more chance of alienating honest employees by controlled errors than by the techniques of surprise cash counts. Other restraints and controls have long been used: time clocks, inspection of lunch boxes of employees leaving a plant, surveillance systems whereby investigators observe personnel in the conduct of their duties, and security questionnaires. Usually, it is the guilty, not the innocent, who object to such controls.

4. The internal audit image should be and most likely is based on how internal auditors conduct themselves during regular audits when they are completely open with their clients. It is doubtful that their responsibility for taking all reasonable means to safeguard enterprise assets will affect that image. Besides, desperate diseases call for desperate remedies. The current welter of frauds and embezzlements demands rigorous cures. Internal auditors should alert senior management to the benefits of controlled errors.

In organizations where controlled tests are considered appropriate and are applied under strict rules of conduct, here are some applications:

- Send improperly authorized request-to-purchase to the purchasing department to see whether they will be accepted and acted upon.
- Place substandard items or an insufficient number of acceptable items in an incoming shipment or in a production batch to see whether they will be passed by inspectors.
- When designated signatures are required on documents, use poor forgeries.
- Send improper paperwork to payroll accounting to see if fictitious employees can be placed on the payroll.
- Send to accounts payable such improper documents as:

  (i) Invoices marked paid.
  (ii) Carbon copies instead of original invoices.
  (iii) Invoices on typed instead of printed billheads.
  (iv) Invoices for material that are not or will not be received.

In each organization, a decision must be made on whether the advantages of controlled testing outweigh the disadvantages. The ultimate decision rests with senior management. Internal auditors may regard the technique as personally repugnant; but when the organization is facing serious problems or system breakdowns, it would seem that they owe a duty to their problem-solving partners in top management to submit the proposition for high-level consideration before they take it upon themselves to reject the concept.

RECOGNITION AS A RESPECTED PROFESSION

As a direct result of the advances made in the profession, what is of signal importance is the improved acceptance by executive management, board audit committees, and external auditors.

Survey after survey has disclosed that senior managers are turning more and more to internal auditors to help in the decision-making process. The Mautz survey emphasized the greater reliance senior managers are placing on the internal audit review of the adequacy of internal control and the monitoring of adherence to internal control procedures.(10) Members of audit committees think highly of the competence of internal audit departments in their enterprises. 70% of the audit committee respondents to Mautz's questionnaires regarded their internal auditors as superior to other members of the organization.(11) A similar view of the increasing competence of and respect for internal audit emerges in the United Kingdom and Ireland.(12)

The Mautz survey disclosed that both managers and board members are seeking even more help from their internal auditors and at higher levels of evaluation. They indicated that they would want their internal auditors to have an increased managerial perspective and expertise.(13) Indeed, a Conference Board Report said that "Once a kind of stepchild function in many companies . . . internal auditing has steadily gained status and influence in the corporate organization over the last decade. Audit committees have been a factor in that progress." The report goes on to say that "The internal audit function, in particular, has benefited from its growing relationship with audit committees."(14)

In this litigious society, with board members subject to suit for wrong decisions, they have greater need for the objective information on tap from the well-schooled internal auditor. Also, the reporting relationship of directors of internal auditing has increased with the passage of time. More and more are reporting to board audit committees technically and to CEOs or CFOs administratively.

The nature of internal auditing—often a transient position on the way to jobs in other parts of the enterprise—draws different pictures in different enterprises. Yet the passage of time has shown some dramatic gains in the support received from the top. Well-established professional internal auditors are invited by higher management to consult on a variety of subjects. These subjects go beyond accounting controls. Internal auditors are asked to provide management studies in a broad spectrum of entity affairs.

Their status and their interesting assignments attract people from within the company to the internal audit ranks. In many companies, new and budding managers are given internships for as much as a year in internal auditing to gain a sound, hands-on understanding of the entity itself and the means of gathering and evaluating information of all kinds. In such companies, the internal auditing department is regarded as a reservoir of talent that thinks like management and acts like management. Strengthened support from the top has been one of the biggest changes in internal audit over the years.

Still, the transient nature of the discipline creates some problems about the identification of internal auditors as true professionals. Degrees and certifications may not do it. After all, only doctors can write prescriptions. Only attorneys can submit legal briefs. Only certified public accountants can certify to financial statements, but anyone can sign an internal audit report.

The leap to true professionalism may have to be made by individual internal audit directors or chief executive officers. They can assert the claim to professionalism by hiring only those people who are certified or are working toward certification. Also, they can declare that only certified internal auditors may sign internal audit reports. When that knowledge becomes current throughout the enterprise, then will the audit department be regarded in the same manner as the legal department is regarded? It will be a long time before The Institute of Internal Auditors achieves that consummation in all internal audit departments around the world. In the meantime, forward-looking audit departments and senior managers can accomplish it within their own organizations.

COMPUTERS

Internal auditors today are faced with two challenges that have been posed by computers. First, auditing the technology that contains so much of the data on which the enterprise relies. Second, using personal computers to assist them in their audits.

Auditing the Computer

Computer literacy for internal auditors was once "nice to have." Now it is absolutely essential if internal auditors are to do their jobs of evaluating the adequacy and effectiveness of internal control throughout the enterprise. The explosive growth of technology, the use of the computer in every function of the organization, and the vastly increased information available to managers, all place a responsibility on internal auditors to understand and evaluate the risks and the opportunities that are spawned by computer technology.

To maintain their independence, internal auditors must now understand and work with business systems that are exceedingly complex. They can no longer audit around the black box. They must be able to delve into its very bowels. And to do so they must have both technical education and hands-on use. They may not rely on others.

Both executives and operating managers depend on internal auditors to provide a realistic assessment of the risks in their organization that the computer brings. With the proliferation of mini–and microcomputers, layer upon layer of networking, vast data storage, decreasing levels of human review of transactions, and rapidly evolving application systems, managers desperately need internal auditors to protect them. This change has not only lifted internal auditing to new heights; it has also placed an enormous burden on the profession.

Computer-Assisted Auditing

Through the computer, internal auditors are able to extend the scope of their activities enormously. They are now able to review and appraise immense collections of diverse, complex, and interrelated data. Paper trails disappear. Some information is available only by aggregating several files—a task almost impossible to deal with manually. Lap computers can be taken anywhere internal auditors go, to access data, select samples, make comparisons and computations, and evaluate results. This change in internal auditing gave auditors a new tool to take much of the donkey work out of their tasks while handling detail with greater speed and accuracy.

Statistical Sampling and Quantification

The ancient standard of auditing 10% of the population, no matter what the population might be, went by the board with the advent of statistical sampling as an audit tool. Internal auditors must now understand the principles of statistical sampling and apply it in their audit tasks where appropriate. Of course, computer software programs take most of the detailed effort out of the job. But internal auditors must know how to use the computer and they must also know how to decide which program or which form of sampling to use and what to make of the accumulated data and the computer-generated analyses.

In the field of quantification, internal auditors are now required to be familiar with quantitative techniques and the means of depicting the interrelationship between and among recognized factors. Managers are turning more and more to quantitative models for assistance in making business decisions. And where management goes, the internal auditor should be prepared to follow. Indeed, when the manager doesn't know the path, the internal auditor should be a knowledgeable guide.

CONCLUSION

Internal auditing has made giant strides in the last half century. It has gained new respect from board audit committees and from managers at all levels of the enterprise. It is well on its way to having its practitioners seen as professional people. Certainly, it is being looked to as an important adjunct to management— indeed, as an extension of management.

The ultimate step toward, and the imprimatur of, a *learned* profession may for some time be achieved only be individual internal audit departments with the support and assistance of management and the board. Some organizations have achieved that goal. As time goes by and the need for professional internal auditors is perceived, the concept is likely to spread.

In the meantime, knowledgeable managers should expect of their internal auditors a new kind of support and assistance—an ability to join in a problem-solving partnership to help solve the most complex of management problems. To that end, they are entitled to demand from their auditors the professional practice of internal auditing.

REFERENCES

(1) Gordon McIntyre, "Auditing for Management Control," *The Internal Auditor,* May–June 1975, p. 37.
(2) *Standards for the Professional Practice of Internal Auditing* (Altamonte Springs, Florida: The Institute of Internal Auditors, 1978), Introduction, p. 1.
(3) R. K. Mautz, Peter Tiessen, and R.H. Colson, *Internal Auditing: Directions and Opportunities* (Altamonte Springs, Florida: The Institute of Internal Auditors Research Foundation, 1984), p. 32.
(4) L. B. Sawyer, *Sawyer's Internal Auditing* (Altamonte Springs, Florida: The Institute of Internal Auditors, 1988), p. 7.
(5) Dale L. Flesher, *The Institute of Internal Auditors: 50 years of Progress through Sharing,* (Altamonte Springs, Florida: The Institute of Internal Auditors, 1991).
(6) F.E. Mints, "Internal Audit Certification—It Makes a Difference." *The Internal Auditor*, February, 1985, pp. 18–22.
(7) Gerald Vinten, "UK Internal Audit Developments—Towards Europe or America?" *Managerial Auditing Journal,* Vol. 6. No. 1, 1991, pp. 16–20.
(8) Gerald Vinten (editor) *Educating Auditors: The Future of the Profession,* MCB University Press, Bradford, England, 1988
(9) T.R. Igleski, "Legal Considerations When Employee Fraud is Evident," *The Internal Auditor*, January–February, 1969, p. 37.
(10) Mautz et al., op.cit., p. 115.
(11) Mautz et al., op cit., p. 124.
(12) Institute of Internal Auditors (UK) Survey of Internal Auditing in the United Kingdom and Eire, IIA, London, 1985.

(13) Mautz et al., op.cit., pp. 113, 124.
(14) Jeremy Bacon, "The Audit Committee: A Broader Mandate," The Conference Board, New York, Research Report: No. 914, p. 1, 1988.

4
Classical Management Theory—Links with Modern Internal Auditing

THE DEVELOPMENT OF MODERN MANAGEMENT

Early History

Management in one sense, is as old as mankind itself. It reaches back to the earliest days when one person led and controlled others. Its seeds were planted in the soil from which governments sprang. But it did not approach fruition until the twentieth century.

Before 1900 there were, of course, private businesses, but they were run by their owners. The people we now call managers were merely assistants to the owners, and the owners ruled as by the divine right of kings. Some kings rule badly, but they rule nevertheless. So too the owners of businesses; they ruled their companies not because they ruled well but simply because they were the owners. Ownership was the controlling factor, not performance, innovation, or vision.

The divine right of ownership died hard. Henry Ford is a case in point: by the early 1920s he had built one of the world's most profitable companies and almost monopolized the automobile market in the United States. By 1927, however, his business was crumbling. He lost millions, year after year. Hindsight now tells us that his difficulties stemmed largely from the fact that he had no managers working for him—only assistants(1) Any assistant who tried to act like a manager, and take management risks was fired. It was the present-day version of "off with his head."

Then in 1944, Ford's 26-year-old grandson took over the company. The young man, short on experience and training but long on vision and managerial instinct, had other ideas. He got rid of the assistants, replaced them with managers who could perform, and brought the company back to its place of pre-eminence.

Like the modern internal auditor, the professional manager is a relatively new breed. He or she follows principles that have but recently been enunciated by the teachers of management theory. But the principles seem to follow natural laws, since they are rooted in early history.

The oft-told tale of Moses and Jethro illustrates some of the management principles. The Book of Exodus, chapter 18, tells us that Jethro saw Moses, his son-in-law, sitting from morning until night judging all his people. And Jethro said to him, "The thing that thou doest is not good. Thou wilt surely wear away, both thou, and this people that is with thee: for this thing is so heavy for thee; thou art not able to perform it thyself alone."

Then Jethro, the archetype of the internal auditor-teacher-counselor, having analyzed the problem and determined the causes, recommended that Moses "provide out of all the people able men . . . to be rulers of thousands, and rulers of hundreds, rulers of fifties, and rulers of tens. And let them judge the people at all seasons: and it shall be that every great matter they shall bring unto thee, but every small matter they shall judge."

In that wise counsel, so simply and succinctly stated, lay a clutch of "modern" principles of management:

- *Span of control.* There is a limit to the number of people a manager can personally supervise effectively.
- *The scalar principle.* There should be a direct chain of authority from supervisor to subordinate throughout the organization.
- *Management by exception.* Only significant deviations should be brought to the manager's attention.

Other sages in history also spoke in terms of modern principles of management. Here are some of them:

Confucius, in the sixth century BC, said, "Require of others only what you first taught them." It is fundamental to the tasks of management that the manager set standards and explain them to subordinates before they can meet the levels of excellence in mind. To achieve understanding, there must be adequate communication between the manager and staff.

Lao-tzu, a contemporary of Confucius, said, "As for the leader at the very top, it is best if people barely know he exists . . . The people are pleased because they think they did it all themselves." That statement is a precursor of what modern teachers of management propound: the worker must organize work with the advice and counsel of supervisors and professionals. The supervisors should be available for guidance, and not for organizing the work for the worker. Only then does the worker feel involvement and only then feels master of the job. No longer need workers feel that the work is master over them. As they are the designers of their own jobs, the organization can hope to get from them the best that they can give.

Mencius, or Meng-tzu (379–289 BC) said, "The person whose sole pursuit is

Profit-and-Advantage can be ruined by a bad harvest. But the person whose sole pursuit is excellence cannot be confused by evil times." Today the teachers of management theory say the same thing when they talk about goal setting, management by objectives, and determining what the business really is. As the teachers now write, profit-maximization is not the ultimate goal of the business.

Hau-fei-tzu (282–233 BC) pronounced that "Leaders should never be exempt from blame or punishment for their failures." Here are seen the principles of responsibility and accountability. Whoever is given the authority for carrying out assigned tasks must be held accountable for performance.

More recently, the oft-maligned but truly brilliant management theorist Machiavelli suggested "examining problems in a practical way in the light of the experience of others who have faced a similar problem in the past." His simple statement would seem to encapsulate the rules of problem solving and decision making.

The principles of management started with the need to govern wisely, and the modern principles of management are, in effect, a continuation of the old art of government. But it took managers to apply the principles to current business problems. They put the principles to work. They thought the problems through. They showed how management as a science can be used by the professional manager to build a business and make it productive.

The Professional Managers

Robert Owen

The early professional managers are of relatively recent origin. Perhaps the first manager worthy of the title was Robert Owen (1771–1858), and it was a long, long time before he had a successor. In him the flesh-and-blood manager first emerged from the abstractions of earlier theorists.

Robert Owen ran a textile mill in New Lanark, Scotland. In that mill, in 1820, he was the first to deal with productivity and motivation, with the worker and his work, with the worker's relation to the company, and with the worker's relation with his supervisor.

Most important, his business was a commercial success. He was able to prove that a profitable enterprise and concern for people can go hand in hand. According to the unanimous testimony of all who visited New Lanark, results were excellent. Children were happy and well brought up. There was health and plenty for the workers. Owen's methods were a demonstrated success. Yet it was a long while before another true manager came along.

Georg Siemens

The next individual to have an impact on the science of management, to start the schism between owner and managers, was Georg Siemens (1839–1901). As a young man of 30, he took over the management of the then puny Deutsche Bank in Germany. And from 1870 to 1880, he built the bank into Germany's leading financial institution.

The Deutsche Bank's rise stemmed not from financial brilliance or baronial ruthlessness, but from managers. Not assistants; managers. Siemens built a top-management team. He analyzed the bank's activities. He assigned responsibilities and granted authority to each member of the team. He saw to it that the job fit the person. And yet, through the delegation of responsibility over all of the bank's functions, every operation was in one way or another covered by a manager. That was a sharp break with the divine-right approach to running a business.

It is a sad commentary that Siemens' successful venture into modern management was not adopted by others, and sadder still that many a promising business was lost through the failure to follow Siemens' methods. The story was there for all to see, but few saw it. The past is prologue; the fruition of the future lies in the seeds of the past. The busy manager may not have the time to study it, but business history should be a part of the internal auditor's store of knowledge ready to be tapped to savour advice to managers.

Ei-ichi Shibusawa

Another management pioneer was Ei-ichi Shibusawa (1840–1931). He was a statesman who became a business leader. He raised some fundamental questions about the relation between business enterprise and national purpose, between business needs and individual ethics. He was perhaps the first to envision the professional manager. In fact, Japan's rise to economic leadership can be traced to Shibusawa's thought and work.

Shibusawa's professional manager was ahead of his time. But then many strokes of brilliance are, and internal auditors should be alert to them. Internal auditors must study the principles and translate them into practical rules for practical people. They must show those people how to apply the rules in their day-to-day tasks and how such an application will help managers reach their objectives. They have a signal opportunity to carry out their mission; for it is they who detect deficiencies, inefficiencies, and ineffectiveness. And as they point out unsatisfactory conditions and identify their causes, they can reach into their store of knowledge and show the practical effect of violating sound management principles.

Pierre S. du Pont

In more recent years, giants in the United States took long strides in advancing our knowledge of the practice of modern management.

Pierre S. du Pont (1870–1954) first developed the principle of decentralization and helped create the modern "big business." He transformed his family-dominated company into modern business by giving it a management structure. Du Pont worked out the system of organization known as "federal decentralization," later perfected by Sloan.(2) Federal decentralization is the organization of a company into a number of autonomous businesses. Each unit has its own management and runs its own business; each is responsible for its own performance and results; each makes a contribution to the entire company and is held accountable for that contribution.

Federal decentralization can be applied to institutions other than business. In a hospital, for example, the entire hospital function can be arranged into units of activity: one unit can take care of intensive-care patients; another unit can take care of short-term and ambulatory patients; another mental patients; still another convalescents; and so on. Common service units, such as laboratories, kitchens, case workers, and physical therapists, can be shared by the decentralized units.

Similarly, certain service units can aid decentralized businesses. For example, a central purchasing department can develop master purchase agreements for suppliers of common items, such as stationery and maintenance supplies, which would be available to the decentralized companies.

The involvement of the du Pont family in the company would seem to be a reversion of the old owner-manager concept, but in the du Pont organization only the family members who can qualify as true managers stay on. Obviously, family has the inside track. But in the case of the du Ponts, as it was of Georg Siemens, being a family member may get you in but only contribution to the business permits you to stay.

Alfred P. Sloan, Jr.

Alfred P. Sloan, Jr. (1875–1966) followed Pierre S. du Pont and improved on what du Pont had done. Sloan developed systematic approaches to business objectives and to strategic planning. After the du Ponts acquired the then floundering General Motors in the early 1920s and put Sloan in as president, Sloan developed the "professional management team" which raised GM to heights of greatness.(3)

Julius Rosenwald

Julius Rosenwald (1862–1932) built the first business based on the marketing approach. Richard Sears founded the business, and it escalated because he was a shrewd speculator. But as the company grew and Sears' reach exceeded his scope, he was forced to take Rosenwald in. Rosenwald was truly a manager. He built an organization in which managers were given maximum authority and full responsibility for results. Most important, he determined early on just what his business was.

That determination heralded Sears, Roebuck's future. Rosenwald thought through the business and decided that its essence was to be the farmer's friend. Simply that. But that simple-sounding concept was central to the success of the business. For the company to be the farmer's friend, Rosenwald had to determine where his customers were and what they needed. He had to develop the mail order catalog as a marketing instrument; the customer had to get what was wanted at a low price, and with assurance of regular supply.

Most important, Rosenwald had to give a warranty of reliability and honesty, because the remote locations he served—this was before the company went into retail sales—made it impossible for the customer to inspect the purchase in advance of delivery. So Rosenwald changed the concept of "buyer beware" to "seller beware." And he made stick the famous Sears' policy of "your money back and no questions asked." Rosenwald was the father of the marketing-and-distribution revolution.

The Advance Guard of the Modern Theorist: Classical Management Theory

In recent years there has been an enormous boom in management texts. Before World War II, the books on management could have fit on an office bookshelf. Since then, hundreds of management titles have been appearing each year.

In this chapter we will speak of some of the theorists who began to formulate management principles and blaze the trail for others to follow. We have selected theorists whose ideas seem to mesh with the work of the internal auditor, ideas that evoke examples of the relation between management theory and modern internal auditing. The examples, described later in this chapter, underscore the feasibility of the problem-solving partnership. The classical management theorists are normally considered to be of two varieties: scientific management and the bureaucratic school. We begin with scientific management, and then explore bureaucracy in the shape of Max Weber and A. W. Gouldner.

The systems school of management theory is reserved for discussion in Chapter 5. And a number of the modern management theorists, particularly those concerned with behavioralism, are identified in Chapter 7.

Frederick W. Taylor

Frederick W. Taylor (1856–1915) laid the foundation for scientific industrial management. In 1880 and 1881, while employed as a gang boss at the Midvale Steel Company, he became convinced that a standard day's work in any operation could be measured and that scientific methods could be applied to work in the shop. He concluded that a large percentage of labor and material was wasted through inefficiencies' both in organizing and in supervising work.

In 1911 he wrote *The Principles of Scientific Management*. His intention was to provide principles of general applicability for managers, but his application was particular. It emphasized time-and-motion studies. Nevertheless, in terms of management theory, he made an important contribution by showing that scientific methods could be applied to management problems.

Taylor's classic pig iron experiment is an illustration. Laborers, relying on brute force and ignorance, could load only $12\frac{1}{2}$ tons of iron per man-day onto a railroad car from a storage yard. By using Taylor's improved methods, which were based on studies of motion, time, and fatigue, along with incentive wages, they boosted daily output from $12\frac{1}{2}$ to 48 tons. The daily pay rose 60% to $1.85 a day—minuscule by today's standards, but much higher than the average rate being paid in the community.

The school of scientific management developed methods of confirming or disproving business propositions. It sought to discover causal relations to business phenomena, and it contributed tremendous knowledge through a structured rather than a catch-as-catch-can approach to problems. The school made use of investigation, experimentation, and the careful interpretation of results. Method replaced intuition.

The very importance of Taylor's contributions emphasized the drawbacks. The great interest in Taylor's scientific methods drew attention away from general management and focused it on shop management.(4) Although born in the shop, however, many of Taylor's principles have equal applicability today in other environments. Some of the principles that have stood the test of time and changing occupations are:

- Replacing intuition and guesswork with the analysis of each element of a worker's tasks.
- Scientifically selecting and training workers.
- Promoting the cooperation of management and labor so as to better accomplish work through scientific method.
- Establishing a more equal division of responsibility between managers and workers.

Some of Taylor's ideas, on the other hand, are becoming less relevant. Taylor advocated systems of incentive pay for labor, but the decline of piecework and of unions has made such systems much less important in the field of compensation and motivation for workers. Nevertheless, it should be noted that Taylor's own motivation was not to be a cold and calculating stopwatch artist; instead, it was to free the nineteenth-century worker from the burden of heavy, destructive toil and break the wage barriers that condemned workers to unremitting poverty. He was responsible for making it possible to increase wages by increasing productivity.

Henri Fayol

If Taylor was the father of scientific management, then Henri Fayol (1841–1925) can be considered to be the father of modern management theory. His was the first rational approach to organizing an enterprise along functional lines. He considered the business function as a "bundle of related skills." It was his answer to the organizational question of which activities belong together.

Fayol's approach may have applied admirably to the relatively small—by present standards—coal-mining company that he ran. Today it may be more important to bring together the contributions that groups make to the enterprise than to bundle the skills. Nevertheless, many of the principles Fayol propounded with brilliant insight are largely valid to this day.(5)

Fayol developed 14 principles from his own experience in managing an organization.(6)They apply primarily to the manager, but, as we shall demonstrate later in this chapter, they are of vital interest to the internal auditor as well. They are summarized as follows:

1. *Division of work.* The division of work involves the principle of specialization: each to one's ability. Fayol first discovered the principle in connection with his study of shop work, but he saw its applicability to all kinds of work, both administrative and technical.

2. *Authority and responsibility.* Whenever authority is delegated, responsibility for the actions taken and the decisions made must be exacted. Authority has two aspects. One is rooted in the manager's official designation of position; the other is rooted in the manager's own ability, experience, intelligence, and moral worth.

3. *Discipline.* Discipline implies conformity to the organization's rules. Fayol said that this principle requires clear and fair agreements and good superiors at all levels.

4. *Unity of command.* Employees should not be required to serve two managers within the organization. They should receive orders from one superior only.

5. *Unity of direction.* Each group of activities that has the same objective should have the same plan and the same direction. Fayol saw unity of direction as related to the organization as a whole and unity of command as related to personnel and their superiors.

6. *Subordination of individual interest.* The interest of the group should always transcend the interest of the individual. It is the job of the manager to reconcile conflicting interests.

7. *Remuneration of personnel.* Payment to people should be fair and consistent and should give maximum satisfaction to employee and employer.

8. *Centralization.* The centralization principle refers to the degree to which authority within an organization is concentrated or dispersed so as to be cost-effective.

9. *Scalar chain.* The scalar chain denotes the line of authority from the highest to the lowest ranks. It derives from the Latin for "ladder." And although it depicts an upward-and-downward movement, with the implication that subordinates should comply strictly with protocol, the horizontal rungs permit a sidewise movement when strict adherence to protocol would be inefficient and ineffective.

10. *Order.* Order involves the organization of people and functions: a place for everyone and everything, and everyone and everything in their places.
11. *Equity.* The equity principle deals with human relations. It calls for fair dealing between supervisor and worker.
12. *Stability of personnel tenure.* Fayol was concerned with unnecessary employee turnover, and he saw it as both the cause and effect of bad management.
13. *Initiative.* Fayol regarded initiative as thinking through problems and devising and executing plans. He looked to managers to stimulate initiative in subordinates, since he saw initiative as one of the "keenest satisfactions for an intelligent person to experience."
14. *Esprit de corps.* The final principle has to do with teamwork and morale; to achieve them is heavily dependent on good communication.

Fayol made a valuable contribution in emphasizing the absolute necessity for general managerial ability. He considered that detailed knowledge about a given function (even the one that constitutes the primary activity of the business) may be largely supplied via departmental heads and staff, but nothing can make up for lack of managerial ability. He also placed much weight on business ethics:

> "Moral flaws on the part of a higher level manager can lead to serious consequences, for a high position in the scalar chain is like the arm of a lever whose length increases its power considerably; good and bad qualities are a hundred times more important in a seven- or eight-striped leader than in a foreman."(7)

Lyndall Urwick

Lyndall F. Urwick (b. 1891) was one of the first management consultants and a leading advocate of Henri Fayol. Like Fayol, he believed in using principles of management to provide criteria for good administration. Among the principles he propounded were:(7)

- *Uniformity.* All reports and figures used to control activities should be the same throughout the organization.
- *Objectives.* Contributions by individuals in the organization will be effective to the extent that they are in gear with the organization's aims and goals.
- *Span of control.* There is a limit to the number of subordinates a manager can supervise effectively.

Ralph C. Davis

Ralph Currier Davis (b. 1894), who taught management at Ohio State University, helped develop a unified theory of management. He was a proponent of the concept of accountability as an addition to the concepts of authority and responsibility. Accountability is the charge laid upon a subordinate to account for the proper discharge of duties.(8)

The Gilbreths

A man and his wife, Frank and Lillian Gilbreth (1868–1924 and 1878–1972), powered the work that is referred to as motion study. They classified work according to motions, such as moving, lifting, and putting down. Their Therbligs (an anagram of Gilbreth) encompass the entire range of manual operations. The Gilbreths sought to develop "the one best way" for each operation. Each of the Therbligs, which look something like Chinese ideographs, depicts the information needed to engineer a motion.

The Gilbreths' purpose was work simplification, not work speed up. For example, they found that, if working conditions were merely held constant so that employees became familiar with the operations of the work, there would be a significant increase in output. Essentially, work simplification is merely applying common sense to find easier, better, more economical ways of doing things. Briefly stated, the steps are as follows:

1. Identify the work that could use simplification.
2. Analyze the job. Break it down into its component parts.
3. Question each component part of the work.
4. Try to improve existing processes or methods by eliminating, combining, rearranging, simplifying, and substituting mechanical for manual means.
5. Put the improved methods into effect and monitor them. All the analysis and creativity in the world go for naught without action, follow-up, and feedback.

One of the weaknesses of that form of analysis is that the analysis may be starting at the wrong end. It usually starts by analyzing the work being done while accepting without question the need for the end product. It is concerned with efficiency, not effectiveness. A similar criticism may be placed at the door of International Standards, which are concerned with documentary process rather than outcome.

Henry Gantt

Henry L. Gantt (1861–1919), another great pioneer in work analysis, fully understood the necessity of determining "what do we want to produce?" His charts started out with the end product and then detailed each step, in proper sequence, needed to attain it; they provided for scheduling work so that the entire process spread before the eye like a road map. In brief, each Gantt chart shows on the left the producing department, the number of operators, and the department's weekly capacity. Each job proceeding through a department is scheduled, day by day. The chart shows which jobs are on schedule and which are not meeting their schedules.

Mary Follett

Mary Parker Follett (1868–1933) did some significant work in the field of administration and the relation between management and the worker and between members of the organization. She pointed out, in the 1920s and 1930s, that effective managership was more than a function of official position within the organization. The senior manager appoints the operating manager and puts him or her in the job. But the subordinates must accept the manager before the manager can function effectively. Follett could see that assigned authority is like a wave breaking on the rocks if the subordinates are not willing to obey. She proposed the "law of the situation," which states that people will be moved not by divine right or domination, but rather by how they regard the manager's ability to interpret the situation in which the group finds itself. She conceived coordination involving direct contacts among people as being the essence of management. She saw coordination as a continuing process that must be introduced at the outset of a function and pursued to the end.

Coordination is conditional to communication, and communication is conditional to how the communicating parties perceive the situation. That perception, in turn, is conditional to the backgrounds, experiences, and prejudices of the parties. What one sees clearly the other sees not at all. Both, according to Follett, are likely to see "reality," but their inner eyes may capture entirely different pictures of reality.(9)

Chester Barnard

Chester I. Barnard (1886–1961), a corporation executive, was one of the first to study the management process of decision making in the functions of the executive and to explore the formal and informal organizations within a business entity.(10) Barnard searched for the universal fundamentals to explain the executive's job and to help the executive improve ability as a manager.

In decision making, Barnard stressed the need to identify the strategic factor that, when recognized and properly weighed, lies at the heart of wise decisions. All systems, conditions, or sets of circumstances consist of elements or factors. When regarded from the viewpoint of the purpose to be achieved, the factors fall into two classes: those which, if absent or changed, would accomplish the desired purpose (provided all the other factors remain unchanged) and the other, unchanged factors.(11)

For example, if an otherwise properly functioning automobile runs out of fuel, the fuel is the strategic, or limiting, factor. In a business seeking to expand, the availability of capital may be the strategic factor. Strategic factors for a particular set of circumstances may vary with different organizations and with points in time within the same organization. Strategic factors may be extremely difficult to identify and isolate, and that is the challenge to the decision-making executive.

Barnard spoke also of formal and informal organizations.(12) The formal organization is represented by the activities of two or more people who consciously coordinate their efforts toward mutual goals. The informal organization comprises the sum total of relations among people who may not have common purposes but from which arise joint results. There need not be a conflict between formal and informal organizations. The informal organization permits individuals to maintain their personalities against the effect of the formal organization, which, through its impersonality and coldness, may tend to disintegrate their personalities. Indeed, informal organizations may be important to the enterprise because they foster a feeling of belonging, status, and self-respect.

The Bureaucrats

Max Weber

Most parts of the public sector may be considered as hierarchic and bureaucratic, but then so is most of the private sector, unless we consider worker cooperatives, and even these display some bureaucratic tendencies. Bureaucracy, as defined by Max Weber, has ten major features:

1. Staff are personally free, observing only the impersonal duties of their offices.
2. There is a clear hierarchy of offices.
3. The functions of the offices are clearly specified.
4. Officials are appointed on the basis of a contract.
5. They are selected on the basis of a professional qualification, ideally substantiated by a diploma gained through examination.
6. They have a money salary, and usually pension rights. The salary is graded according to position in the hierarchy. The official can always leave the post, and under certain circumstances it may also be terminated.
7. The official's post is the sole or major occupation.
8. There is a career structure, and promotion is possible either by seniority or merit, and according to the judgement of superiors.
9. The official may appropriate neither the post nor the resources which go with it.
10. The official is subject to a unified control and disciplinary system.

Despite criticism that this "classical" view of management is incomplete as a synoptic view of management, it is nevertheless true that it has a number of abiding principles. Even Weber did not make absolutist claims for his theory:

"Thus, contrary to many interpretations, Weber did not maintain that bureaucratic organizations operate as efficiently as "slot machines". He said rather that such organizations operate more efficiently than alternative systems of administration and that they increase their efficiency to the extent that they "depersonalize" the execution of official tasks."

Weber did recognize the inefficiencies that could accompany bureaucracy, what we call red tape, but he coined no word for it, and has been frequently criticized for choosing to de-emphasize it.(14) He did perceive that bureaucracy could separate staff from the means of production and lead to a growth of formalism in organizations, and he seemed to view this prospect with resigned pessimism.

Alvin W. Gouldner

This American sociologist provides a contemporary up-dating to Weber, and demonstrates the lasting value of Weber's ideas, although, as we have argued, it would be an anaemic management theory that restricted itself to this perspective only, valuable as it has been. Gouldner was particularly interested in studying the problem of establishing or changing the basis of authority. In his book, he makes the distinction between three manifestations of bureaucratic behavior, all of which it is possible to find co-existing in the same organization:(15)

1. Mock bureaucracy, in which unwelcome rules are imposed on the organization, or part of it, from the outside, and both supervisors and subordinates go through the motions of complying, but in reality disregard the rules. Morale can be quite high in this circumstance as the common enemy of the stupidities in the system unites staff to find ways to work around it. In the days in the United Kingdom when strikes were more common than the rare event they are nowadays, they would often show up as a work to rule. This was always a paradox, for how could obeying the rules amount to a strike? The reason was that the rules were completely unworkable, and so any attempt to implement them would bring the organization into chaos. In normal working conditions, the workers ignored the rules invented by management, and the organization functioned relatively efficiently.
2. Representative bureaucracy, in which rules are made by experts whose authority is accepted by all members of the organization, with deviations being assumed to be the result of ignorance or lack of care. This is a participatory culture, with staff working well towards a common end.
3. Punishment-centred bureaucracy, in which either supervisors or subordinates force the other into submission on particular issues, resulting in gains or losses in relative status. Deviations are viewed as deliberate disobedience, and it is not surprising that tension and conflict abound.

Apart from the conflict just identified, Gouldner emphasizes two other sources inherent in even the more healthy versions of bureaucracy:

1. The gain of the bureaucratic approach is reducing conflict through substituting the impersonal rule for personal authority. The trouble is that this sets a minimum acceptable level of performance, which then becomes the norm. The consequent reduction in efficiency necessitates more supervision, an increase in

interpersonal conflict, the concoction of further rules, and so the vicious circle continues.

2. Managers tend to be either "cosmopolitans"—with loyalty primarily to their professional affiliation rather than to the organization—or "locals"—the dedicated company person. This choice between expertise and loyalty, both of which are desirable, can make decisions at appointments difficult.

Elton Mayo

Elton Mayo (1880–1949), an Australian working at Harvard, developed the concept of "human relations," the study of people working together in an enterprise. He perceived the dominance of interpersonal relations within the work group and the fact that the human character of business organizations had been largely ignored.(16)

The project that had the most to do with the concept that human relations was an integral part of business was the Hawthorne experiment, 1927–1932, of the Western Electric Company. The researchers sought to prove the validity of accepted management principles by observing employees at their tasks. Different variables were introduced into the work group, and the results in terms of production were measured. For example, a rest period was introduced where there previously had been no rest period, and increased production was noted and measured. Additional benefits to the workers were introduced, and each brought about an increase in production. That the researchers had expected. What they had not expected was that, when the amenities were gradually withdrawn, there was no decrease in production. Evidently there were uncontrolled and unknown factors in the experiment.

To find the uncontrolled factors, Mayo, along with F.J. Roethlisberger, followed up the experiments with an intensive counseling program and learned that the way managers perceived workers was not the way the workers perceived themselves. The workers saw themselves as members of a group, and they regarded interpersonal values as superior to individual or managerial values. The interpersonal relations brought about by the experiment itself carried on despite the removal of amenities. Some questions have been raised about the validity of the methods used in the Hawthorne experiments and whether those methods would stand up under modern scientific scrutiny. Be that as it may, the experiments brought about new thinking about manager-worker relations and have had a lasting effect on the study of scientific management.

Mayo showed that, unless the manager understands the values of the group and gives them full consideration, he will not get much enthusiasm out of the workers. Instead of trying to get across what management wants, the manager should try to find out what subordinates want, need, and have to know. That includes making the worker responsible for work and giving the authority to structure the job—with the advice of experienced supervisors, of course. When that condition obtains, the manager can expect to see commitment and involvement on the part of the worker. But workers structuring their own jobs is not a practice often seen. Usually, the manager or the supervisor or the industrial engineer structures the job and expects the worker to follow the dictated operations.

Yet the concept of involvement is being used in other areas. For example, it has become general practice in many organizations to have those who are subject to budgets and schedules be party to establishing them. The budgets and schedules are then *their* budgets and schedules and there is less resentment in trying to achieve them.

LINKS WITH INTERNAL AUDITING

The writings about management evoke a sharp echo from the work of modern internal auditors. There is a link between the two: in the way professional management and modern internal auditing developed, in the application of management principles to internal auditing practice, and in the dealings between managers and internal auditors. In this section, several of those links will be examined in relation to the work of some of the theorists just discussed.

Taylor: The Focus on Manufacturing

Taylor's work was criticized for being focused on shop management. Similar criticism is leveled at writers on modern internal auditing on the ground that much of the literature is focused on manufacturing. But in the growth of a profession, that is a fault to be expected. It was in the large manufacturing companies that internal auditing made its first great strides. The principles developed there are now in use in financial institutions, hospitals, government, and service industry.

Fayol: Principles of Management

Fayol's principles can be seen to be operative in many of the conditions internal auditors find in their examinations. For that reason we shall discuss at some length a number of actual conditions found by internal auditors and key them to many of Fayol's principles. A useful anthology of audit improvement suggestions has been published by the Institute of Internal Auditors.(17)

Authority and Responsibility

Fayol saw responsibility as a corollary of authority; the internal auditor may see the emphasis reversed. For example, the procurement department has the responsibility for purchasing materials and services for the organization. It should have the commensurate authority to be the only group in the enterprise to make commitments of that kind. Because of its responsibilities, it develops strict rules to make sure that buyers place orders without favoritism and in the best interests of the organization.

In one case an internal auditor found that the purchasing department's authority was not being fully exercised or protected. The manager of the transportation department was buying automotive equipment and supplies directly from suppliers; he was making commitments and consummating purchase agreements. All that was done without the strict controls imposed on buyers.

When the internal auditor observed the conditions and the dangers inherent in them, he counseled senior management to issue directives to all department heads that the authority to commit the company's funds was vested exclusively in the purchasing organization. Authority was thus made commensurate with responsibility.

Done without finesse, such an audit action would not sit well with the transportation manager, since it implies doubt as to that manager's objectivity. But the internal auditor pointed out the dangers the manager was facing in the event of a purchase, made with all the good intentions in the world, turning out to reek of favoritism. The manager was convinced that the new rules were designed to protect him as much as they were to protect the organization.

Discipline

Internal auditors have a responsibility for seeing that the rules are followed as intended. They also have a responsibility for seeing that the rules are reasonable and are in accordance with organizational objectives. In some companies internal auditors were instrumental in having formal conflict-of-interest programs developed. Under such programs each employee answers an annual questionnaire designed to disclose potential conflicts. Everyone is informed of the rules and of the penalties for disobeying them. The rules apply to everyone in the company from members of the board of directors to junior buyers within the purchasing department.

Conflicts may include ownership in a company supplying goods or services to the organization, acceptance of gifts from suppliers, and kickbacks from suppliers. Internal auditors in a company will be concerned with learning whether the rules are reasonable, will protect the company, and are not unnecessarily onerous to employees. Then they will see to it that all questionnaires are executed completely and that any deviations are appropriately dealt with. As a part of their responsibility for determining that the rules are followed as intended, they will be sure to review questionnaires executed by senior management, including the board of directors.

Division of Work

The concept of specialists working together toward the common good is high on the internal auditor's list of audit priorities. For example:

- When auditing purchase orders, the internal auditor wants to be sure that representatives from the traffic department have checked and approved routings and that representatives from the accounting department have approved the accounts or contracts shown as being charged.
- When auditing contracts, it is necessary to ensure that reviews and approvals were obtained from the general counsel's office, the tax department, and the insurance department.
- When rules and regulations that affect employees' rights, such as charges for lost equipment, are issued, the auditor wants to make sure that specialists within the personnel department agree that no union agreements are being violated.

Unity of Command

In one company, the manager of quality control was organizationally responsible to the director of manufacturing. The manager prescribed rules under which her inspectors were to operate, and the rules were in agreement with contract specifications governing the quality of delivered products. But the director of manufacturing and the managers working for him bowed more deeply to the gods of cost and schedule than to the god of quality, and inspectors were constantly being pressured to accept nonstandard products. The inspectors, working for two masters, were confused and resentful. They were not sure which was the last authority—the rules written by their manager or the oral demands of manufacturing managers to bend those rules.

The internal auditors recommended autonomy for quality control—a level in the organization that was equal to the level of the director of manufacturing. The difficulties of the inspectors' jobs were not eased, but the frustration and confusion on the part of the inspectors were eliminated. Now there was no question which manager was their superior.

Unity of Direction

One internal auditor encountered a violation of unity of direction in the audit of scrap generation and sale. The scrap sales department was trying to receive the most dollars from scrap no matter how much it cost the manufacturing department,where the scrap was generated, to sort and segregate the scrap.

Now, scrap *should* be segregated into types, because when different types of metals are mixed together, the value of the total will not exceed the value of the cheapest ingredient. If, for example, aluminum were mixed with titanium, an extremely expensive metal, the whole batch would command only the lower price offered for aluminum. So segregation is important, but segregation can also be expensive, particularly if the metals are already mixed.

Unity of direction would require the departments in the company to work together for the highest *net* return. If the cost of segregating the materials exceeded the return that could be obtained, it would make no economic sense to insist on high-cost segregation.

The answer was to seek segregation at the source of the scrap. If initial segregation was impossible, then the expensive chore of assigning production workers to sort the scrap was to be avoided. At the same time, the manufacturing managers were to be given monthly reports of the cost of different types of metals on the scrap market to alert them to the benefits of segregation. Also, their superiors were to be given reports of unnecessary contamination of expensive metals with cheaper types of metals. Unity of direction resulted in lower costs to the enterprise.

Subordination of Interest

Internal auditors should have an abiding interest in whether supervisors and managers know what their people are doing. During a defense contract audit, the government auditors made floor checks to determine the probable extent of idleness. The auditors observed that employees in the second and third shifts were spending time in places other than their assigned working areas; their individual interests took them there. The foremen should have known where their employees were, and so 33 of them were asked to name the employees assigned to them, state the employees' job assignments, and locate the individual employees. Over half of the foremen quizzed did not have lists of the people assigned to their supervision. Five of the foremen had to admit that they did not know the whereabouts of one or more of their assigned workers.

When the matter was reported to management, the system was promptly improved. Each foreman was required to have in his possession at all times an up-to-date crew list annotated to show absences, loans, and transfers. Managers were to make periodic observations to be sure the foremen were following the new rules. It was estimated, by the management people themselves, that about $1 million was saved through the institution of the improved controls.(17)

Centralization

In one company, the electronic data processing department was under the control of the chief accountant. All requests for data processing work by the chief accountant were complied with promptly. Other requests, sometimes of greater significance to the company as a whole, were given lower priorities. The internal auditor analyzed the requests and presented his findings to senior management.

The result was an organizational change. The head of data processing was elevated to a level equal to that of the department managers for whom he performed services.

Order

Internal auditors are beginning to get involved in the appraisal of organizational structure. A classic research study by the Institute of Internal Auditors examined the internal auditor's involvement with organizational control.(18) The report explores the basic concepts of organization, the nature and scope of organizational control, and the auditor's relation to such control. In addition, it provides audit guides for evaluating organization control.

The study cites a number of examples of the results of organizational audits. One of them describes a food company's thrift store operation in which a number of factors contributed to inefficiency, many of them organizational. For example, the central director lacked adequate authority over the field units. As a result there were no uniform policies for pricing, staffing, or store hours. Also, the field units lacked coordination with other company operations. Once the internal auditor identified the reasons for the inefficiencies, recommendations could be made for changes in the organizational structure, and increased authority for the central director.(19)

Equity

Equity, perhaps the fourth E after the internal auditor's concern with the three Es of Economy, Efficiency and Effectiveness, is a nebulous field and one in which the internal auditor's application of objective evaluation and the quantification of results may not be appropriate or possible. Nevertheless, the human resource is valuable and poor morale reduces productivity and the value of that resource. Senior managers are, or should be, concerned with employee morale, yet they cannot always be close enough to the workers to assess the level of morale.

Internal auditors are close to people as they do their audit jobs. They are, or should be, sensitive to feelings and attitudes, so they can obtain impressions that can be objective even if they are not quantifiable. Such judgements can be of considerable importance to managers. In some internal audit organizations, the auditors present an informal report to senior management that sets out impressions and judgements on such matters as working conditions, employee attitudes, availability and experience of supervisors, and employee morale.

Those reports, judiciously presented, can be very helpful to senior management and beneficial to the employees themselves. Management interest is heightened when observed conditions can be traced to morale and working conditions.

Stability of Tenure

In audits of a personnel department, the internal auditor will usually want to know if, in exit interviews, an effort is made to find why departing employees are leaving. The internal auditor will try to determine whether turnover rates are reasonable or excessive and how those rates compare among departments or among major divisions of the organization. High turnover is costly, and the internal auditor will want to know whether managers at appropriate levels receive information on reasons for excessive turnover and what they are doing about the causes.

Initiative

Innovation is the key to growth. A climate that restricts initiative inhibits growth, but initiative is hardly a simple thing to audit. It does, however, come within the purview of the internal auditor's impressions about an organization. When visiting a department and finding that there is no provision for self-appraisal, for seeking to do new things or to do the old things in new ways, the internal auditor has a responsibility to discuss the matter with management people.

Certainly, the discussion calls for tact and delicacy, but even the asking of a pertinent question may get the manager thinking if the internal auditor asks "To what extent and how do you stimulate initiative and innovativeness?" The internal auditor may receive an offhand response, but the manager may have started thinking about a program to tap the innovative wellsprings of employees. Also, the informal report to senior management may insure the continuance of such thinking.

Urwick: Principles of Administration

Urwick's principles, like Fayol's, find echoes in the work of the modern internal auditor. Illustrations, as they relate to two of the principles previously mentioned, follow:

Uniformity

Internal auditors usually review policies on employee wage and salary rates in the personnel department. They are particularly concerned with consistent treatment. If one employee of a group received a certain salary and a co-worker in the same wage classification received even a minor amount more, the lower-paid worker will conceive the difference as a reflection of standing in the company. It will be considered justifiable for the lower paid worker to produce less than the higher paid co-worker.

That applies to travel allowances as well as to pay checks. In multidivisional organizations, each relatively autonomous, there are often a good many transfers between divisions. The internal auditor will pay particular attention to reasonable consistency among the divisions to prevent employee dissatisfaction.

Objectives

The first rule of modern internal auditing is to know the objective of the activity under review. This does not necessarily mean the published statements or policies. They may be just window dressing. It means understanding the true, the real objective and how it relates to organizational objectives.

The basic objective of accounts payable is not merely to process payments to suppliers. That's the ostensible objective. The real objective must be much broader if it is to carry out the mission of the activity. A much better audit is made if the internal auditor sees the objective of accounts payable as approving payments to creditors when due, for what is done, while achieving the maximum conservation of cash. When internal auditors view the accounts payable activities in that light, they can perform an audit that is management-oriented, not merely a clerical verification.

Span of control

There is an old proverb that says the best fertilizer for the soil is the shadow of the owner. To the internal auditor that means that the best form of control is knowledgeable, available, respected supervision. Hence, internal auditors must be concerned, as they perform audits throughout the organization, about the supervision of employees:

- Do supervisors appear to know their jobs, and do they have the respect of their employees
- Do supervisors seem to be exercising control and providing direction to employees?

When supervision is inadequate because there are not enough supervisors to go around, or when, on the other hand, the ratio of supervisors to employees is higher than necessary to perform an adequate job, the matter of span of control becomes significant to the internal auditor, who should report the conclusions to management.

Davis: The Concept of Accountability

Davis was responsible for many important concepts and principles of management theory. We have singled out his concept of accountability because it has particular meaning for the internal auditor.

In large organizations, accountability is evidenced in reports to superiors. Such reports are usually the means by which top management learns what has been accomplished and how performance measures up to the goals that have been set. Also, they provide data on which decisions are based. The reports must therefore be accurate, timely, and meaningful. Most internal auditing organizations maintain a list of the key operating reports and see to it that the reports are reviewed periodically during the audits of related activities.

The managers who receive the reports must rely upon report integrity, yet operating managers may have a tendency to put the best face on things and gloss over unsatisfactory conditions or accomplishments. The internal auditor, as the partner of senior management, must insure the integrity of the reports. As partner to operating management, the internal auditor should point out defects and recommend improvements. Moreover, when the internal auditor perceives the need for accountability and an absence of reports, there is the responsibility to report the need for preparing the reports.

The Gilbreths: Simplifying the Work

The Gilbreths were concerned with work simplification, and so are internal auditors. Internal auditors need not be industrial engineers, but they must know enough about work methods to be able to tell when an industrial engineer should be called upon to help simplify work. If they know the steps of work simplification, they could probably suggest improved methods themselves. Some of the questions internal auditors can ask themselves as they approach any ongoing process, are:

- How can this process be improved?
- How can this form be combined with another?
- How can this flow of work be re-routed for greater efficiency?
- How can this step be eliminated completely?
- How can this amount of copying be done away with?

As internal auditors address themselves to the simplification of the work, they will start with determining whether the means justify the ends. They do not begin the analysis of an operation until they have determined the objective of the activity they will review. They will want to know precisely what end product is desired and needed.

There is a big difference between efficiency and effectiveness. Efficiency implies doing a job expeditiously and well. Effectiveness implies doing the right job. What profits it a person or an organization if the wrong job is done with the utmost precision and dispatch? The internal auditor, before analyzing the operation, will always ask:

- Is this operation needed?
- Does it accord with the organization's objectives?
- Will it further the organization's goals?

Gantt: Scheduling the Work

Many variations of the Gantt charts are now in use, but all emphasize the significance of time values in planning work. In industrial companies, the internal auditors concern themselves with production schedules, and they regularly audit the Gantt charts or the modern-day counterparts. Internal auditors are interested in the premises on which schedules are based. They want to know if there is coordination between the company's master schedules and its detailed schedules, between the sales organization and the manufacturing organization, between scheduling and both man loading and machine loading.

Internal auditors are particularly concerned with whether off-schedule jobs are highlighted and brought to the attention of higher management and whether appropriate steps are taken to recover from off-schedule work. One of the most important services the internal auditor can perform for higher management is to make sure that the reports it receives on schedule accomplishment are supported by the facts.

Follett: Perception and Communication

The internal auditor can be the catalyst to obtain congruence of perception among interfacing groups within the organization. Traditionally, accounts payable is at odds with purchasing, engineering is at odds with production, sales is at odds with production scheduling, and budgeting is at odds with just about everyone. The mutual objectives are the same—the good of the enterprise—but perception of those objectives and how to achieve the objectives may vary widely. In specific situations in which conflicts abort goals, the internal auditor can bring the parties together to reconcile divergencies and meet mutual objectives.

The internal auditor endorses Mary Parker Follett's preachments that good communications are absolutely essential. Many of the problems that the internal auditor runs into have their causes in faulty communications. For example, inspectors might be evaluating products against outdated specifications because new specifications were not promptly and properly communicated to them. In one audit, an internal auditor observed that new specifications were posted on a bulletin board for a week and then taken down. The inspectors were supposed to read and study those specifications, but the auditor found that many of them paid no attention to the bulletin board. Also, the auditor was able to trace a number of customers' rejections of inspected parts to the problems of communication.

At the internal auditor's urging, the chief inspector took these steps:

- Inspectors were instructed to initial and date a master copy of all new specifications, and the master copy was then filed in a binder available to all.
- Supervisors were required to hold weekly meetings with their people to discuss all new and revised specifications.

Barnard: Decision Making and the Executive

The auditor can play an important role in the decision-making process of the executive. This role is not that of the decision maker; that would be an unwarranted usurpation of authority and responsibility assigned to the manager. Instead, the role is to make sure that the executive is provided with the proper information and factors needed for a knowledgeable decision. Information submitted to executives by subordinates may be incorrect, incomplete, not meaningful, or not timely.

The auditor must be aware than informal organizations exist and are important to the workers within the enterprise. Then findings, conclusions, and recommendations become related to the "real world" and not the plastic world of organization charts and procedures. The auditor is more readily accepted by worker and manager alike when the audit program is geared to activity objectives rather than sterile rules. If those objectives are being met by bending the rules, the auditor will fault the rules instead of the performance.

The Bureaucrats—Weber and Gouldner

Rule-by-rule has advantages over seat-of-the-pants styles of management. Yet even in the more rule-bound public sector there is a need for leadership and knowing when to let go of the rules. The auditor needs to be aware of the sensible and healthy use of the bureaucratic approach, and contexts, such as financial regulation, where tight and virtually immutable rules are called for. Elsewhere there will be dangers in harping on this approach to the exclusion of others.

CONCLUSION

Books and articles on the principles of management are rapidly inundating the management community. Many of the principles set forth have stood the harsh test of time. Field studies and surveys have pointed to business downfalls when those principles have been violated. But the busy manager, beset on all sides by the problems faced each working day and pressed to make the decisions needed to overcome those problems, has little time to study or research those principles and put them into effect.

Yet the modern internal auditor, in day-to-day encounters with operational difficulties, can trace most of the difficulties to violations of management principles or good administrative techniques, and so must understand and keep abreast of studies in management. Internal auditors must be counselors and teachers so that they can aid busy managers in putting the principles and practices to practical use—to help managers make decisions that not only solve a problem but keep it from recurring.

REFERENCES

(1) Peter F. Drucker, *Management,* Oxford, Butterworth-Heinemann, 1991, pp. 307–308.
(2) A. D. Chandler, Jr., and Stephen Salisbury, *Pierre S. du Pont and the Making of the Modern Corporation* (New York: Harper & Row, 1971).
(3) A.P. Sloan, Jr., *My Years with General Motors* (Garden City, N.Y: Doubleday, 1964).
(4) Harold Koontz and Heinz Weihrich *Management* (New York: McGraw-Hill, 1988), p. 28.
(5) Henri Fayol, *General and Industrial Administration* (London: Pitman, 1984), trans. from the French, originally published in 1916.
(6) Ibid, chap. 4.
(7) Lyndall F. Urwick, *The Elements of Administration* (New York: Harper & Brothers, 1943).
(8) Ralph C. Davis, *The Fundamentals of Top Administration* (New York: Harper & Brothers, 1951).
(9) H. C. Metcalf and L.F. Urwick, eds., *Dynamic Administration: The Collected Papers of Mary Parker Follet* (New York: Harper Brothers, 1941).
(10) C. I. Barnard, *The Function of the Executive* (Cambridge, Mass: Harvard University Press, 1938).
(11) Ibid., pp. 202, 203.
(12) Ibid., chap. 9.
(13) R. Bendix, *Max Weber: An Intellectual Portrait*, Methuen, London, 1966, p. 427.
(14) M. Albrow, *Bureaucracy,* Macmillan, London, 1970, pp. 45–46.
(15) A. W. Gouldner, *'Patterns of Industrial Bureaucracy'*, Routledge, London, 1955
(16) Elton Mayo, *The Human Problem of an Industrial Civilization* (Cambridge, Mass: Harvard University Press, 1933).
(17) H. J. Mintern, ed., *How to Save Millions Through Internal Auditing* (Orlando, Fla: The Institute of Internal Auditors, 1988) p. 174.
(18) V. Z. Brink, "The Internal Auditor's Review of Organizational Control," *Research Committee Report* 18 (Orlando, Fla: The Institute of Internal Auditors, 1972).
(19) Ibid., p. 44.

5
Management, Managers and Internal Auditors

THE NATURE OF MANAGEMENT AND MANAGERS

The Field of Management

The boom in management theory since World War II let loose a Niagara of thoughts, ideas, and theories about management into the libraries of the world. To dissect the anatomy of management, hundreds of scalpels busily probed the core of the growing profession.

Not all the words were in English, and not all the scalpels were made in America. Management is not a very precise word, because it is used to describe both a function and the people who carry it out.

The function is universal, but the significance of the word varies. In hospitals, universities, and government, administrators manage. In the armed services, commanders manage. In businesses, managers manage. And in many organizations, executives are the counterparts of top managers.

Managers are professionals. Their function is now generally independent of the function of ownership. Although they use the tools of many disciplines—economics, quantification, and behavioral science—they practice a separate discipline called management. Managers may be indifferent technicians; but if they have absorbed the skills and techniques of management, they may be superb in evoking and putting to use the best from the skilled technicians.

Some theorists call management a science; some call it an art; some call it a practice; some call it a discipline. Perhaps it is an amalgam of all four. It has a body of systematized knowledge, predicated on persuasive principles. It seeks to bring about desired results through the application of skill. It calls for intensive, disciplined training and application to meld together a multitude of efforts and activities to reach desired goals.

On the quality of managers hinges the success or failure of business, government, churches, universities, and other organizations. It is becoming an aphorism that what goes well or what goes badly within an enterprise depends on how well managers innovate, function, and produce. So the search for the ingredients of this phenomenon on the human scene has been feverish.

Management and Manager Defined

Each student of management has a favorite definition. Here are a few from among a myriad:

Koontz and Weihrich say that "management is the process of designing and maintaining an environment in which individuals, working together in groups, accomplish efficiently selected aims."(1) It is "getting things done through and with people." Kreitner places the two Es of Effectiveness and Efficiency at the centre of his definition:

> "Management is the process of working with and through others to achieve organizational objectives in a changing environment. Central to this process is the effective and efficient use of limited resources."(2)

The internal auditor upholds the three Es of Economy, Efficiency and Effectiveness, but of these the weakest of the brethren is economy since:

- Economy is doing things cheap
- Efficiency is doing things right
- Effectiveness is doing the right things

Efficiency without effectiveness produces a "much ado about nothing" situation, and we have all heard of false economies.

A slightly more complex definition, which emphasizes the perpetual striving towards achieving the organization's stated goals, is supplied by Stoner and Freeman:

> "Management is the process of planning, organizing, leading, and controlling the efforts of organization members and of using all other organizational resources to achieve stated organizational goals."(3)

Charles Handy dismisses attempts at definition as either being so broad as to be meaningless, or so stereotyped as to become part of the background.(4) Certainly definitions, however provisional, do have value in providing orientation, but we can agree with Handy's suggestion that individual managers write their own set of precepts, and with his use of the medical analogy of the general practitioner.

Drucker views management through the functions of defining the specific purpose and mission of the enterprise, making work productive and the worker achieving, and managing social impacts and social responsibilities.(5) Along with his broad view of management, he sees the manager in a different light than most other writers. He sees as managers not only the leaders of others but also those whose actions and decisions are intended to have a significant impact on the business and its ability to perform and the direction it will take. In that context, the internal auditor, as one of those whom Drucker calls the "knowledge professionals," has a place on the management team.

A little tale illuminates this view of what a manager is: Three stonecutters, busy at their jobs, were asked what they were doing. The first said he was making a living. The second said she was doing the best job of stonecutting in the entire country. The third, with a look upward, said "I am building a cathedral."

The first stonecutter knows what he wants out of the job, and being a manager is not part of it. The second may think she's a manager, but her view is too narrow. The third is the true manager: a craftsperson and not a leader of others, but identifying with the enterprise and its goals. This contribution transcends personal needs or competence as a craftsperson; it is identified with the prime purpose of the job and not with the individual's parochial concerns.

Internal auditors may see parallels in the work of the stonecutters. One may perform an audit in strict compliance with the established audit program. Another, following the same program, may apply imagination and innovation in detecting deficient conditions that require special skills to unearth and develop and to bring articulately and persuasively to management's attention.

The third goes a step further, learning the underlying causes of the defects, and counseling managers on why the difficulties occurred and how recurrence may be prevented. This third internal auditor seeks out other activities within the enterprise in which like defects might exist and other managers might need similar counsel. More than a craftsperson, this individual is a "knowledge professional," a member of the management team.

The Management Theories

Each theorist who examines management sees it as the blind people "saw" an elephant: a rope, a tree, or a wall depending on what they touched. The varied views have become a tangle of strands each seen by someone as the sole line to the truth: this *is* the management theory jungle. A host of theories and combinations of theories seek to explain the management function. Here is a brief explanation of some of them.

Classical

Together with the classical school can be considered the school of scientific management, and the operational and empirical schools of management theory.

The classical school started as a system of management in the eighteenth century when handcraft at home with personally owned tools gave way to factory systems. People were brought together. They worked for someone else with someone else's equipment. Formal organizations were developed. Rules and regulations were imposed. The owners ruled chiefly by reason of ownership and by instilling feelings of fear.

Then, with the advent of Taylor, Fayol, Gantt, and the Gilbreths, some order was imposed on the haphazard organizational structures that had been built at the whims of individuals. In the late nineteenth and early twentieth centuries, management began to emerge as a science as Taylor and others concentrated on the study of processes and on systematic planning.

The operational approach was fashioned by Fayol. It made use of a universal body of knowledge, theory, and principles and applied them to all types of enterprises. Fayol viewed management as a process that can be understood by analyzing the functions of the manager. Past experience can be the source from which basic principles can be distilled. The principles can serve as standards for managers and, with time, be either refined or disproved. The proven principles remain valid whether the manager uses them or elects to ignore them. But the operational approach is encapsulated; it is isolated from other fields we now know to have a profound effect on the enterprise: economics, sociology, psychology, and other sciences. Therein lies its weakness.

The empirical view relies on experience. The premise is that a study of how other managers solved specific problems will reveal helpful techniques that have universal applicability. That may often be true, but it may just as often be misleading. It is rare indeed that today's problem is precisely the same as yesterday's. Also management is not so exact a science that precedent will be completely applicable in all cases.

One thread runs through the fabric of all these schools of management theory: the approach is relatively mechanistic; it leaves little room for the human being who is subject to the decisions, rules and principles. The single beam of the spotlight illuminates the manager as the unquestioned authority. The law flows down. Those beneath may not question; they may not disobey; they may not even debate or suggest.

Yet that approach is most prevalent today; indeed, in some organizations, suborganizations, or environments, no other is appropriate. Still, different schools of management thought are making themselves felt, as we shall point out.

Behavioral

Starting with the 1920s, observers of the management scene began finding some blind spots in the scientific view of management. The discovery began with the work of Mayo and Roethlisberger, who carried out organized research into the subject of humanities in business. The school is variously called "human relations," "behavioral science," and "leadership." It focuses on the human side of management and the worker. It seeks to obtain greater understanding to accomplish group objectives. The research has been able to buttress the proposition that, if the needs and desires of people are satisfied, the organization's output will increase.

The followers of the behavioral approach see the manager not as a doer but as an accomplisher through others. There have been significant contributions in the use of participation and in dealing with organizational conflicts. Besides, new understandings have been reached about the motivations of people, the effect of authority, the place of irrationality in behavior, and the all-important informal relations within an organization.

On the other hand, some proponents have sought to elevate the behavioral approach to unattainable heights. They see it as the core of management. They equate human behavior with the entire field of management, whereas, at most, it is only a tool of management and one of the many tools the manager must master in order to do the job.

If the worker is to be productive, the manager must understand not only the work but also the physiological, psychological, social and community, and economic dimensions of working. These four dimensions are outlined as follows:

1. *The physiological dimension* Workers are human beings and not machines. They lack the strength and stamina of a machine, but exceed machines in coordination and imagination. The machine works best at a steady speed, but workers perform at varying speeds, and so their work is best organized to provide diversity.

2. *The psychological dimension.* People are conditioned to work; unemployment creates severe psychological disturbances. As an extension of personality, work gives the individual a feeling of worth and accomplishment. The Western work ethic gives respect and dignity to working.

3. *The social and community dimension.* Belonging to a work group satisfies an individual's need. Outside the family, the person's job is the one great bond with others.

4. *The economic dimension.* Work is the basis for the individual's economic existence. It creates power relations between management and labor.

Those four dimensions are important to the manager in dealing with people; the manager cannot avoid them or will them away. The manager must be concerned with the behavioral and human relations approach to the job. There are several reasons why. First, human relations can contribute to greater productivity. Second, if the manager is not concerned with human relations, something else, like the labor union, will step in to force that concern. Third, the government may intervene, as witness Fair Employment Practice laws. Finally, every organization must meet certain moral objectives, and concern for the human being is a paramount objective.

Decision Making

Some theorists contend that decision making is the pivotal job of the manager. Whatever the manager does involves selecting a course of action from among different choices. The theorists have studied decisions for improving communication, incentives, reactions of workers, and human values in terms of enterprise objectives. Thus the decision theory school has expanded its concepts. It has gone beyond evaluating alternatives. It has reached into the entire bag of the entity's functions, including value considerations about the enterprise goals.

As in many schools of thought, adherents seek to use the decision-making umbrella to cover every conceivable enterprise activity. However, there may be a question whether decision making is the center of the management universe or just one of the spheres within the totality. There is more to managing than making decisions; there is also implementation, evaluation, and feedback. Nevertheless, decision making as a key function of management cannot be underestimated.

Systems

The systems management school sees every organization as a complex system made up of integrated subsystems. The manager functions through systems grappling with a huge system by dealing with the many smaller systems that constitute the whole. Each system has the elements of input, processing, output, and feedback, and all are governed by some means of control. The input is received from an upstream system's output. The output is passed on to a downstream system.

The systems concept simplifies dealing with the numerous and varied activities within a large organization. Also, it brings about a coalescence of disciplines usually considered isolated: economics, engineering, psychology, sociology, and anthropology. It crosses organizational lines. It penetrates the departmental capsule.

In similar fashion, the internal auditor, as occasion warrants, may depart from the review of a single department or group—the organizational audit—and cross organizational lines to trace a function from headwater to delta—the functional audit. In a functional audit of purchased products, the internal auditor might trace the various interlocking subsystems that begin with preliminary design and drafting—where the purchased products needed are identified—through production planning, purchasing, receiving, and storing and the incorporation of the procured products into a final assembly. To the internal auditor, as to the manager, the functional or systems approach leads to a completely different view of the organization's operations.

The multitudinous interrelations among subsystems call for the assimilation of masses of data. Thus the advent of the computer added muscle to the management system concept by permitting new, complex control devices to function. This important subject receives full length treatment in Chapter 6.

Quantitative

The quantitative, or mathematical, school traces its heritage to Taylor's scientific management and its birth to World War II. In the 1940s what is now known as operations research was developed in England to solve war-related problems. Professor P.M.S. Blackett of the University of Manchester gathered a team of physiologists, mathematical physicists, mathematicians, astrophysicists, and other specialists to study combat and logistical systems. That group, as well as others like it set up in the United States, had excellent results from using mathematical models to solve difficult problems. They determined the best size for war convoys and the depth at which charges should explode in an attack on submarines.

The results were so good that the approach was adopted by business enterprises. The development of the computer simplified handling great amounts of statistical data dealing with numerous variables and solving complex problems. Calculus can be used to determine the extent of change in one factor with respect to another factor. The businessperson is given answers to "what if" questions: How are overhead rates affected by changes in the labor base, or productivity, or greater sales? What is the best geographical location of warehouses? What is the proper size of sales territories? What will be the effect of lowered or raised prices?

Models can be developed to represent systems and to assist in decision making. The techniques used include probability theory, regression analysis, linear programming, Monte Carlo simulation, inventory theory, queuing theory, sensitivity analysis, game theory, dynamic programming, and exponential smoothing.

Nevertheless, the quantitative approach is no more the whole story of management than accounting is. It offers assistance in decision making and even in evaluating risks. It contributes to orderly thinking. It forces managers to identify and think through problems thoroughly, establish goals, and measure effectiveness. It fosters the development of logical systems of management. But it is less a school of management than a tool of management.

The early promise of substituting operations research for management thought and the computer for the manager has not been and cannot be realized. Management in many ways is still an art. The quantitative approach places emphasis on techniques, not on principles.

Communications Center

In the communications center approach, the manager is a walking information center. Managers are the focal points for receiving, storing, and processing information and then disseminating it as they direct people and control activities. The approach gained greater popularity with the advent of the computer and management information systems, and it is akin to the decision-making theory of management. However, the reliance on computers overshadows a simple fact of life: managers have always been communications centers. By being privy to bits and pieces of information not available to their subordinates, they emerge as the nerve centers of their organizational units. By contacts with peers, their own superiors, and their own people, they become depositories of information that goes beyond anything known by their people. Then that information puts them in the position of being able to make more knowledgeable decisions than their people can make. Like other schools, however, communication is not the whole story.

Social System

The social system school is related to the behavioral approach. It conceives of the organization as a series of cultural interrelations within the organization. It seeks to integrate those relations into a system. The emphasis is on cooperation to solve the organization's problems and assist in making decisions. It looks toward the balanced interests of the entity and rejects courses of action that benefit one group alone.

The social system school pays particular attention to ethics, to what is seen as right and moral. Hence it is concerned with the relations among the organization, the internal and external environment, and the forces for change. The ethics of the manager are brought into sharper focus; the manager is not an island and personal life affects the organization and the organisms within it.

The concepts of the social system school are significant, but are they really the entire structure of management?

Integration

Managers are practical people. They do not see themselves as chameleons who must change management colors with each new task or problem. They want some unified theory that selects the best from all theories and leads to increased productivity while preventing or reducing employee alienation.

Many attempts have been made to integrate the varying approaches that we have just identified. Some theorists see valuable lessons in all the concepts propounded by each of the schools of management and have sought to extract and meld the best from each. The attempts at amalgamation go by many names. They include but are not limited to the fusion process, the modified theory, and the organization overlay. Here are brief explanations of these three:

1. *The fusion process* declares that, so long as the individual and the organization are in contact, they must in time coalesce and integrate their needs and desires. The individual, while remaining in the organization, must somehow change behavior to meet the needs of the organization. The organization must also change; its plans and structure must not be so rigid that they fail to accommodate the individual's needs. If both parties satisfy their needs in that accommodation, then there is a successful fusion. Perfect fusion is hardly ever possible because of

basic differences in goals; indeed, may not be desirable, because progress is born in the crucible, not in the easy chair.

2. According to *the modified theory of management,* the classical approach succeeds only through the liquidation or erosion of human assets. Drives for short-run productivity increases are bound to result in employee alienation. In the participative approach, an effort is made to obtain cooperation between employee and employer to the end that production increases and alienation is dissipated. Studies by Rensis Likert have indicated the practical benefits from the approach.(6)

3. *The organization overlay* school suggests that the formal structures of the organization, as depicted by the familiar organization charts, are too rigid; they exclude the human element and are out of touch with reality. Additional relations are vital and essential. Those relations include the employee and group, influences of intellectual leaders, decision-making centers, the power residing within groups and individuals, and the flow of informal communication.

Such patterns, guides, and networks can be laid over the official organization chart and hence display the "real world" organization. The resulting picture is extremely complex and serves to demonstrate, if nothing else, that the true organization chart is not as clean and crisp as it appears to be. The intelligent manager must take the human relations into account.

Models of Managers

Models of management have certain counterparts in models of managers. The schools of management theory produce echoes from the people who perform management functions. The correlation is not precise, but it is close enough to deserve attention.

The affluent society depicted by John Kenneth Galbraith owes its growth to many factors, including improved education, innovation, and an expanding technology, but central to all those factors are management and managers. Managers have responded to the needs of society and to the opportunities for improved productivity. Many shifts in the way managers function have occurred in response to the changes in society, the outlook of workers, and the findings of researchers who have probed management theory. As a result, new models of organizational behavior have evolved, and many are still evolving. The models are not merely catchwords or labels. The concepts that give rise to the models influence the managers: their thinking, the way they see the world around them, and their attitude toward the people they deal with.

When managers influenced by a new school of behavior think in new ways, they begin to act differently. On their actions depend the productivity of the organizational unit. If they follow outmoded or inappropriate models, they may be jeopardizing their jobs or their organization.

Four distinct models of organizational behavior have evolved during the last 100 years or so; they are the autocratic, custodial, supportive, and collegial. The autocratic model, the traditional bull of the woods, held sway 75 years ago. Then, with the proliferation of studies on organizational behavior during the 1920s and the 1930s and with the growth of the unions, the more successful custodial model emerged. More organizations, however, are now beginning to turn to the supportive model, particularly among white collar workers. Just beginning to make itself felt in some advance organizations is the collegial model—the group of colleagues. Actually, no one organization follows a single model, nor does any manager use one model exclusively. Yet one model will tend to be dominant and will guide the methods of the organization and the thinking of the manager.

Within the organization's suborganizations, different models may be appropriate. The security department may use the autocratic approach; the production department the custodial approach; the internal auditing department the supportive approach; and the research department the collegial approach. The four models will now be analyzed in terms of the manager, the employee, and performance.

Autocratic Model

The autocratic model is rooted in history; it prevailed during the Industrial Revolution. It is based on power pure and simple. It uses threats, and motivation is negative. It sees people as passive, resistant, and lazy. Managers assume that employees have to be pushed into doing their jobs, and so they develop formal, structured organizations interwoven with detailed rules that are violated at the employee's peril. The manager gives the orders; the worker obeys "or else."

Employees bow to the authority of the boss, who *is* a boss rather than a leader. The worker has a psychological dependency on this boss, who holds the power of the job's life or death. The worker may like the boss, as a respected individual, and may perform because of basic drives. However, all that is attributable to the worker and not to the managerial model.

Modern observers tend to condemn it, but the autocratic model had its measure of success in building empires during the 1800s: the railroad systems, the steel mills, and an industrial society. Yet questions arise: Is there a better way? Can the same or better performance be achieved with enthusiasm instead of passive resistance? Can needs other than basic subsistence be filled in the employee and result in improved productivity? Those questions turned attention to other models of managerial behavior.

Custodial Model

The custodial model took form in the 1930s when interest started turning from the despotic organizations to the "happy shop." Psychologists, industrial relations specialists, and economists pointed out that a satisfied employee could be a more productive worker. Under the autocrat, the compliant worker might be afraid to speak, but couldn't be stopped from thinking. Somehow or other seething frustrations and suppressed aggressions would be taken out on productivity, the family, and the community.

So began the development of the custodial model, with its fringe benefits, social security, and numerous programs to cater to what were seen as the needs and wants of the employee. Generally, the programs depended on the economic resources available to carry them out, and managerial orientation was toward material rewards for the worker. The employee saw security in the model. Morale improved; the employee tended to transfer dependence from the boss to the organization that provided the security blanket.

But the roseate picture that had been painted for the custodial model began to fade. People may have been happy, but they were not being fulfilled. A warm bath is relaxing, not invigorating. Security and happiness are important, but they are not the whole answer to work. People need to be motivated beyond what they think they are capable of doing in order to be achieving and in order to be fulfilled.

Observers began to see that neither the custodial nor the autocratic model provided the ultimate truth. Clearly, there may be some jobs and some people—insecure, timid, weak, not needing or desiring self-fulfilment—who function best in a custodial atmosphere. They see the job as a source of income and necessary evil. If the evil can be made tolerable through pleasant relationships, there is nothing further to demand—at least they will not be alienated. For others there is more to work than a relaxed way to earn a living.

Supportive Model

The supportive model found adherents when researchers, particularly in the Hawthorne experiments, showed that the happy employee was not necessarily the most productive employee. The supportive model moves away from the economic support of the custodial model to the psychological support provided by a leader-manager.

The supportive model depends on leadership and a climate that helps the employee grow vigorously, not languorously. The manager has positive feelings about staff. They *do* want to work. They *do* want to grow. They *do* want to be productive. They *do* want to take responsibility. They *do* want to achieve.

Since what is being supported is performance—rather than happiness—the employee is oriented toward that goal instead of obedience or security. Psychologically there is a feeling of participation and involvement. The worker and organization become "we" instead of "me and them." The model awakens drives that the worker may never have been aware of.

The supportive model is a rung that is high in the ladder that reaches toward employee motivation and progress, but it is not the top rung of the ladder. That may well be the fourth model.

Collegial Model

The fourth and latest model is still beginning to take shape. It developed from research, especially by Likert and Hertzberg.(7)(8)It depends on management building a feeling of mutual contribution. The manager and the employee are joint contributors; they are not boss and worker. Since much is expected, much is given. Each contributor—worker, co-worker, manager, and executive—is respected for what he can offer to meet organizational goals.

The manager is oriented toward teamwork instead of toward superior and subordinate. Performance is improved because there is an inner need to perform at maximum effectiveness, not to please the boss or the inspector, but to please the inner monitor that rejects everything but the best.

The result from the employee's standpoint can be self-discipline, responsibility, self-fulfilment, and enthusiasm.

Summary

Models are evolutionary. They grew out of the needs of organizations and of people. They are not static, and none as yet answers the needs of all situations, but managers must be aware of the models that exist. They must realize that no one model is the full-spectrum cure to organizational maladies. Low-skilled routine work and the people content with that kind of work may respond best to security and motivational rewards, that is, to the autocratic and custodial models. Other jobs, more professional in nature, may be made most productive in a climate of teamwork and self-motivation, that is, the climate of the supportive and collegial models.

As time goes by, as employees strive for more than a 9:00-to-5:00 existence, and as greater premiums are placed on innovation and commitment, the trends for all kinds of workers can be toward the supportive and collegial models and whatever lies beyond.

THE NATURE OF MODERN INTERNAL AUDITING

Models of Internal Auditing

Evolving models of management have counterparts in evolving models of internal auditing. There too the classical and autocratic beginnings are giving way to more enlightened schools of thought. The classical internal auditor was an adjunct of the autocrat. The autocrat made the rules; the internal auditor accepted them and checked to see whether they were being followed. The primary function of the classical auditor was to examine financial transactions, accounts, and reports and to evaluate compliance with applicable rules and regulations. To that end there was need for a basic knowledge of accounting theory and practice and a facility for applying auditing techniques and procedures. The numbers came first; people came afterward if at all. A deviation was a deviation whether it was merely a smudge on the pillars of the organization or an earthquake that rocked the pillars.

The classical internal auditor performed, and still performs, a needed function, but that function is restricted and is sometimes warped. Besides, it looks to the past, not to the future. The classical auditor belongs to the "protective" school that concentrates on the conservation of resources and the detection of deviations. The high point in an auditing career would be to find fraudulent transactions and see to it that the thief or embezzler was put behind bars. It should be emphasized that being on the alert for fraudulent transactions is still a necessary function of internal auditing, but it is not the whole function.

Concepts and theories of internal auditing have advanced in many organizations in both the public and the private sectors. They have marched forward with the development of innovative and imaginative auditing organizations, with the establishment of The Institute of Internal Auditors and its motto "Progress Through Sharing," and with the writings of the modern thinkers in the profession.

The scope of internal auditing expanded to a review of effectiveness, efficiency and economy in the use of resources. "Resources" came to embrace more than what was recorded in the books of account; they now mean people, materials and money. The range of the internal auditor has widened. The internal auditor no longer remains bound to the books of account, but roams at will through every activity in the organization where there can be a service to management. The preoccupation is no longer solely with assets and numbers, but with all resources and operations. In the "constructive school," the purpose is to evaluate all relevant and significant operations and make appropriate recommendations for improvement.

A third school of internal auditing is now forming. It is taking shape as the internal auditor takes on a new responsibility: to determine whether desired results are being achieved effectively. That is a quantum jump, but it is more than an increase in the scope of internal auditing. It is a change in thinking and a change in the levels of people with whom the auditor primarily deals.

To examine transactions calls for dealing with workers and supervisors. To review operations calls for adding operating managers to the clientele. To evaluate program results requires bringing executive management into the auditor's compass of concern.

Evaluating desired results and the effectiveness with which they are achieved calls for determining more than whether activities are being carried out with due concern for cost, quality, and schedule. It calls for determining whether the right activities were carried out to begin with, whether those activities mesh with the organization's objectives and goals, whether people are employing appropriate management and administrative techniques, whether people know what they should be achieving and are using their resources wisely to achieve, and whether people need counsel and guidance to do the right thing in the best way.

That is the newest school of modern internal auditing theory: the school of the counselor, teacher, and problem-solving partner.

Understanding Models of Management

The schools of management theory are not merely textbook caricatures. Research has identified and delineated them. Different managers follow different philosophies of management. If the internal auditor were to deal with a classical environment as if it were a collegial one, the certain results would be conflict and misunderstanding. Also, the auditor would be prevented from achieving own audit goals.

We shall outline the schools of management theory in relation to the internal auditor:

- *In a classical environment* the internal auditor emphasizes transactions and deviations. That classical managers understand: they make the rules; they want them followed. Once they are convinced that deviations have occurred— and they alone must be convinced—they will take the steps to correct them and to see that they do not recur. The auditor is not debarred from evaluating effectiveness and results, but treads softly and recognizes the need for a selling job.
- *In the behavioral school environment* the internal auditor must take a different tack, and must speak of goals and objectives, of values and needs. When people of the behavioral school are made aware that they are not achieving what was intended, both they and the auditor may not only assess production but reassess the goals themselves.
- *In the environment of the decision-making school* the internal auditor's orientation will be toward the elements of the decision. Has the problem been formulated precisely in terms of goals? Does the decision tree take into account the controllable factors and those beyond control—the fixed factors and the variable factors? Have the possible solutions been tested? Have the solutions been put into effect? Have feedback systems been established to help determine whether objectives are being met?

  Internal auditors should be careful not to become second-guessers of management decisions; 20-20 hindsight is easy to develop and difficult to appreciate. But they can evaluate the *methods* used in making decisions, and make sure that managers are receiving the kind of prompt, accurate, meaningful information they need for their decision-making process.
- *In the systems school environment* the internal auditor might describe problem

areas in terms of input, processing, output, feedback, and control and point out how breakdowns in any of those elements result in difficulties that need correction.

- *In the environment of the quantitative or mathematical school* the internal auditor can use analytical ability to assure senior management that appropriate quantitative approaches and techniques were used, that the input is relevant, accurate, and complete, and that the methods employed can be tested objectively. There may be a tendency to place overreliance on numbers; it is easy to forget, in the passion for mathematics, that the end result must pass the test of reason and must make good sense.

- *In the communication school environment* internal auditors can provide a service in seeing that the communications received are relevant, current, complete and usable. They can also perform a service by looking at the economies of the communication received. Is the flood of information necessary? Is it all raw data that are useless to the recipient? Can it be synthesized to have more meaning and be made more readily usable?

- *In the social system school environment* the internal auditor should keep abreast of new legislation on safety, the environment, and social impacts. Managers are not always kept informed of new laws that have an immediate effect on their work. When government inspectors come around to check on compliance, it may be too late. Hence, as counselor to management, internal auditors should be alert to new laws that will affect systems and controls. They should bring them to the attention of managers and point out the steps needed to bring activities into compliance.

The schools of management theory proliferate. There is no unanimity: no one seems to have the whole answer. Yet each school, in its way, has some effect on management thinking, so internal auditors should have more than a nodding acquaintance with the schools to keep attuned with the managers they must deal with.

Dealing with Models of Managers

Each manager the internal auditor deals with has a unique style. Some managers may be exclusively autocratic, custodial, supportive, or collegial. Others may be amalgams of two or more of the model styles, although usually one model style will predominate. Internal auditors should be aware of the individual styles, which may affect the audit approach. They may have a bearing on how they "get through" to the manager to present their findings, make recommendations, and decide how to proceed to be sure that corrective action is taken and is effective.

The internal auditor needs to consider the individual style of the managers:

- *The autocratic style* should signal to the internal auditor that workers and subordinate managers lack independence. They will be fearful of taking any action that might conflict with the autocrat's views—or with their views of the autocrat's views. To aid the autocrat, the auditor should look for clear instructions, tight controls, and a rigid system of review and approval. Also if the auditor encounters defects or proposes improvements, he or she will find it necessary to clear them with the autocrat, for nobody else within the group has authority to approve changes. If defects are traceable to an environment of repression, the auditor may have to counsel the autocrat or the superior on the benefits that may flow from other management styles.

- *The custodial style* calls for the internal auditor who encounters unsatisfactory conditions to point out how much easier matters will be if defects are corrected and recommendations are adopted. At the same time, the auditor should be aware of the faults inherent in the custodial style. The relaxed atmosphere is not always the climate in which productivity grows. Perhaps realistic goals and measurements need to be established—with the cooperation of those who will be measured.
- *The supportive style* gives the internal auditor the opportunity to take both managers and employees into confidence from the time the audit starts until it is completed. Recommendations gain readier acceptance when he can show how they will improve production and better achieve goals and objectives.
- *The collegial style* beckons the auditor to be a contributor to the group and offer recommendations and contributions to the greater good of the organization.

Acceptance into the Partnership

In law, a partnership is an association of two or more persons to carry on, as co-owners, a business for profit. Although the manager and the internal auditor are not co-owners, they can carry out their responsibilities only if they act as though the business were theirs and its profits depended on their working together to meet its objectives. Indeed, before an internal auditor makes a recommendation for improvement, the question "What should I do if I owned the enterprise?" would be asked.

Another definition of partnership more precisely describes the hoped-for affiliation between management and internal auditing: a relationship involving close cooperation between parties who have specified and joint rights and responsibilities. A partnership is a delicate relationship. It is founded on mutual trust. It should combine complementary skills and assets that each partner brings to the undertaking. It calls for mutual respect and for agreement on what each partner demands of the other.

One of the most serious and recurring complaints from many internal auditors is the lack of acceptance of the internal auditing function by managers within the organization. Internal auditors, hearing of the high regard in which many of their colleagues are held in some organizations, become frustrated when their own managements fail to provide them with the status and support they feel they must have to carry out a topnotch audit job.

No one formula will provide the key to management acceptance, much less the hoped-for problem-solving partnership. Not all managements are the same, and certainly not all internal auditors are the same. Some have not thought through what their role and function within their organization is and how it fits into the particular management style or management needs. Clearly, the needs in a bank or insurance company vary widely from the needs in a government agency or a university.

Many more internal auditors have not equipped themselves with the skills, techniques, and know-how that bring respect and acceptance. Still others have not mounted the right campaign within their organization to parade their wares before management and determine what management really wants and what it really needs.

Some hints of what management expects from the internal auditor can be gleaned from the words of high-placed managers themselves. And what better source for such intelligence than the people who pay the bills? From a sampling of those thoughts, the same theme seems to recur: enlightened managers see the respected internal auditor as more than a verifier and a checker, more than a chronicler of things past, and more than a faultfinder. They see such an internal auditor as more of a counselor, more of a teacher, and more of a problem-solving partner. So we have grouped these thoughts under the more respected headings as follows.

Counselor

Ward Burns, when controller for J.P. Stevens Company, Inc., laid down ten commandments for the internal auditor:

1. Are the company's systems being properly controlled? Can management be sure, for example, that cash is protected by proper internal controls from receipt to disbursement, that excess cash is invested advantageously, that cash is borrowed at competitive rates for the shortest possible time, that "goodwill" bank accounts are minimized, and that foreign currencies are promptly exchanged at the best rates?
2. Be familiar with the organization and its controls. Be sure of the facts. Be expert in the methods of evaluation, the techniques of control, and the development of practical recommendations.
3. Be able to prepare clear, concise reports. Avoid trivia. Include matters that top management can do something about and also matters that were resolved but about which top management should be informed.
4. Inform management immediately about any significant deviations that need correction; do not wait for the final written report.
5. Resolve all disputes before the report reaches top management. Review draft

reports up the management ladder. Report irreconcilable differences and give both sides.

6. Review data processing operations as top management would review them if it had the time and knew how.

7. Be available for consultation on matters and techniques of control. (Burns says, "Happy is the internal auditor who has so conducted himself over a period of time that he is invited to participate in establishing procedures and concepts at the start of a new venture of operation. It is the ultimate proof that the internal auditor is wanted and needed and that his skills are, at long last, clearly recognized.")

8. Have guts. Once sure of the facts, certain of the relevance and significance of recommendations, and perceiving a clear and present danger if recommendations are not followed, the internal auditor must have the fortitude to stand up and be heard, even if that takes going to the very top.

9. Be ethical. Be competent. Be professional.

10. Be interested in every aspect of the enterprise. Be concerned with the impact of accelerating technological, economic, regulatory, or social changes.

To Burns the most important thing top management should expect from internal auditing is the ability to welcome, evaluate, and assimilate change. The thrust of the internal auditor's work may have to be the evaluation of activities, transactions, and probabilities of the future rather than the present or past and counseling management on the findings and conclusions.

William O. Beers, as president of Kraftco Corporation, wrote:

> "The prime goal of business will not change. The goal is profit. But to obtain that profit, more than ever it will be necessary to plan accurately—plan with the help of the latest available information [while] considering the dynamics of our society, our environment, and our economy.
>
> In this endeavor, the internal audit function will be crucial . . . 'the uninspected inevitably deteriorates.'"

Stephen F. Keating, when president of Honeywell, Inc., expected the internal auditor (or operations analyst as was called at Honeywell):

- To know the total business.
- To think like the managers.
- To develop, communicate, and sell ideas.
- To keep evaluating his own function.
- To be sensitive and diplomatic.
- To be objective.
- To be a coordinator of good business practice.

In connection with the coordination function, Keating said that because analysts study so many parts of the company, they are in a perfect position to perform a cross-pollinating function, and they are looked upon to some extent as operating a consulting service.

Stuart D. Watson, when president, chief executive officer, and a director of Heublein, Inc., saw internal auditing as follows.

1. It must aid the chief executive in the planning process by ensuring the integrity of the information systems. Those are the systems the executive must rely upon in devising effective plans.

- Have all the risks been identified?
- Has there been adequate research on markets and on competition?
- Are sales forecasts, pricing strategies, and projected costs sound?
- How good are the budgeting methods for establishing goals and monitoring performance?

2. It must alert the chief executive in the organizing process when it encounters problems traceable to the organization structure: duties, responsibilities, and personnel policies.

3. the audit function should help head off and resolve business problems. The more exposure to company operations it has the better equipped it will be to identify and work on the more significant problems.

4. It is important to know how management thinks: its plans, its objectives, and its operating concepts; in short, its management model.

Teacher

Raymond Plank, as president of Apache Corporation, which is involved in oil and gas exploration, used his internal auditors to advise him on company acquisitions, on whether there was compatibility of interests and policies. Then, when a company was acquired, the internal auditor helped advise management on making necessary transitions to bring the new company into gear with Apache in terms of policies, procedures, and systems.

Plank also asked his internal auditors to help owner-managers of subsidiary companies find ways to improve profits, ways to balance long-term and short-term profits. Above all, he wanted the internal auditor "to get through to people" if they are to get results.

Dudley Stewart, as vice president and comptroller for the Industrial Acceptance Corporation Group of Companies, in speaking about the internal auditor of the future, said:

"The internal auditor must function as an integral part of the management team. The chief internal auditor will become more and more a creative executive. The more effective he becomes, the more he will find that a great deal of his time is spent on teaching those who report to him and teaching very subtly those on whose work he is reporting."

Problem-Solving Partner

Charles R. Gollihar, Jr., as vice president, finance and treasurer for Douglas Aircraft Company of Canada Limited said:

"Overall, I recommend to you the principle and belief that the audit report should settle each question in the mind of management, not raise questions to which an answer must then be found.

The message I most wish to convey is that I feel strongly that in the area of management audits, the auditor can and should be an integral part of the *problem-solving team*. I do not feel his role is to stand apart and say 'I warned you!', but rather [he] should roll up his sleeves and jointly with other managers report to top management: 'we fixed it.'"

Kenneth W. Bahler, assistant to the president, Union Carbide Corporation, includes in his catalog of what management expects from the internal auditor:

• Act and perform like a professional.
• Serve as an extension of management in doing the type of verification the manager would do personally if he could.
• Participate as a member of the management team to find better ways of doing the job.

William G. Phillips, former president and chief executive officer of International Multifoods Corporation, draws these conclusions about internal auditing:

"Now let me sum up by saying that the internal auditing profession has a tremendous opportunity to expand the service it provides to companies. In our company, for example, we have changed the name of the internal audit function to audit services so as to communicate an expanded concept of the function throughout the organization.

An area of increasing importance to American business is the planning process. Within our company and many others, planning has been improved, and added emphasis placed on more and better attention to implementation, by defining proper action steps.

Why shouldn't auditors be asked to become working partners in reviewing the basic assumptions and inputs which result in operating plans? This is one of the many new and exciting areas in which the profession can make a contribution.

In today's vigorous and expanding business climate, you either move forward or you regress. If you rise to the occasion, the sky is truly the limit for today's internal auditor.

With this change in the role of the internal auditor, the definition, of course, would have to be revised to read something like this:

"The typical auditor is a beautiful person, intelligent warm and considerate with an ability to be in the other person's shoes and understand the problems; polite in contact and helpful, but at the same time objective, calm and as composed in crisis as Stravinsky on opening night; a human person with a heart of gold and with the charm of a friendly poodle, plus brains, business foresight and a sense of humor. Happily they train others in their image and all of them finally go to Heaven."

THE INTERNAL AUDITOR'S BILL OF RIGHTS(9)

William R. Howell, as Chairman of the Board and Chief Executive Officer of JC Penney Company, suggested that as an antidote to the plethora of articles on what senior managers should expect of internal auditors, he would like to see something on what internal auditors have a right to expect from their senior management. The articles of his suggested Bill of Rights are that auditors have a right to:

1. A precise and detailed definition of their responsibilities.
2. A full understanding of the corporate policies they are expected to monitor.
3. Know what kind of moral behavior management expects of its people.
4. Be problem solvers as well as problem identifiers.
5. Be brought into the mainstream of the company.
6. Complete understanding of the company's goals and aspirations.
7. A career path in the company.
8. The total support of their company's management.
9. Expect senior management to set the right tone for the environment in which they work.
10. To feel important—indispensable in fact—to corporate management.

Geoffrey Bowes, Executive Director of the Institute of Directors of New Zealand considers that the internal audit function is quintessentially a tool for directors, and that this point receives insufficient emphasis in the professional standards.(10) This certainly gives more empowerment to the internal auditor, although it is important to serve equally the needs of the wider constituency of managers at all levels.

The ultimate seal of approval came from Sir Adrian Cadbury's 1992 committee on corporate governance. The following quotation shows that internal audit is now placed at the centre of the debate on corporate governance:

"The function of the internal auditors is complementary to, but different from, that of the outside auditors. We regard it as good practice for companies to establish internal audit functions to undertake regular monitoring of key controls and procedures. Such regular monitoring is an integral part of a company's system of internal control and helps to ensure its effectiveness. An internal audit function is well placed to undertake investigations on behalf of the audit committee and to follow up any suspicion of fraud. It is essential that heads of internal audit should have unrestricted access to the chair of the audit committee in order to ensure the independence of their position."(11)

Management acceptance of the modern internal audit function takes work. It must be founded on demonstrated professional competence and on the communication of the benefits of the function to managers through comprehensive long-range audit programs, through professional audits, through crisp, incisive audit reports, and through periodic summary reports to management on the accomplishments the internal auditor has made. There are no shortcuts or easy ways, but the benefits both to the auditor and to the organization are worth the effort.

CONCLUSION

The classic authoritarian form of management is being challenged by a host of new schools—new theories of how best to run an enterprise and motivate people. It would seem that, as more theorists address themselves to the subject, additional schools will blossom in the jungle of management theories. Yet each has something to commend it, and both managers and internal auditors should be aware of what current research is bringing to the management table.

Certainly internal auditors should know the nature of the manager they are dealing with and how best to cope with each type of manager, whether autocratic, custodial, supportive, or collegial. Also, if they are to gain acceptance in a problem-solving partnership, they should know how thoughtful executives regard the internal audit function and thereby bring to the partnership complementary assets needed to help the organization thrive.

REFERENCES

(1) Harold Koontz and Heinz Weihrich, *Management* (New York: McGraw-Hill, 1988), p. 4.
(2) Robert Kreitner, *Management*, 4th edition (Boston: Houghton, Mifflin, 1989),p. 9.
(3) JA. Stoner and R. E. Freeman, *Management*, 4th edition, (New Jersey: Prentice-Hall, 1989), p. 4.
(4) Charles B. Handy, *Understanding Organizations*, (London: Penguin, 1985), p. 361.
(5) Peter F. Drucker, *Management*, (Oxford: Butterworth-Heinemann, 1991), p. 36.
(6) Rensis Likert, *New Patterns of Management* (New York: McGraw-Hill, 1961) and *The Human Organization* (New York: McGraw-Hill, 1967).
(7) Likert, *The Human Organization* pp. 3–11.
(8) Frederick Herzberg, Bernard Mausner, and Barbara B. Snyderman, *The Motivation to Work* (New York: Wiley, 1959).
(9) William R. Howell, "The Internal Auditor; Bill of Rights," *The Internal Auditor* February 1986, pp. 24–27.
(10) G. Bowes, "Ensuring Internal Audit Meets the Needs of Directors," *Managerial Auditing Journal*, Vol. 6, No. 4, 1991, pp. 4–10.
(11) Cadbury Committee, *The Financial Aspects of Corporate Governance*, Gee, London, 1992.

6

Managing Chaos—The Art of the Impossible?

In this chapter we examine whether it is possible to manage, and hence to audit, chaos. Managers and auditors in their problem-solving partnership will come out of reading this section with a degree of modesty and humility, as well as regard to the creativity necessarily present in such endeavour, a theme which is picked up later in the text.

By "managing chaos" it is not intended to suggest that we manage in a condition of constant chaos, although most managers can readily identify chaotic elements in their work patterns, and their attempts at time management. Rather it is a reference to a theory beginning to grip the imagination of physicists, but with ramifications far beyond this subject(1) These ramifications have not yet been fully explored in relation to management, but when they are explored, they must affect our approach to the management task. They have been explored in relation to the capital markets in a book which it is believed is the first of its kind.(2) In this article we make one of the few emerging attempts to relate chaos theory to management.

Planning for chaos is unlikely to be at the head of any strategic or operational plan. Nevertheless, chaos is an important, yet generally unrecognized, substratum in the workings of an organization. Strategic management deals with both the uncertain and the unknowable, with feel and intuition being important. In this process, reality is likely to be confused, complex, and messy.(3) Have you ever carried out an evaluation of such creative but less stable and predictable areas such as research and development or advertising?(4) In order to accomplish this, you turn to one of the standard texts, and you search for a list of standardized performance indicators or inter-firm comparison criteria. Armed with these, and with a false confidence, you begin to ask all manner of operating staff questions based on your sources. All you then have to do is to write a report based on the findings. However, you feel that something is missing. You have failed to capture the essence of the activity, and have been working to an artifact that is only approximately connected with the activity under review.

The reason is likely to be chaos. Chaos theory is gradually taking the scientific establishment by storm. Its ramifications are, however, much wider than the physical sciences, and the purpose of this article is to place managers to the fore in understanding a theory that will become increasingly pervasive over the decade, and which will be applied and re-applied to every aspect of human endeavour.

A CLOCKWORK UNIVERSE?

The seeds for the present debate were already sown in ancient Greece. What was lacking until recently was the means of progressing beyond debate to scientific evidence. Aristotle represented one side of the debate. He gave credence to those who view the universe as a coherent whole, with a large number of sub-components which cooperate and co-exist to achieve some greater end. Individual objects and systems were seen as subordinating their behaviour to an overall plan or destiny. This was exemplified par excellence in living organisms which perpetually strive to achieve their designated end according to the great cosmic blueprint. This idea fed through into Christianity, and has been highly influential on Western thought.

In opposition were the Greek atomists, such as Democritus, who taught that the world was nothing other than atoms moving in a void. The universe is a machine in the grip of blind forces. There is no overall plan or final cause to which the world evolves. The only means of change is the erratic movement and the shape of other atoms.

The deep rift between these two views, respectively holism and reductionism, has existed ever since. Although reductionism seems barren as a complete explanation of the world, it nevertheless came to dominate scientific thinking. It is also possible that it has had more than its undue influence on operational audit. Only with chaos theory has it been possible to realise that both holism and reductionism are needed, but that of the two the greater is holism.

SCIENCE ACCORDING TO NEWTON

Sir Isaac Newton in the 17th century was very much in the tradition of the Greek world-view, with its rigid geometry in a clockwork universe, governed by immutable laws. Newton's famous three laws of Motion suggest that the motion of a body through space is determined entirely by the forces that act on that body, once its initial position and velocity are fixed. Newton was able to describe how gravity rules the motion of the planets. It followed that since all physical systems obeyed these laws, that the key to accurate prediction was simply accurate measurement. The French mathematician Pierre Laplace drew the conclusion in

1819 that nothing is then uncertain, and that the future and the past would be equally present to the eyes of any intelligence able to comprehend all the forces controlling nature. Even though the future may appear uncertain in our eyes, in reality it was already fixed in every minute detail.

Newton, therefore, believed that the macrocosm of the whole could be easily reduced to the motion of its constituent parts according to his mechanistic laws. This procedure of breaking down physical systems into their elementary components and then looking for an explanation of their behaviour at the lowest possible level is referred to as reductionism. The aim is to identify the fundamental fields or particles and then to study their dynamic behavior in interaction. The theorist then comes along and seeks to reduce everything to a mathematical formula, known as a Lagrangian, after the French physicist Joseph Lagrange who provided a neat formulation of Newton's laws. With a Lagrangian for every system, the system is "explained" and no mystery remains.

GLIMPSES OF CHAOS

It was towards the end of the last century that Laplace's fellow countryman, Henri Poincaré, questioned that if the universe were driven by clockwork, then it ticked in a strange, complex and even unpredictable way. Through applying a new geometry to Newton's Laws he tried incessantly to achieve a deeper insight into the dynamics of nature. Repeatedly he was repulsed as he approached the edge of a mathematical abyss, and came face-to-face with unpredictability and chaos. Newton had served us well, and was fine as far as he went. If we are aware of the initial conditions, then we can predict the outcome the laws assert. The big problem is the two letter word *if*. We rarely have perfect knowledge of nature, and so it is impossible to determine precisely the position of, say, a particle in space.

The hope then became that by studying complex systems in many different disciplines, new universal principles would be discovered that might shed light on how complexity grows with time. The Newtonian vision had failed to meet the needs of complex systems in four major respects:

1. Complex systems are generally non-linear. To treat them as simply linear approximations will do varying degrees of injustice to the subject matter. A linear system is one in which the whole is simply the sum of its parts. This ignores the element of synergy which is so important, business applications just being one example. Businesses, after all, exist to produce value-added synergy in the form of profit and customer satisfaction. Management accounting data may also be non-linear, but it is traditional to ignore this in the interests of simplicity, and to reduce cost behavior to the four basic types of fixed, semi-fixed, variable and semi-variable.(5)

2. Complex systems may also have a very large number of components, or

degrees of freedom. The attitude of traditional science is to ignore complexity with which it cannot or does not wish to deal. We could thereby be throwing out the baby with the bathwater. In any case complex systems are not just complicated versions of simple systems. They have identities of their own.(6)
3. Complex systems are rarely closed. Indeed it is their very openness to the external environment that provides their driving force. Entrepreneurial or marketing-led organizations are an example.
4. Complexity generally appears abruptly and unpredictably rather than being formed by a process of slow and continuous evolution.

THE BUTTERFLY EFFECT

Integrally associated with chaos is the butterfly effect. Half in jest this suggests that the wing beatings of a butterfly in Taipei can somehow impact on storm formations in Orlando, Florida. The weather example is well worth pursuing as an example of chaos in action. England, with its few extremes of weather conditions, has trivial variations in the weather as one of its great talking points. Weather prediction has long been a major global pastime. Earthquakes in San Francisco and elsewhere are particularly graphic reminders of chaos and the consequent problems of prediction. Modern weather prediction usually depends on a grid of points around 60 miles apart. Even so ground stations and satellites cannot fathom everything, and so some starting data have to be presumed. Let us assume that we place computerized sensors a foot apart on the earth, and then rising at foot intervals right up into the atmosphere. Even with this over-sophistication it will still not be possible to predict whether a manager visiting New York will need umbrellas to attend a business meeting after the flight from London Heathrow. The reason is that the spaces between the sensors will still hide fluctuations from prediction of which the computer will remain ignorant, and that these will create small errors a foot away, magnified to the ten foot scale, and so on across the globe.

The Waterwheel

The waterwheel is an example beloved by Eduard Lorenz, one of the most distinguished chaos scientists.(7) Everyone knows the regularity of waterwheel rotation, yet when the flow becomes faster, the rotation can become chaotic, and non-linear aspects appear. The spin will even reverse itself many times but the pattern never becomes stable or predictable.

Order and disorder, form and chaos, are competitors fighting for supremacy in the universe. Indeed, both may be regarded in part as subjective concepts,(8)and this may explain their interdependence. One of the amazing paradoxes of chaos theory is that there is complexity in apparent simplicity, and simplicity in apparent complexity. Computer representations of an apparently straightforward equation such as $x^2 + C$ can produce lavishly complicated results. Conversely there is order underlying the disorder and chaos as the simplicity of the formula suggests. The impressive patterns of fractal geometry are a case in point.

Fractals

A fractal is a geometric shape, not being a straight line, which has one very special property. This is that the closer you look and the closer you come to it, you still see the same thing. The same applies to a straight line. A circle is different. From a distance it looks like a circle but as you come closer it becomes a straight line. A familiar example of a fractal is the coastline. As you come closer and closer you see more of its irregularity, but it looks very much the same whether you look at it from a distance or up close. Other fractals have this property of invariance. Although every snowflake is different, they all obey the same "snowflake" rules—variations on a six-sided geometric shape. One of these rules is branching which is a fractal process. As each crystal grows, minute differences in form are magnified—the butterfly effect again. The computer, using the fractal rules, can recreate mountain growth. The most complex fractal, the Mandelbrot Set, with the seahorse tails and mystical beauty, obeys the same simple set of rules.

ORGANIZATIONAL CHAOS

It is time for us to consider the application of chaos theory to organizations. A number of writers have come near to doing this, but have stopped short of making an explicit connection with chaos theory. Donald Schon's title *Beyond the Stable State* provides an appropriate flavour.(9) Alvin Toffler then wrote his book *Future Shock* in which he talked of an adhocratic society accompanied by massive societal change.(10) Three waves have characterized world history. First wave (agricultural) and second wave (industrial) are now being superseded by the third wave (electronic information). Humanity now faces a quantum leap forward in the process of which future shock is encountered. This manifests itself as "the shattering stress and disorientation that we induce in individuals by subjecting them to too much change in too short a time." The reference to quantum physics is apposite. Quantum processes are inherently unpredictable and indeterministic; it is generally impossible to predict from one instance to another how a quantum system will behave. Spontaneous change is very much of the essence. Quantum theory restricts itself to the microworld, and so its influence never spilled over into the wider concerns. Future shock was certainly a fitting scene-setter for chaos theory.

Tom Peters

Tom Peters is the latest management thinker to give prominence to the idea of chaos, this time in name but with reference to chaos theory as such. In *Thriving on Chaos* he indicates how his two previous best sellers presuppose a relatively stable and predictable world which no longer exists.(11) Indeed it certainly did not exist at the time, not light years away, when Peters was first writing. This may well account in part for why some of the "excellent" companies have subsequently failed. In actual fact there was some acknowledgement of chaos in the initial *In Search of Excellence.*(12) The emphasis in the text was on keeping things simple in a complex world. However, it was recognized that it was necessary to tolerate some chaos in return for quick action and regular innovation. One can also see this in the final attribute of the eight attributes which they found characterized all excellent US companies, namely simultaneous loose-tight properties. Tight control is exercised around the few essential core values of quality, reliability, action, regular informal communication, and quick feedback. Tightest of all is attention to the customer, but this is not through massive documentation and other controls, but through self and peer discipline and the "soft" concept of philosophical values. Paradoxically these "soft" concepts may be the most hard-hitting of all, but their precise impact is more difficult to predict.

Peters reflected on whether to call his next title *Thriving* amidst *Chaos* or *Thriving* on *Chaos*. "Amidst" suggests doing our best despite the chaos. This is too reactive. The more radical "on" suggests dealing proactively with chaos and seeing this as leading to market opportunities. Now, Peters maintains, merely to be excellent is insufficient. We need to be able to constantly adapt, and to be able to continually create new market niches and add new value (quality) to products and services in response to the ever-shifting desires of customers. Creating total customer responsiveness, pursuing fast-paced innovation, achieving flexibility by empowering people, learning to love change, and building systems for a world turned upside-down are the essential ingredients for riding on the back of chaos.

CHAOS AND MANAGEMENT THEORY

Rather like Molière's character M. Jourdain, who discovered that he had been speaking prose all his life, with an awareness of chaos theory, we can begin to see how it infiltrates management theory, implicitly or explicitly, at every twist and turn. A few examples will suffice.

Differentiation and integration

Paul Lawrence and Jay Lorsch consider that the twin needs of differentiation and integration play the key role in organizational effectiveness.(13) To deal effectively with their external environments, organizations need to develop segmental units, each of which is charged with dealing with the response to a particular aspect or aspects of this external environment. Each segment may need a different orientation. Thus the research and development department may have a long-term horizon but informal structure, whereas production may require more immediate time-scales and more rigidly formal systems. The greater the degree of uncertainty (read chaos) within each segment, and the greater the diversity between them, the greater is the need to differentiate, in order to be effective in each sub-environment. However, this necessity also brought with it the potential for increased inter-departmental conflict as the various groups developed their own methods of coping with the peculiar uncertainties of their own sub-environments. Hence the need for integrative devices, such as cross-functional teams at different levels of management.

Thompson's matrix

The American sociologist James D. Thompson, who was founding editor of the *Administrative Science Quarterly,* was concerned with how members of organizations aspire to be orderly and rational despite circumstances which may work in quite the opposite direction.(14) Decision making involves beliefs or assumptions as to what will happen as a result of one course of action rather than another, and preferences as to what is most desirable. Thompson's matrix in Figure 6.1 illustrates the possibilities:

The bottom right-hand box in Figure 6.1 corresponds to chaos when there is all-round uncertainty, and the only strategy can be an inspired leap in the dark.

		Preferences regarding possible outcomes	
		Certainty	Uncertainty
Beliefs about cause/effect relations	Certain	Computational Strategy	Compromise Strategy
	Uncertain	Judgemental Strategy	Inspirational Strategy

Figure 6.1 Thompson's Matrix

Information cost of transactions

The US economist Oliver Williamson makes the information cost of transactions as the chief explanatory variable for the workings of organizations.(15) A market is the best way of conducting transactions when all the necessary information is communicated through the price mechanism, and this alone is sufficient. A hierarchy, by contrast, is to be preferred when much more needs to be known, uncertainty prevails, and there are ethical aspects, since the organizational hierarchy brings a degree of control to the inadequately informed parties to a transaction. Transactions move out of markets into hierarchies when "information impactness" is high, that is when the uncertainties and distrust inherent in transactions exceed the point at which prices may be easily determined. There is a lack of knowledge, the discovery of which may be prohibitively expensive, and notions of quality may be ill-defined. Incidentally one of the gains Williamson attributes to hierarchies is that parties cannot use gains entirely for their own purposes, and what they do can be more effectively checked and audited.

The three "forces of misdirection"

Peter Drucker in his prolific writings is well aware of the workings of chaos.(16) He fully admits that the measurement which is so crucial to determining organizational effectiveness is still at a very crude level in most areas of business activity. He refers to three "forces of misdirection." These are the specialised work of most managers, the existence of a hierarchy, and the differences in vision that exist in organizations. All of these encourage breakdown and conflict. Drucker believes that *management by objectives* is the means of overcoming these problems, and putting at the fore the overall goals of the organization.

Closed circles

Rosabeth Moss Kanter has emphasized how managers, rising to the top, need to cope with increasing degrees of uncertainty.(17) The way in which they cope with this, and the need for easy communication, is to become a closed circle. Homogeneity reigns supreme, and social conformity is the norm. Women were considered unpredictable and incomprehensible (chaotic) and so were generally excluded. "I'm always making assumptions [about women] that turn out to be wrong" was a typical male manager comment. Predictability was an attribute highly prized. Being controversial was not completely ruled out, as long as there was consistency, loyalty and adherence to the hard work ethic. Closed male circles is a familiar ostrich-like approach to managing chaos, and one that is akin to taking aspirins for headaches—it does little for the underlying problem, but provides transient relief.

Male and female risk-taking

A dissertation by Conlan gave some support.(18) The first part of the research design failed to find any male-female differences on risk-taking. The second part was more complex in that it involved a situation in which risk was not easily perceived. Subjects had to choose between the two matrices (Game Theory). One involved low monetary payoff but with absolute decision-making power, the other high monetary payoff with shared decision-making power, the other high monetary payoff with shared decision-making power and the risk of exploitation by the other participant. The ease or reluctance with which subjects chose the second matrix was taken to be an indicator of risk-taking. A lower number of females made this choice and this, plus questionnaire data, was interpreted as showing lower female risk-taking tendencies.

Another study centred on menstruation in a garment manufacturing factory over a thirty three week period.(19) Most women's work performance was not affected detrimentally by menstruation. Indeed where performance did vary, it was more likely to vary across the days of the week rather than across menstruating and non-menstruating days. A second part of the survey examined the attitudes of factory women, female managers and male managers to menstruation. All three groups viewed it in negative terms in relation to women's performance and emotional stability. The female managers' attitudes were often more negative than those of the women workers. Women who expected their performance to deteriorate at menstruation usually performed as well or better when their behavior was compared to other parts of their cycles. It would seem from these glimmerings of research that much of the chaos is male-imagined or invented, but that does not make it any the less real. Freud's patients certainly thought they were dealing with reality. As to differences on risk-taking there is a need for alternative perspectives, and conservatism will on occasions be appropriate.

Uncertainty and power

For a French perspective we turn to Michel Crozier, who is equally at home in the US.(20) To him uncertainty explains power. Conversely the routinization of uncertainty removes power. Crozier gives the last example of the French nationalized tobacco company in which everything in the local factories was subject to detailed control, except the work of the maintenance workers. They steadfastly resisted any documentation of their art since they thereby had power through the uncertainty of machine stoppages. The same can equally apply to the rise and fall of finance specialists, production controllers, and others. Authoritarian reformer figures will wait amidst the bureaucratic routine for that moment of crisis or chaos when the system will have need for them. The rationalization that resides in organization produces incessant effort to encapsulate areas of uncertainty, within the range of formal controls. Paradoxically experts become the agents of the very rationalization that diminishes their own power.

Programmed and non-programmed decisions

The quartet of Herbert A. Simon, R. M. Cyert, J. G. March and Charles E. Lindblom emphasize the limited problem-solving capacity under the deluge of information that confronts the manager.(21)(22)(23) Simon distinguishes the two polar opposites of programmed and non-programmed decisions. It is with this last that we increasingly encounter chaos. We can regard the work of these famous four as attempts to cope with chaos.

On the theme of paralysis by analysis, we have the warning of strategic planning processes that become inflexible, formalized and excessively quantitative.(24) An excess of rationality can become counter-productive, particularly the pursuit of one-dimensional approaches to multi-dimensional problems. The dual forces of administrative efficiency and planning effectiveness can pull in opposite directions. If you want more of one, you may have to sacrifice some of the other. Innovative thought and entrepreneurship are not so easily achieved through the rigidity of budgets and timetables. We need to reach an equilibrium between control and no control, which is a return to the theme of order and disorder.

THE MANAGEMENT OF CHAOS

Unlike quantum physics, chaos theory has already come out of its closet, and has universal significance. It has entered into management thinking, implicitly rather than explicitly, and therefore managers need to begin to take it on board. Are not the complementary paradoxes shown in Figure 6.2 perfect descriptions of the situation generally confronting the manager?

The farther we move away from the short-term and easily quantified, with a ready determinism, to longer-term strategic issues, in which much in the external and perhaps internal environment is uncertain, the more we can appreciate the

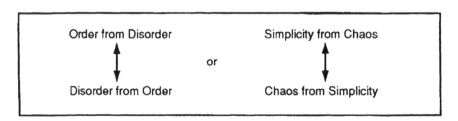

Figure 6.2 Complementary Paradoxes

contribution of chaos theory. Systems theory, which has infiltrated most areas of management thinking, has traditionally dealt with systems that are relatively closed, and capable of being flowcharted. As we move towards more complex open systems we encounter disagreement as to the meaning and significance of the constituents of the system, and how performance is to be measured and evaluated. The lure of the familiar, whereby we concentrate on a variable or group of variables in a problem situation simply because they fit our preconceptions or professional training, can do grave injustice to the subject matter. Charles Handy has indicated that selective focusing also unfocuses a lot of other variables, and that "reductionism," in which each variable is disentangled in turn, may suit some academics and analysts, but will not serve the manager who has to put the whole together and make it work.(25)

It was Professor Reg Revans, management thinker and father of "action learning," who distinguished the puzzle from the problem.(26) The puzzle has a known solution, which it is only a matter of time to discover. The problem, however, has no known solution, and, indeed, there may be no neat and tidy outcome. Top management and executive training programmes which require managers to tackle issues in departments and professional areas other than their own are frequently in the domain of the problem, and the problem is in the domain of chaos behavior. It is possible to distinguish increasing degrees of chaos in the matrix in Figure 6.3:

Quadrant A is relatively trouble free, but may still contain an element of unpredictability and chaos. Quadrants B and C contain a mixture of the familiar and unfamiliar, and quadrant D contains the greatest potential for chaos to exhibit itself.

DIRECT VERSUS PREVENTIVE CONTROL

The management text that has over the years given the highest implicit recognition of chaos theory is that of Koontz and Weihrich.(27) In the ninth edition a distinction is drawn between direct and preventive control. Direct control attempts to dampen deviation from a pre-set norm. Of course this may fail because of uncertainty and risk, and through lack of knowledge, experience or judgement. There are five additional questionable assumptions underlying direct control:

1. That performance can be measured. Where do creativity, foresight and judgement enter in? This is particularly true in areas such as assessing new product development or marketing.

2. That personal responsibility exists. It is sometimes true that nobody is individually responsible. Exchange rate fluctuations are good examples of the

		PROBLEMS	
		Familiar	Unfamiliar
	Familiar	A	B
SITUATION			
	Unfamiliar	C	D

Figure 6.3   Matrix Showing Degrees of Chaos

workings of chaos and the butterfly effect, and may have catastrophic impact on a business, but whose responsibility are they?

3. That the time expenditure is warranted. Is it worth the time and energy second-guessing past decisions?

4. That mistakes can be discovered in time. Discovery often comes too late for effective action.

5. That the person responsible will take corrective steps. What happens when the main cause of the problems is the chairperson or managing director?

Again these five points tend to be the traditional province of the manager, yet we can see that although they will have a role, they have their limitations. What then is preventive control? It is simply the application of the fundamentals of management. The higher the quality of managers and their subordinates, the less will be the need for direct control. The trouble is that as yet we are lacking a comprehensive and universally agreed set of management principles. On the other hand a Likert panel of experts would probably reach reasonable consensus on part at least of matters under consideration. A mixture of university education, on-the-job-experience, coaching by superiors, self-education and development, and management and enterprise self-audit may all be ways of achieving this. We are, then, left with a substantial residue of chaos to cope with as best as we can, and with few ground rules.

CONCLUSION

Chaos enters into organizations and their management, as much as everywhere else. This should not lead to despair. We have seen that order and chaos are reciprocally related. There will be elements of both in any management situation. In the determined situation of managing a payroll department it may be mainly order. In other cases the chaos element may be more obtrusive. Mintzberg and Waters rename the two elements as deliberate and emergent strategies.(28) Encouragingly, the emergent strategy does not have to mean that everything is out of control. Rather it permits management to act before all is understood, and to respond to an evolving reality, as opposed to focusing on a stable fantasy. Mergers and acquisitions would be one application area for the emergent strategy. Recognition of the inevitable limitations of management and planning is necessary if we are to be realistic. Some have sought to draw a distinction between mere management and leadership, and it is the leader who needs to thrive on chaos.(29) It is also in the chaotic areas that we can give full reign to the creativity that is so important.(30)

By giving reign to the creativity, the management task and that of the internal auditors, may become as beautiful or mystical as the cascading color of the geometric shapes and patterns produced through chaos theory. At least there will be humility on all sides, and a wish to assess the true balance of order and chaos that characterizes both the universe and the organizations in which we work.

REFERENCES

(1) J. Gleick, *Chaos. Making a New Science*, Cardinal, London 1987.
(2) E. E. Peters, *Chaos and Order in the Capital Markets. A New View of Cycles, Prices, and Market Volatility*, John Wiley and Sons, London, 1991.
(3) D. Asch and C. Bowman, Editors, *Readings in Strategic Management*, Macmillan, London, 1989.
(4) G. Vinten, "The audit of Advertising: A No-Go area?" *Internal Auditing*, Vol. 10, No. 5, May 1987, pp. 135–139.
(5) C.T. Horngren and G. Foster, *Cost Accounting. A Managerial Emphasis*, Prentice-Hall, London, 1987, pp. 363–365.
(6) G. Vinten, "The Auditor and Systems," *Internal Auditing*, Vol. 10, No. 11, December 1987, pp. 331–334.
(7) K. Lorenz, "Deterministic Nonperiodic Flow," *Journal of the Atmospheric Sciences*, Vol. 20, 1963, pp. 130–141.
(8) P. Davies, *The Cosmic Blueprint*, Unwin, London, 1989.
(9) D. Schon, *Beyond the Stable State—Public and Private Learning in a Changing Society*, Penguin, London, 1973.
(10) A. Toffler, *Future Shock*, Pan, London, 1970.
(11) T. J. Peters, *Thriving on Chaos*, Macmillan, London, 1988.
(12) T. J. Peters and R. H. Waterman, *In Search of Excellence: Lessons from America's Best Run Companies*, Harper and Row, New York, 1982.
(13) P. R. Lawrence and J. W. Lorsch, *Organization and Environment*, Harvard, Mass., 1967.
(14) J. D. Thompson, *Organizations in Action*, McGraw-Hill, London, 1967.
(15) O. E. Williamson, *Markets and Hierarchies: Analysis and Antitrust Implications—A Study in the Economics of Internal Organization*, Free Press and Collier Macmillan, New York, 1975.
(16) P. Drucker, *Managing in Turbulent Times*, Heinemann, London, 1980.
(17) R. M. Kanter, *The Change Masters*, Allen and Unwin, London, 1984.

(18) A. D. Conlan, "A Study of Sex Differences in Decision-making under Conditions of Risk," Unpublished MSc dissertation, Queen's University, Belfast, 1987.
(19) G. J. I. Bates,"Menstruation, Performance and Attitudes: An Industrial Study. Unpublished PhD, Queen's University, Belfast, 1987.
(20) M. Crozier, *The Bureaucratic Phenomenon*, Tavistock Publications and University of Chicago Press, 1964.
(21) H. A. Simon, *Administrative Behaviour*, Macmillan, London, 1960.
(22) R. M. Cyert and J. G. March, *A Behavioral Theory of the Firm*, Prentice-Hall, London, 1963.
(23) C. E. Lindblom, *The Policy Making Process*, Prentice-Hall, London, 1968.
(24) R. T. Lenz and M. A. Lyles, "Paralysis by Analysis: Is your planning system becoming too rational?", *Long Range Planning*, Vol. 18, No. 4, 1985, pp.64–72.
(25) C. Handy, *Understanding Organizations*, 3rd edition, Penguin, 1988.
(26) G. Vinten, "Internal Auditing and Action Learning," *Managerial Auditing Journal*, Vol. 3, No. 3, 1988.
(27) H. Koontz and H. Weihrich, *Management*, McGraw Hill, London, 1988.
(28) H. Mintzberg and J. A. Waters, "Of Strategies, Deliberate and Emergent," *Strategic Management Journal*, Vol. 6, 1985, pp. 257–272.
(29) H. Sungaila, "The New Science of Chaos: Making a New Science of Leadership?," *Journal of Educational Administration*, Vol. 28, No. 2, 1990, pp. 4–23.
(30) R. D. Stacey, *The Chaos Frontier. Creative Strategic Control for Business*, Butterworth-Heinemann, London and Boston, 1991.

7
Patterns of Behavior

THE WORKER AND THE MANAGER

Work

Nature of work

The origins of work are veiled in the mists of antiquity. The scriptures told Adam to till the ground from whence he was taken because of his fall from grace. He was told also that if any would not work, neither should they eat.(1)

Two giants of Greek poetry wrote about work. Hesiod in his *Work and Days,* says, "Before success the immortal gods have placed the sweat of our brows." First came work, then came the rewards. But Homer, in the *Iliad* and the *Odyssey,* wrote of glorious ideals, of epic deeds, and of gods and demigods whose work flashed like comets across the skies of mythology. Homer's heroes were fulfilled in their very work. Hesiod's man worked for his bread, not for fulfillment, and because work is man's estate. Homer dealt with myths; Hesiod dealt with reality.

Today's worker is beginning to reach for more than bread alone, with fulfillment in work seen as more than a myth. The enlightened manager is learning that fulfillment for the worker and profit for the company are not mutually exclusive. Also of course, whatever concerns the manager concerns the internal auditor.

Work has been examined and tested in myriad research studies. Conclusions have been drawn and pronouncements have been made, each professing to be the ultimate truth. Some have been tested by time and still stand firm; others may bow to the counter thrust of studies leading to opposing conclusions. As a result, managers may be reluctant to put their trust in the pontifications of any particular pundit. However, among the profusion there may be some principles that will retain fast colors even in the harsh sunlight of reality. They can be extremely useful to manager and internal auditor alike, both of whom should therefore be aware of what is being done and said about work and the worker—the two factors that are so critical to the success of the organization. We will present some of the principal views here. They may be adopted or rejected in the light of the law of the situation and the bent of the reader, but they should be considered.

The fact that a person has a job and receives a pay check is no guarantee of satisfaction. Every job has its constraints. Every job implies in some degree rules, deadlines, standards, measurement of results, and accountability that may conflict with the employee's ideas of what he needs and wants.

Satisfiers and Dissatisfiers

Work is seen differently by the worker's manager and by the worker. The traditional manager sees the workers as coming on the job to further the organization's goals and objectives. The worker, however, may march to the beat of a different drummer and see work as a means of satisfying many basic needs.

Herzberg regards work as providing two separate and distinct factors: the hygienic factors and the motivators.(2) The research that led to his conclusions was based on face-to-face interviews with workers, not anonymous answers to cut-and-dried questionnaires. Each of many subjects was asked to tell when they felt very bad on the job and when they felt very good.

The hygienic factors—pay, interpersonal relations, supervision, company policy, working conditions, status, and job security—surfaced when the worker spoke of feeling very bad. The motivators—recognition, achievement, and the potentials for growth and advancement—were cited when the worker spoke of feeling very good. From that Herzberg deduced that the hygienic factors form a continuum from *dissatisfaction* to *no dissatisfaction.* Those factors are negative. Their absence makes the worker feel bad. But their presence does not awaken *good* feelings, just as one does not pay attention to the temperature in a room that is completely comfortable.

On the other hand, the motivators form a continuum from *no job satisfaction* to *job satisfaction.* If the job is routine, there is no satisfaction. If the job is exciting, challenging, and fulfilling, there is full satisfaction. The motivators concern the work; the hygienic factors concern the environment. The motivators relate to productivity; the hygienic factors relate to employee turnover.

Job Enlargement and Enrichment

The worker generally has no personal control over the environment—over matters like pay, supervision, and organization policies. No gratification can be achieved from them. However, an interesting and absorbing job can provide personal satisfaction, and the degree of satisfaction is under the worker's control. The more the worker does in a job that stimulates, the more the satisfaction.

Many jobs that are routine and repetitive provide no satisfaction or gratification to the worker. True, many workers want no job gratification. They just want a pay check; they see their jobs as the penalty they must pay for the wages they receive. Yet many others live their lives of quiet desperation in jobs that give them no fulfilment.

Some managers are becoming aware of the adverse effects of undemanding jobs. The phenomenon is being brought to their attention by the new breed of workers with higher education and changing attitudes toward authority. The trend is therefore toward job enlargement, job rotation, and job enrichment. Mass production's demands for more routine and simpler jobs is being given a hard look. Efficiency may be destroying effectiveness.

Job enlargement implies adding more steps to the routine job. *Job rotation* implies switching workers, and managers as well, from one job assignment to another at horizontal levels to reduce boredom and display a more comprehensive panorama of the organization to the employee.

Job enrichment tends to relieve the poverty of job satisfaction by providing greater responsibility and more opportunity to exercise independent judgement. Job enrichment is not new. At least one company, IBM, has been practicing it with considerable success for a long time.

It is said that IBM's founder and then president once saw a woman sitting idly at her machine. When he asked her why, she said that she was waiting for the setup man to change the tool setting for the new run. He then asked her if she could do the setup work herself. She replied, "Of course, but I"m not supposed to." It was found that a great deal of time was wasted in that manner and that only a few days of additional training would qualify workers to set up their own machines.

The success of that simple enlargement and enrichment of a job sparked a systematic program at IBM to engineer employee interest in the job. The operations themselves are kept simple, but a number of them are put together into one job and always the job is designed to require some skill or judgement. In addition, the variety of operations permits the worker to vary the rhythm of the work. Satisfactory experience with job enlargement and enrichments is put to use in the introduction of each new product or product change at IBM. Production supervisors and workers participate in production layout and job planning.

IBM is not unique. During World War II, workers had to take on added responsibilities because of the shortage of industrial engineers and skilled supervisors. In one aircraft company, entire engines were assembled from start to finish by separate teams. The teams organized their jobs differently, and different staff did different jobs at different times. Each had been trained for the enlarged job, and each had continuing learning through weekly meetings with supervisors and the engineering staff to discuss problems and improvement. In each case the teams exceeded the output norms that the engineers had suggested.

Similarly, in Sweden, under pressure of labor shortages, teams are set up to build entire automobiles. The plant sets the output and quality standards, but the men themselves work out the structure and organization of the jobs with the help of industrial engineers. The industrial engineers assist rather than prescribe. The results are reduced turnover and increased productivity.

Enriching jobs is neither a simple matter nor a panacea. Nothing is simple when people are concerned. Studies show that job complexity is related to job enrichment, and what is complex for one individual may be simple for another. The worker's *perception* of the job's complexity becomes central to job enrichment; hence, that perception should be examined before the job enrichment program is carried out. What generates interest in worker A may frustrate worker B.

People do respond to attention and interest; the Hawthorne experiments proved that. But a challenging job should prompt and maintain more employee interest and response then a pat on the head. The new breed of worker is more concerned with essentials than with supervisory soothing, particularly if the positive reinforcement is contrived and manipulative rather than sincere. Also the strain may be more than the supervisor could bear for long. Certainly positive reinforcement will have its benefits for the people who need it, but it too is not the whole answer.

Workers

Work and the Workers

The relation between workers and work, the way employees perceive the job, what rewards they expect, and how they and the job relate to the community around them are complex, mysterious phenomena that are largely unexplored. Yet dealing with a problem calls for an understanding of the problem elements; and although the theorists explore and research, neither the worker nor the manager can stand around while they dredge up the answers.

Managers generally understand, as the old saw has it, that one does not hire a hand—the whole person goes along with it. Experienced managers are also well aware that there is no such thing as the average worker. How much easier managers would find life if they could deal with all people alike.

Although rules tend to be standardized, human beings are not standardized units. They are not standardized in their reactions or in their goals. It would be naive to think that all employees work to their full potential and that all people rise to a challenge. The reasons to the contrary are various: work restrictions by employees, tenure and protected job security, poor discipline, or belief in the propaganda of exploitation.

The Knowledge Workers

Changes in the workforce have taken place. Larger percentages of the labor force in the developed countries do not work with their hands; instead they work with ideas, concepts, and theories. They perform what Peter Drucker calls "knowledge work."(3) That form of work need not be restricted to the college graduate. File clerks, after all, deal with a high level of abstraction: the alphabet.

Knowledge workers are a new breed to the classical manager, and the new breed has an elevated level of what is to be expected of life and work. They are highly educated compared with their counterpart of a century ago. They challenge traditional management with questions that managers are hard put to answer. They want more from work than the economics of the job. They want work to be fulfilling; they want more than material rewards. As Drucker puts it, they want more than a living out of work; they want work to make a life as well.

Knowledge workers need careful treatment by management. They are moved more by self-motivation and self-direction than by fear. This tends to frustrate the traditional manager. The knowledge worker's jobs are complex. Owing to the variables with tasks, productivity is hard to define or measure. Achievement is still more difficult to appraise.

What managers will have to accept is that, for the knowledge worker especially, the worker and work are tied together. If the job is to be dealt with effectively, it needs to be analyzed into its component parts, it needs to be synthesized into a process, and it needs to be provided with feedback so that the knowledge worker can control his or her own work. Also managers will have to understand that the job cannot be designed *for* the knowledge worker. It must be designed *by* the knowledge worker.

The Needs of the Worker

The Hierarchy of Needs

All human beings have certain needs. The needs may vary with ethnic background, levels of skill and professionalism, social position, and family upbringing. The urgency of the needs may also vary with the needs that are filled and those that remain unfulfilled. Such needs have been identified, and the hierarchy, suggested by Abraham Maslow, is widely accepted:(4)

1. *Basic physiological needs.* The basic physiological needs constitute what the human being requires at the barest subsistence level: air, water, and food. Until those needs are satisfied, the higher needs have little meaning. On the other hand, once those needs are satisfied, offering to fulfill them has no power to move the employee to greater productivity.
2. *Safety and security.* The safety and security needs ask for assurance that the basic physiological requirements will be met. That calls for job security and the ability to continue working in a risk-free environment. The two needs are physical, and both need to be satisfied to an acceptable degree before the worker feels the stirrings of other needs.
3. *Love and acceptance.* From the need for love and acceptance arises the need to

be part of a family, a gang, a club, a political organization, or a work group. It is a social need that is due to being gregarious and needing the comfort of being wanted.
4. *Esteem and status.* When physical and social needs are satisfied, the individual can become concerned with psychic needs. The psychic needs call for recognition of work, achievement, status in the organization, and standing among peers. Under the first basic physiological need, the bread to fill the belly may occupy full attention. Under the fourth need, for esteem and status, sustenance means nothing since it is already achieved. The thickness of the pile of the carpet in the office or the achievement of acceptable quality and schedule within budgeted costs may become uppermost.
5. *Self-realization and fulfillment.* Meeting the need for self-realization and fulfillment provides the highest psychic or ego satisfaction. The satisfaction arises from self-actuating, from setting goals for ourselves and achieving them.

The higher-priority needs—basic physiological needs and the need for safety and security—must be satisfied before the lower-level needs cry for satisfaction. Indeed, not all needs will be fully satisfied, and Maslow suggests as a hypothetical example, the worker who is 85% satisfied in physiological needs, 70% in safety needs, 50% in love and acceptance needs, 40% in self-esteem needs, and 10% in the need for self-realization and fulfillment.

The needs are not followed in a rigid pattern, and under some circumstances a lower-priority (psychic) need may block out a higher priority (physiological) need. For example, a research scientist may disregard physiological needs and go without food and sleep while spurred by creativity. It is suggested that the hygienic factors of Herzberg, discussed earlier, correspond to Maslow's physiological, safety, and security needs. Also, the motivators correspond to Maslow's needs for esteem and self-realization. But Maslow's proposed needs suggest a continuous sequencing, and Herzberg does not stipulate the satisfaction of hygienic needs before the motivators are felt. Yet one study found that a challenging job in a poor environment will not necessarily result in greater worker satisfaction than a routine job in a good environment.(5) That simply proves what the experienced manager and the modern internal auditor have known for some time: principles are useful, but the law of the situation as observed by the perceptive manager still obtains, and the ability to read the individual worker's capacity and maturity is still significant.

Maturity

Behavioralists regard human nature, to some extent at least, as a function of maturity in the human being. Chris Argyris has suggested a series of continuums in a person's maturation from infant to adult. Some grown people, of course, may never mature in some or many of the dimensions presented by Argyris. Others may mature in all or most of the dimensions. In any case, perceiving the degree of maturation is important to the manager who deals with the individual. Argyris's dimensions are as follows:(6)

Table 7.1 Dimensions of Maturation

From (infant)	To (adult)
Passivity	Increasing activity
Dependence	Relative independence
Limited behavior patterns	Complex behavior patterns
Shallow interests	Deeper interests
Short-time perspective	Long-time perspective
Subordinate position	Superordinate (superior) position
Lack of self-awareness	Self-awareness and self-control

Wants and Expectations

In addition, a person's personality, wants, and needs are affected by preferences or expectations. Vroom's preference-expectation theory, therefore, warrants consideration by the manager. His theory is based on two premises:(7)

1. A person considering the expected outcomes of different courses of action, will assign subjective values to them and thereby have certain preferences for them.
2. How the person reacts to situations will depend on two factors: (i) the person's hopes to accomplish and (ii) the extent to which it is believed by the person that own actions will affect the outcome.

If workers can be convinced by a manager that an outcome is desirable to them and that their actions can affect the outcome, they will be more prone to act. However, there are some behavioralist's who contend that people can and will adjust to the structures and strictures of the organization. Where Argyris sees subordination to the entity as a sign of immaturity in the individual, Dubin thinks that most people will adjust to tight regimentation. Also, he cannot see everybody having a high degree of interest in every activity every day. He regards some indifference as a normal characteristic and believes that a certain amount of self-actualization will come from work outside the job.(8)

Yet one cannot lose sight of the fact that the human being is a wanting creature. Not all the wants are the same for either the individual or for classes of individuals. The white collar (knowledge) worker may be more concerned with work content, whereas the blue collar worker may be more concerned with such environmental factors as security and pay. Technological, economic, and educational advances have emphasized the wants and needs of the knowledge worker. As a result they find a movement among managers toward self-determination, wider participation in decision making, and application of the worker's judgement in the performance of the job.

In addition to the needs of the manual worker and the knowledge worker, there are the needs of the knowledge professional. Improved technology calls for more professionals in business. The professionals are of crucial importance to the organization, because they are the fount from which pour the ideas and innovations without which the entity cannot grow. Yet the professional is bound more to the profession than to the organization. Newly hired scientists and engineers may be committed to their professional rather than to the organization's values.

With all those conflicting wants, orientations, and levels of maturity, the manager has the unenviable job of supplying what the worker needs within the bounds that the organization has set while still fostering the kind of morale that knits people together for the common good and evokes voluntary cooperation. This job is complicated further by the variety of subcultures within the organization, each with its varying needs and affiliations.

However, the difficulty of the problem does not excuse the failure to seek solutions. The success of any organization lies in the ability to provide values to the members as compensation for the burdens imposed.(9) Management, therefore, in laying its plans, must do so in the light of an understanding of the workers' needs. When the needs will frustrate the meeting of the organization's goals, constraints must be placed on the worker. But when personalization of tasks to satisfy needs will bring a *net* gain to the organization after the cost of personalization is considered, the plans should provide for acceding to the needs and raising employee morale. Autocratic adherence to structured restrictive plans must take into account that, as a result, the worker:

- Has reduced independence and self-control.
- Is subject to boredom and apathy.
- Loses valued participation in forming goals and objectives.
- Does not relate to the organization.
- Engages in a running conflict between his own needs and the organization's demands.

The Manager and the Worker

Self-esteem

The worker, according to Skinner, is a malleable instrument who is conditioned by managers and can be shaped as a sculptor shapes clay. The process is gradual; but if the shaping has been through positive reinforcement by rewarding desired behavior, the worker develops a feeling of freedom. If it has been through negative, punitive reinforcement, the worker is left feeling controlled and coerced.(10)

So the way managers regard workers has a powerful effect on how workers will see themselves, their organization, and the people around them. Douglas

McGregor, observing managers in operation, perceived a duality in how they saw workers. The duality, which McGregor labelled Theory X and Theory Y(11), paralleled Argyris's view of worker maturity. Theory X paints a picture of infantilism; Theory Y paints a picture of maturity. The Theory X manager, the classical, traditional Bull of the Woods, regards workers as follows:

1. The average person dislikes work and will avoid it if possible.
2. Because of that characteristic, workers must be controlled, directed and threatened with punishment to obtain from them the effort needed to achieve organizational goals.
3. The average worker really wants to be directed, avoids responsibility, has little ambition, and more than anything else wants the security blanket of strong, autocratic leadership.

In contrast, the Theory Y manager, a behavioralist who believes in the innate goodness of people, gives the following assessment of workers:

1. Work is as natural to people as play or rest.
2. If workers are committed to an objective, they will direct and control themselves.
3. Commitment to goals is a function of the rewards associated with achievement.
4. The average worker, if given the opportunity, will seek and accept responsibility.
5. A majority rather than a minority of the population can and want to exercise imagination, ingenuity, and creativity in their work

McGregor maintains that how the manager treats people and how they react depends on the manager's philosophy and attitude towards people. Accordingly, a manager who is predominantly X presents a climate that is coercive and restrictive. Also, managerial philosophy about the worker—X or Y, mature or immature, the seekers of hygiene or the thirsters for motivation—will affect how management designs its organization, establishes its personnel policies, and develops its rules and regulations.

Theory Z

A number of writers have considered that Theories X and Y are too simplified and generalized. Edgar Schein formulated his complex model according to which human needs fall into many categories and vary with the person's stage of personal development and life situation,(12) This means that motives will vary from one person to another, one situation to another, and one time to another. Incentives can equally vary in impact: money, for example, while generally satisfying basic economic needs, can produce self-actualization for some. Employees can certainly learn new motives through organizational experiences, and can develop responses to different kinds of managerial strategies. The most important determinant of motivation is the psychological contract, an unwritten set of expectations. This includes economic aspects (pay, working hours, job security), but also implicit matters such as opportunities to learn and develop, degree of work autonomy, and being treated with dignity.

William Ouchi bases his analysis on a comparison of Japanese and American organizations:(13)

Table 7.2 Comparison of Japanese and American Organizations

Japanese	*American*
Lifetime employment	Short-term employment
Slow evaluation/promotion	Rapid evaluation/promotion
Non-specialized career paths	Specialized career paths
Implicit control mechanisms	Explicit control mechanisms
Collective decision making	Individual decision making
Collective responsibility	Individual responsibility
Holistic concern	Segmented concern

Ouchi uses the term "Theory Z" to describe the Japanese model as applied to the West, and it therefore represents an extension of McGregor's Theory Y. Z organizations place greater emphasis on human-relations management both from an individual and a group perspective. Decision making now becomes a participatory activity for a widened circle of employees, and responsibility is collaborative, being the domain of group or team processes. In his later book, Ouchi shows how the strongest companies are M-form—multidivisional—with middle managers competing with each other but working together to iron out their differences, before approaching top management with unified proposals.(14) He also indicates how Japan is an M-form society, with the three essential components of strong interlocking trade associations, a responsive governmental organization, and the active participation of banks, often as stockholders. However, it is possible for the West to emulate, and Minneapolis is cited as an example.

Richard Pascale and Anthony Athos have been keen to argue that East and West have much to learn from each other.(15) Japan has borrowed extensively from the West, and owes its emphasis on quality to US experts, notably Deming and Juran. The potential problems with Theory Z organizations is that they can de-emphasize professionalism, and can be sexist and racist, preferring to recruit clones. Nevertheless, such organizations are among the long-term successes, their graduates eagerly sought by head-hunters. In the UK Marks and Spencer is an example. Highly successful, but heavily rule bound, the rules may triumph over commonsense. For example, they used to refuse to sell small numbers of bananas when these were all that were left, and they would be either thrown away or given to charity. It would never occur to them to give them to customers who present them at the checkout. The rule says no sale, confiscate the bananas from customers, and be totally inflexible in administering the rule. Safeway is much more flexible, and the customer is not aware of being subjected to rules. Table 7.3 suggests the likely audit response to various management styles:

Table 7.3 Linking Management Style and Internal Audit Response

Dimensions of Auditors	Management Styles			
	Theory X Autocratic	Theory X Modified Custodial	Theory Y Supportive	Theory Z Cooperating
Set-up meeting:	Authorization: This is what we plan	Instructive: This is what we plan	Dialogue: Here is what we plan: any suggestions?	Mutuality of interests: How should we proceed?
Progress meetings	Only if further direction of auditee needed	Only if further instruction of auditee needed	Discuss status and important findings and request input	Quality circle approach with regular meetings for discussion
Closing meeting	Summarize the report in a factual manner	Summarize the report in a consulting manner	Discuss the planned report and permit input	Joint report
Formality of report	Very formal	Formal	Informal and formal	Informal
Method of reporting	Written	Written	Oral and written	Jointly Oral and written
Timing of reports	Final report	Final report	Interim and final	Interim and final
Education of auditee regarding the audit	None required	Some advisable	Some necessary	Essential
Scope of audits	Restricted	Financial systems plus	Managerial systems	Comprehensive

Participation

The relation between manager and worker was also studied by Rensis Likert.[16] Likert sees the most effective manager as the one who practices participative management, is strongly oriented toward the worker, and engenders a mutual and genuine interest in the goals of both the organization and the worker. In an experiment reported by Likert, data were collected from 31 different departments doing substantially the same kind of work. To develop participation, group meetings were held in some departments but not in others:

• Group A, ten departments. Both the men and the supervisors thought the meetings were useful.
• Group B, seven departments. Group meetings were not held at all.
• Group C, fourteen departments. Group meetings were held; the men thought them a waste of time even though the attending supervisors thought they were useful.

Production was then measured and, on a scale of 0 to 100, group A measured 64, group C measured 32, and group B, with no meetings at all, measured 54. It appears that no meetings at all are better than meetings from which the participants feel they are gaining nothing—indeed, in which they may feel that they are being manipulated.(17)

Indifference and apathy on the part of the worker are a constant concern of the manager. Some writers, like Likert and Argyris, feel they can be countered with participation and job enlargement.(18) Others say they must be accepted as a fact of our structured lives and that the worker must satisfy psychological needs off the job.(19) It may be that we just have not given enough attention to the totality of the worker's universe; task and job, perception and personality, work community, and rewards and power relations. The universe may be so complex that it may never be truly understood.

Despite the lack in some quarters of enthusiasm for participation, real-life studies and examples have shown definite improvements in productivity as a result of the participative approach. The first is from Coch and French.(20)

"In a textile factory changes were to be made in work methods and piece rates. Four groups were established. Group 1, the control group, was told about the change in the classic autocratic manner. From group 2, representatives were selected to be told of the change and to instruct their fellow workers in the revised methods. Groups 3 and 4 were accorded total participation. Previously, production had been 60 units per hour. A month after the changes were made, the production rates were as follows:

Group	Units per hour
1. Control	48
2. Representation	68
3. Participation	74
4. Participation	72

In the control group, not only did production decrease, but 17 percent of the employees quit and conflicts arose among workers, method engineers, and supervisors. In the other groups, the cooperation was high."

The following study is from Fleishman.(21)

"A dress manufacturing firm's operations were subject to major style changes during the year. Each change brought reduced productivity. A participative approach was used on 30 sewing machine operators. The operators were asked to do what the managers used to do: prescribe the sequence of operations, bundling methods, and pricing the individual operations. Based on past experience, management figured that the 750 dress lot would be run in eight days. The participative group did it in three days. After that run, the old autocratic approach was reinstalled. On the next run, performance levels *ran even higher*. But with the continuation of the autocratic approach, the productivity eventually declined to former levels."

The third study is from Likert.(22)

"A pajama manufacturing company, A, which had long used the participative approach, took over a competitor, B, which used autocratic methods and which had been having unprofitable years. B's managers were retained, but their philosophy was changed to that of A. The change was accompanied by a 30 [percent increase in earnings of piece-rate workers, a 20 percent decrease in labor turnover, and a change in profit on investment from minus 17 percent to plus 15 percent."

Performance Appraisals

A point of potential conflict between manager and worker, one which has a serious effect on relations, is the appraisal of employee performance. There is no easy or perfect way to appraise people, to tell the people the truth as the supervisor sees it, and to satisfy equally the needs of the job and the wants of the employee. Yet people want to know how they are doing and how they can improve, so long as the appraisal process is not abrasive to them. Some guidelines for a system of appraisal include:

- Keep it simple. Develop a cutoff point between above- and below-average performance and concentrate on the extremes.
- Keep it separate. Do not tie it into other systems, such as promotions and raises.
- Keep it contained. Restrict the collection of data. Be chiefly concerned with the appraisal of performance and potential, not with peripheral character evaluations.
- Keep it participative. Solicit the subordinate's point of view; ask the subordinate to appraise himself.

Groups

Group Dynamics

Most workers spend more time with their work groups than with any other groups; hence, work groups and group behavior demand the attention of the manager. Most people enjoy a social environment, and their work group becomes extremely important to them. It can be another family for them, so managers should cater to the group idea if it does not interfere with productivity. Certainly it is the height of optimism for managers to think they can control every relationship. They may therefore have to deal with the group instead of the individuals within it.(23)

Groups may be formal or informal. They can be assembled for a specific task, or they may form naturally because of mutual attraction. Personal attraction in both formal and informal groups can be extremely important in meeting group goals. People tend to agree with those they like and reject ideas of those they don't like—the very same ideas they would accept from someone they liked.

Kurt Lewin popularized the term "group dynamics" in the 1930s and helped establish an organization devoted exclusively to the study of group phenomena:

The Research Center for Group Dynamics. A group is defined as two or more people who are interacting and interdependent and who have the ability to behave in a unified manner with shared purposes and objectives. Lewin's work confirmed the importance of the control that groups can have over productivity and output.(24)

Groups have personalities of their own—composites of the personalities of the members. The personality of the group can over-power that of the individual member. As for structured groups, those brought together by management, a group of five members is best and seven is a maximum. In groups of those sizes, members feel more comfortable and are willing to participate. Also, the odd number prevents deadlocks. anything larger leads to the formation of cliques within the group and loss of participation.

Participative leadership promotes involvement of the members in the group objectives, whereas authoritarian leadership prevents it. Through constructive participation the group members display an interest in informing, clarifying, orienting, mediating, and encouraging. The leader has to watch for and control the orators, needlers, and fence-sitters.

Cohesiveness within the group is important if the members are to constitute a working entity. If the goals of a cohesive group are aligned with those of the organization, then the group is a powerful force for good. The other side of that coin is that if the goals of a cohesive group run counter to those of the organization, the group represents a major threat and needs to be dissolved.

In forming a potentially useful group, managers must do more than merely assign people to it. They should:

- Demonstrate to the group the interdependency of group needs and organizational goals.
- Enhance the status of the group and thereby give the group importance and the members self-esteem.
- Stimulate participation by promoting democratic techniques of leadership.
- Promote maintenance of the group as a productive force.
- Reduce perceived threats from the environment and management that might tend to foment group rebellion.

Managers and task leaders must understand the dynamics of the group and how to deal with it. The task leader may at times not be the same person as the group leader. The task leader must seek and the manager must promote harmony between the two. The task leader promotes the task goals. The group leader promotes congeniality and unanimity. When they agree, tasks get accomplished. When they are at odds, the task goals may never be reached.

The task goals are derivatives of organizational goals, and their achievement should help meet the organization's goals. For the task leader to push toward task goals unremittingly may disrupt the cohesiveness of the group, so chit-chatting and some relaxation may be useful in releasing frustrations and hostility. Also, trust is engendered, and that opens up the creative forces within the group and promotes originality and exchanges of ideas.

Formal organizations have their policies and procedures; social groups, those brought together by common interests, have their standards of behavior: how hard to work, the degree of commitment to the organization, and how much to cooperate with the establishment. The formal task goals may impinge on group norms, so the formal group leader should promote openness, cooperation, reduction of criticism, support for novel ideas, and participative leadership. Otherwise, informal group pressures can be stronger than official regulations.

Group Behavior

The individual in the group will not normally change behavior from that which the group finds acceptable. Re-educating a group member individually and returning this person to the group to disseminate newfound knowledge can spell trouble for this individual and the group. It is far better to have a group member propose group changes. The group will listen to the group member more readily than to an outsider. When someone works with a group, this person must identify with the group.

Indoctrination in group behavior is provided by various methods. Currently, the most popular method is sensitivity training, also known as T-group and laboratory training. The goal is to improve the individual's self-understanding including impact on others. It seeks group participation under controlled laboratory conditions, and its expected outcomes are openness with others, greater concern for the needs and more tolerance for the differences of others, improved listening skills, and more realistic standards of behavior. Positive changes in behavior as a result of sensitivity training have been reported.

Yet sensitivity training has some disadvantages. It is difficult to administer, and participants have had breakdowns under the stress of the sessions. Also, although there may be an enhancement in personal relations, there is no perceived correlation between T-group training and performance. Training one group member and returning this person to the group usually has little effect; the entire group needs the training. Under proper supervision, however, sensitivity training can open people's eyes to the importance of tolerance for others and the need to try to understand them.

Further aspects of informal organizations will be discussed in Chapter 13, Organizing.

Creativity

Workers will produce under the lash of the disciplinarian, even though the output may not be all that is desired. They will satisfy certain of their basic needs even under a domineering, authoritarian manager. They will find certain satisfying relationships in sharing the security blanket of a group; but in a cold, repressive climate, they cannot hope to harvest the fruits of creativity.

An organization must have creativity and innovation if it is to have growth. Some forms of creativity can take place under the classical manager: creativity that is based on logic, science, planning, and the calculated research for new combinations of existing ideas. That approach evokes artificial creativity through such structured techniques as brainstorming. However, primary creativity, which draws upon the wellsprings of inspiration, insight, incubation, and seeing things from within, needs a mild and unrepressive climate.(25)

Primary creativity may be stifled by an organization that insists on tight controls and demands blind adherence to procedures. As a result, the creative flame may go out or the creative individual may leave the organization. Large organizations, therefore, have a smaller chance of nurturing the creative spark. Although the laboratories of AT&T developed the transistor, it took the smaller, new Texas Instruments to conceive its use in something other than the telephone.

Hence, in larger companies especially, managers should be able to identify the creative worker and give the special kind of freedom needed. A summary of several studies shows that such people have certain characteristics:

- They are not necessarily more intelligent than the less creative. They must be intelligent, but intelligence does not insure creativity.
- Their view of authority is that it is not absolute; thus authority does not inhibit.
- They are less dogmatic, because they look for the various sides of a situation—not just one. Hence, they tend to make fewer black-and-white distinctions.
- They are not inhibited from expressing impulses the less creative might think irrational.
- Their sense of humour is generally better than that of the less creative.

As we would expect intuitively, the creative person's patterns of behavior exhibit greater freedom and greater tendency to reject rigorous control by others.

Tapping the Worker's Creativity

Japanese products, in the first half of this century, were often characterized by shoddiness and inferior quality. After World War II, the Japanese government made better quality a national priority. It solicited a number of Americans to help instill the concept of and desire for superior quality in Japanese managers, and workers alike. The excellence of modern Japanese products testifies to the success of the program.

Two Americans in particular, W.E. Deming and J.N. Juran, influenced Japanese thinking about quality. Deming taught the statistical aspects of problem identification and correction. Juran advanced the proposition that quality is everyone's responsibility and must be everyone's commitment. The combination of quantitative analysis and individual striving for excellence led to management support and worker training in what became known as QC circles.(26)

The QC circles made their appearance in Japan in 1962. Each circle is a group of about eight to ten workers and a supervisor. The objective of a circle is to identify and solve quality problems and thereby improve quality, reduce the costs generated by rejections, repairs, and rework, and stem the flood of customer dissatisfaction.

In 1972 Japan boasted about a half million circles with some six million members. The use of circles expanded enormously as the circle concept proved its worth and fired the enthusiasm of its participants. The circles build people, not use them. The ordinary worker is trained in such applications as brainstorming, data gathering, cause-and-effect diagrams, sampling techniques, and Pareto curves (curves that identify the vital few from the trivial many; for example, 20% of the problems are responsible for 80% of the costs), check sheets, graphs, histograms, frequency tables, correlation analysis, basic quality costs analysis, and Ishikawa diagrams (mapping out variables that might cause problems).

Participation is voluntary. People receive no additional pay for their QC circle work. The rewards are a feeling of self-actualization and the recognition received when the group presents proposals and status reports to a higher management that listens respectfully to the workers' recommendations. All projects are carried out in teams that have a collegial orientation in which each learns from the others. The circles are project-oriented, not individual-oriented. They are synergistic in effect, since the united effort exceeds the total of the individual part.

Training is provided both to workers and to managers. Top management supports the effort and encourages creativity. In circle operation, no idea is stupid and no proposal is ridiculed. Since each project relates to the members' work, it becomes personal to the worker. Two hours of regular working time each week is allotted to circle deliberations, but many employees continue working on projects on their own time.

What Americans taught the Japanese has returned to America to create QC circles in American industry with gratifying success. Wayne S. Reiker, Lockheed's manufacturing manager in its Missiles and Space Division at Sunnyvale, California, learned about QC circles from a group of visiting Japanese. He then started the most encompassing in-depth study of QC circles ever undertaken by an American company. After their installation at Lockheed, the QC circles not only expanded workers' horizons and generated increased quality consciousness but also saved $ millions over the years.

Thus through innovative management that taps the sources of creativity in people, the Japanese made a startling turnaround in product quality by successfully integrating the findings and teachings of behavioral scientists with the application of quantitative problem-solving techniques. Then the bread cast upon Japanese waters by American experts floated back across the Atlantic to help American companies improve quality and reduce costs.

THE WORKER AND THE INTERNAL AUDITOR

Work

The internal auditor, also a worker, has a dual concern with the behavioral patterns of workers. First the internal auditor is concerned with either being a subordinate or a supervisor. Second, there is concern with the people whose work is being reviewed. Often the role scripted will influence the way the internal auditor will work as an appraiser of the work of others.

The tasks of the internal auditor call for the talents of an architect, a pick-and-shovel worker, and a builder. When they are all put together, the audit assignment can lead to a complete structure of job satisfaction, because the job is then "my job." As an architect, the internal auditor develops the program. As a pick-and-shovel worker, the internal auditor delves into the details and gathers information. And as a builder, the internal auditor constructs conclusions and recommendations to assist management.

Of course, each professional needs a period of apprenticeship and training in which to learn the principles, techniques, and methodology of the calling. Auditors must learn to differentiate between significant findings and nit-picking. They must learn to deal with people professionally and with empathy. They must learn the difference between a significant and relevant line of inquiry and one that merely satisfies idle curiosity. They must know when to hang on doggedly and when to let go.

After novices have learned the fundamentals, they should not be kept exclusively on pick-and-shovel work; the continued, routine listing and checking of transactions can be stultifying. They should be given a "piece of the action." They should be shown the overall audit program for the entire internal audit project. They should be told what the thrust or "theory" of the job is. Also they should be given a part of the job to carry through to conclusion.

Assume, for example, that they are assisting in an audit of the marketing organization, which encompasses the activities of marketing research, advertising, sales promotion, credit, customer service, and budgets and costs. The assistant internal auditor who has been indoctrinated and taught the basics could be assigned one of the elements, such as advertising, or one of the subelements, such as advertising budgets, agency agreements, department purchases, or agency charges.

It would be up to them to carry out the assignment to conclusion under the watchful eye of the auditor-in-charge. The assistant internal auditor would:

• Study the literature on audits of advertising and records of any prior audits.
• Learn the objectives and the systems of control for the activity he is reviewing.
• Prepare the audit purpose for the subject of the audit.
• Determine the total population of the relevant activities and transactions.

- Propose to the auditor-in-charge the extent of tests, the size of the sample, and the sampling plan and technique.
- Examine the transactions selected in the sample
- Discuss any deviations with the people responsible.
- Record the results of his tests in a structured form that will facilitate the final report writing.
- Accompany the auditor-in-charge when the latter discusses any serious deficiencies with the department manager and division chief.
- Review corrective action proposed or taken and offer suggestions to the auditor-in-charge on whether the action is designed to cure the defects.

This is job enlargement and enrichment. It brings the novice internal auditor into the mainstream of the audit project, gives responsibility, and if the job is carried out properly, gives job satisfaction.

The modern internal auditor has a dual concern: concerned with not only own job enrichment but also that of the workers within the organization, looking for circumstances that tend to create encapsulated impoverished jobs, looking for indicators such as:

- Communications units. An example is the telephone units that handle the flow of requests and perform narrow, routine functions.
- "Checking" functions, which may remove responsibility for quality.
- Troubleshooting jobs, which take coordinating, expediting, and control away from the line.
- "Super gurus"—consultants and analysts who can erode the completeness of others' jobs.
- Job title elephantiasis. Overspecialization can unnecessarily narrow the job.
- One-on-one relationships (Fig. 7.1). If A is strong, B has nothing more than paper-shuffling to do.

- Dual-reporting relationships (Fig. 7.2):

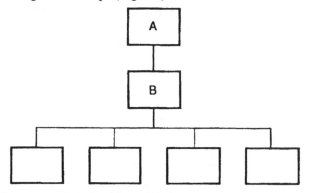

Figure 7.1   One-on-one Relationships at Work

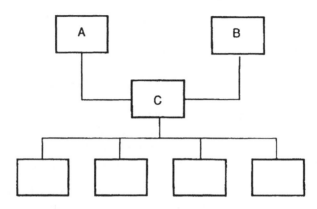

Figure 7.2   Dual-reporting Relationships at Work

This organization tends to erode C's job, because if A and B are strong, C is merely a conduit between them and their subordinates.

- Unclear division of responsibility. Uncertainty as to its nature may result in shunning responsibility.
- Overly complicated work flow. Jobs may be poorly delineated; nobody feels complete responsibility for the full job.
- Duplication of functions. Staff groups may overlap.
- Labor pools. These may destroy "ownership of work."

Workers

To grow a good crop, the farmer needs good seed. To build a good organization, management must hire people with potential. Yet many personnel hiring policies are archaic and many hiring practices involve the hurried search for and adoption of the first warm body that comes along.

The internal auditor can perform a signal service to management by including a review of the hiring practices in the long-range audit program. The review should be concerned not only with practices that search for potential but also with practices that prevent the hiring of villains and misfits.

It is an unfortunate fact of life that many companies shun the publicity that attends the prosecution of an embezzler or a thief. When they detect wrongdoers, they will usually walk them to the gate and let them be hired by another, unsuspecting company. The hiring organization must therefore protect itself by paying close attention to reasonable hiring practices.

Before employees are hired, attention should be given to the careful screening of applicants. Not only should prior employers be questioned but applicants should be queried and investigated about past histories of gambling, unusual expenses, and high living—conditions which may force people to steal.

Psychological tests have been designed to point up a tendency toward dishonesty. Organizations that are hiring employees for sensitive positions such as purchasing agent should consider full-scale background investigations by reliable investigators.

The polygraph, or lie detector, is being used more and more by commercial organizations for pre-employment testing. The questions that are asked relate to thefts from former employers, lies on the application form, use of narcotics, length of time the applicant intends to stay with the organization, and whether female applicants are pregnant. Internal auditors who recommend polygraph tests in place of the more expensive background investigations should, however, be aware of the strong opposition to such tests by many unions and legislators.

The internal auditor's tests in audits of personnel records should include these steps:

- Review applications of employees in sensitive positions.
- Find out whether adequate explanations were obtained for time gaps on the application forms.
- Make sure all employment and school references have been verified.
- If reference replies are unfavorable, make sure that the personnel people inquired of the prior employer whether the applicant was discharged for dishonesty.

The audit program used by one company lists the following questions that are pertinent to hiring and to other personnel practices within the organization:

- Is the company's application form laid out in a well-organized manner?
- Is the application form designed to weed out undesirable applicants rapidly?
- Have employment standards been established in written form?
- Have interviewing procedures been standardized and have interviewers been carefully selected and trained?
- Are tests used in the selection and placement of new employees?
- Are the tests related to the jobs for which the prospective employee is applying, and do they accord with federal government requirements?
- Does the personnel department check local credit investigating organizations to obtain information that might be helpful in evaluating applicants?
- Does the personnel department check former-employment references?
- In checking references, has the personnel department developed a list of specific questions that should be asked to obtain information to help in evaluating the applicant's potential?
- Is a manual or booklet given to each person who is employed to inform of the company's rules and regulations?
- Are new employees required to undergo a probationary period? Does the personnel department check responsible supervision to make sure the requirements of the job have been satisfactorily met.
- Do the personnel files contain a full history of each employee, including data

on special talents, ambitions, and personal achievements?
- Does the company have a program for helping employees solve personal problems?
- Are employees kept informed of management's objectives, plans, problems, successes, and failures?
- Do supervisors periodically review individual progress with employees?
- Does the company encourage and help employees to further their education?
- Does the company maintain a training program?
- Are the more progressive and talented executive personnel selected and enrolled in advanced management courses?
- Does personnel carry on a university recruiting program?

The Needs of the Worker

Management can be reasonably sure that its workers' needs are not being satisfied if the level of worker morale is low. Morale is reflected in the degree to which people cooperate voluntarily in group efforts toward group goals.

Managers are, and should be, deeply concerned with employee morale, if for no other reason than that morale directly affects productivity, safety, security, absenteeism, and turnover. The internal auditor must therefore be equally concerned with the attitudes of workers. The internal auditor, who is usually most comfortable with objective standards, units of measurement, and quantitative evaluations, is hard put to it to appraise that subjective quality in objective terms. Yet the importance of morale will not let the subject be swept under the rug of the regular audit program. There are relatively objective appraisals to be made, and there are some subjective appraisals to be applied.

Answers to the following questions might help the internal auditor make objective appraisals:

- Do supervisors observe their workers' behavior and periodically report to higher management on employee morale?
- Do safety inspectors consider the question of morale in appraising causes for accidents and do they report their findings?
- Is there a program of nondirective interviewing by employee counselors in which the counselor makes no judgements and offers no interpretive or associative comments, but rather encourages the worker to full and honest expression?
- Are all terminating employees given exit interviews, and is employee morale discussed?
- Are the number and types of grievances analyzed?
- How do grievances compare in number and seriousness with those in comparable organizations?
- Are production quantity and quality unduly affected by absenteeism?

- What is the degree of labor turnover, and how does the turnover compare with that of other departments in the organization and with other organizations?
- Are attitude surveys calling for anonymous replies carried out, summarized, and acted on?

The internal auditor can also make subjective appraisals; and although they may not be couched in quantitative terms, they can be valuable. In audit assignments, the internal auditor usually works with the employees, observes their demeanour, working habits, relations to their supervisors, and feelings about their department and the organization. Being subject to the same physical environment it is often possible for the internal auditor to find causal relations between deficiency findings and morale.

At the end of his audit assignment the internal auditor can prepare a record of impressions on such matters as morale, working habits, organization and staffing, supervision, interface with other organizations, and working areas. Impressions can then be discussed—best not refer to them as findings—with appropriate managers and executives. The subjects are best handled informally and not included in the written audit report.

The Internal Auditor—Appraiser and Subject of Appraisals

Performance reviews affect internal auditors from the standpoint of first their own and subordinates' performances and second the organization's personnel procedures and practices.

Performance of Internal Auditors

Appraising performance of internal auditors is complicated by the fact that no two audit projects are the same. It is further complicated by the many contracts the internal auditor must make at the various levels within the organization. Thus, besides technical and professional ability, the way the auditor deals with others can be extremely important. An abrasive personality can undo in one meeting the participative relationship the auditing department has been trying to build for years. On the other hand, the internal auditor who glosses over serious deficiencies in an attempt to be liked by the auditee can present an even greater hazard to both the organization and the profession.

The evaluations of internal auditors must therefore be considered carefully. To be effective, they should be frank, fair, frequent, and friendly. However, not all evaluators have the innate or even the developed ability to perform useful evaluations. One auditor-in-charge may have a built-in bias against an assistant auditor, whereas another auditor-in-charge may regard the assistant with complete objectivity. Also, every audit assignment may call for different talents from the same auditor. An assistant or an auditor-in-charge may perform superbly in an audit of the accounts payable department and fall flat on the face in an audit of production control.

Hence, a compromise to the evaluation of internal auditors is to appraise the auditor after each audit assignment. The director of internal auditing should develop an evaluation form that gives appropriate weight to the various demands of the job. Here is an example:

Planning and organizing	20%
Fieldwork (working papers, testing techniques, evaluation of findings, etc.)	50
Oral expression	10
Writing ability	15
Meeting budget and schedule	5
Total	100%

The various elements within those characteristics may then be evaluated as excellent, very good, fair, and unsatisfactory and a numerical rating given each. The measurements can be followed by an evaluation of other characteristics such as initiative, energy, pleasantness, cooperativeness, work habits, and readiness for promotion. Since those qualities do not lead themselves readily to quantification, adjectival ratings can be used. The numerical and adjectival ratings should be supplemented by the narrative comments of the rater; the comments can be more descriptive of ability and potential than the structured ratings.

At the end of a period—semi-annual or annual—the evaluations of the various raters can be combined and the results can be discussed with the individual. Various forms and approaches are used to evaluate internal auditors. Whichever one is used, it should be applied consistently and should be fair to both the individual and the organization.

Auditing the Performance Review Function

The internal auditor must understand that performance evaluations serve two basic purposes:

1. To determine the best possible utilization of the human resource.
2. To help individuals improve their value to themselves and the organization.

The internal auditor must also understand that people generally dislike playing the role of judge of their fellow workers. When the judging involves reducing the evaluations to writing and discussing defects in performance or character face-to-face with the worker, the chances are that the responsibility will be avoided or put off. Also, if the materials of evaluation are arbitrary, bookish, and not relevant to the work, the chances for successful evaluations become even more remote.

Accordingly, the internal auditor will want to determine whether:

- The personnel department has prescribed reasonable policies, procedures, forms, and records for the evaluation process.
- Evaluations are performed and reported on at prescribed periods.
- Adequate records are maintained.
- The evaluations are used when the employee is considered for raises or promotions.
- Management has done a creditable job of indoctrinating workers and evaluators in the purposes and uses of the evaluations.

Internal Audit Groups

The internal audit team assigned to an audit project is a group, and the psychology of groups is applicable to it. Large teams may have their formal and their informal leaders. The formal leader—the auditor-in-charge—is responsible for the conduct of the work and the final report. However, the success of the project will depend on how well the leader welds together a successful team and elicits the cooperation of the members. In seeking cooperation, the informal leader must be identified and dealt with.

Some team captains operate as autocrats. They lay out the program, parcel out the assignments, review and correct working papers, deal alone with operating managers, and take over completely the writing of the audit report. However, standoffishness can impoverish the job. Each of the team members makes contacts and develops understandings that may be useful and helpful to the team leader and the other team members. Periodic meetings whereby each member can contribute ideas that will further the audit purposes can be useful. Also, if the team leader promotes a feeling of cohesiveness, the individual contributors can present lines of audit thrust not dreamed of in the original program.

Similarly, in large internal audit organizations deploying a number of teams, periodic staff meetings can be helpful. They promote a feeling of belonging. They can provide a sounding board for ideas. The internal auditor reviewing the shipping department might have some pertinent points for the internal auditor reviewing accounts receivable. The internal auditor reviewing accounts payable might point to problems the auditor reviewing purchasing should be aware of.

Staff meetings should be so structured that people are given an agenda of what will be covered and the time allotted for interchanges among members. They should also have their unstructured moments so that people will feel free to get things off their chests or contribute information to the group.

Internal auditors are also concerned with the groups in the organization: the ad hoc, temporary, or permanent committees set up to carry out specific functions. They should be interested in whether each such committee is given a formal written charter for all to see. Also, they should want to know whether any of the committees have overlapping functions or whether some activities or functions that top management thought were covered have somehow slipped between the assigned responsibilities of contiguous committees.

Internal Audit Review of Groups and Committees

Certain functions within an organization do not require the day-to-day attention of an operating department yet may represent a responsibility that requires periodic attention and must not be forgotten. Safety and security matters, separate from the ongoing policing function, are a case in point. Management sets up committees to meet monthly or quarterly to consider matters of fire or disaster prevention. Charters are established; chairs are appointed; and representatives from operating departments are assigned to the committees.

Having done its job of organizing the committees, management will usually turn its attention to more pressing matters. Usually, no one executive has the responsibility for seeing that all committees function effectively, cover all activities that need coverage, and do not overlap. The job of making such a review and analysis should fall to the internal auditor. If auditors see that committees are carrying out their functions as prescribed and are adequately covering the activities needing committee coverage, they can provide assurance to executive management. If, on the other hand, some relevant activities are not covered, they should make appropriate recommendations to management.

A case in point involved the review of safety and security in a large corporation that had a central corporate office and a number of operating divisions. The internal auditor of one of the divisions reviewed the charters, meetings, agendas, and reports of all committees involved with or charged with responsibility for safety and security matters. Findings showed that there were 11 committees concerned with such matters:

1. Corporate Disaster Prevention and Safety Committee
2. Divisional Disaster Prevention and Safety Committee
3. Divisional Disaster Control Committee
4. Divisional Industrial Security Emergency Planning Committee
5. General Safety Committee
6. Managers' Safety Committee
7. Workmen's Safety Committee
8. Fire Hazard Committee
9. High Hazard Committee
10. Isotope Committee
11. Skills Training Committee

The internal auditor prepared a chart showing side by side the names of the committees, the frequency of their meetings, the chairpersons and the members of the committees, the detailed functions and responsibilities of each committee, the authority under which each committee was established, and citations to the implementing instructions.

For the first time executive management was able to see what it had wrought over the years: the interrelations among the committees, the overlapping responsibilities, and the necessary activities that somehow had been forgotten in developing the committees. As a result of this work and report, the internal auditor provided certain assurances to executive management on the adequacy of its safety and security systems. At the same time recommendations were made for improvements and consolidations that became apparent when the entire record was spread out for management to see. The auditor demonstrated the importance of taking a good, hard look at groups and committees within the corporate structure to make sure the groups continue to do their jobs and are disbanded when they are no longer needed. The effectiveness of using the management viewpoint in making audit appraisals was also demonstrated.

Appraising Creative Activities

The Creativity of Others

The internal auditor's review of the organization's creative activities, such as sales promotion, advertising, and research and development, is often centered on the control aspects. The auditor may determine whether plans have been devised, organizational structures established, approval systems prescribed, budgets prepared, and costs evaluated. However, management's interest in creativity exceeds measurable performance. As it looks to the future it is also interested in the abilities of its creative and professional people. Are those people competent? Are they innovative? How do they compare with their counterparts in competitive organizations? The immediate managers of those people may have a vested interest in protecting their professionals by extolling virtues and hiding defects. The managers may not always be objective, but the internal auditor is. Executive management has, of course, a right to expert, objective evaluations of any activities that affect the organization's current and future operations. Properly done, such evaluations can be useful.

The key criterion in assessing professional ability is how the professionals are regarded by their peers. In the case of scientists, for example, a test of standing in the professional community is the frequency of publication of papers. In one audit of an international company's research department, the internal auditors analyzed the department's publications over a period of years. They found that 20% of the scientists and engineers had not published in two years. That was considered by all to be a significant percentage. The matter was turned over to the department head, who agreed to determine the reason why some of his people published 12 to 14 papers a year and others published none.

In the same research department, the internal auditors found that section supervisors evaluated the performance of their scientific and engineering personnel but failed to communicate the results to the employees evaluated. The major benefits of an evaluation of a professional by a peer were therefore being lost. The difficulty stemmed from the fact that evaluators look upon the job of employee appraisals with repugnance and try to avoid the embarrassment of bringing defects to the attention of their people. Nevertheless, the job still has to be done, and management has to be told if it is not being done.

On a more traditional note, the audit of the research-and-development activity had a direct effect involving a good deal of money. In their tour of the laboratories, the internal auditors counted six electron microscopes. Those monsters cost about $100,000 each, and a couple were not being used. Several weeks later, during a budget audit, the auditors observed that another laboratory division had listed in its budget the procurement of an electron microscope. The auditors brought the two division heads together, had one of the six microscopes transferred, and saved $100,000.

If we take Peter Drucker's 10 Rules of Effective Research, it is immediately apparent that the internal auditor can play a valuable role in ensuring that such insights are not lost on an organization.(27) The rules are:

1. Every new product, processor or service begins to become obsolete on the day it first breaks even.
2. The company bringing about the obsolescence is the only way to prevent a competitor from so doing.
3. If research is to have results, the nineteenth century distinction between "pure" and "applied" research is best forgotten.
4. In effective research physics, chemistry, biology, economics and the like are not "disciplines," but tools.
5. Research is not one effort, but three—improvement, managed evolution, and innovation.
6. Aim high! Trivial corrections are usually as hard to make and equally resisted as fundamental changes.
7. Both long-range and short-range results are required.
8. Research is separate work, but not a separate function.
9. Organized abandonment of research projects is required.
10. Research has to be measured like anything else.

Whenever the internal auditor feels out of depth in evaluating specialized and professional activities, the services of a respected peer of the professional worker should be enlisted. In the world of academe, it is standard practice for professionals of known stature to be assigned to evaluate their peers. The evaluation is accepted as a matter of course by those evaluated and creates the least amount of personal problems. It is the experience of internal auditors who have been part of such evaluations that the resulting reports should be made orally to both operating and executive management and not be incorporated in formal reports.

Internal Audit Creativity

The modern internal auditor also is deeply involved with creativity. Creativity need not be the inspirational flashes of genius associated with the nuclear physicist. Nor does it have to be; for creativity has been defined as "the ability to formulate new combinations from two or more concepts already in mind."(28) Seen in that way, creativity is as available to the internal auditor as it is to the sculptor or the poet. Creativity is there within all of us; psychologists are convinced that all people are to some degree potentially creative—all ages, all cultures, and all fields of human endeavor.

Imagination and originality, by and large, are qualities that all of us were born with and which made our childhood days a kaleidoscope of incredibly interesting dreams, experiences, and ideas. As the years went by some of those qualities may have dried up as we developed hardening of the attitudes and fell into patterns and ruts. Perhaps we learned that in this demanding world of ours there was no real independence, no complete freedom from fear. In the absence of freedom from fear, imagination and originality find the climate too severe to grow to fruition, much less survive.

Sensible internal auditors understand that in such positions—that of careful, conservative counselors—they cannot tolerate some of the mistakes other experimenters can afford to make. Management is looking for what is tried and true, not what may be merely an ephemeral wish or hope. Nevertheless, within the confines of the profession, there is still room and need for innovation—sound innovation, practical innovation. Management does not generally get critical of new ideas as such. It is critical of new ideas that don't work, of half baked ideas that need more time in the oven.

With that in mind, the auditor may still recall the imagination and originality of childhood, but now this can be harnessed by using the reins of practicality, reasonableness, and usefulness. Hemholtz, the German physicist, gave three elements of the creative process: saturation, incubation, illumination.(29) *Saturation* is soaking up the facts, observing, gathering information. *Incubation* is carried on without conscious effort. It means carrying the facts, observations, and information in the deep dark recesses of the subconscious where they come into contact with other experiences and other knowledge to form new combinations. *Illumination* is that flash of understanding, after the incubation, when the new ideas come at the most unexpected times to give us a key or a solution to a problem.

To the three elements of saturation, incubation, and illumination the internal auditor will add verification: evaluation and the elaboration or development of ideas. The internal auditor should not, dare not, take action until verification has been accomplished. But when it is carefully developed, creativity can take place almost anywhere in the broad spectrum of activities the internal auditor engages in.

The internal auditor may be innovative in the long-range audit program. There may be built up fences to help protect the company against fraud and theft.

Each company will present different forms of risk: the internal auditor, through research, survey, and knowledge of the company, should identify and list the forms. They will include such disparate matters as blank check stock, receipt of currency in the mails, bank reconciliations, deliveries bypassing the receiving department, sole-source procurements, drugs in the medical department, rotation of employee assignments, assurance that all people in sensitive positions take vacations, conflict-of-interest programs, and many others. Once identified and listed, the activities should be referred to and covered in a programmed examination or dealt with as a separate examination.

The internal auditor can create new ways of performing fieldwork, perhaps by questionnaires sent out in advance of arrival. Computer systems can be designed with special loops to spin off particular types of transactions for special study or random selections for examinations. In the examination of processes and methods, the auditor can be creative by doubting and questioning all that is seen. The fact that something has been done for a long time in the same way is no guarantee of its propriety. Here is an example:

> Large rivets and fasteners have to be used around certain doors in an airplane under construction. Before a fastener is installed, a hole is drilled for its shank. The hole is then countersunk so that the top of the fastener's head will be flush with the surrounding metal. The internal auditor found that inspectors were rejecting some of the installations. The reason they gave was that the heads weren't flush with the surrounding metal. Since there seemed to be quite a few rejections involving a lot of rework expense, and since feelings were running pretty high between production and inspection people, the internal auditor looked into the matter.
>
> The auditor found that there were two kinds of rivets, both of which were perfectly acceptable. One had a so-called knife-edge head; when it sat in the countersink, it fitted snugly. Both to touch and sight, the fastener was a perfect fit. The other fastener had a blunt or rounded edge to its head. When it was seated in the countersink, it left a moat—a slight, almost imperceptible space around the head. When the inspectors looked at and touched the head of the rivet and the surrounding metal, they got the impression that the head wasn't properly seated and rejected the assembly.
>
> The internal auditor, using some creativity, demonstrated by using a straight-edge strip of metal that the fasteners were indeed properly installed. As a result, rejections fell off and extensive, expensive rework was avoided.

C.S. Whiting observed that three positive factors will permit creativity to show itself: constructive discontent, observation, and facility of combination.(30)

1. *Constructive discontent.* To be constructively discontented is to be dissatisfied with existing methods and never to accept "This is the way we've always done it" as gospel. It is to question, to ask why, and to refuse to be put off. But it must be *constructive* discontent: an urge to make better and not merely overthrow.

2. *Observation.* Observation comprises the gathering of facts, the watching of processes, the discussions with production workers, inspectors, engineers, and managers so that the process is understood and all sides have been seen.

3. *Facility of combination.* The ability to combine and recombine information in a variety of ways amounts to the facility of combination. It seems plain that the greater our fund of knowledge, the more likely we are to be creative. The more hooks we have to hang the problems on, the more factors there are to combine and recombine.

One of the most significant assets the modern internal auditor can offer to the problem-solving partnership with management is the ability to be creative in attacking the problems that beset every organization.

CONCLUSION

Both the manager and the internal auditor must deal with workers. To deal with workers effectively, the partners in problem solving must understand the workers' needs, wants, abilities, and potentials. The two partners must understand both the psychology of the individual and the psychology of the group. Disregarding the group will not make the group go away. It must be considered, and its goals must be meshed subtly with the goals of the organization. When the goals are diametrically opposed, the group unit must be disbanded lest it do harm to the organization.

Managers and internal auditors alike must appreciate the importance of growth, innovation, and creativity to the organization and how to foster it and evaluate it. What is extremely important is that internal auditors should seek to tap the wellsprings of their own creativity to help further the needs of the problem-solving partnership.

REFERENCES

(1) Gen. 3:23 and 2 Thess. 3:10.
(2) Frederick Herzberg, *Work and the Nature of Man* (Cleveland: World Publishing, 1966).
(3) Peter F. Drucker, *The Frontiers of Management* (London: Heinemann, 1987), p. 35.
(4) Abraham H. Maslow, *Motivation and Personality* (New York: Harper & Row, 1954).
(5) Richard Kosmo and Orlando Behling, "Single Continuum Job Satisfaction vs. Duality: An Empirical Test," *Personnel Psychology*, Vol. 22, No. 3, pp. 327–334.
(6) Chris Argyris, *Personality and Organization* (New York: Harper & Row, 1957).
(7) Victor Vroom, *Work and Motivation* (New York: Wiley, 1964), pp. 17–33, 121–147.
(8) Robert Dubin, *Human Relations in Administration*, 2nd ed. (Englewood Cliffs, N.J: Prentice-Hall, 1974), pp. 126–129.
(9) C. I. Barnard, *The Function of an Executive* (Cambridge, Mass.: Harvard University Press, 1951).

(10) "Conversations with B. F. Skinner," *Organizational Dynamics*, Vol. 1, No. 3, p. 31.

(11) Douglas McGregor, *The Human Side of Enterprise* (New York: McGraw-Hill, 1960). pp. 33–34, 47–48.

(12) E. H. Schein, *Organizational Culture and Leadership*, (London: Jossey-Bass, 1985).

(13) W. Ouchi, *Theory Z: How American Business Can Meet the Japanese Challenge* (Addison-Wesley, 1981).

(14) W. Ouchi, *The M-Form Society. How American Teamwork Can Recapture the Competitive Edge* (Reading, Mass: Addison-Wesley, 1984).

(15) R. T. Pascale and A. G. Athos, *The Art of Japanese Management* (London: Penguin Books, 1986).

(16) Rensis Likert, *New Patterns of Management* (New York: McGraw-Hill, 1961) and *The Human Organization: Its Management and Value* (New York: McGraw-Hill, 1967).

(17) Likert, *New Patterns of Management*, p. 123.

(18) Argyris, op. cit., pp. 187–200, and Likert, *New Patterns of Management* chaps. 2, 7.

(19) H. J. Leavitt and T. L. Whisler, "Management in the 1980s," *Harvard Business Review* Vol. 36, No.6, pp. 44–45, and Dubin, op. cit., p. 79.

(20) Lester Coch and J. R. P. French, Jr., "Overcoming Resistance to Change," *Human Relations*, Vol. 1, No.4, pp. 512–532

(21) E. A. Fleishman, "Attitude versus Skill Factors in Work Group Productivity," *Personnel Psychology*, Vol. 18, No. 3, pp. 253–266.

(22) Likert, *The Human Organization*, pp. 31–38.

(23) G. C. Homans, *The Human Group* (New York: Harcourt, Brace & World, 1950).

(24) Kurt Lewin, *A Dynamic Theory of Personality* (New York: McGraw-Hill, 1935) and *Field Theory in Social Science: Selected Theoretical Papers* (New York: Harper & Brothers, 1951).

(25) Abraham H. Maslow, *Toward a Psychology of Being* (New York: Van Nostrand, 1962), p. 141.

(26) W. E. Deming, "What Happened in Japan," *Industrial Quality Control*, August 1967, pp. 89–93; J. M. Juran, "The QC Circle Phenomenon," *Industrial Quality Control*, January, 1967, pp. 329–336.

(27) Peter F. Drucker, *Managing for the Future*, (London: Butterworth-Heinemann, 1992), pp. 224–228.

(28) C. W. Taylor, *Creativity: Progress and Potential* (New York: McGraw-Hill, 1964), p. 5.

(29) C. S. Whiting, *Creative Thinking* (New York:Reinhold, 1958), p. 6.

(30) Ibid., p. 20.

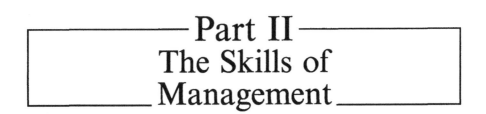

Part II
The Skills of
Management

8
Decision Making

STRATEGY AND THE MANAGER

"I sometimes think that strategy is nothing but tactics talked through a brass hat."(1)

There may be some confusion as to the difference between business strategy and business policy, but the confusion clears when we realize that the difference is simply in the Greek *stratiotes,* meaning soldier, and *polis* meaning city. It is military versus civil. The quotation is questioning whether there is any such thing as military strategy, reckoning that all one has is a tactical approach conveyed through the like of a general. There is obviously some support for such a statement although equally government departments of defense certainly have a strategic dimension. Nowadays the two terms are simply alternatives, although early management theory often concerned itself with the military, and we still encounter generals running management courses, and books on the management lessons to be gained from Atilla the Hun! Presumably Machiavelli on management is the civil equivalent.

In the development of notions of business strategy, there was a move from a pre-occupation with the internal, exemplified in the so-called management principles, to a concern with an external orientation, aided and abetted by the insights from marketing in the 1950s, and from systems theorists about the same time. It was only really in the 1960s that the notion of strategy was being worked up into a coherent framework by major players such as Kenneth R. Andrews, H. Igor Ansoff, and Alfred D. Chandler Jr. Peter Drucker had presented an earlier, less developed formulation in his 1954 *The Practice of Management* (Harper and Row), with the distinction of tactical and strategic management.

Although there are differences of emphasis among business strategists, similar to the definitional footwork that applies to the term "management," there would be broad agreement to the classic expression of Ken Andrews:

"Business policy is the study of the functions and responsibilities of the senior management in a company, the crucial problems that affect the success of a total enterprise, and the decisions that determine its direction, shape its future, and produce the results desired. The policy problems of business, like those of policy in public affairs, have to do with the choice of purposes, the development and recognition of organization identity and character, the unending definition of what needs to be done, the mobilization of resources for the attainment of goals in the face of aggressive competition or adverse circumstances, and the definitions of standards for the enforcement of responsible and ethical behaviour."(2)

We seem to be returning towards our definitions of management when Andrews tells us that business policy is essentially the study of the knowledge, skills, and attitudes constituting general management. However, general management is used to designate members of the office of president, executive and senior vice presidents who have interfunctional responsibilities, and presidents or managers of divisions.

It is impossible to discuss strategy without mentioning the contribution of Michael Porter.(3) His model of competitive strategy has been extremely influential (see Fig. 8.1).

The model is useful for analyzing both a company, and the competitive situation of the internal audit service. Equally useful are the accompanying notions of overall cost leadership, differentiation (offering a product or service that is perceived industrywise as being unique), and focus (directed at serving a particular buyer group, segment of the product line, or geographical market more effectively or efficiently than competitors who compete more broadly),

Business process re-engineering was infiltrating many corporations in the mid 1990s. It is defined as "the fundamental rethinking and radical redesign of business processes to achieve dramatic improvements in critical, contemporary measures of performance, such as cost, quality, service and speed."(4)(5)

As an example of the reengineered corporation, James Champy, in conversation with Professor Vinten, named British Airways as his favorite carrier for business class. His ticket is marked as a frequent flyer, and about once in every four trips, he is expedited through customs. He likes the catering arrangement on the transatlantic flight. On one flight he asked a question to which there was no immediate answer, and he presumed that the flight attendants were too busy to be able to find out, but when he landed he was paged, and handed a written answer. He is also recognized and greeted on flights in a personal way.

DECISION MAKING AND THE MANAGER

The Anatomy of Decision Making

The Futurity of Decisions

Decision making is problem solving. If there is no problem—and in this context

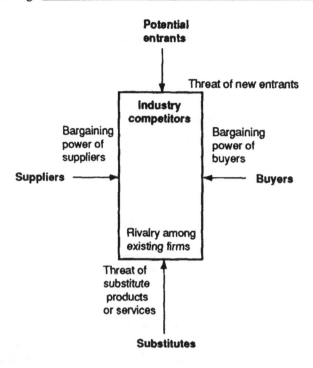

Figure 8.1 Model of Competitive Strategy . . .

we include difficulties and conflicts in the term "problem"—there is no need for a decision. Whether to launch a new product, how to procure needed parts that are in short supply, and how to get the warring directors of sales and manufacturing to see eye-to-eye, all call for decisions.

Whether the matters requiring decision are called problems, difficulties, or conflicts, the means of resolving them have one thing in common: they relate to the future.

What sets the manager's decisions apart is that they are made in a fishbowl.

The Manager's Decisions

Day-to-day decisions affect most of the people within the unit. More important decisions affect people and colleagues in interfacing units. The most important decisions affect the entire enterprise and perhaps the community as well.

Decision making is perhaps the manager's key skill. Impact on the organization is measured by the results of decisions. Indeed, the decision theory approach to management holds that decision making is the sole function of management.

Decision making is rational selection. It is not a mechanical job. It is a taking of risks, because to anticipate the future is always a chancey undertaking. It is a challenge to judgement because it is more than a mere intellectual exercise and because it calls for vision and energy and for the deployment of the organization's resources to achieve effective action.

Rationality

Yet complete rationality in decision making is rarely achieved. Rationality can relate only to what has already happened; and since managers must deal with the future, they will have to settle for limited rationality. It can, however, be a well-founded rationality if the conditions of decision making are understood. The decision maker should:

- Be trying to meet some goal that could not be met without taking positive action
- Fully understand the limitations within which decisions on the action will be taken
- Realize that any choice made must be consistent with the goals
- Know that rarely is there one best choice, one best selection that will satisfy everyone. Instead, the final selection will most likely be a compromise between no action at all and some elusive Holy Grail.

More than that, the manager must keep in mind that every decision made must take into account the responsibility to manage the enterprise, manage the worker and the work, consider the community and society. Yet when we ask an executive how decisions are made, we get about the same answer as to the question: "How do you ride a bicycle?" The actual answers are usually like these:

"I don't think we businessmen know how to make decisions."
"I don't know how I do it, I just do it."
"There's no formula for effective decision making."
"Thinking only causes mistakes."

In recent years, however, particularly in the nonroutine decisions, intuition is relinquishing its place to reasoning. Certainly there must always be a place for individual judgements, but the managers are turning more and more to attempts to reduce the number of occasions on which intuition is the sole basis for the decision. A person who has nothing but background is a theorist. A person who has nothing but practical experience is a business mechanic. A professionally trained executive is one in whom there is an effective integration of these two general types of experiences, combined with adequate intelligence.

Classifications

Decisions and approaches to decisions can be classified in a number of ways. Here are some of them:

1. There are planning decisions and controlling decisions. Planning decisions

make the rules. Controlling decisions enforce the rules. Planning decisions specify organizational objectives, develop programs, and set policies and procedures. Controlling decisions call for the steps to be taken to bring performance into line with the standards specified in the plans.

2. Decisions can also be classified as:

Routine. Repetitive decisions that follow well-defined patterns and established procedures.

Nonroutine. Unique problems that require individual analysis and solution, including those that are concerned with people.

Ends. Broad decisions that are concerned with goals and objectives and are often nonrational; that is, they are influenced by the politics of a situation, the setting of objectives for an organization, or the personal drives of the executive.

Means. Specific decisions that relate to the ways by which goals and objectives are reached. They should be rational or they will not be effective or efficient.

Strategic. These decisions involve the relations between the organization and its environment or concern such matters as product mix and diversification.

Administrative. Under this head come organizational decisions that include establishing authority, determining the flow of work, and deciding where to locate facilities.

Operating. Here may be grouped the decisions related to pricing and marketing and those concerned with production.

3. The bases for decisions may be classified as:

Nonquantitative. Those based on intuition, facts, experience, and considered opinions.

Quantitative. Those based on such mathematical techniques as operations research, linear programming, simulation, Monte Carlo, queuing, and gaming. They will be discussed in Chapter 11.

Experience and Decision Making

Managers who use and defend the intuitive approach to decision making point to the success of the decisions they have made and to the effectiveness and efficiency of their operations. That kind of intuition may be a valuable asset and certainly should not be abandoned entirely. However, the intuitive manager must recognize that intuition is based on learning from limited experience. Such learning is usually haphazard rather than structured and extensive. All managers have learning experiences, but there is no certainty that they learn from those experiences. Besides, conditions change, and the problem under consideration probably is not exactly the same as the successfully solved problem dredged out of experience. Decision making is often identified with the final choice. Actually, it is a process.

Arriving at a decision takes four steps:

1. Defining the problem: determining whether there really is a problem. Identifying the real issues, estimating when a solution must be reached, and estimating what it will cost to solve the problem.
2. Defining expectations: clarifying what will be gained by solving the problem and setting the goals which must be considered in all the steps of finding the most satisfactory solution.
3. Developing alternative solutions: Which of the options available best meet the goals and are surest to avoid that which is undesirable and unexpected?
4. Knowing what to do with the decision after it is reached.

If a manager pays attention to those four rules, he or she will keep from falling into such traps as:

- Finding the right answer for the wrong problem.
- Making the decision at the wrong time. The premature decision may not take into account enough knowledge. Postponement, which is also a decision and sometimes a bad one, can be irrevocable and may defeat the goals that the manager is trying to achieve.
- Making decisions to act that result in no action. To leave such a decision unimplemented is an abortion.

For the purpose of this chapter, we have expanded the steps in the decision-making process to include the evaluation of the developed alternatives and the making of the final choice. Accordingly, the portion of this chapter devoted to the manager's decision making will be subdivided under the following topics:

- Recognizing and defining the problem
- Defining expectations
- Developing alternative courses
- Evaluating possible courses
- Selecting the best choice
- Taking action

Recognizing and Defining the Problem

Problems are brought to the manager's attention in many ways. Some surface routinely as the manager reviews reports and compare actual occurrences with occurrences that have been scheduled and budgeted. The significant variances rise like flares to capture attention. Others are brought by the operation of well-designed controls and checks, the most important of which is the functioning of an alert internal auditing staff. The broader the scope of the internal audit program the more certain the executive can be that problems throughout the organization—not only in the accounting areas—will be brought to attention. The internal auditor's role in the decision-making process will be discussed at length later in this chapter.

Some problems arise from the setting of new objectives, and they are self-generating. New objectives, goals, and product lines foretell the problems that are bound to accompany them, and the executive has at least an inkling that in those activities decisions will have to be made.

Other problems burst unexpectedly in the manager's face: contract cancellations, catastrophic acts of God, death of key people, an unexpected flood of orders. However, by far the largest volume of matters calling for decision come before the manager in the following three ways:

1. *Decisions or directives passed down by higher authority.* Executive decisions and directives require implementation. That implementation calls for decisions at the lower level, and sometimes the higher decision was made without giving full consideration to the circumstances that prevail where the implementation must be carried out. The manager may be hung on the horns of a dilemma. Carry out the executive decision and create chaos, or refuse to carry it out and be found insubordinate. Those are the situations that try managers' souls and create great actors; for some managers have the consummate skill of making insubordination appear to be the highest form of loyalty. Usually the dilemma occurs because the manager responsible for the action was not included in the process that led to the higher decision.

2. *Submissions by subordinates for management decision.* It is a sad fact that most people would rather respond routinely to stimuli than take the responsibility of making decisions, so they pass the decisions to the boss. Also, conflicts or jurisdictional disputes in the lower ranks bring pleas for decisions, but the good subordinates understand their responsibilities and authority to make decisions. They settle on their own the matters within the compass of their assignment and seek help only when matters are clearly outside that compass. Again, however, most people would rather leave the deciding to the boss. The wise manager must let it be known that self-reliance and initiative is expected from subordinates, and so forces them to make the appropriate decisions. Similarly, managers do not create a climate in which they make every decision, large or small, or in which the penalty for mistakes is so severe that decisions are avoided.

3. *Decisions imposed by the situation.* Many decisions are required neither by the imposition of superior decisions nor by submissions from subordinates; they are an inherent part of the responsibilities defined by the plan of organization. The first two kinds are not elective; the manager will have to respond one way or another. The situational decision is a matter of choice, however, and it is by far the most significant test of the manager's executive ability. Situational decisions are made on the manager's own initiative; and when initiative is lacking or when fear of failure is overweening, the tendency is to avoid the decision. The hesitant manager fears the consequences of a wrong decision more than those of no decision.

Problems, whatever their source, do not come with clear, incisive labels on them. Difficulties that identify themselves as one thing on the surface often mask the true identity of the underlying problem. The manager may then commit the cardinal sin of rendering the right judgement on the wrong case.

The first question that the manager should ask when faced with a problem or difficulty that presents itself is this: "Is a decision necessary?" If it is likely that the matter will clear itself, or, although annoying is of no importance and if corrected will not make much difference, the best course for the manager is to leave things alone. Strangely enough, not everyone abides by that seemingly self-evident truism. The project manager, with the help of a dedicated team, may accomplish miracles of production effort under adverse circumstances but then dismiss an employee for some minor infraction just to prove that there is a "tight ship."

The rule the project manager should have followed is really a simple one: *Act if on balance the benefits greatly outweigh the cost and the risks.* A corollary to the rule, of course, is: *Act or do not act, but do not hedge or compromise.* If a disease warrants a cure, prescribe the full dose. Half a dose is worse than none. Cutting off one finger when the whole hand is gangrened inflicts all the trauma and provides none of the benefits.

The first phase of decision making, therefore, is diagnosis: to identify and clarify the problem. Too few managers fully practice or even understand that element of decision making, yet it is clearly the first sure step toward the solution of the right problem. Failing to give adequate attention to that step may lead the decision maker in the direction of a solution of the wrong problem. The perils of improper problem identification are seen in this short case study:

> A company was having great difficulty meeting its production schedules. Shipments were late despite a great deal of overtime. In desperation, management decided on plant expansion to ease production problems. Large sums were budgeted for the expansion and plans were being laid. Then somebody decided that perhaps the real problem had not been identified. When she started asking questions the key issue was unearthed.

> The fault lay not with production but with sales. Sales staff were promising rush deliveries to all customers, marginal customers as well as good customers. No priorities were being set. Orders were being rushed through no matter whose orders they were. As a result of the problem identification, the sales staff were given new instructions on rush orders and priorities. The orders of marginal customers took a back seat. and production was able to meet schedules.

> Management took a small risk, of course, that some marginal customers would be lost. But the greater risk of losing good customers because of missed schedules was avoided.

Some managers, accustomed to the intuitive snap judgements that they feel have worked for them, may reject the thought of spending large amounts of time in problem identification and definition. They are probably right if they are thinking of problems that are routine or will have no serious impact on their organizations' operations. But when decisions involve long stretches of time, considerable expenditure of funds, and the lives of people, the time so spent is economical in the long run. It is a sad waste of energy and funds to make decisions about the wrong problems. As many a manager is aware, there always seems to have to be time to correct the mistakes and so little time to forestall them.

Defining Expectations

After the problem has been identified and defined, one further step is needed before the search for alternatives: the objectives to be achieved by the decision—what the manager can expect to see accomplished by a decision on the issues and what hazards are faced by taking some new course of action prompted by the decision—must be identified.

Defining the problem is the first step, of course. But the most precise definition will not identify the objectives to be met by the decision, isolate the obstacles to the decision, or point out the constraints laid upon courses of action. And those objectives, obstacles, and constraints may have a profound effect on the relevance of the alternatives available to the decision maker.

The objectives must be in consonance with the overall organizational objectives. A decision that may appear brilliant, practical, and feasible may founder on the shoals of executive veto if it runs counter to executive policy. Similarly, an otherwise valid decision may prove to be a useless exercise if there are no resources for carrying it out. So the decision maker should take certain constraints into account before embarking on the search for solutions:

- *Policy constraints.* A manager's decisions on a new product may be constrained by a company policy that all such decisions are to be made by the board of directors.
- *Financial constraints.* The decision for plant expansion may be blocked by the utter unavailability of funds.
- *Technological constraints.* The decision to provide added strength and resiliency to a product may be barred by the absence of any materials that offer such qualities and the lack of funds to develop them.
- *Contractual constraints.* Decisions involving workers may run directly counter to union agreements.
- *Government constraints.* Government is a factor that lurks in the background of many decision processes. A perfectly reasonable decision to merge two firms may run foul of laws concerning restraint of trade. Similarly, the influence of the government must be considered in seeking decisions involving such matters as pricing, financing, and stock options.
- *Physical constraints.* Decisions on plant expansion may be meaningless in the absence of any space in which to expand.
- *Personnel constraints.* Decisions calling for special qualities in people cannot be carried out unless those qualities are available or procurable.

The consequences of decisions also must be taken into account before opening the field to certain alternatives. Every decision expectation must be concerned with "what if." Every decision involves some change. Every change has a ripple effect and the ripples can turn to tidal waves for the unwary.

Second-order consequences with some rough ripples can result from what appeared to be a perfectly reasonable decision, as shown in the following example:

> The Australian Yir Yorunt aborigines had from time immemorial used stone axes as their primary cutting tool. Missionaries, in the hope of improving the life of the Yir Yorunts, gave them steel axes. But the missionaries decided to give the steel axes to all the Yir Yorunts, men, women, and children. What the missionaries failed to take into account, however, was that stone axes played important roles in the lives of the aborigines, over and above their use in cutting wood. The men were the ones who had always owned the stone axes; and these were held to be symbols of masculinity and generated respect for the elders.

> Older men, having less respect for missionaries, were not likely to accept the steel axes, but as they saw them in the hands of others, it soon became obvious that the steel axes were far more efficient. So the elders, once respected, were forced to borrow steel axes from women and younger men. And thus the previous status relationships, so important to the stability of the culture, where thoroughly upset. . .

Certainly a manager cannot be expected to be a Delphic oracle able to anticipate every contingency or be aware of every constraint. That is why the intuitive decision maker who usually rides the crest of successful decisions can sometimes be capsized by the unexpected waves. However, in most large organizations, planning staffs are available to explore the contingencies and the constraints. Their advice and assistance on major decisions should be sought before the decision is made, not after.

At the same time there can be a tendency for some planners to live in ivory towers, out of touch with reality. The wise manager, in seeking counsel from such staffs, should make the realities known to the planners and create a good marriage between planning and doing. "First get all the facts," a common exhortation to decision makers, puts the cart before the horse. If followed, it may produce factual information on a host of irrelevancies, including matters that should not concern the decision maker because they are excluded by constraints or adverse contingencies or because they run counter to the expectations of the decision maker.

On the other hand, opinions and hypotheses that relate to decision expectations should be encouraged during this step of decision making. Facts relate to the past, hypotheses to the future. Hypotheses are born of experience with similar circumstances and are an integral part of decision making. The manager should entertain such hypotheses, but should demand that they be well thought out. What must be known to test hypothesis validity, how can the validity be tested, and how can the hypothesis be measured? Those are the "facts" that are relevant.

In the conflict of opposing opinions and hypotheses, the purpose and expectations of the decision emerge. The next step, the creative development of alternatives, can take place in greater safety.

Developing Alternative Courses

Whenever a decision is called for, there are at least two alternatives: overt action and no action at all—to change things or leave them as they are. However, it is a mistake for the manager to jump to the conclusion that there are only two choices.

It is rare for a number of alternatives to be lacking. In fact, it is a good idea for every manager to take the position that, if there seems to be only one way to go, it is the wrong way. Some decision makers have an unfortunate tendency to see only the extremes—the either-or situation. They are usually the people who pride themselves on their intuitive decision making and their snap judgements. They see no value in the difficult, often mind-bending search for potential alternatives, as seen in this scenario:

> A firm was losing money because production was inadequate. Survival depended on increased output to reduce costs and serve an expanded market. But the losses had shrunk both capital and credit. The equipment needed for expanded production just could not be financed. The sole course of action appeared to be no action at all; and that meant bankruptcy. With that end facing them, the officers went to work and found two other alternatives:
>
> 1. A manufacturer had the needed equipment. It had been bank-financed, and the manufacturer had been unable to sell it. The bank agreed to let the manufacturer sell the equipment to the firm without down payment, accepting two-name paper instead of the one-name notes already held.
> 2. A competitor of the firm had new equipment on order and offered to sell the old machines without requiring a down payment.

The workable alternatives don't come begging for attention. They must be hunted down; and that hunt has more than one purpose in decision making. The best thought-through decisions may be rendered inoperative by changing, unforeseen circumstances. There should be an alternative waiting in the wings if the star is unable to perform:

> Both the Schlieffen Plan of the German Army in 1914 and President Franklin D. Roosevelt's initial economic program in 1933 were disproved at the time they were supposed to be effective.

> The German General Staff had concentrated on one plan only; it had no alternative plan to fall back on. Hence, when the Schlieffen Plan failed, there were no other well-thought-through alternatives. And the ensuing series of gambles all failed.

> On the other hand, while Roosevelt's first plan was based on orthodox economics, he had people working on an alternative plan. The collapse of the banking system

showed economic orthodoxy to be suicidal for the times. He then switched to a more radical policy, based on economic and social reform. He had a well-conceived, alternative policy to follow.

The soil from which innovative alternatives grow must be planted with the seeds of discontent and disagreement. A meeting of people anxious to avoid conflict and please the boss produces few alternatives, because by definition a number of alternatives implies different, and perhaps diametrically opposed, approaches to a problem. Tough, hard disagreement that raises the competitive instinct forces innovativeness. It is up to managers to foster that fruitful disputation by permitting people to disagree with them and with each other in the search for alternatives. The consensus and compromise come later.

Also, in the search for alternatives, the manager must not brush aside the novel options and thereby stifle creativity within the organization. Creative thought needs freedom and "thinking time." That is another reason for avoiding the haste and stress of snap decisions, decisions made under pressure at the last moment. Creativity is enhanced when it is rewarded—if only by the appreciation of the manager for new ideas and if there is a reduction in levels of stress. That is the sort of climate the manager must generate to permit the growth of viable alternatives: the appreciative consideration of innovative proposals and the absence of severe penalties for novel ideas, which do not always work.

In the development of alternatives, the wise manager is also looking for opportunities, and an opportunity for novel courses of action:

A small plumbing supply manufacturer had both excellent products and customers. Sales kept climbing, but profits remained the same. The manufacturer could not produce efficiently in his old location, and space constraints blocked expansion. The only alternative which came to mind was to build a new plant. But he had not considered the financial constraints, and he had not searched for other alternatives. The new plant was built, the manufacturer became overextended, and he went out of business within the year. He could have considered other alternatives, some of which might have been excellent opportunities to move in new directions and improve his financial position. He could have:

- Subcontracted some of the work under appropriate quality control.
- Rented a new plant instead of building one.
- Given up the inadequate facility and had all his goods made by an outside supplier.
- Become a distributor for another supplier.
- Merged with another manufacturer.

With the opportunities they offered, any of those alternatives could have been preferable to the position in which he finally found himself.

The successful search usually produces some alternatives that seem equally appropriate. If that were not so, there would be no problem of choice. The best alternatives would stand high above the rest and would automatically eliminate the others. However, there is rarely one clear-cut solution that provides without doubt all the answers to a problem. The alternatives must be weighed and evaluated to determine which offers the most benefits with the fewest side effects.

Evaluating Possible Courses

With a number of alternative courses laid before them, decision makers must measure each alternative by the standards of the decision objective within the constraints posed by existing circumstances. The easy way is to select the course that they proposed or personally like, but effective decision makers give each alternative its day in court. They try to understand why others proposed different courses. It could well be that they had a different understanding of the problem and perhaps theirs was the better understanding.

All knowledge is less than perfect because of human or technical limitations. If all knowledge were complete, ultimate, and immutable, the totality could be spun into the computer and the readout then accepted as gospel. However, knowledge is not perfect, and for that reason the decision maker has a function to perform in evaluating the alternatives. That evaluation may take subjective or objective forms.

The subjective form does not necessarily imply an intuitive ranking of alternatives. Certain criteria that are available to the decision maker may provide the subjective evaluation with some rationality:

- The availability of resources in staff, material, money, and machines.
- The amount of risk faced in seeking the expected goal.
- The costs to be borne in achieving the hoped-for results.
- The time frame within which the decision and its implementation should take place.

Techniques that may guide the decision maker in assessing what the uncertain future may hold relative to the decision may be:

- The best alternative method is the one that offers the least "potential surprise." The executive must make a subjective judgement that the alternative selected will result in no unpleasant surprises.
- In the "regret" criterion method, to the extent maximum goals are not achieved, the decision maker will experience regret. The difference between the maximum payoff and the payoffs resulting from various conditions measures the degree of regret.
- The "maximum criterion" method follows the principle that "whatever can go wrong will." The decision maker assumes that the worst will happen to each alternative, and then chooses the best of the worst states.
- In the weighted combinations of pessimism-optimism method, the decision

maker assigns a level of probability to a conception of the best and the worst of available courses of action.

Those approaches do not yet provide hard and fast rules for today's decision makers, but they do show the thinking being applied to the evaluation in the light of uncertainty. The techniques make use of probabilities that can be objectively measured, but the probabilities assigned usually come from the subjective feelings of the decision maker based on judgement and experience.

In weighing alternatives, the decision maker must account for limiting factors. Those are the factors that block the accomplishment of a desired objective. Until they are identified and removed, the objective cannot be met. The factors can be tangible: time, fixed costs, operating costs. They can also be intangible: labor relations, technological changes (the unknown unknowns), political climate, the economy, strikes, and the nature of people.

Finding the limiting factor can sometimes be a difficult task. But, we can break through surface symptoms and come to grips with the real problem by isolating the critical factor, the strategic element:

> In one firm, eight men in rapid succession were given the job of executive vice president. All either left or were removed. In desperation, the president interviewed all eight in an attempt to determine why the job seemed to be too much for eight highly qualified people. He learned that the critical factor was himself. He had not been permitting those men to do their job. He had issued orders to vice presidents without informing the incumbent executive vice president. He had all vice presidents reporting to him. He just couldn't keep his hands off operations. Each executive vice president was forced to function in the dark, and he inevitably stumbled. The strategic element was responsibility without authority. The solution eliminated the limiting factor. This was done by elevating the president to chairman of the board and selecting a new president from among the eight former executive vice presidents.

Between the subjective evaluation and the objective, mathematical evaluation lie evaluations that can be weighed by cost-effectiveness analysis. The technique is used to determine the best choice when the objective sought does not have the clean specificity of such qualities as sales, costs, or profits. Among the objectives may be those of reducing pollution or training unemployables, but certain standards still may be used to measure effectiveness in such activities. For example, if the general objective of the decision were to improve employee morale, the alternatives to be evaluated would be those best calculated to reduce turnover, absenteeism, or the number of grievances. To the inputs might be added the judgement of qualified experts. The features of cost-effectiveness decisions are generally:

- Objectives are generally imprecise.
- Alternatives are concerned with systems, programs, or strategies.
- Although not always subject to quantification, the measure of effectiveness

must be directly related to the objectives and must be set in as precise terms as feasible.

- Costs are traditional measures, but nonmonetary terms also may be used.
- The decision criteria involve trade-offs or call for achieving desired objectives with available resources at the least possible cost.

When uncertainty reigns, the theory of probability can be employed to determine mathematically the degree of certainty that postulated events will take place. The physical sciences have long relied on mathematics. The methodology of quantification is now being adopted by decision makers to evaluate the probability of success or available alternatives.

Selecting the Best Choice

Making the final decision is a lonely task. It is also a risky task, so some managers turn to group decisions. There may be some merit to that route. It gives the group a feeling of belonging, and it improves commitment to carry out the decision because the group participated in the selection. The complexities caused by our galloping technology cry for input from different disciplines to find the right direction. A shared responsibility enhances chances of cooperation. All members of the group, when they see that their differing attitudes have been considered, feel that they have been dealt with fairly.

However, the arguments against decision by consensus may be more powerful than those for it. Clearly, a certain amount of cooperation can be assured if the group is made part of the development of alternatives and if its members know that the alternative they propose will be given careful consideration. The ultimate selection from among those alternatives does not lend itself to debate, however. A committee moves with the speed of its least-informed member. Some members speak louder than others. Some stand in awe of others and are fearful of making their choices known. Committees generally lead to vacillation and delay; and the consensus solution may be a mediocre average instead of a best and innovative choice.

In the final analysis, the authority for any particular decision lies with the responsible individual even if that individual is sitting with other council members. This does not mean the selection of the best alternative should be made in mahogany row. The final decision should be made at the lowest feasible level and as close as possible to where the work is being done and the implementation will take place. Executives must learn when to let go. Many of them carry all the decision-making prerogatives with them as they move up the corporate ladder. That can create bottlenecks and overburden top executives with excessive detail.

Besides, if top management reserves to itself all decision making, it may very well make a brilliant judgement on an operating decision but not be aware later of the sudden hazard when things do not go according to plan and swift changes must be made. It is really all a matter of degree. Some decisions are routine. Others, by their nature, should be moved up to higher levels. Here are some guidelines:

- *Range.* Is the commitment long- or short-range? How readily can the course be changed if unfavorable results become apparent?
- *Effect.* Does the decision have impact on only the decision maker and his organization or on other organizations as well?
- *Values.* Does the decision concern ethics, morality, or social and political beliefs? Does it affect human beings?
- *Rarity.* Does the decision concern recurrent affairs, or is it rare and unique?

With our institutions and technology growing more complex, it becomes all the more important that the authority to make particular decisions be clearly spelled out and assigned to those who are capable of making wise choices. Decision making calls for a particular temperament. It has less to do with learning and intelligence than with decisiveness. For example, the brilliant scientist may be a poorer decision maker than the pragmatic executive. The scientific discipline creates indecisiveness because of the strictures it places on the scientist to question everything that is not supported by scientific knowledge.

Managers, however, must be decisive without the support of full knowledge. They are dealing with futurity and uncertainty, and so must be willing to rely on subjective feelings of "conviction," "certainty," and "self-reliance" under the most uncertain conditions. Having made the decision, they must speak positively about it, no matter what the inner feelings so that others will feel confident that the best decision was made.

The selection process becomes still more difficult when it is concerned with aims and ends. The ends and aims are usually affected by nonrational factors as distinguished from profit-based goals, which are supported by the rationality of quantification. The nonrational decisions that involve morality or social considerations cannot be called right or wrong by scientific standards, but they have to be made. The executive is better equipped to make them than the moralist or the sociologist. Both the latter become entangled in the web of social responsibility, which is rarely clear-cut, and they lack decisiveness. The executive must take action that may call for aiming at one social goal at the expense of others. The Gordian knot must be cut; rarely is there time to untangle it.

The executive usually calls upon intuition or experience in making the final selection. Unfortunately, intuition implies an absence of analysis; intuition cannot be explained. If the basis of the ultimate selection is not clear, even to the decision maker, the chances for success become dimmer. Similarly, experience can be helpful or dangerous. Many people have experiences without gaining from them. Good decisions are tested against future events, whereas experience is rooted in the past. It may well be that experience is given greater reliance than it deserves in decision making. It is for this reason that Peter Drucker talks about coming to grips with the new realities, rather than those long past.(6)

There are some rules the decision maker can follow when the time comes to make the final choice, rules that make use of but do not rely wholly upon intuition and experience:

1. *The decision must contribute to achieving stated goals.* The alternative that best meets the established goal or objective is most likely to resist the eroding effect of time.

2. *Employ creativity.* The best solution may be a novel one, a grouping of familiar ideas in a new and novel way. The decision maker should not hesitate to leave his warm, accustomed bed and brave the chill morning of innovation.

3. *Every decision must be converted to action.* The choice selected must be capable of being implemented by existing or available money, men, and materials.

4. *Consider the ripple effect.* Every decision brings change, and the change often extends beyond the circle of the intended and expected decision field. So the decision maker must consider what can go wrong and how seriously it can go wrong, what safeguards should be employed and their cost, and how to monitor the results.

5. *Maintain stability.* Continually opening decisions for revision leads to frustration. Unless new facts or views become extremely compelling, the decision made should be let stand.

6. *Trial runs can determine feasibility.* Full resources need not always be committed at the outset. A trial run can point up unexpected defects, or a series of checkpoints can be established to guard against disastrous and irreversible effects.

7. *Decisions should not be made before their time.* Managers should not vacillate. They must be decisive, but the more time they have to make the final decision the better the decision is likely to be. The effort spent on the final selection, however, will be reduced if sufficient time and thought were allotted to developing the alternatives from which the selection must be made.

8. *A decision should not be defaulted.* The worst action is deciding not to decide. Needless delay may result in a waiver of the decision making, and that will create a vacuum that others may have to fill.

9. *The decision maker must recognize that everyone will not be pleased.* Someone usually disagrees with the decision. That is a condition that the decision maker must live with. After reaching the decision, it is necessary to try to explain the thinking and win cooperation. In the face of uncertainty, it may not be possible to maximize but instead, as Simon puts it to "satisfice"—take a share of the market rather than all of it, make an adequate profit rather than a maximum, or obtain a fair price rather than the highest price.(7)

Taking Action

The end result of any decision must be action. Defining problems, establishing expectations, developing alternative courses, evaluating possible courses, and selecting the best choice are sheer exercises in futility without action. Many a brilliant task force has pointed out the unmistakable way to go—but nobody went. Often it was because people were not presold or informed or made a part of the decision process.

Anybody who is needed to make a decision effective—or who could cripple it—should be part of the decision process. The alternative could be disastrous. The decision maker must understand that decisions may not be acted upon unless the actors receive their scripts early on:

> A decision was made within a company producing industrial equipment to discontinue a model which had long been in production but whose sales were falling off. The customers who owned the model were dutifully notified. They recognized that the model would soon be unobtainable, and those who liked it hurriedly placed orders for the equipment against the day that it would be unavailable. Accordingly, there was a brief but sharp spurt in sales.

> In the meantime, the company's buyer who was assigned to procuring parts for the discontinued model was unaware of the decision not to produce it any more. His instructions had been—and to him still were—to buy parts in ratio to sales. The upturn in sales sent him scurrying to buy more parts. And the company wound up with enough parts in inventory for eight years of production, none of which would take place.

Every decision must provide for implementation; and whenever action is desired, there must be feedback to make sure the action is appropriate and effective. The armed forces have long known that. When an order is given to a subordinate, the superior or the aide personally verifies that the order was carried out. There is never reliance on reports from the subordinate. The skepticism does not necessarily stem from distrust of the subordinate; it stems from distrust of communication.

Once the selection from among alternatives has been made, the decision maker must then consider:

- The sequence of steps to be taken in implementing the decision.
- The people who should be charged with carrying out each step.
- The controls to be installed to see that the steps are taken.
- The clear line of communication to those charged with implementation.
- The tangible results expected.
- The reports required to provide feedback on the action taken.

STRATEGY AND THE INTERNAL AUDITOR

The Internal Auditor's Responsibilities

Most internal auditors reckon that they have a pretty good idea as to what business strategy is. At one time internal auditors were not allowed anywhere near it, and tended not to have one of their own! Although they had moved from economy and efficiency towards effectiveness, effectiveness was often defined in terms of existing policy, rather than in terms of what the external market might have been dictating. Effectiveness was, therefore, only seen in a half light. The fault was not just that the internal auditors were lacking in being pro-active, but that this was a reflection of the state of the art at the time.

The internal audit neglect of strategy changed with the onus on internal audit to prove its worth, even in areas like the public sector, where it had traditionally been part of the furniture. With a growing realization as to what internal audit was, came the challenge for it to perform at ever more ascending and challenging levels. A special edition of the *Managerial Auditing Journal* (Volume 6, No. 4, 1991) was entitled "The Strategic Audit", and was able to include contributions from the Head of a National Institute of Directors, and the Group Chief Executive of a TV company, with a commentary from the Group Internal Audit Manager.

We can, therefore, be operating in a rarefied atmosphere of the board of directors which is less familiar territory to the internal auditor. One can take the view that internal auditors need to understand business strategy as an important given in their work, but not as something to audit. It is, however, difficult to concur with the usual definition of effectiveness as "doing the right things" without invoking strategy. We could look for doing the right things within a functional area, but this is scarcely the expanded scope auditing that was announced over a decade ago. It would also be inconsistent for the IIA to seek to be a significant contributor to the corporate governance debate, without individual internal auditors being able to contribute within their own organizations.

In the USA, it is more common for internal auditors to have business-related degrees or even MBAs. This makes them more able to contribute at strategic level. This is less common in other countries such as in the UK and Eire. It is important that the opportunity to be ready and available to make a strategic contribution is not lost. Some are already achieving this, and many auditors may be close to it. Others need assistance to achieve this goal. This is an area where the IIA through its examinations, courses and publications has a vital role, as do the members who are prepared to share best practice.

Two professional publications inculcate the need for internal audit to adopt a strategic perspective itself, not just as a luxury item, but as a matter of survival and growth. It is no coincidence that both were produced in the early 1990s as the recession had taken its toll, and organizations had been downsized, and had become flatter and less hierarchical, with outsourcing, also called the contracting out of services, compulsory competitive tendering or market testing, impacting on internal audit. The public sector had seen many of its functions transferred to the private sector in cultures that were less favorable to internal audit. This in turn led to a fraud culture which became a matter of huge public concern, and a backlash in which internal auditors could again flourish, although with the need to indicate that internal audit is not primarily about fraud investigation, but about internal control in its wider sense. The European Union has been accompanied by scandalous levels of fraud, particularly around agricultural subsidies, with a response that has tended to be complacent. The larger accounting firms increased the size of their internal audit service provision, and the internal audit profession was not sure initially whether to regard this as a threat or an advantage, but has generally settled for the second.

The first publication, *Promoting Internal Audit*, by the Audit Panel of the Chartered Institute of Public Finance and Accountancy, drew upon a national survey it had conducted.(8) The publication emphasized the need to obtain the client's perspective, to have strong marketing skills, and a risk-based approach with a business plan based on service level agreements and performance indicators. Eleven overhead projector slides are supplied to assist in the audit presentation to management. The second publication, *Survival Pack for Internal Audit*, was written by the IIA-UK in association with Coopers and Lybrand, and is divided into two main sections: Marketing and Presentations, and Tendering and Contracting.(9) Particularly helpful is the detailing of the stages of the tendering process showing how to assess your own positioning against the competition, and how to manage successfully an audit service contract. The publications catalogues of these two bodies are replete with items of considerable assistance for empowering and enhancing the internal audit service. Addresses are included in the references. In addition the catalog of the IIA Inc is a fruitful and voluminous source. The address is Institute of Internal Auditors, 249 Maitland Avenue, Altamonte Springs, Florida 32701–4201. This book features in the two IIA catalogues. Those wishing to subscribe to the *Managerial Auditing Journal*, a forum for debate and contribution between managers and auditors, may write to MCB University Press, 62 Toller Lane, Bradford BD8 9BY, England.

Internal audit has always shown itself willing and able to take on board and baptise into its panoply of techniques the best of current management techniques. This applies whether it was the MbO (Management by Objectives) of a previous decade, or the more recent Business Processing Reengineering. Professionals who obstruct Reengineering tend to think in a linear and hierarchic way. The internal auditor should be able to adopt Reengineering and avoid the pitfalls. Too many companies downsized and thought it was Reengineering. Cost reduction also was not it—this did not motivate, whereas a dynamic new vision or product for the future did.

James Champy has no time for establishing staff officers, since it removes responsibility from line managers. This leads us into the latest internal audit response, variously called the Control Risk Self Assessment (CRSA), Control Self Assessment (CSA), Self Assessment Programme (SAP) or Self Review (SR). the IIA—UK's Professional Briefing Note *Impact of a Control Assessment Approach upon the Role and Practice of Internal Auditing* (1995) provides a definition:

"A control self assessment programme is a process which allows individual line managers and staff to participate in reviewing existing controls for adequacy (both now and in the predicted future) and recommending, agreeing and implementing improvements (modification, addition or elimination) to existing controls. It is likely to include the application of risk criteria to the process of control assessment, and may extend to confirming that key, identified controls and processes are operating efficiently and effectively—and are likely to continue to do so."

The CSA is the latest response to external demands for effective internal control made by the market place. In fact it is nothing new, since both authors of this book practiced it and have recommended it for years. Equally, companies such as British Petroleum have had versions of it since the late 1970s. However, it is now becoming more prevalent and something of an accepted wisdom. It is a good example of what Michael Porter calls focusing—in this case re-focusing. Internal auditors should become the product champion of CSA, and monitor its implementation, since if it is falling down anywhere there may develop immediate and potentially serious internal control weaknesses. It is a valuable supplement to internal audit activity, although one that comes with a cost, and a need for constant maintenance. Like other past initiatives, it may experience a lapse of enthusiasm, and then an organization will recognize the abiding value of it possessing an internal audit service.

DECISION MAKING AND THE INTERNAL AUDITOR

The Internal Auditor's Responsibilities

Modern internal auditors can be an important contributor to the decision-making process. Their position in the organization, objectivity and independence, and analytical ability combine to make them an indispensable part of the problem-solving team. They have much to offer in all but one of the steps in the process. That one step is the final selection from among the choices open to the decision maker. That is a line management function, not a staff function. For the internal auditor to make the selection would be to usurp line prerogatives. Also, it would tend to erode the auditor's own objectivity and independence. The Statement of Responsibilities makes that point clear when it says: "Objectivity is essential to the audit function. Therefore, internal auditors should not develop and install procedures, prepare records, or engage in any other activity which . . . could reasonably be construed to compromise the independence of the internal auditor."

Making the selection of a course of action for the manager could compromise the internal auditor's independence. The internal auditor owes it to the manager to suggest *a* course; but should never insist on *the* course. But in the remaining steps he or she can provide a signal service.

Recognizing and Defining the Problem

Busy executives are worried not only by the problems they are aware of but also by those that may be lurking in the dark corners and have not yet come to light. They rest a little easier, therefore, if they know there is an independent force dedicated to shining a light into the corners and spotting the problems that need management attention. The charter that gives the internal auditor access to all records, areas, and personnel within the organization adds an extension to management's antenna. When that access is restricted, the antenna's reach is correspondingly reduced. Management gains, therefore, by eliminating restrictions on the internal auditor's activities.

The extent of the antenna's reach can be measured by the internal auditor's long-range audit program. Many internal auditing groups prepare long-range programs that cover spans of three to five years and list the specific audit projects to be undertaken. An indication of the depth of coverage for each audit project is seen in the number of audit days assigned to particular projects. The long-range audit program provides guidelines to the auditor and assurance to management about the activities to be examined. Management is thus made aware of the corners in the organization to which the audit lamp will be directed and can add corners of its own if it wishes.

Two examples out of many highlight the service the internal auditor can provide in identifying and defining problems.

During an audit in one of his company's plants, the internal auditor saw that cartons of finished goods were being invoiced at amounts which assumed that all the cartons contained uniform quantities. He made tests of carton contents over a period of time. And he found that on the average the cartons contained about 10% more than the invoiced quantity. At the internal auditor's recommendation, management issued instructions to prepare invoices for actual quantities shipped. The identification of the problem resulted in annual savings of $1.3 million.

An internal auditor for a manufacturing company was making an audit of perishable and durable tools. While checking tool inventories in the tool cribs, he observed that one expensive tool used to install fasteners was causing difficulties for production workers. There seemed to be a constant parade to the tool cribs for replacements of that tool. The production workers complained pungently to the tool crib attendant; but since repairs were not his responsibility, he turned a deaf ear, replacing the broken tools with new ones and ordering replacements and repairs as needed. The internal auditor began to dig deeper and finally identified the problem.

- Repairs on this tool were costing $2.25 million a year.
- Excessive breakage was caused by misuse in some instances and poor tool design in others.

The internal auditor then brought the matter to the attention of the appropriate manager with the following results:

- The production workers were instructed in the use of the tools.

- Improvements were made in tool repairs.
- Some tools were replaced with tools of heavier design.
- Fundamental weaknesses inherent in the tool were investigated by the manufacturer.

As a result, repair costs were reduced by $1.5 million.

Management decisions relate to the future, and so for the manager to "get all the facts" is irrelevant. Internal auditors, however, in identifying and defining the problems needing management attention, must get all the facts needed to establish that there is a problem and that it warrants attention. They must know the population they are dealing with, in this case the number of tools, their value, and the cost of repairing them. They must isolate the causes leading to the problem, because they know that no problem will ever be truly solved unless its causes have been identified. In this case, the causes were employee carelessness, poor tool design, and ineffective repair practices. They must know the effect of failure to solve the problem. In this case it would be employee frustration, lost production hours, and excessive expense.

Internal auditors, if they have truly arrived in their organization, are often called upon by executive management to perform management studies in addition to programmed audits. The executive, on seeing the need for improvement in some areas, may ask the internal auditor to evaluate conditions, determine their seriousness, and recommend solutions. However, the assignment of the study to the internal auditor may be an impulsive statement of what is desired from a frustrated manager who has not had or did not take the time to think the matter through. Throwing his or her hands up at some perceived difficulty, or upset by the inability of other staff people to solve it, the executive may simply say to the internal auditor, "Take a look at so and so and tell me what you think."

Wise internal auditors will not jump on their steeds and go galloping off in different directions. They will first determine whether there is a problem and, if so, how it is conceived. Then, having identified and defined the problem, they will carefully present to executive management a thorough analysis of what they see the problem to be, how they will carry out the study to provide the information they think management needs, and how much the study will cost. Very often management's conception of the problem becomes crystallized when the auditor defines it.

Defining Expectations

The experienced internal auditor sees, as the first rule of operational auditing, determining the objectives of an activity or an assignment before laying out the audit plans. Without the lodestar of objective, goal, or aim, it is easy to get off course, and that is often why managers find the right solution to the wrong problem.

The internal auditor can help management chart a straight course and avoid the hidden reefs of constraints during the decision process. Constraints are not restricted to laws, executive policies, and technology. They may surface—often too late—when a decision in one department of an organization runs afoul of existing practice in another. The internal auditor can be very helpful in identifying those constraints.

Nobody in an organization has the intimate, extensive knowledge of practices and procedures that is possessed by the experienced modern internal audit staff. Executive management has a general knowledge of operations throughout the organization. Operating management has an intimate knowledge of its own operations and perhaps of operations in contiguous departments, but not of operations in departments with which it has no contacts or only rare ones. The deficiencies that internal auditors bring to the attention of surprised operating managers indicate that manager knowledge may be intimate but not necessarily complete.

Only the far-ranging internal auditor is aware of practices throughout the organization, and to exclude such a person from the decision making process is to don blinders deliberately. For that reason, wise managers will ask their internal audit staff to read new policies and procedures and changes in operating instructions. The object is not to obtain internal audit approval for those matters; rather, it is to learn whether the internal auditor is aware of constraints that might impair the success of proposed actions. This is not to say that internal auditors can be a guarantor of that success; it is merely to say that, if they have knowledge of some impediment to the sought-for accomplishment, they will make management privy to that knowledge.

Similarly, executive management should think long and hard before it bypasses the internal audit function in favor of a management consulting firm to help solve some management problem. It is not that consulting firms are without experienced, able personnel. They are capable of fine analyses and suggestions. What they lack, however, is the intimate knowledge of the organization. The authors of this book have observed expensive, extensive management studies by outside consultants that culminated in thick, hard-cover reports that contained dozens of recommendations. The trouble is that generally only a small percentage of those recommendations were adopted. The recommendations may have been valid enough in principle. But often they were not relevant to the particular operations in the particular organization.

As a member of management study teams staffed by the organization's internal auditors, the authors have found that a rejected internal auditor's recommendation is a rare exception. The ingredient for success is usually a knowledge of the constraints within the organization that would make otherwise rational recommendations inoperable.

Developing Alternate Courses

Some writers on internal auditing hold that the internal auditor should identify problems but not make recommendations to solve them. The reason cited is the auditor's potential loss of objectivity and independence. Such a position runs counter to both the internal auditor's Statement of Responsibilities and good sense. The Statement, under the heading Objective and Scope, lists "Recommending operating improvements" among the activities the internal auditor should carry out to attain overall objectives. Denying management the benefit of experience with workable solutions would seem to be an abdication of responsibility.

Internal auditors have no business telling management that their recommended course is the one course to follow. That involves them in the selection process, where they do not belong. What they should offer is one of the courses the manager should evaluate and consider before making the final selection:

> Incoming raw materials are usually tested for conformance to specifications. The internal auditor during a routine test found that his company's inspectors often omitted these tests. He asked why and was told that the specification tolerances were so wide that materials invariably fell within an acceptable range. For example, the supplier might have been committed to a stated specification of .9. But the inspector's instructions permitted acceptance of a broad leeway—like a range of .7 to .11. Even at .7 the quality of the material would not adversely affect the quality of the company's processes. What had been overlooked, however, was the fact that the supplier would charge a higher price to meet a quality of .9 than a quality of .7. So the internal auditor suggested considering negotiation in appropriate cases with suppliers to ease the specifications and thereby reduce prices.

> The internal auditor did not prescribe how much to ease the specifications, which materials to apply the revisions to, or what suppliers to negotiate with. Those were management decisions. Management moved ahead to renegotiate specifications with suppliers, and the eased requirements resulted in substantial savings in the cost of raw materials.

Evaluating Possible Courses

Internal auditors can and should provide managers with assistance in weighing alternative courses of action. They have many products in the inventory to use in assessing the courses available. Knowledge of company records and ability to analyze values can be brought to bear:

> A company had switched from coal to oil as fuel for steam boilers. Yet the coal inventory was carried on the books at purchased cost. Disposal had been recommended. But no evaluation had been made of the economics of that course. The market value was deemed nil; and still the inventory had been maintained.

> The auditor encountering the situation made the appraisal for management. She learned that a market value did indeed exist, and at 75% of book value. Besides, she found that maintaining the inventory cost about 12% of book value for taxes, insurance, pile turnover, and the like. She also found that the company could recover 56% of the book value after paying delivery charges.

> When the auditor presented her evaluation to management, she suggested two

alternative courses:

1. Reduce inventory to the recoverable amount, thereby saving substantially in taxes.
2. Dispose of the coal if the cost of keeping it for backup purposes was considered too high.

Management decided to sell the coal. The cash recovery after taxes was about $250,000 and annual maintenance expense was eliminated.

It will be observed that the internal auditor did not make the decision. She helped management make it through her proffered courses of action and by her evaluation of available courses, including the course of doing nothing.

Internal auditors need not be specialists in operations research or in other quantitative methods. But they should have a broad enough knowledge of all management techniques to know where to turn and whom to consult in order to aid managers. One of the authors of this book became involved in just such a situation:

Executive management received a proposal from a young budget manager to use multiple regression analysis to estimate overhead rates. The budget manager had a master's degree in business administration and a thorough command of both quantitative analysis and computer programming. He had developed the formula and the computer program and had presented the proposal to the executive in a detailed report. The executive was stumped. He was not technically competent to evaluate the program himself, but he did not want to reject out of hand a plan which might cut hundreds of man-hours from the development of overhead rates. Yet he could not bring himself to make a decision solely on the recommendation of his young budget manager.

He turned to the internal auditor and asked for help. The internal auditor was not an expert on the subject either. But he knew where to look. In a book of mathematics for management, he found a multiple regression problem comparable with the one at issue. The problem provided detailed input data, formulas, a computer program, and the correct answers.

At the internal auditor's request, the budget manager introduced that problem's data into the computer, using his own program. The internal auditor observed every step of the input. After the lights had flashed and the tapes had whirled, the computer displayed the answer—and it was not correct. So the budget manager had his computer program reviewed and a programming error was found. With the error corrected, the auditor's data were again fed into the computer. This time the answer in the book and the one provided by the budget manager's program were identical. Buttressed with this support, the executive adopted the corrected program.

Selecting the Best Choice

Selecting the final course of action is a lonely task. It is a management decision, and it can rarely be shared—certainly not with the internal auditor.

The internal auditor is the monitor of the organization's controls, and must monitor and evaluate with objectivity and independence. Internal auditors lose that objectivity when they espouse a single course of action, so they must be careful to avoid being associated as sponsor with any one course. Such an association could come back to haunt them if later found wanting. It is human for the internal auditor to want to be able to say, "That is what I told top management to do, and that's precisely what they did." But the path is strewn with traps. There is no need to walk it. That auditor's partnership agreement with management doesn't require it or even sanction it.

Taking Action

Once the decision is made and implemented, internal auditors must deal with it as with any other important activity in the company. They must appraise the control system. They must evaluate the effectiveness of the action taken. They must see to it that managers are provided with the feedback that will assure them that what they ordered came to pass. The best-laid plans oft go astray. That is the reason for the modern internal auditor, and here is a case in point.

> In any large manufacturing process, product changes are a way of life, even though they are the bane of the production manager's existence. Every change has its inexorable ripple effect. Every care is, or should be, taken to make sure the ripples do not unduly rock the organization boat.

> As a part of the decision to make a product change, there must be an instruction that every engineering revision be communicated to the purchasing organization. Engineering changes often affect the parts or materials in the product. As a result new parts and materials will have to be purchased in time to meet production schedules.

> As a part of a regular audit of the engineering organization, an internal auditor examined a sample of significant engineering changes and traced every ripple the changes caused. The internal auditor found that the changes had been communicated to Purchasing so that new parts and materials could be procured to help implement the change. To management's dismay the internal auditor also found that the orders for the superseded parts and materials had not been canceled, so the company was receiving both the new needed items and the superseded needed items. Needless to say, corrective action was swift in coming.

Internal auditors can be management's safeguard in helping to monitor the results of decisions and make sure desired effects are achieved. With the broad scope of their review program, they can provide managers with a feedback mechanism that is needed to round out the decision-making process.

CONCLUSION

The steps in decision making are similar to those in problem solving; they call for identifying and defining the problem, defining the expectations or objectives of the decision, developing alternatives and evaluating them, selecting the best possible choice, and then taking action. The key to decision making is the element of futurity; it is too late to make decisions about the past. So uncertainty and risk are always involved in decision making. Quantitative techniques are, however, available to measure the degree of risk.

Internal auditors can help the manager in the decision-making process because of the broad scope of their activities within the organization, their analytical ability, and their understanding of modern evaluation methods. One step of the process is outside the scope of their responsibility: selecting the final choice. That is a management prerogative, and any attempt to usurp it would lead to a loss of objectivity and independence of the internal auditor.

REFERENCES

(1) R. V. Jones, *The Most Secret War.*
(2) Kenneth R. Andrews *The Concept of Corporate Strategy*, Third Edition (Irwin, Homewood, Illinois, 1987).
(3) Michael E. Porter, *Competitive Strategy, Techniques for Analyzing Industries and Competitors* (New York: Free Press, 1980).
(4) Michael Hammer and James Champy, *Reengineering the Corporation* (Nicholas Brealey, London and HarperCollins, 1993).
(5) James Champy, *Reengineering Management. Managing the Change to the Reegineered Corporation* (HarperCollins, London, 1995).
(6) Peter Drucker, *The New Realities* (Heinemann, Oxford, 1989).
(7) H. A. Simon, *Administrative Behaviour* (New York: Macmillan, 1957).
(8) Chartered Institute of Public Finance and Accountancy, *Promoting Internal Audit. Towards an Effective Audit Service—How to Improve Image and Profile. Guidance Manual* (3 Robert Street, London WC2N 6BH, 1992).
(9) Institute of Internal Auditors—UK, *Survival Pack for Internal Audit. An Essential Guide to Marketing & Presentations, Tendering and Contracting* (13 Abbeville Mews, 88 Clapham Park Road, London SW4 7BX, 1992)

9
Communications

COMMUNICATION AND THE MANAGER

Importance of Communication

The textbooks generally classify communications as a function of directing, but its importance to the enterprise cries for separate treatment. If some omnipotent power were bent on surely destroying an organization, it need but transform the organization into a tower of Babel, confounding "their language that they may not understand one another's speech." Then would the people be scattered and the organization abandoned.

That is more than a flight of fancy. Clarence B. Randall, former president of Inland Steel once said, "The businessman today must be able to write and speak the English language with clarity and felicity, or stand aside and let his chair be occupied by someone who can."

This does not mean that all who communicate well are sure to be good managers. Successful communication is not the cause of good management; it is a result. A competent manager will almost invariably be a good communicator. Indeed, what may be considered a problem in muddled communication may be a matter of muddled management. Barnard said that the first function of the executive is to establish and maintain a system of communication.(1) The executive must act as the center of a communication network and receive and disseminate information needed to keep the enterprise functioning effectively. Without such a network the manager would be incapable of functioning, like a human being without a network of veins and arteries carrying blood to and from the heart.

Communication is equally important to the manager's subordinates, who exchange ideas, concepts, needs, purposes, and problems through personal communication more effectively than through any other means. In the absence of open communication, common and personal goals become difficult to achieve—

because they are not mutually understood. Too, planning often fails because those responsible for or carrying out plans do not have access to information about high-level objectives or policies. As a result the subsidiary plans are either not made or are inexactly implemented. The line of communication from top to bottom must remain unbroken if the members of the enterprise are to understand and work toward common objectives.

If communication is so significant to the proper functioning of an enterprise, why is it a topic which only recently has been explored? Perhaps because the ancients felt that, since everyone seemed to be engaging in communication, everyone was fully aware of communication's essentiality. However, everyone is not aware of its significance, nor does everyone fully appreciate how its presence can lubricate the mechanism of the enterprise and its absence permit the rust of impotence to form.

A dramatic example of the benefits of good communication was reported by Texas Instruments:

> Texas Instruments found that new assemblers were having difficulty in learning their jobs. Three months was considered sufficient to develop an adequate level of competence. Yet the level was rarely being achieved within that span. The root cause was traced to anxiety about the unknown and that cause brought about high rates of turnover, excessive training time, high levels of tardiness and absence, and unacceptable quality of work.

> So Texas Instruments inaugurated an experiment. One group of new employees was given a full day of orientation instead of the usual two hours. The expanded orientation period was specifically directed to reduce anxiety. The new employees were told of the kind of hazing they could expect from the old hands. They were briefed on the idiosyncrasies of their future supervisors, and they were urged to take the initiative in communicating with their supervisors. For example, they were told that one supervisor was friendly despite the aura of strictness that he wore; he was a shy man, but he really liked to talk to subordinates who made the first overtures toward him.

> At the same time, control groups received the same kind of indoctrination as before, and the difference in orientation methods was not known either by the experimental group or by the control group.

> The results were astonishing to management:

> - Training time was cut in half.
> - Training costs were cut by two-thirds.
> - Absenteeism and tardiness were cut in half.
> - Waste and rejects were cut by four-fifths.
> - Costs were cut by 15% to 30%.

> The lesson learned in communicating with new assemblers was then carried up to new supervisors and managers. They too were anxious about how well they would do in their new assignments, dealing with experienced subordinates. Texas Instruments devised a plan whereby seasoned operators helped train new supervisors.

This had several salutary results. The supervisor learned to rely on subordinates for problem solving. The subordinates were given an interest in the success of the new supervisor. The supervisors, anxiety reduced, felt sufficiently competent to communicate openly with their managers instead of keeping to themselves problems which they felt guilty about.

In this chapter, we shall seek to define communication, examine its symbols and forms, explore both the problems and opportunities it presents to managers, and discuss the internal auditor's place in the scheme of the comminations network.

Communication Defined

Within the definition of "communication" lie both the essence of communication and the reason why communication is difficult to accomplish. It derives from the Latin *communicare* "to make common, to share, to impart, to transmit."

To achieve communication, there must be a commonality, a complete sharing of ideas, facts, and courses of action. But static commonality will not be enough. For communication to take place there must be an interaction between or among people. It is the interaction that distinguishes communication from other transmissions, and it is interaction that stresses the desired effect of a message: action on the part of the receiver.

In every communication there is always a giver, a message, a receiver, and symbols. The giver wishes to convey what he or she has in mind to the receiver by couching a message in appropriate symbols. The success of the effort to communicate depends on a minimum of distortion during the process of communication.

Until that is understood, there can be no communication. The early sages understood well the elements of communication. Their understanding was encapsulated in the riddle posed by the Zen Buddhists, the Sufis of Islam, and the Rabbis of the Talmud. They asked: "Is there a sound in the forest if a tree crashes down and no one is around to hear it?"

The right answer, of course, is no. The crashing of the tree creates sound waves, but nothing is heard until those waves impinge on the receiving eardrum and are converted into sound. The ancients understood the phenomenon that escapes many of us today: it is the recipient who achieves communication. If it is impossible for reception to take place, there is no commonality, no sharing, no communication.

Communication differs from information. Information is logic. It is mechanical. It makes no demands. Communication does make demands. Its elements are perception, expectation, and action. Unless the receiver perceives, there is no communication. Perception, roughly, is the awareness that a living, sentient thing has of its environment. That awareness is developed by all of us in different ways. It is molded by heredity, environment, family, friends, teachers, predilections, biases, and prejudices.

What cannot be perceived cannot be shared, and the effort to achieve communication fails. So the person who is sending the message must comprehend the receiver's ability to perceive the message before the message is understood. When the perception is absent, the sender must first help the receiver perceive before he transmits the message.

People will tend to select from a message that which fits their needs. And they will tend to "recode" the message to fit into their perception. The result is often distortion and no communication at all. Try to communicate the color blue to a person blind from birth. It is impossible. The same impossibility is true of any message that does not fit into the receiver's perception.

Another indispensable element of communication is expectation. People hear or read what they expect; if it is not what they expect, they do not hear or perceive it. The recipient looks to fulfill expectation. The unexpected is rarely received at all. It is ignored, or it is misheard. That is why it is so important both for the manager in instructions and the internal auditor in reports to set the stage, explain what will be said, and then use terms and concepts that fall within the range of perception of the recipient.

Finally, communication is action, communication is purposeful. Ideas are transmitted to achieve a particular response. Therefore, the communication must be so couched as to facilitate the response. If the communication is to warn against some anticipated peril, the terms and structure must convey urgency, directness, and the inherent dangers. If, however, the purpose of the message is to achieve goodwill, it must be so planned and couched as to promote good feelings.

In communicating, whatever the medium, the question must be, "Is this communication within the recipient's range of perception, is it what would be expected to be heard, and will it promote the action desired?"

Symbols

All language is made up of symbols. The spoken words are symbols; the written words are symbols; and so are smoke signals, Morse code, shorthand, bits of magnetic tape, proofreaders' marks and mathematical notation. So too are the manager's frown, raised eyebrows, or darkening scowl. Semantics, the science of language, is concerned with the study of symbols and their meaning.

Like maps, symbols are labels for the object or the concept; they are not the object or the concept itself. Therein lies the difficulty in communication. When two people observe the same pencil, then the same picture is likely to impinge on two brains. On the other hand, if one person says "pencil" to another, the picture in the other's brain may be of a wooden pencil with or without eraser, a gold pencil, a silver pencil, a black pencil, or a small brush for fine art work.

As terms become less concrete, the chances that the same symbols will evoke different concepts in different people increase in geometric proportion. The meanings of words are influenced by association. Increasing the opportunity for personal association correspondingly increases the probability that different people will look at the same map and see different terrains.

So the manager is more likely to achieve communication with the use of symbols less capable of being misunderstood: pictures instead of words, concrete words instead of abstract words, examples to reinforce principles, and illustrations to illuminate procedures.

Forms of Communication

Choosing the right form or channel of communication may be as important to the effectiveness of the communication as the information presented. Managers have many channels to choose from. If they pick the right one, they may meet the objective. If they pick the wrong one they may meet hostility.

For example, a controversial subject should not be sprung for the first time in a formal staff meeting. It would be more politic to obtain informal support from colleagues before the meeting opens. Similarly, hearing about an important change in a major program from the newspapers creates employee resentment. Being told of such changes informally before the public hears about them puts the employees in the know and enhances the feeling of belonging. On the other hand, an announcement of changes in a retirement plan demands a formal communique; the subject is too important to all employees and too readily misunderstood to be communicated without a formal, carefully thought-out presentation.

Every enterprise uses various forms of communication. Here are some of them:

1. *The chain of command.* Messages may be given orally or in writing, and formal messages travel down through the established organizational levels. Oral communication is quicker, but the messages can be thoroughly garbled by the time they reach the ultimate recipient. Some limited studies have been made of communication penetration. Starting with a board of director's meeting—ranked at 100%—the penetration of a statement passed by the board and communicated from the president to the vice president to the department director to the foreperson to the worker had dwindled to 20%.

Written chain-of command-communications are as effective as the writer's ability to be understood. One executive would ask his two teenage daughters to read every instruction he wrote before he published it. If they failed to understand what he was driving at, he would rewrite it until they did.

2. *The order.* Among the most important forms of communication to the employee is the order. This is the form managers use most often to get specific jobs done. It is essential to the execution of management tasks, but it is often badly communicated. It should tell what is to be done, who is to do it, and when, where, how, and why.

The successful manager considers all those elements in the orders so that there will be no misunderstanding about what is to be accomplished. The order should be subjected only to the interpretation intended.

The order "Test the incoming shipment of bolts 100%" may lack a host of elements that could easily lead to confusion. When is the shipment coming in? Who is the supplier? Why 100% for this shipment, when bolts are usually sampled in receiving inspection? What priority should be given to the tests? Where will the bolts arrive? How should they be tested—by standard or special tests?

3. *Poster and bulletin boards.* The bulletin boards and posters should not be used as primary devices, because many employees refuse to read them. In one instance internal auditors found that receiving inspectors were being informed of new test requirements by revised instructions posted on a bulletin board. When the auditor queried the inspectors about the new specifications, she found that a considerable percentage were unaware of them.

4. *Company periodicals.* A bright, attractive periodical can do much to convey information about the company. Employees soon learn, however, that generally only self-serving declarations, statements that are consistently beneficial to the company, are permitted in the paper. Specificity and accuracy are therefore desirable. Also since people love to see their names and pictures in print, a periodical can play a significant part in the company's social life.

5. *Letters and inserts.* The personal letter addressed to the home gives the employee a feeling of importance. Pay inserts insure exposure at the very least, but the communications are usually read rapidly and with partial attention. They should be written clearly and simply.

6. *Employee handbooks and pamphlets.* During the orientation process and when special programs such as pension and insurance plans are introduced or changed, handbooks and pamphlets are often given to employees. Unfortunately, many remain unread even though the employees sign statements that they understand the contents. If the pamphlets are considered important enough, supervisors may have to hold meetings with their subordinates, to discuss them and then test the subordinates' knowledge about the information.

7. *Annual reports.* Annual reports were originally prepared for the owners, but more and more they are being expanded to provide information to employees as well.

8. *Labor unions.* The union can be helpful in combining with management to offer information or persuasion on some significant issue. That can boomerang, however, if the employees get the notion that the management-union relationship is not in their best interests.

9. *The grapevine.* The grapevine is the underground railroad of communication in an organization. It exists wherever people work together; much of what an employee learns within an organization comes from the informal network of communication that springs up in all enterprises. An employee receives information from the colleague at the next desk, from a spouse who may have picked it up from another employee's spouse, from the coffee break chatter, from social

activities, and from daily associations in the company. There is a bit of the town crier in all employees.

The grapevine produces rumor aplenty, but it also carries fact. A study was conducted to trace thirty rumors occurring in six different companies. Sixteen turned out to be just that—unfounded rumors. But nine turned out to be fact; and the remaining five were at least partly fact.(2)

Opinions about the grapevine vary. Some executives regard the grapevine as closely related to poison ivy. Others see it as playing a positive role that should be enlisted. They counsel that management cannot possibly plan every channel of communication in the network. So why not use the informal network? If the canny manager would make use of the grapevine, however, he or she should recognize the "informal communication" leaders and keep them well informed. Thus the grapevine can transmit more accurate information.

The greatest drawback of the grapevine is its capacity to disseminate inaccurate information. The best antidote for the poisoned grape is a dose of truth. When false rumors are rife, managers should hasten to counter fiction with fact. Some companies print both the rumor and the truth, but that may tend to underline the fiction and insure its remembrance. Some organizations use the company newspaper to scotch rumors in a column of letters to the editor. Employees are encouraged to make inquiry on any subject relating to the company that may interest or concern them. Authoritative answers then tend to dispel the unfounded rumors.

10. *The meeting.* Probably the most used channel of communication is the meeting. Indeed, it has been said that the manger who is not attending a meeting is either going to one or is leaving it. Untold hours are spent in meetings and wasted there because the chairs do not handle the meetings effectively. Yet there are some commonsense rules for the chair that can improve communication and reduce the length of meetings.

- Use meetings when all else fails. Don't substitute them for deciding simple issues or using the telephone.
- Inform the conferees in advance what will be discussed, what is expected of them and what material to bring.
- Set a specific starting date and time and estimate the duration of the meeting.
- Tell the conferees about the purpose of the meeting. Is it to inform, to consider a proposal, to arrive at a decision, or to offer advice?
- Develop a meeting agenda and consider the questions that the conferees might raise.
- Make sure each conferee is informed, and have your secretary call him in advance to remind him that his attendance is expected.
- Use visual material to convey complex data, but don't let the "dog and pony show" take the full time of the meeting.
- Don't allow monopolies of conversation. If comments are not needed the

member probably should not have been asked to attend the meeting.

- Don't let the meeting get off track. Stick to the specific issues and get the wanderers back home.
- Sum up significant points. Ask if your summation accurately conveys the thoughts expressed. Make sure all understand what has been said.
- Do not permit telephone calls to be transferred to the meeting room, but allow the quiet delivery of notes in emergent circumstances.
- Present facts before offering or asking for solutions.
- Write up all proceedings of the meeting, including action items, persons responsible for action, and the dates of completion. Distribute copies to the conferees and to their superiors.

Studies have been conducted to determine which forms of communication are most effective. Interestingly enough, the speediest are found to be first the grapevine and second oral communication received from the supervisor and the manager. The least effective are memos, letters, and bulletin boards. It appears, therefore, that face-to-face communication is far superior to other forms if speed is desirable. In accuracy and permanence, however, the written word must take precedence.

Feedback

Good managers leave little to chance. They are fully aware of the ease with which communication breaks down, messages are misunderstood, and orders are ignored. Many a business communication is like a message scrawled on a piece of paper, corked in a bottle, and tossed into the sea. Feedback is the means by which managers learn whether their communications have been effective. Feedback returns to the sender the signal "message received and understood" if the message has been clear and the recipient is on the proper wavelength.

In face-to-face conversation feedback may be a light of comprehension, a puzzled look, or a blank stare. Perceptive managers can tell whether they are getting through or whether they need to say things another way, amplify statements, illustrate them, or ask whether they are fully comprehended. The face-to-face discussion has a better chance of achieving understanding if the sender is watching for the signs of feedback.

Written messages require feedback built into them or into the communication system. There is no assurance that a query will be answered or that a request will be carried out as expected. It is rare indeed that the desired action will be prompt and satisfactory. The manager should as a matter of course have a follow-up system for all written communications. When a written message asks for some action, a copy should be placed in a tickler file and marked with a follow-up date. On the appointed date the recipient should be called or written to again, with a request for information on the status of the inquiry or request. The individual who receives and acts on each message as requested is unique. The manager's feedback loop must take that into account.

Achieving Communication

The Difficulties

Successful communication, like a successful marriage, requires an earnest willingness to share. From the sender's standpoint there must be an aggressive willingness that plows through obstacles until the goal of understanding is achieved. Successful communication also requires a willingness to understand, fully understand, the process of communication. Without that understanding, there is merely a clashing of symbols that emit noise without achieving comprehension. Let us therefore summarize some of the concepts that may help the manager cope with problems in communication.

The pivotal term in communication is "perception." When that term is fully comprehended, the difficulty of achieving successful communication is finally realized. Perception means seeing the same picture in the same way—sharply focused and undistorted. No two mental cameras are the same. No two learning experiences are the same. No two sets of biases, predilections, prejudices, families, and friends are the same. Yet each set affects perception, how the individual perceives both what is told and how it is told.

Seen in that light, true communication, the transfer of an identical picture from one mind to another, along with the words and accompanying music, is an utter impossibility. At best the picture will be an approximation, but how can even the approximation be gained? The answer lies in determining how the recipient perceives the message and adjusting the focus as necessary. So reasonable communication is achieved less by sending messages than by receiving them, less by speaking than by listening, providing for feedback, and by earnestly trying to find out just what picture was thrown on the recipient's mental screen by the message.

A friend of ours, president of a small business, was stimulated to try an experiment after we had expounded on the hazards of achieving communication. It was his practice to provide new hires with an orientation course about the company and its processes. After our conversations about communication, he had his new hires for technical and administrative positions carry a small notebook with them and record their impressions each day for a period of time. Then each day he read the record they had made.

The results were eye-opening. The perceptions often varied widely from those he thought the new hires had. He was gaining an insight—and sometimes a humbling one—into his ability to communicate. He was beginning to achieve reasonable communication, because he was making the effort, because he was earnestly trying to share, because he was not only sending messages but listening as well, and because he was not only giving instructions but obtaining feedback on how effectively he was instructing.

Misunderstandings are bound to occur in the communication process. They can be the result of many differences: in vocabularies, in the meanings associated with certain words, and in the status of the people sending and receiving the messages. All of them place impediments in the path of communication. Direct conversation is therefore the best way of removing the blocks; it not only permits speaking and listening, statements and questions, and recapitulations and restatements but also permits the use of nonverbal symbols that heighten understanding and signal comprehension. Often it is the light in the listener's eye, and not the spoken word, that reflects the extent of comprehension.

Written Communication

Yet the written word, with its permanence, preciseness, and the opportunity it provides for analysis, is essential to the communication process in large organizations. However, the writer of messages must take the hazards into account. One of those hazards is failing to recognize that communication is also expectation. As we have pointed out, one hears what one wants to hear or expects to hear. So written communication must always set the stage, focus the expectation, and tell the reader what is to be expected. This is only part of the story.

Written communications must have clarity, believability, and integrity. The writing must be as clear and simple as it is possible to make it. Simple words. Concrete words. Words that bring pictures to the mind—sharp, clear pictures that the sender wants to flash on the receiver's mental screen.

A message could merely say, "This project exceeded budget by $10 million." But how much more graphic is the picture if the message were to say: "The budget was exceeded by $10 million, which is equal to a person working 40 hours a week, 50 weeks a year, at $20 an hour for 250 years."

The message must have believability. It must carry the aura of accuracy and propriety. Getting the message is difficult enough; its transmission should not be garbled by doubts as to its authenticity.

The message must support the integrity of the organization. Among other things, that calls for the executives to buttress the positions of their subordinate managers. And unless emergent circumstances demand simultaneous messages to all in the organization—like a bomb threat in a building—the messages from on high should not bypass those in intermediate positions who have a need to know.

Perceptions

The great leap in understanding comes from the superior's comprehension of the subordinate's perceptions: values, beliefs, hopes and goals. The comprehension comes only when the superior tries to get into the skin, the heart, and the head of the subordinate. This is only possible by receiving messages, not sending them.

Superiors should ask their subordinates to record carefully and thoughtfully how they see themselves in the organization's scheme of things, how they perceive the superior's position, how they can contribute to organizational goals and objectives, what standards they should seek to meet, how they can measure themselves to see if they have met those standards, how they should be expected to perform, and what they should be held accountable for.

Such communications seldom fail to surprise the superior, whose perception is rarely the same as his subordinate's. Nevertheless, they do show where bridges need building. They show where the downward messages got garbled in the transmission and how badly the subordinate misconceived the superior's job, its complexities, and its constraints. The superior and the subordinate may not see eye to eye, but the veils may start to lift and there may be at least an approximation of communication, even where the subordinate's proposals may need to be overridden.

COMMUNICATION AND THE INTERNAL AUDITOR

How the Internal Auditor Can Help: The Communications Audit

Communication is the internal auditors' food and drink. Without it they cannot do their job properly, and they cannot adequately convey the results to those who need to know. They must be able to communicate both to obtain information and to pass the information on.

Checkers of numbers, sitting alone and incommunicado in a corner, are anachronisms. They do not play the role management expects of the modern internal auditor. The role they do play gives little emphasis to listening, speaking, and writing—primary tools for the comprehensive internal auditing job. They must be first-class communicators to learn from others what the conditions are and then to explain to others how the conditions deviate from standards, how they may be improved, and how they may be corrected.

Sometimes the conditions are complex, esoteric, and technical, and they may be enshrouded in arcane language known only to a select few. So internal auditors must be translators for management. As they ride the circuit in their organization, they sojourn for a while in strange lands with strange languages. They must learn those languages so as to be able to speak them fluently.

Internal auditors must be conversant with the following:

- Remainders and reversionary interests in the legal department.
- Drawback, demurrage, and switching costs in the traffic department.
- Packing sheets and receiving memos in the receiving department.
- Work-in-process and process costs in the accounting department.
- Contaminated metals in the scrap department.

- First-article inspections in the quality control department.
- Traveling requisitions and acknowledgments in the purchasing department.
- Attachments and garnishees in the personnel department.
- The safety department and relevant safety legislation.
- Interperiod tax allocations in the tax department.
- Euro-dollar issues in the treasury department.
- Area quotes in the contracts department.
- Budget realizations in the production department.
- Design change control in the engineering department.
- Tear sheets in the advertising department.
- Program loops and accumulator registers in the data processing department.

All of these—plus an anthology of other terms—are compounded by a proliferation of form and procedure numbers, abbreviations, acronyms, and nicknames.

The internal auditor must therefore be able both to appraise management's systems of communication and to communicate his findings clearly and understandably to management. The remainder of this chapter will be devoted first to the internal auditor's appraisal of the information system within the enterprise and second to his reports, which inform managers of the conditions that are not brought to light by the information systems.

Appraising Operating Reports

Managers in large companies function and make decisions largely on the basis of information received from operating levels. The decisions are generally no better than the information on which they are based, and that information, flowing to the decision maker, may leave its recipient either parched or inundated.

Clear, current, accurate, meaningful reports are desperately needed, but the perfect report is a rarity. The executive, poring over the data needed to help in planning, directing, and controlling the activities of the organization, is generally at the mercy of the report writers. Often the reports can be more like self-serving declarations than full statements of existing conditions.

The professional internal auditor, analytical, objective, and unbiased, is the chief defense of the report recipient. When the auditor has done the job, executives can breathe more freely for knowing that the data on which they may be staking their managerial reputation are reliable. Every internal auditing organization should have a complete and constantly updated listing of "management" reports—the reports prepared in the operating departments and destined for the organization's top executives.

The list should be referenced to regular audits scheduled in the long-range audit program. To make sure that there are no slip-ups in the review process, each "permanent file," the repository for all information relevant to repetitive audits, should contain instructions to review appropriate management reports. To further insure against slips, each internal auditor embarking on an audit assignment should fill out a reminder list that provides for the steps to be taken in any audit, and in that reminder list should be an instruction to determine which management reports are relevant to the audit and to review them. The loop is not closed until the audit supervisor makes it a practice to review the reminder lists for compliance.

The management reports, because of their significance in successful decision making, are among the known "risk areas" in an organization. An auditor cannot be held responsible for a risk area that a prudent practitioner has no reasonable way of identifying. However, management reports come within the purview of the internal auditor's responsibility, and the auditor owes a duty to management to review them regularly.

An individual internal auditor, on beginning an audit of operations, should determine which reports are issued and received within the organizations whose activities are being reviewed. They may not be the kinds of reports submitted to the organization's top echelons, but they may be of significance to operating managers. Also the internal auditor can provide the operating managers a service by reviewing the reports.

The extent of the internal auditor's review of reports will depend on the nature of the reports themselves, but generally the auditor will be concerned with elements of accuracy, timeliness, and meaningfulness. Let any one of those elements be missing and the report may be a waste of time, effort, and money because it will be valueless to the recipient.

An audit of a report that is expensive or significant enough to warrant a thorough review might go something like this:

1. Determine the purpose of the report and learn the names of the report's recipients and scheduled due dates, the source of the data on which the report is based, the process used in preparing and reviewing the report, and the cost, in staff hours, of preparation.
2. Test the report for accuracy by comparing it with source data and recomputing its calculations.
3. Test it for timeliness by comparing due dates with release dates for a reasonable period.
4. Test its meaningfulness by:
   (i) Evaluating the format to determine whether it summarizes and provides the information needed to carry out the report's purpose.
   (ii) Questioning recipients as to the usefulness and derivable benefits from the report.
   (iii) Determining the regularity with which report preparers question report recipients as to a continuing need for the report. In one case the head of an accounting department queried executives about their need for a

37-copy report. All of them said they needed it, but the chief accountant had doubts, and the next month withheld all the copies. There was never a request for the report, so it was discontinued.

Appraising Policies and Procedures

Superiors promulgate policies and procedures that subordinates may follow, circumvent, or pay lip service to. Whether those policies and procedures are successful therefore depends largely on how well they are understood and accepted by subordinates and how relevant they are to real-life situations. Hence, superiors should have a healthy interest in how well their policies and procedures are faring at the working level.

Without professional help, obtaining that information may be a catch-as-catch-can affair. Part of every internal audit program is devoted to appraising adherence to existing policies, procedures, and other instructions. Also internal auditors are usually concerned with more than mere compliance; they will evaluate the relevance and propriety of executive instructions under changing conditions.

The internal audit program can take many forms. The simplest is testing transactions by comparing them with the standards set up in operating instructions. For example, in an audit of purchase orders, the internal auditor might test compliance with rules such as these:

- All orders valued at over $10 000 require at least three written bids.
- Lists of potential bidders must be reviewed by the buyer's supervisor.
- Orders valued at less than $200 require no signatures other than the buyer's, but orders of greater amounts must be approved at designated levels, depending on the amounts involved.

Those are but a few rules among very many that apply to the purchasing function. The internal auditor's test of a sample of purchase orders is designed to appraise compliance with the rules. The auditor would also ask questions such as these:

- Is the $10 000 level for written bids reasonable? Should it not be $5000 or $50 000 The volume of orders and the existence or absence of other checks might make the $10 000 rule no longer practicable.
- Is the review of bidder lists for each purchase reasonable? Do the reviews of all lists result in inundating supervisors so that the lists get no more than perfunctory approval? Would it be better to have a general list of all approved bidders that the buyers must use and ask for supervisor approval only in exceptional cases?

A level of $200 for orders issued solely over buyers' signatures may seem reasonable on its face because of the small amounts involved. However, it has been found that repetitive orders under $200 can represent large total amounts, and they can be the dark little corners in which favoritism may lurk. Hence the question whether the supervisors regularly select random samples of such orders for review and evaluation. The uninspected inevitably deteriorates.

Inspectors of products must work under a host of rules and regulations, standards, and specifications and they must have an intimate understanding of those rules, regulations, and so on to do their work accurately and with dispatch. One internal auditor selected a sample of important rules that such inspectors must follow and quizzed the inspectors on how well they understood their instructions. The results discomfited the inspection manager but brought about improved training programs.

Appraising Downward Communication

Superiors often have difficulty in communicating successfully with subordinates. The communication gets distorted, filtered, and diffused by the time it reaches the ultimate recipient. The internal auditor can put a finger on the pulse of downward communication and inform managers how well the communications are reaching the people for whom they were intended.

Hired consultants are often employed to listen to employees, but the internal auditor is eminently suited to carry out the same function. Here is an example of the usefulness of the technique:

Because of economic conditions, management of a company had been forced to hire new employees at rates which were higher than those paid older employees. Also on occasion, to avoid short-term layoffs, some employees were transferred to other jobs. Management had thought that it had ably communicated the reasons for its actions to its employees and had even expected applause for its efforts in preventing the short-term layoffs.

However, production dropped and puzzled management could not tell why. A consultant was hired to find out. He questioned 600 employees over a 6-month period. The results of the questions showed that there were strong feelings on the part of many employees that work standards were too high, the older employees resented the higher wage scales of the new, and that the temporary transfers to avoid layoffs were resented, much less applauded.

As a result, management undertook a broad communication and action program:

- Methods men were set to roaming around the factory floor to be available to employees on questions about standards.
- Vacations were lengthened for older employees to compensate for the higher wage scales necessary to recruit new employees in a tight labor market.
- Service clubs were established for older employees. A new plant organ was developed to improve the social life in the plant and instill a pride in company products.

- A rotation system was installed in conjunction with the temporary transfers, and management carefully explained the alternative, which would have meant layoffs.

Obviously the sensitive, tuned-in manager might have arrived at the same solution, but the sad fact is that they often just do not have the time, and perhaps the skills, to carry out such an appraisal program. Therefore they need the skilled internal auditor, the problem-solving partner. And the professional internal auditor needs a thorough grounding in the behavioral sciences to conduct such an appraisal.

Personnel policies are often the bone in employees' throats. Also generally, it is not so much the policy itself as the way employees perceive it that causes resentment. Personnel policy audits have been undertaken to assess that perception. The policies are listed and employees are interviewed to obtain their views on the policies. The data gathered are arrayed and summarized, and the internal auditor may consult with behavioral scientists in the personnel department to interpret the information gathered and recommend action to solve any problems identified by the audit.

Audit Reports

Of all the skills the professional internal auditor needs, communication must surely top the list. The most brilliantly developed findings, the most innovative, cost-saving recommendations may lie moldering in the internal auditor's working papers unless the auditor can communicate them successfully to the person able to act on them. Ability to communicate effectively takes training and effort; it requires ingenuity and innovativeness; and it calls for an understanding of what managers want and need and how managers think. It also calls for the realization that managers at different levels have different needs, different understandings of conditions, and differing spans of time they can spend on reading audit reports, to say nothing of different perceptions, expectations, and responsibilities for action.

All those things the professional internal auditor must take into account in communicating findings and getting recommendations accepted. The most appropriate forms of reporting are needed to obtain attention and achieve correction. The reporting process should not be reserved exclusively for the formal, final report that concludes the audit assignment. Communication for the auditor should be an always thing.

At the very outset of assignments internal auditors should report orally to the operating manager on how they propose to carry out the audit project: what they plan to cover and what they plan not to cover. Through that communication they can avoid such astonished questions from the manager at the end of the project as "You mean to tell me you fellows never looked at our XYZ unit . . . training program . . . indirect expenses . . . procurement policies . . . reporting systems . . . etc., etc.?"

The communication process is carried out when the internal auditor detects a condition that needs prompt correction; and reporting unsatisfactory conditions calls for special techniques and qualities. Certainly, the internal auditor should not become enmeshed in minutiae. Minor defects not warranting management attention should be discussed with operating personnel, corrected on the spot, and reported only in the internal audit working papers. They should not be used to take up the time of the busy manager.

However, significant findings usually demand prompt action to correct the unsatisfactory conditions that were found, and the urgency of the situation can be conveyed to the manager if the auditor performs a professional job. The techniques of developing findings and the elements of a properly presented finding are as follows:

1. *Statement of condition.* This statement should describe the condition and its scope. It should, for example, indicate the population involved: the total value of purchase orders, the total number of people on the payroll, the total number of safety boxes, the total number and value of cars and trucks, the total number and severity of accidents, and the total volume of blueprints. The information puts the findings in perspective and indicates its importance in the company's scheme of things. The statement should show exactly what happened, objectively and fairly, with verifiable specificity.

2. *Standards.* Internal auditors should show not only what happened but what should have happened. They must show the standards or criteria for the particular operation and the path that should have been followed. They must always be ready to tell the operating manager: "This is the way it should have happened according to the rules and regulations, and this is the way it did happen," An understanding and agreement between the internal auditor and the manager on the standards the internal auditor used in measuring the effectiveness of an operation is pivotal to an agreement that things are not what they should be.

3. *Effect.* Every manager confronted with a reported condition calling for action has the right to ask: "So what?" Every auditor reporting an unsatisfactory condition should be prepared to answer that question in terms of dollars or days lost or potential hazards that should be avoided. The effect of the condition should be presented in such a way that managers become convinced that they may not achieve their own objectives if the condition is not corrected.

4. *Cause.* Rare indeed is the manager who does not pose to the internal auditor a question like "How in the world did this happen?" The auditor should be prepared to show the cause or causes for the condition. Besides, the purpose of determining cause goes beyond satisfying someone's curiosity; for no problem is truly or permanently solved until the cause is isolated and identified—the cause that, if not corrected, will surely permit the condition to recur.

5. *Recommendation.* The problem presented to management calls for a decision.

As we discussed in Chapter 8, each decision is a choice from among alternatives, and the internal auditor can help managers by offering feasible alternatives. Thus the internal auditor has a duty to offer a recommendation for management's consideration. The recommendation should be feasible, economical, and workable. Perhaps it will not be followed, but that does not matter. Management must make the operating decisions. The internal auditor is not responsible for having recommendations put into effect, but for seeing that the conditions get corrected.

Interim reports of a condition—presented during the course of the examination—can be made orally or in writing. The complexity of the condition will generally dictate the medium. What is significant is for the matter to be reported promptly so the defect can be corrected without unnecessary delay.

The final, formal report should be testimony to the internal auditor's communication abilities. It must demonstrate understanding of: "Who are my readers and what do they need or want to know?" If ability to communicate is demonstrated, the internal auditor will have a wide following of interested readers from managers at the operating levels to executives who guide the destiny of the entire organization.

The operating manager and superior generally want to know what the auditor covered and what was not covered, what was found to be satisfactory and what was found to be unsatisfactory, and what they can do to correct unsatisfactory conditions. Also generally, they want the information in sufficient detail that they have a comprehensive picture of what the internal auditor found. For that reason, the formal audit report generally contains the following elements:

1. *Introduction.* This section of the report should, obviously, come first. It sets the stage. It defines the area, activity, function, or organization that was reviewed. Familiar activities—receiving, purchasing, accounts receivable, for example—need little introduction, but volume statistics about the number of employees, transactions, and dollar amounts help put the operations in perspective. Less familiar activities—research and development and tool liaison, for example—may require some explanation to improve the reader's perception.

2. *Purpose.* This sets out specifically what areas or activities the internal auditor planned to cover. It develops the reader's expectations of what he can hope to see discussed in the remainder of the report. In effect, it is a map of where the reader will be led.

3. *Scope.* This section is particularly helpful in defining the limitations of the internal auditor's detailed examination: purchases in the last three months only; invoices in excess of $500 only; tool cribs in plants A and B, but not in plant C; payrolls for hourly but not salaried employees; the control systems but no tests of transactions. The section should also show, of course, the reasons for any limitations of the audit coverage.

4. *Opinion.* Some audit organizations report exceptions only. Their reasoning is that top managers operate on the management-by-exception principle. We think

that is wrong. It portrays the internal auditor as a predator instead of an objective evaluator and it denies management the benefit of the internal auditor's overall appraisal of the activity audited.

If the opinion is satisfactory, executive management need not read further. If it is satisfactory, with certain exceptions, or unsatisfactory, the executive may wish to dig more deeply into the exceptions and assure himself that appropriate corrective action is being taken.

Expressing an overall opinion provides a service that may assure managers of satisfactory operations, alert them to problem areas that have been detected, or sound a call to action when emergent circumstances warrant high-level attention.

5. *Findings*. The findings support the opinion. They may be satisfactory and provide information on the steps the internal auditor took to be assured that conditions were free of defects. On the other hand, they may be unsatisfactory and be accompanied by explanations of the conditions found, the standards or criteria from which the actions taken deviated, the causes, the effects, and the recommendations for improvements. Also, each statement of finding should include the reaction of the operating manager to the finding and the action the manager proposes to take.

The elements just described make up a comprehensive audit report. Such a report may be long and detailed to provide operating managers with the information they need. In a large company, in which hundreds of audit reports may be issued in a year, it would be a physical impossibility for executive managers to read each report in detail. Yet the audit reports describe the company's administrative health and are important sources of information for executives on company operations.

The internal auditor should therefore provide executive management with a summary statement that offers a quick overview of the auditor's opinions and findings. Many auditing organizations give that information in a one-page summary that becomes the first page of the internal audit report. The summary can be constructed to offer opinions about and brief explanations of the results of the internal audits. One approach is to provide opinions on the three elements generally constituting the scope of the auditor's work: compliance, efficiency and effectiveness. They may be defined as follows:

- *Compliance*. How well the auditee complied with laws, regulations, policies, procedures, instructions, and other standards of performance and whether those standards of performance are still valid.
- *Efficiency*. How promptly and economically the auditee carried out his assigned tasks.
- *Effectiveness*. Whether desired results were being achieved, whether assigned missions were accomplished, and whether the work done was consonant with the entity's overall objectives and plans.

To provide opinions on those qualities, the internal auditor would have to be aware of the organization's objectives, determine whether appropriate plans, policies, procedures, and systems had been devised to meet those objectives, determine whether people met acceptable standards of cost, quality, and schedule, and whether people were complying with acceptable practices and procedures.

A one-page summary for an audit report covering marketing activities is shown in Table 9.1. The summary provides opinions on the five marketing activities covered in the audit. Opinions are given, by adjective ratings, under the three elements of compliance, efficiency, and effectiveness. The rating of A, B,C,D, or F is followed by the number of the deficiency finding, identified under the heading Deficiency Finding, that caused the rating to be assigned. The meanings of the ratings appear in the legend at the bottom of the summary page.

A minor deficiency is one that requires correction and warrants reporting to management but cannot be said to prevent the activity from meeting a major objective. A major deficiency implies failure to meet one or more of an activity's major objectives. A complete breakdown of an activity's functions would merit a rating of F.

The deficiency findings cited briefly are referenced to the page numbers in the body of the report, where the conditions are discussed in more detail. Management is also interested in the status of the corrective action taken to cure the defects reported, and that information also is provided in the summary.

The comments in Table 9.1, near the bottom of the summary, are extremely important. They place the audit findings in perspective. A catalog of errors, unrelieved by positive comment when warranted, can give a completely erroneous impression to executive management and can result in misguided punitive action.

In the illustration, the comments indicate that the chief difficulty—one often found in technical organizations—was administration. When the man in charge is concerned more with technical activities than with his people and his systems of control, the kinds of findings cited are almost inevitable.

Summary statements such as the one in Table 9.1 can provide valuable insights for the executive without demanding too much time. With such an overview, executive managers may become as interested in reports on the organization's administrative health as they now are in the reports of its financial health.

CONCLUSION

The manager who cannot learn to communicate had better move over and make room for one who can. Each manager must be the center of a communication network passing messages upward and downward. Through communication understanding is created and action is promoted. Precise downward communication—the flashing of the same picture on two or more minds—is a virtual impossibility because no two people have the same perceptions, the same

Table 9.1 Internal Audit Report on a Marketing Division

Activity Reviewed	Compliance	Efficiency	Effectiveness
Marketing research	A	C(1)	C(2)
Advertising	B(3)	A	A
Sales promotion	A	D(4)(5)	A
Credit	A	A	A
Customer service	A	A	C(6)

Deficiency Findings
(1) Marketing research was performed exclusively through field polls and questionnaires at a cost of $57,000 when substantially the same information was available from the U.S. Census Bureau and trade reference guides (page 3).
(2) The data that cost marketing research $350,000 to gain through market-testing product Q were already available in trade publications (page 3).
(3) The advertising department, instead of the purchasing department, dealt directly with the suppliers in a number of instances in violation of company policy 123 (page 4).
(4) Orders for sales promotion material were not issued on time, and as a result excessive overtime and transportation costs were incurred (page 6).
(5) Costs were not being monitored, and hence the sales promotion manager was not informed that the sales promotion program overran budgets by $63,000 (38 percent) (page 8).
(6) Instructions to customers on the use of company products were written in technical terms not readily understandable to the layman (page 9).

Corrective Action
Corrective action was completed on findings 1 and 2 through revised procedures. Findings 3 and 4 were corrected through improved instructions to employees and closer supervisory review. Corrective action was initiated but not yet completed on findings 5 and 6; written reply is requested.

Comments
Despite the six deficiencies we observed, we believe that people in the marketing division are highly motivated and technically proficient. The advertising and sales promotion products are of excellent quality and have received commendations of merit in trade publications. Prompt action was taken and is continuing to correct the conditions we found; and while we consider some of the conditions to be serious deviations from good practice or policy, we believe that they are not material when considered in terms of the marketing organization's overall mission. The marketing director has assured us that he plans to devote increased attention to administrative matters in the future.

Legend
A–No deficiencies   C–Relatively major deficiency
B–Relatively minor deficiency   D–More than one major deficiency
                        F–Failure to accomplish major missions of the
                        activity

backgrounds, the same qualities, and the same feelings. An approximation of communication can be achieved if managers can comprehend the channels of communication, the symbols of communication, and the barriers to communication and if they try aggressively to reach their employees.

Internal auditors can play a significant role in the communication system by evaluating and appraising the channels of communication, by determining whether management's communication of policies of procedures are being complied with, and by assessing whether instructions communicated are still valid. Internal auditors must be adept at communication to be able to report their findings clearly and compellingly to the various levels of management within the organization.

REFERENCES

(1) C. I. Barnard, *The Functions of the Executive* (Cambridge, Mass.: Harvard University Press, 1938), p. 226.
(2) Robert Hershey, "The Grapevine—Here to Stay but Not Beyond Control," *Personnel,* Vol. 43, No. 1, pp. 62–66.

10
Measurement and Evaluation

MEASUREMENT AND MANAGERS

Performance

The ultimate test of a manager's ability is performance. That and that alone is relevant to the organization's aims and needs. The manager may be endowed with sterling qualities that dazzle the eye: ambition, charisma, dedication, drive, forcefulness, and initiative. However, all those qualities are merely surface glitter unless they are wrapped around a central core of demonstrated performance.

Managers are truly measured, then, by how well they perform. Effectiveness as a manager emerges only as a direct result of the performance of the people who look for leadership. "Wherefore, by their fruits ye shall know them."

Productive managers are the organization's most valuable resource. It must be weighed as carefully as such other resources as money, inventions, and marketable products, yet it is often measured less thoughtfully than the cost of stationery.

Management Inventories

Weighing and measuring remains the weakest link in the organizational chain. Although the valuation of product inventories has become almost an exact science, the evaluation of management inventories and potentials is still pretty much a groping in the dark. Many executives evaluate their management inventory as of the present or for the short range. Is this worker capable of managing? Should this manager of the general accounting department be promoted to controller? We've just lost one of our branch managers; who should replace her?

How much more comfortable and secure is the executive who has a properly evaluated management inventory that names candidates and lists their strengths and potentials. It is useful for each segment of the organization to have a chart of the key people in that segment. After each name might be two facts (age and number of years in the position) and an assessment. (Ready for promotion. Promotable within one to three years. Has the potential for promotion. Does satisfactory work but is not promotable.)

Some companies maintain data banks of skills that include education, current and previous experience, and performance ratings. Obviously, such an inventory needs periodic updating and objective valuations.

Thoughtful attention to the management inventory has some valuable side effects. It forces an organization's executives to think through its objectives and reevaluate them as circumstances present new opportunities or obstacles. It requires executive management to ask itself: "What are the specific responsibilities of our managers and workers and how important are they in meeting organizational goals?" "What tasks should be undertaken, and how shall people be held accountable for their completion?" "How can we help people help themselves and thereby build a better management inventory?"

The failure to answer the last question is the reason for many appraisal breakdowns, the reason why appraisals of and by managers remain a chronic weakness. Evaluations should not be the province of the superior alone. The subordinate manager and the worker should be provided with the information that will help them appraise themselves.

Trait-based and Quantitative Measurements

Executives and managers have long recognized the need to appraise their people. Varied means of appraisal were developed, but they often did more harm than good. They were based on traits rather than performance. They asked superiors to evaluate such qualities as judgement, dependability, attention to detail, qualities of leadership, and getting along with people.

True such qualities are highly desirable, but their appraisal is highly subjective. They are colored by the appraiser's biases and predilections. They require the appraiser to play God without anything resembling superhuman insights. Indeed, the appraisals may be untrue or, if they are true, they may be unconvincing to the person being appraised. They lack objectivity. They lack predictability. Also when they directly affect the appraised person's economic interests—salary increases or management compensation plans—they can lead to dissatisfaction and bitterness.

Fair-minded executives, feeling that trait appraisals require them to toy with people's souls, tend to lean over backward by giving high trait ratings. In support of that thesis, a rating of Navy officers showed that some 98.5% were outstanding or excellent and only about 1% were average.(1) Trait-based measurements have therefore generally fallen into disrepute.

Many executives then replaced trait appraisals with evaluations "by the numbers." Certain mathematical goals are set for the manager and the worker, and accounting reports then determine whether the goals have been met. The method is obviously more objective. However, there is more to people and jobs than numbers and when managers have the numerical crutch to lean on, they may let the numbers do their deciding for them. Then only blacks and whites predominate. The person either reached the quantitative goal or didn't. Inequities, inconsistencies, and external forces are disregarded. The appraisal becomes a robot performance.

Enlightened management, however, has arrived at an amalgam in evaluating managers—and more particularly potential managers—that combines both objective appraisals of performance and judgements on the qualities of management. The managerial qualities cannot be overlooked. There is a temperament that resides in the true manager that is lacking in the technician. The superb technician can easily meet and exceed personal performance goals that are set for the average worker, but a manager must meet those goals through staff. The managerial temperament provides the aura of confidence that people feel and that makes them feel comfortable under their superiors. It is comparable to the judicial temperament that some able attorneys have and others have not: the ability to sift evidence quickly and surely, the ability to judge people, the ability to ask the right questions, the ability to make a quick decision—one that is usually correct—and then cleave to it.

Measurements for Managers

What, then, is a reasonable measurement for managers and for potential managers? Fundamentally, measurement is the ascertainment of the quantity or capacity of some well-defined entity. The entity must be identified. Its characteristics must be established. The units of measurement must be determined. Finally, a count must be made of how many times the unit is contained in the entity.

It sounds simple, but when the entity is a manager, a human being, the inherent capacities cannot be measured by such yardsticks. Yet *productivity* can be measured. Measuring characteristics in terms of production can be translated into determining how the individual manager did what was expected. This expectation can be translated into objectives, goals, policies, programs, indexes, and standards.

"Objective" stems from the Latin and is literally a thing thrown before the mind—some purpose to be gained. It is often general in character, and it is usually expressed in broad and qualitative terms extending over long periods. As an example, suppose we plan to increase our penetration into the world market of Texas-size belt buckles.

"Goal" stems from the French *gaule* —a "stick" or "pole." It has a tangible quantifiable connotation and governs a shorter, well-defined term: We plan to market 200 000 buckles in the coming fiscal year.

Plans and programs are the elements of work scheduled to achieve established goals: we will produce belt buckles in lots of 1000, using existing equipment; we will inspect them on a nondestructive basis; we will mount an advertising program in both developed and developing countries in selected media.

Indexes and input-output ratios are measures that are useful to managers in weighing performance. An input may be the number of sales calls; the related output the number of sales; and the input output index the sales per sale call. Similarly, an input may be the number of employees on the workforce; the output may be the number of employees leaving the organization; and the input-output index may be the employee turnover rate. In our present example, the ratio might be the number of belt buckles handled each hour by each worker producing the buckles.

Standards are the desired goals or measures—the ratios that the workers and the manager should equal or exceed. A worker should be able to produce 20 acceptable buckles an hour. The belt buckle production manager's workers should be able to produce 4000 acceptable belt buckles a week.

Each organization and each unit within the organization must develop its own objectives, goals, plans, programs, indexes, and standards. Then only to the extent that they are clearly understood, acceptable, and attainable will they be met by worker and manager.

Standards

The keystone in the structure of measurement is the standard—the statement of results expected of an operation, the yardstick by which performance will be measured. New factors are as important in weighing performance. For how are the worker, the manager, and the executive to know whether they have done a good job if they do not know what a good job is?

If standards are appropriately set, appraisals of performance become easier to make and are more readily accepted by the evaluator and the one evaluated. The unfairness of trait-based measurements is avoided. The capricious, subjective, often biased likes and dislikes are replaced by thoughtful judgements guided by reasonable standards.

Some standards are relatively easy to construct. In repetitive activities, for example time-and-motion studies supply measurable standards on clearly calibrated yardsticks. However, if an item is custom-made or requires a high degree of judgement to produce, effectiveness of performance is more difficult to measure. Managers may shy away from developing standards that cannot be readily quantified. There is little choice, however. If performance is to be objectively measured, then acceptable, reasonable, and usable standards must be set.

Tasks should be divided between quantitative (structured) and qualitative (nonstructured) work. The quantitative work can be measured; the qualitative

Table 10.1 Structured and Nonstructured Work in the processing cycle

Properties	Structured	Nonstructured
Input	Invariant; non disturbances to input	Variable; random disturbances
Processor	Machinelike	Man or man-machines system
Control	High reliability	Wide range of reliability
Output	Predictable; structure stable	Unpredictable; statistically unstable
Feedback	Self-organizing	Output not automatically reintroduced

work must be judged. Yet all processes, whether they are simple or complex, mechanical or thoughtful, have certain elements in common:

- The incoming work is received into the processor.
- The processor acts upon the work.
- The processor operates under certain controls or constraints.
- The work leaves the processor as "output."
- The results of the output produce a feedback mechanism that influences the input: satisfactory output will maintain or increase input; unsatisfactory output will have an adverse effect on input.

The nature of the work, quantitative-structured or qualitative nonstructured is generally evidenced by certain attributes in the processing cycle. Table 10.1 provides clues to those elements.

After its nature is determined, the job must be divided into manageable segments. As each segment is examined, it should be questioned:

- Why are we doing this job?
- How necessary is it to meet the established objectives for the job?
- What units capable of being measured or judged make up the segment?
- What is the hallmark of a job well done for this segment?
- How do the worker, supervisor, and manager know when the job is done well or poorly?

If at all possible, individuals whose work is to be measured should participate in the setting of both objectives and standards. Their willingness to be measured by the standards has a better chance of improving if they take part. That does not mean that their proposals or decisions will prevail. The manager must have the last word; for there rests the final responsibility. However, the worker or the subordinate manager can feel that thoughts, needs, and capacities have not been overlooked in the process.

The very process of setting standards can be beneficial. The job is analyzed; it is put in perspective relative to the entity's needs. There is dialogue between manager and subordinate. The purpose, importance, priority, and relations of the job to other jobs are explored. Ways of doing the job better, quicker, and more economically are bound to come up. The individual takes a fresh interest in and has an improved attitude toward the job.

For some jobs the task of setting measurable standards can be frustrating, but if enough thought is given, some criteria can be developed. After all, each job has some purpose, or else it should be eliminated. If that purpose can be defined and spelled out clearly, there will be some way to determine when the job is achieved efficiently and effectively. Often the boss may not be able to set relevant standards. However, if the manager enlists their aid, subordinates, those who are on the firing line and intimately know the work being performed, may be able to propose some kind of standards. True, the boss may have to review, change, add to, or even veto the proposal, but from the dialogue may emerge ways by which all can see whether efforts have achieved expected goals.

It is so much easier to measure that which is quantifiable that standards for the nonquantifiable or partially nonquantifiable are often ignored. Attention is then focused on what can be readily measured by the numbers and turned away from that which can not be. Yardsticks to measure the performance of a seamstress, a buyer, a salesperson or a draftsperson are readily constructed. On the other hand, performance yardsticks for a secretary, a doctor, a scientist, or a vice president of industrial relations are not easily calibrated. Yet the need for the objective measurement of such positions is as important as, or maybe even more important than, the need for measuring those previously mentioned.

Each job has its hallmarks, its techniques that can be performed well or badly, its elements which, when put together, show a goal to be achieved. Not all the elements are tangible or mechanical. The manager's job, for example, includes more than technical skills. The chief engineer in an aircraft company must be expert in the technical fields of aerodynamics, stress, weight, and producibility. In addition because the manager is responsible for the work of others, proficiency in the fields of planning, organizing, directing, and controlling is necessary.

Those elements are the heart and marrow of management. If the chief engineer is good at only the technical aspects this may be nothing more than an elevated technician, certainly not a manager. Requiring managers to be measured by standards related to the principles of management has the happy faculty of making better managers of them.

Appraisals

Setting standards without appraising results is like buying the groceries but not making the dinner. Appraisals represent the final purpose of the measurement process. They should not wait for the end of the job, however, or for the end of the year. Managers should probably be appraised at least every quarter against verifiable goals and standards. That which is going off track can be corrected more easily and economically than that which has left the rails entirely.

Appraisals call not only for the ability to compare one number with another but also for the application of wisdom and understanding. Often the standards and criteria—set for events in the future—may not have been accurately established. Unforeseen events, the unknown-unknowns, can provide 20-20 hindsight, but they can also result in unfair evaluations. The appraisal process calls not only for a review of performance but also for a look at the yardstick used to measure performance. Were the goals really attainable? Did unanticipated factors completely frustrate the attainment of goals thought reasonable when set? On the other hand, did luck play a part, so that under the circumstances the poorest of managers could have reached the promised goals?

Here is an example of the dangers of evaluating by the numbers without taking other relevant factors into account:

> A number of production control supervisors had been removed from their jobs for failing to set production schedules which would bring about scheduled deliveries and make the best use of facilities. The performance evaluation system in use had led to the transfer or dismissal of the supervisors because deliveries were late and facilities were ineffectively used.
>
> A frustrated management called in an independent agency to determine whether the computer could do a better job of scheduling. As in many computer feasibility studies, the analysis disclosed inherent defects that not even the computer could cure. It seemed that the manufacturing division comprised a number of sections, some of which did their own scheduling. From the managers of these sections the supervisor could get no adequate information. So when he prepared schedules for other divisions, he was working in the dark. He was being frustrated by an organizational deficiency. This was ultimately cured by a reorganization which put all production scheduling in his hands. Evaluations which took into account these frustrations could have pointed up the problem.

Appraisals, like other functions, do not sit in a vacuum. They too have purposes and the chief purpose is to improve performance. The purpose is not to demean or embarrass people, to exhibit biting wit and sarcasm, or to punish. The purpose is not to dwell on weaknesses but to underscore strengths for the greater good of the individual and the organization.

Evaluation, therefore, should be regarded by both the evaluator and the one evaluated as a learning process for development. This process works best when the evaluation focuses on the problem and not on the individual.

Financial Measurement

The financial branch of the organization is fortunate in dealing with a unit of measurement that is commonly accepted: the dollar, the pound, the franc, the yen, the mark, and the ruble, to name a few. Financial executives have a variety of financial yardsticks for measuring organizational performance. Ordinarily, measurement is applied to "divisions" within a company that represent responsibility centers having compatible products, services, and markets.

Measurements encompass both the manager and the operation for which he or she is responsible. The results of such measurements may be different. The measure of the operation is a mechanical one. The measure of the manager may have to take into account matters outside the manager's control, such as executive decisions, fire, flood, strikes, and shortages. Commonly used yardsticks and some problems in their application are, very briefly, as follows:

- *Profit as a percentage of sales.* Along with sales increases and decreases, profit as a percentage of sales is probably the most commonly used index of financial health. It is readily available and easily comparable with forecasts and similar figures for prior periods. However, it has little usefulness in comparing the results of one division with those of another or determining true profitability in each division. Yet it can be a useful early-warning system.

- *Return on investment.* Although return on investment is considered a simple and valuable measure of operating efficiency, in practice the variants in use can make its application quite complex. Yet within the total organization, common methods should apply to all the divisions of the organization. Some companies tend to oversimplify ROI computations, particularly when investments, fixed-asset valuations, and controllable and noncontrollable expenses are concerned. That may make for easier understanding by the executive, but statistical accuracy may be reduced. Some middle ground needs to be established.

- *Residual income.* As a profitability index, residual income answers the complaint that ROI induces divisional managers to emphasize the *ratio* of profits to investments and underplay the *total* of dollar profits. Hence the managers may abandon projects that promise increased earnings but will show small ratios. Residual income, however, is an index that shows the dollar contribution to the corporate weal. It is computed by allocating to each division the organization's current cost of capital and determining the consequent positive or negative amount of divisional residual income. Emphasis on residual incomes ties in directly with the organization's objective to maximize earnings on stockholders' equity.

- *Earnings per share.* The earnings per share index is concerned with the appeal that the company's stock carries with its investors and in the marketplace. Certainly, the executive gives high priority to improving return on investment and raising the profit level. However, good market performance cannot be overlooked, and concern with earnings per share will direct the executive spotlight toward the larger problems. More current attention should be given to a division that accounts for two-thirds of the company's earnings, but has low profitability, than to a profitable division that accounts for but a small fraction of the company's profit per share.

- *Cash flow per share.* In a manner similar to earnings per share, cash flow per share figures are computed by dividing divisional cash flow by the number of the company's outstanding common shares. The device can be useful in determining which division is contributing most to the company's well-being.

A sustained high cash flow is a good index of satisfactory contribution. The cash flow per share yardstick is receiving increased attention because reported profit may have questionable validity as a result of the relative elasticity of "generally accepted accounting principles" and the application of "creative accounting." For example, depreciation allowances may often be considered inadequate because they are based on original asset costs and may not cover actual replacement costs. On the other hand, maintenance costs charged to current expense keep current facilities in repair and prolong their life. Hence, depreciation costs in terms of cash flow per share, as they affect reported profitability, have no relevance.

All these yardsticks have their uses, but, like any other measurement devices, they need careful interpretation. When management performance is appraised, variances must be evaluated by whether they are controllable by the manager.

MEASUREMENT AND INTERNAL AUDITORS

Standards

Within the scope of measurement and appraisal, internal auditors can contribute to organizational performance in two ways:

1. By measuring their own performance so that they may improve efficiency and effectiveness.
2. By providing executives with new means of measuring the administrative health of the organization.

Internal auditing has its own criteria and standards of excellence. The truly professional internal auditing organization makes them known to its people and measures the performance of its personnel against them. The subjects covered are planning the audit project, organizing the work, directing and carrying out the audit steps, controlling the audit resources, and reporting the audit results. For each of those subjects there are criteria for judgement and standards for measurement. For example, some criteria calling for objective judgements from an audit supervisor are as follows:

- Were audit programs geared to the key objectives of the operations audited?
- Were working papers developed in a professional manner?
- Were all audit findings fully developed in terms of determining operating standards, gathering facts, evaluating effects, assessing causes, and recommending improvements?
- Were audit man-hours expended only on material matters?
- Was the audit report properly supported by the evidence accumulated in the working papers?

- Was corrective action taken or initiated during the audit?
- Were cooperative relations maintained with the auditee?

Some of the standards that the supervisor can use to measure the work of the auditor quantitatively are these:

- Was each programmed audit step carried out or otherwise accounted for?
- Were working papers accurately and completely cross-referenced?
- Was the approved audit report format employed?
- Was the audit accomplished within the work-days budgeted?
- Was the audit completed by the scheduled due dates?

Appraisals

The director of internal auditing can make use of all the objectives, goals, and standards to appraise the organization and to permit executive management to appraise its performance. Such performance appraisals can be presented in oral and formal performance reports that say: "Here are the matters that, with your knowledge and concurrence, we set out to do; and here is what we accomplished."

The value of performance appraisals can be enhanced by imagination and innovation. Through performance reports, the director of internal auditing can not only appraise accomplishments but also use the opportunity to provide executive management with objective summaries of information not elsewhere available: information on the administrative health of the entire organization with which top management can apply new yardsticks of performance to appraise its operating managers.

Executive managers receive reports on the entity's financial health. The reports are developed by the controller's organization and are validated by the external accountant. Ordinarily there is no counterpart to those reports to cover evaluations of other operations in the organization.

However, because internal auditors make wide-ranging appraisals of operations, they are in a position to offer objective, quantitative indexes of the entity's operating performance. Each of the internal audit reports normally expresses an opinion. That opinion may be favorable or unfavorable. (See Chapter 9, Communications). The opinions are most likely supported by audit findings, but the opinions of the findings are indexes of the effectiveness of the operations reviewed, and they can be arrayed quantitatively according to area and subject matter. The array can be given additional meaning if comparisons among divisions of the entity and against operations performed in prior years are made. Trends portrayed by graphs can be particularly helpful.

Appraisals of administrative health can be made especially useful to management by pointing to the causes of deficiencies described in the audit reports. A host of defects haphazardly listed can portray serious weaknesses within the organization, but they can also be confusing and valueless to executives concerned with the

Table 10.2 Causes of Deficiencies

Cause	Number
Planning	
Need for control not recognized	55
Management decision not to take action	50
Failure to develop policies and procedures	40
Organizing	
Failure to assign appropriate authority	60
Failure to assign appropriate responsibility	50
Failure to assign appropriate priorities	30
Failure to assign sufficient personnel	5
Failure to provide adequate equipment	5
Directing	
Failure to provide coordination	60
Failure to provide adequate training	55
Poor morale	5
Controlling	
Insufficient management attention	60
Failure to see that standards are met	40
Failure to obtain feedback	20
Human error	10
Employee attitude	5
Total	550

steps needed to correct the basic problems. If, however, the listing emphasizes the causes, the reasons, and the endemic difficulties, then they may aid executives in planning for improvement and in decision making.

For example, assume that internal audit reports described 550 different deficiencies during the past year. Let us also assume that the individual defects had been corrected during the audits or soon thereafter. However, in the background may lurk a basic problem that is not being corrected because it is not being addressed, and executive management is not addressing the problem because the problem has not been identified.

Let us suppose the internal auditing organization were to classify the 550 deficiencies according to cause and were to report them to top management, under the four functions of management, as shown in Table 10.2. The signposts raised by the causes listed point unmistakably to operating managers who are not carrying out their management functions. Whether sales are good or profits are high or return on investment seems satisfactory, the fact remains that conditions could be still better if managers were doing their job of managing. The individual deficiencies must have had an adverse effect on costs and profitability, and the catalog of causes hints why.

Measuring Operations

If internal auditors are to perform a management-oriented audit, they must think like a manager; they must structure audits along management lines. Hence, they must be concerned with the same tools, the same principles, and the same methods that competent managers use when examining their own performances.

The internal auditor's first job, therefore, is to identify as specifically as possible the objectives of the organization being reviewed: the organization's purpose, reason for being, and desired contribution to the well-being of the entire entity. This is not as simple as it sounds. Many an internal auditor—and manager as well—confuses objectives with activities. The resulting audit is then designed to see whether the activities are being carried out in accordance with established procedures.

However, this is not the be-all and end-all of internal auditing; it would not satisfy the able executive who installed internal auditing in the organization. What the executive expects to learn from the internal auditor is whether the operations under review *achieved their objectives* and, incidentally, whether those objectives were achieved efficiently and economically. Clearly, then, the first step is to learn what the objectives are. If the objective of an accounts payable operation is regarded simply as processing invoices for payment, the ensuing audit may probably be restricted to matching invoices with receiving memos and purchase orders and verifying signatures evidencing executive approvals for services.

A different audit might result if the true objectives are identified and used in the audit appraisal. Those objectives may be regarded as follows: to process for payment what is due when due; distribute expenditures to appropriate accounts; and facilitate conservation of the organization's funds.

Seen in that light, the audit may take a different turn. The auditor may start asking questions that are management-oriented and keyed to the operation's central objectives. For example:

- How do people who sign invoices for services assure themselves that the services have actually been received?
- What studies have been made to determine the point at which lost discounts are counterbalanced by improved cash flow?
- How are accounts payable clerks instructed on account distributions and changes in the charts of account, and how is the accuracy of account distributions monitored?
- How promptly does accounts payable receive copies of purchase order change notices from the purchasing department?
- Should feasibility studies be undertaken to computerize the accounts payable function?
- What contacts have been made with companies using the computer for accounts payable processing?

The usual detailed verifications are still appropriate. Indeed, they are essential.

However, if the audit were to stop there, some important insights might be lost.

Even so simple a matter as petty cash is elevated to a management view if the true objectives are identified. The objective is more than making cash available for small purchases. It will include that, of course, but the complete statement might make the auditor's thoughts rise above paper verifications. For example, the objectives of petty cash may be to:

- Provide cash for expenditures too small to warrant application of formal disbursement procedures. (The auditor should know when the cost of controls over formal disbursements warrants the use of petty cash funds instead.)
- Restrict funds to an amount that will cover normal expenditures. (The auditor should determine what is normal and what is the least amount of petty cash needed to meet normal needs.)
- Provide funds for a reasonable period. (The auditor should determine the optimum period between replenishments of the funds.)

The list of activities in the fields of human endeavour is almost endless. The practices and the circumstances may differ widely, but in each case the audit approach must be the same: the first and most important step is to determine, in concert with the manager, what the manager's objectives are or should be. Once the objectives have been identified, the internal auditor must determine the means devised or needed to achieve them and the controls needed to see that what has been planned will indeed come to pass.

For example, one of the objectives of the purchasing organization is to buy goods and services at the right price. One of the means of achieving this objective is a system of competitive bids, when they are appropriate, from acceptable suppliers. The system of control needed to see that the objective is met may include a bidder's list of suppliers who have been approved for quality and financial stability. Another is the requirement that supervisors review requests for bids to see that all appropriate bidders have been asked to bid. Still another is the requirement that all requests to bid be mailed and all bids obtained be received by someone other than the buyer. Those precautions provide assurance that the buyer will not play favorites by discarding some requests to bid before mailing them and some submitted bids after receiving them.

The audit measurement process is completed when the auditor examines a representative sample of purchases to determine whether the system is working as intended and evaluates any deviations for materiality and cause. Findings are then brought to the attention of management and, as the case may be, either provides assurance that the system is a good one and is working effectively or recommends improvements to prevent the recurrence of any significant deviations from acceptable standards of control and performance.

The internal auditor generally uses four standards in measuring performance. A brief discussion of each follows, along with examples of actual audit findings that relate to the standards.

1. *Effectiveness.* Is the operation that is being performed necessary to the objectives of the unit and the organization? Does it mesh with the overall organizational objectives? Is it the right operation to meet those objectives? And is it meeting them?

> An internal auditor investigated production control practices because of production line stoppages; in other words, production control was not meeting its objective of keeping the line moving on schedule. It was found that the dispatching of material to the line was not being controlled. For example, materials were being sent to the wrong areas, and nobody was checking bins for adequate supplies until shortages occurred. New orders were being placed to cover line shortages. Using investigations the auditor was able to locate and put into use parts whose replacement would have cost $220 000. As a result of the auditor's recommendations, the production control procedures were overhauled and improved.

2. *Compliance.* Are operations conducted in accordance with applicable policies, procedures, and instruction? And are such directives still valid to meet current organizational objectives?

> An internal auditor was verifying compliance with procedures set forth in a manual dealing with emergency situations. The manual called for specific assignments to individuals designated by name. The internal auditor found that three of the 25-man squad of security people were no longer employed. Of ten men questioned, only two had adequate knowledge of their responsibilities and only five had copies of the manual. Meetings were to be held every six months to review practices and procedures. Seven of those questioned said that they had never attended a meeting, and three said that there had been no meetings in three years. No one could remember a fire-drill. The internal auditor was unable to report savings in terms of dollars, but his report of conditions sent a chill through top management and prompted speedy corrective action.

3. *Efficiency.* Are the resources of people, money, and materials being used and managed with the least possible waste and extravagance? Are operations being carried out in a manner best calculated to achieve desired results?

> An internal auditor was evaluating the need for preemployment physical examinations. During a period of 18 months, 7 025 examinations were given at a cost of $380 000. Only 35 applicants had been rejected, and 18 of the 35 were rejected for pregnancy and varicose veins. The remaining 17 were rejected for heart trouble and high blood pressure. At the internal auditor's suggestion, the medical history questionnaire was expanded to obtain an indication of potentially serious problems, and examinations were required only in those cases. Savings were estimated at $170 000 a year.

4. *Economy.* Are operations being carried out in the least expensive way while still meeting acceptable standards and the objectives set?

> An internal auditor asked a transportation manager the reason why all trucks were equipped with four-wheel drives; the internal auditor saw no logical reason for such equipment for the entire fleet, since most of the work was being performed on paved roads or flat terrain. As a result of the questions, the transportation manager

established a policy of equipping 50% of the fleet with two-wheel drive and 50% with four-wheel drive. Savings amounted to $2.7 million a year.

Management Inventories

A periodic summary report to management on the administrative health of the organization can point to incipient or widespread ailments. Almost invariably, the major causes of defects are management-related. People who are elevated to management jobs don't always know how to manage.

In each audit, the internal auditor deals with managers and supervisors, develops organization charts, evaluates productivity, becomes acquainted with management strengths and weaknesses, and assesses the capability of employees now and for the future. As a result of in-depth analysis of operations, the internal auditor develops some shrewd impressions of the inventory of both managers and workers. Certainly, it is not within the auditor's responsibility to report formally on evaluations of individuals. Such evaluations are the responsibility of the individual's supervisor.

Besides, if the internal auditor started reporting on individuals, there would be antagonisms and hostility that would make the internal audit task almost impossible to accomplish. On the other hand, as a counselor to operating managers the internal auditor could point informally to the desirability of developing, within a department, branch, or division, a management inventory. The inventory would specify a backup for each significant position—insurance that the loss of an individual would not result in the collapse of a function. For example:

> In an audit of personnel services, an internal auditor found that the task of dealing with wage garnishments and credit letters was the responsibility of one employee, who acted without supervision because nobody knew anything about her job. The manager was unconcerned because the employee was doing a superb job. She was handling some 160 garnishments, 5 summonses and complaints, and over 500 credit letters a month. She dealt with company counsel, marshals, and sheriffs, and she knew them all by name. She had a complete and detailed working knowledge of what was involved in the often complex actions, including the relevant legal aspects. She had grown with the job and she handled it competently and knowledgeably. But everything she knew was stored in her head. Not another individual in the company, including the company's legal counsel, had any idea of the steps required to carry out the varied phases of her job. She had not recorded or imparted to anyone else what was needed to perform her tasks. When she was on vacation or was ill, the work simply piled up until she returned to her desk. Her death or separation from the company would have resulted in utter chaos.
>
> The internal auditor, in appraising the activity, made a detailed flow chart of the steps required to carry out the employee's function. He then presented it to the department manager and suggested that it be used to develop a manual for the garnishment and credit letter function. He further suggested that the indispensable employee be assisted by another employee, if only on a temporary basis, to learn the system and forestall catastrophe in the event the key employee went elsewhere.

In another situation, an internal auditor, reviewing a facilities engineering function, observed that 85% of the people in the department were within five years of mandatory retirement. For some reason, the chief facilities engineer, who was abundantly aware of the condition, had not communicated the potential problem to his own superior. The audit report corrected that defect and resulted in a more appropriate mix of ages in the department.

Besides the appraisals of people inventories conducted during regular audits, the director of internal auditing might offer to conduct a management study throughout the organization to see whether key positions are backed up with knowledgeable replacements and executive management is supplied with an up-to-date record of its management inventory.

Financial Measurement

The yardsticks of financial ratios discussed earlier in this chapter are useful tools, but like any other tools they must be sharp and they must be accurate. Most important, the results must be properly interpreted.

The data used by executive management in connection with financial measurement come from accounting and financial records translated into summary reports. The reports are put together by human beings or summarized from computer printouts. The probabilities of error, missing data, misinterpretation of instructions, and misconceptions of management needs represent an ever present danger.

Hence one of the functions of internal auditors is to keep a watchful eye on the matter of information gathering and reporting. Auditors will want to know if people developing information are aware of the purposes and uses of the reports they are putting together. They will want to examine the worksheets used and see how accurate they are. They will be concerned with cross-checks and failsafe mechanisms to insure accuracy. They will make sure people are employing such simple but important techniques as initialling and dating the working papers they develop so that accountability is assured. The internal auditor's job, reduced to essentials, is measurement. Managers should find the internal auditor an expert ally in honing its own measurement techniques.

CONCLUSION

The ability to manage is important, but how well employees perform to meet goals is the true measure of the manager. Performance is the key. To learn how individuals perform, whether manager or workers, it is necessary to determine what people are supposed to do and how well they are supposed to do it. That calls for objectives and goals and for criteria and standards. Only then can people's individual performance be measured objectively both by themselves and by others. The criteria are usually qualitative and must be judged. The standards are usually quantitative and can be measured. Established financial measurements are employed to measure profit performance of an organization. Each of the forms of measurement has its uses and its weaknesses.

Internal auditing is an operation that can measure and be measured in terms of goals and standards. The program of internal audits can also produce indications of the administrative health of the organization through summaries of audit opinions and audit findings. The internal auditor's standards of measurement must take into account the objectives and goals of the operation reviewed, and the audits should be designed to measure effectiveness, compliance, efficiency, and economy. The internal auditor can provide an important service for management in assessing management and people inventories and in assuring the accuracy of financial measurements.

REFERENCES

(1) Harold Koontz and Heinz Weihrich, *Management* (New York: McGraw-Hill, 1988) p. 343.

─── 11 ───
Scientific Methods

SCIENTIFIC METHODS AND MANAGERS

The Complaints

Many a disgruntled manager, after failing to reap expected benefits from quantitative analysis, has growled. "This new-fangled management science is a lot of malarkey." This may have been justified. The high hopes for applying systems methodology, long used in the physical sciences, to management decision making and planning have often gone aglimmering. The dreams that mathematical formulas and computers will replace managerial decisions may have vanished with the cold dawn of unredeemed promises.

To understand the purposes and limitations of "management science." we should first put the term in perspective. Management science, or operations research, seek to solve business and economic problems mathematically. The approach is generally through models that represent the operation or system being examined. The model is usually reduced to mathematical formulas that seek to take into account all relevant variables. The number of variables in a business situation often makes the formula so complex that it can be solved only with the aid of computers. And the ordinary manager, faced with the awesome combination of arcane formulas and mysterious computers, either abdicates managerial responsibilities to the scientists or avoids the scientists altogether.

Early Models

Actually, management science, formulas, and models are not new-fangled. One scientific method reaches back into the fourteenth century, and managers have been using it ever since. Through the years it has remained a powerful and indispensable servant. The formula associated with the method is:

$$Assets - liabilities = owner\ equity$$

The model is double-entry bookkeeping. It is simple, symmetrical, logical, and beautiful. It is not the enterprise itself, the concrete and steel and blood and brains of the physical plant and its people. But it is an accurate representation of the financial structure made in quantitative terms.

The Difficulties

Many problems come equipped with enough variables and interrelations to call for mathematics that exceed the grasp of most managers, even those who can be termed mathematically literate. In fact, John von Neumann, a mathematical genius, discovered that his awesome mathematical limits were soon reached during his development of the game theory.

However, a manager does not have to be a bookkeeper or a mathematician any more than an author has to know how to construct a typewriter. Anyone can use a tool without knowing how to build it, but should know what the tool can or cannot do. The double-entry system will not foretell the future. If properly used, it will accurately portray the past. It will tell of past profits, losses, receipts, and disbursements. That information can provide the base from which the manager—not the double-entry system—will seek to anticipate what is yet to come. Scientific management can provide answers to appropriate questions, but the manager will have to ask the questions.

Uses of Operations Research

Some companies have been successfully using operations research (OR) methods; among them are American Airlines, AT&T, Chase Manhattan, Du Pont, Eastman Kodak, General Electric, General Motors, Gulf Oil, Metropolitan Life Insurance, US Steel, and Xerox. All have saved thousands of dollars through the scientific approach, and the approach has other benefits as well. The structured method gives managers insights that are not gained from intuitive, darts-at-a-dart-board decisions. The approach, which categorizes the OR methodology, is as follows:

1. State the problem. Articulate the objective of the search. Identify the variables, both those within management's control and those that are uncontrollable. Determine the constraints under which the operation functions, such as limits of productive capacity and lack of qualified personnel. Often the exercise of thinking through the problem in such a fashion can remove blinders from the manager's eyes or at least alert the manager to the difficulties to be faced.
2. Build a model. The model, in mathematical terms, should represent the real system. There are basically three types of models that represent systems:
(i)   The *iconic* is a scaled reproduction, like a model bridge or a model railway.

(ii) The *analog* portrays one kind of property by another property that is graphic in character, like solid or broken lines on a map representing different kinds of roads.

(iii) The *symbolic* is portrayed in mathematical terms. Symbolic models are most used in OR work and are constructed by mathematicians. However, the input, the probabilities that some things will or will not happen in the real world, must be supplied by the experienced manager or by consultants such as economists, industrial engineers, and actuaries.

3. Test the model, Try various values, subject to control, to see what the results would be. Too often what shines on paper fades in real life. So the model should be applied to known, proven historical data to see if the results derived from it are the same as those determined from actual experience. Make any needed revisions as a result of the tests.

4. Put the model to work. Obtain alternative solutions to the problem for which the model was designed. The reliability of the solution will, of course, depend on how faithfully the model represents the real system. Select the best solution among the alternatives.

5. Put the solution into effect. Apply it to the system. Determine its effectiveness. See if it has indeed fulfilled its promise. Then, most importantly, update it as needed; changed conditions must be incorporated in the model to represent the changed system.

Opportunities Available Through OR

The What-If Questions

If the manager and the scientist fully understand their own and each other's role, OR can be a powerful tool. Farseeing managers, looking over the horizon of a year or a decade, are constantly asking themselves the what-if question. What if we reduced prices? What if we increased prices? What if we changed credit terms? What if we located a warehouse in Ashtabula? What if we closed our warehouse in Cucamonga? What if we phased out our product X? What if we changed our product mix? The assumptions could, of course, be put to work immediately by executive edict, or they could be tested. Testing assumptions can be an important service that the management scientist can render for managers. However, the manager must ask the question and work with the scientist to make sure there is complete agreement on objectives.

The fact that the manager has asked it does not make a question the right one. The scientist, in concert with the manager, must make sure the right question has been asked before putting to work the extensive, expensive process of quantitative analysis. The manager may have asked, "What if we were to mechanize the costly manual inventory system in warehouse D?" Perhaps the question that needed asking is: "What if we eliminated warehouse D altogether?"

Managers are the ultimate decision makers. They should not, therefore, seek solutions from the OR scientist. They should ask for alternatives together with the risks attached to each. The scientist provides numerical responses. The manager must weigh each response in terms of its effect on the entire enterprise—its aims, its people, and its responsibilities. That is hardly a job for the scientist.

The manager should seek understanding rather than formulas and mathematical answers. When understanding the results of the scientist's work, the manager retains command and responsibility, which can never be delegated or abdicated.

In the subsections that follow, some of the more common forms of quantitative analysis are described.

Regression Analysis

Regression analysis is the most widely used analytical technique for describing relations among variables. It measures the change in one variable when one or more related variables change. Simple regression is applied to the study of two variables; multiple regression relates to three or more variables.

Regression analysis is based on the principle that one variable, called the independent variable, will affect the behavior of a dependent variable. For example, there is a direct relation between packaging costs and the volume of packaged items. Increase the production of packaged items (the independent variable) and the packaging costs (the dependent variable) should increase because, clearly, there are more items to package. Hence, regression analysis would help the manager predict packaging costs at varying levels of production. Whenever there is a consistent relation between two or more variables, regression analysis can be used.

Standard computer programs are available to compute both simple and multiple-regression analyses. The technique has been used to:

- Study price behavior.
- Forecast general and administrative rates.
- Analyze market demand for a product.

However, the manager must be aware of the controls needed and the hazards attendant upon the use of regression analysis.

The reliability of the relation shown by regression analysis must be tested. The degree of correlation between the variables is measured by the coefficient of determination. A high coefficient shows good correlation; a low coefficient shows poor correlation. However, there are hazards even in determining reliability. An apparent high correlation can be the result of too few observations made during the analysis, and there is always the possibility that two or more sets of observations may indicate a relation when in fact no such relation exists. As in all things, the manager must apply judgement and experience to see whether the results presented by the scientists agree with expectations and make sense in the real world.

Relations that existed in the past may not persist in the future; external constraints may alter them. The manager working with the scientist must evaluate the validity of the relations and be satisfied that what was true yesterday will be equally true tomorrow. Constraints like inflation, potential government controls, unavailability of materials, and discontinued demand must be considered.

Probability Theory

In many cases the value of one or more variables is not known, yet decisions must be made despite uncertainty as to outcomes. By using probability theory, the manager can estimate the likelihood that the value of the variables will be at certain levels.

For example, based on experience, a manager can estimate that there is a 75% probability that demand for a product will exceed $25 000 in December and only a 25% chance that it will exceed that amount in January. Using such estimates does not remove the risk, but it points out the degree of risk the manager faces and offers a guide that may help him minimize the hazards.

In making use of probability theory, the steps are usually these:

1. Identify the available choices open to the manager.

   Example
   Produce one of three products, since facilities are not available for all three. Product X will appeal primarily to the mass market, product Y to the middle-class market, and product Z to the upper-class market.

2. Determine the probable result of each choice.

   Example
   Net profits for each product are estimated as follows:

Choices	Mass	Middle	Upper
Product X	$100 000	$30 000	$10 000
Product Y	16 000	100 000	30 000
Product Z	10 000	50 000	150 000

3. Assign probabilities to the achievement of the net profits, based on judgement and experience; that is, assign the probability of achieving profits from each of the three markets.

   Example

Choices	Probability
Mass	.5
Middle	.3
Upper	.2

4. Calculate the expected value of the estimated results by multiplying each expected profit by the probability of achieving it. Then sum the results.

Example

Choices	Mass	Middle	Upper	Expected Result
Product X	$50 000	$9 000	$2 000	$61 000
Product Y	8 000	30 000	6 000	44 000
Product Z	5 000	15 000	30 000	50 000

5. Select the choice with the highest estimated result.

Example

Product X appears to be the most likely choice, based on estimated profits and the likelihood of achieving those profits in the three markets.

In real life the problems and choices are much more complex; here the example has been made arithmetically simple for the purposes of illustration. In some applications of probability theory, a decision tree is used. The branches springing from the trunk—in the case just discussed there would be three branches—display alternative results and the probabilities of meeting them in graphic form that is more easily visualized.

Certainly, an exercise in probability theory would not be warranted when the amounts involved are small, but the theory is now being put to use in industry. For example, at General Electric all investment requests exceeding $500 000 must be accompanied by an assessment of the probabilities of success. Ford, Du Pont, and General Mills also use probability theory as an aid to decision making.

Queuing Theory

The queuing theory, also called the waiting-line theory, helps managers decide how to staff service facilities. It has been used in providing optimum service at minimum cost whenever "customers" must wait in line for some form of service: at banks, tool cribs, loading docks, supermarket checkout stands, hospital clinics, insurance adjusting offices, repair departments, and the like. Too few attendants can result in customer dissatisfaction or customer idle time. Too many attendants can be unnecessarily costly and inefficient.

Actual experience is used in queuing theory computations: the rate at which customers arrive and the time required to serve each customer. The information needed can be gained by observation with the use of stopwatches, and the sample results can be projected to estimates that provide reasonably sound bases for determining staffing and facility needs.

Monte Carlo Simulation

In many cases, analytical solutions based on observed data—as in queuing theory—are impossible because the data are unavailable or too expensive to obtain. It is therefore necessary to simulate actual conditions.

For example, in a large city, data on the frequency and length of telephone calls may be extremely difficult to accumulate. Accordingly, a model is developed. The number and length of telephone calls are simulated by using random digits that correspond to the random placing of telephone calls. In earlier days, experimenters used modified roulette wheels to estimate the expected frequency of events, hence the term Monte Carlo. Recently random-number tables have been used.

Here is an example of the use of Monte Carlo simulation:

> In a supermarket the manager could determine from records the expected sales volume of quarts of milk. But it was impossible to know how the demand by customers fluctuates over a period of days, weeks, or months. By using the Monte Carlo method, random digits for moments in the period under study would simulate the random customer demand and help the manager decide on the amounts of milk he should have available at all times.

Linear Programming

Resources in any entity are rarely, if ever, unlimited. Managers must decide how to allocate limited resources of staff, money, materials, and equipment to provide the best contribution to earnings. Managers must determine what their objective is—maximize profit or minimize cost, for example—and then solve the problem by mathematics. Linear programming helps solve the resource allocation problem, but the problem must have certain characteristics.

1. A stated objective.

Example
To reduce transportation costs between factories and warehouses when a company's factories must deliver to scattered warehouses.

2. Resources are limited and can be put to alternative uses.

Example
Several factories, each with a maximum output capacity, must deliver goods to a number of warehouses, each with minimum requirements.

3. The elements of the problem must be subject to quantitative measurement.

Example
The factory outputs are known. The warehouse needs are known. and the cost of transportation from each of the factories to each of the warehouses is known.

4. The relation must be linear; that is, all elements must be proportional.

Example
A 12% increase in the distance shipped must cause a 12% increase in transportation costs.

The H. J. Heinz Company was one of the first firms in the United States to use linear programming. It was distributing products from six plants located throughout the country to 70 warehouses that were widely scattered. One of the difficulties was that, in the eastern half of the country, demand exceeded production capacity and, in the western half, capacity exceeded demand. When it substituted linear programming for seat-of-the-pants allocations, H. J. Heinz saved thousands of dollars in freight bills.

Inventory Management Techniques

Decisions on inventory are common to most entities in varying degrees. Retailers must maintain stocks of goods to meet customer needs. Manufacturers must maintain stocks of raw materials, parts, and finished products. Offices must maintain stocks of stationery. Hospitals must maintain stocks of medical supplies. Lack of needed inventory can result in loss of customers, line stoppage, or serious dislocations. Excess inventory results in unnecessary investments in goods and in excessive storage space, handling costs, insurance, spoilage, and shrinkage.

Somewhere a balance must be struck because, as every manager knows, as order quantity increases, order costs drop and inventory costs rise, and vice versa. The goal of inventory management, then, is to minimize the total of all associated costs: both the costs of carrying inventories and the costs of not carrying them. Hence the inventory manager has two decisions to make: how much to order, and when to place orders. In deciding how much to order the manager must consider:

1. Needs for a period of time–month, quarter, year.
2. Setup costs—issuing purchase orders for procured materials or setting up equipment for production runs of manufactured products.
3. The costs associated with carrying the items for the need period

In deciding when to order, the manager must consider:

1. Lead time—the period between placing the order and receiving the goods.
2. The demand for the goods during the lead time period.
3. How sure he is that the lead time and demand can be reliably forecast.

Formulas are available for determining economic quantities, lead time, carrying costs, and stock-out costs.

Breakeven Analysis

To assess the effects of alternative courses of action, managers often use breakeven models. The models relate total cost to total revenue. The values are recorded on a chart, and the point at which benefits equal costs is the breakeven point. After that point, when fixed costs have been absorbed, profits begin to expand with increased output. Breakeven charts are useful in determining:

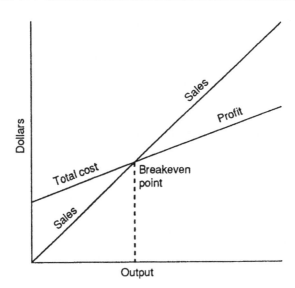

Figure 11.1 Breakeven Chart

- The possible effect of raising or lowering prices.
- Effects of changed plant capacity.
- Whether a new product should be added or an old one dropped.
- Whether a firm should lease or purchase a fleet of cars for salesmen.

Any situation that permits a plotting of costs versus anticipated benefits can make use of breakeven charts, but the charts do have limitations. They may not be useful for long-term decisions, since costs that are stable in the short term may very likely vary over the long term. They may not provide reliable information when the environment is dynamic and fluid. A simplified breakeven chart is shown in Figure 11.1.

Network Analysis

Managers often find it necessary to control complex, interrelated systems that are nonrecurrent, as in large programs or projects. They need control measures to insure coordination, to see that essential steps are not forgotten, and to make certain that step A will be completed before step B begins. That need gave rise to the demand for some means of visualizing the system. A view of the network of steps and actions can disclose places where resources can be redeployed and both cost and time can be reduced.

Network models make use of a set of points connected by lines. The paths indicated by the lines represent the work to be performed to achieve system goals. The network can be useful in controlling projects involving many activities that must be coordinated or must be completed before other activities take place.

Two networks to assist management were devised at about the same time: 1957 and 1958. The Program Evaluation and Review Technique (PERT) was developed by a team of experts from Lockheed and Booz, Allen & Hamilton and was used on the Polaris project. Originally, PERT was chiefly concerned with time. It is designed for projects in which time spans are uncertain. The network emphasizes events. Cost was not considered, but for the Polaris project PERT helped cut two years from the scheduled span, so cost reduction most likely did result.

The Critical Path Method (CPM) was developed by operations researchers from E.I. du Pont de Nemours & Company and the Univac division of the then Remington Rand organization. CPM's purpose was to help schedule and control activities concerned with constructing chemical plants. It is used when there is reasonable certainty as to time spans, and it emphasizes activities. Cost is a major concern in CPM networks. As the name implies, the path is critical because a delay in the completion of any activity in the path can mean a delay in meeting project objectives.

PERT and CPM models have common elements and are developed in much the same way.

1. Define the objective to be achieved.
2. Specify the time and/or cost factors that must be controlled.
3. Determine the order in which tasks are to be accomplished.
4. Estimate the time required to complete each activity.
5. Design the network.

Clearly, the network, as a management tool, is useful only in complex projects. Also, the manager must understand that the model's success is contingent upon the reliability of the information on which the network is based and an understanding of the methodology. Often, the discipline required to plan PERT and CPM networks can have significant benefits without going through the mathematics.

Other Techniques

Other quantitative techniques, less well known, have been used as management tools. Some of them are as follows:

- *Dynamic programming* is termed a "maximization theory." It is used when a whole series of states of action take place and a decision on each state is dependent on the decision made on the preceding state. It permits a mathematical determination of the period-by-period consequences of decisions. It can be used to calculate the desirability of incurring temporary losses for the sake of long-term gains. For example, through dynamic programming a manager could calculate the benefits of expanding large sums on research and development and incurring losses during the immediate period in the hope of making much greater profits in later periods.

- *Game theory* is used to establish a basis for decisions in a competitive environment. It takes into account the consequences of the action by one party upon the actions of an opponent who is choosing from among alternatives. Game theory goes beyond the classical theory of probability, which is limited to pure chance. In game theory, strategic aspects, that is, aspects controlled by the participants, are stressed. The theory is therefore well adapted to the study of competition in which there are present several common factors such as conflicting interests, incomplete information, the interplay of rational decisions, and chance.
- *Exponential smoothing* is used to correlate later values with earlier ones in the same series. It is used to base predictions on past observations and give the greatest weight to the latest observations. It can be applied to determining the production of optimum lot sizes to meet forecasted sales.
- *Markov process,* like regression analysis, is based on mathematical probability principles and combines objective fact and subjective judgement. The process has been used in market research, hospital planning, and reliability engineering.
- *Sensitivity analysis* is used in connection with linear planning. In formulating and solving linear programming problems, we make certain assumptions, at least initially. It is assumed that all values of the coefficients are derived from the analysis of data and that they represent average values or best-estimate values. Accordingly, the method is useful in analyzing the sensitivity of the solution to variation in the coefficients or estimates of the coefficients. Said differently, we seek to determine the ranges of variations of the coefficients over which the solution will remain optimal.

SCIENTIFIC METHODS AND THE INTERNAL AUDITOR

The Benefits

Quantitative analysis gives internal auditors a chance to help themselves and the organization's managers. They can help executives and managers by verifying the data used in scientific decision making, validating quantitative techniques, providing protection against the misuse of mathematical procedures to the detriment of his organization, and recommending appropriate techniques.

The modern internal auditor has a working knowledge of mathematical analysis. Work throughout the organization and familiarity with the computer show the internal auditor how to put that knowledge to practical use.

Statistical Sampling

Audit Sampling

Auditors have for years sampled transactions instead of examining all of them. From the sample results they have drawn conclusions about the population of interest to them: all the travel vouchers or shipping tickets or sales slips or receiving memos or purchase orders or cancelled checks or requisitions for some specified period. The auditors knew that there was a risk in sampling, but they were willing to take the risk in deference to the shortness of life and the limit on funds an organization could afford for the examination of transactions. So auditors would select some haphazard group or bundle of items and verify their validity.

The trouble was that auditors could not measure the risk taken; they could not tell whether it was big or small. They could not defend the sample objectively; they could not demonstrate that it was a reasonable representation of the whole. True, they would try to reduce the risk by examining all expensive items and sampling the rest sparingly. However, the large items are often given reviews by several levels of management, whereas the small ones, reviews of which are sparse, may be the very ones mishandled.

Mathematicians and statisticians, on becoming interested in auditing as a proper field for statistics, pointed out the errors of the auditor's ways. A haphazard groping for transactions was no guarantee of a representative sample. The scientists demonstrated that the time-honored 10% sample could be woefully inadequate or ludicrously expensive. For example, under certain conditions of desired sample reliability, a population size of 50 will call for a sample size of 31 and a population of 100, only 50 items more, will call for a sample size of 46—50% more than the size of the sample for 50. *But* a population of 10 000, to have the same desired sample reliability, requires a sample of only 86 and a population of 500 000—50 times greater—calls for a sample of only 87.

As auditors became more mathematically literate, as they learned to make use of the enormous capabilities of the computer, they turned more and more to the benefits offered by statistical sampling and learning various sampling plans and selection techniques. Some of the more useful plans are as follows in the subsections below.

Attributes Sampling

This plan provides information on "how many." It is concerned with yes or no, go or no-go results. It is used, for example, to estimate from a sample the number of purchase orders issued during a year without competitive bidding. It will not estimate the value of the orders issued without competitive bidding, merely the number of them. Also it will not tell *why* competitive bids were not obtained. That must be tracked down by inquiry and verification.

Variables Sampling

The variables sampling plan provides information on "how much." It is most often used to produce an estimate in dollars. It can be used to estimate from a sample the dollar difference between book values and actual values of inventories. It is somewhat difficult to use, since sample sizes are dependent in part on the variability of the population. The more variable the population, the greater the difference in value between the lowest and the highest amounts of the items in the population, the larger the sample size to achieve the desired sample reliability. To measure that variability, auditors are required to compute the standard deviation of the sample and estimate the standard deviation of the population.

A newer form of dollar estimating goes under the various names of dollar unit sampling (DUS), cumulative money amount (CMA), and combined attributes variables (CAV). The dollar estimating plan, as the last description indicates, makes use of both attribute and variables sampling in estimating dollar values from a sample. Each dollar in a population is considered a sampling unit. A population of invoices totaling $1 million is considered to be made up of that number of units. If .1% of the population were to be examined, every thousandth dollar would be selected. Of course, if that dollar were "attached" to others in an invoice valued at $1 500, the entire invoice would be selected for examination. Proponents of the system argue that it provides greater sample reliability and insures the selection of all invoices of a given value. In the case just cited, since every thousandth dollar will be selected, every invoice valued at $1 000 or more would have to be examined.

Discovery Sampling

Sometimes called exploratory sampling, discovery sampling is used to identify, by a sample, at least one suspected item and to discontinue sampling when the item is located. Obviously, if there were only one suspected item in a population, auditors would have to examine every single item to find it. But if they can stipulate some given number of suspected items—5, 10, 15, and so on—then they can select a sample that will give some measurable assurance—90, 95, 98%, and so on, depending on the sample size—of finding at least one of the items in question.

Discovery sampling usually involves fairly large samples, and the hazard of overlooking an item demands high sample reliability. Its use is therefore restricted to areas of extreme risk to the organization: potential phantoms on the payroll, bank loans without collateral, duplicate payments, unauthorized shipment of goods, shipments not billed, and the like.

Stop-or-Go Sampling

Often auditors may have used attributes sampling on populations that called for a large number of items to examine only to find, at the end that the population could be considered relatively error-free. As they looked back on wasted energies, they wistfully wished they could have obtained some measurable assurance much earlier. Stop-or-go sampling offers that objective measurement. They can start with a small sample of 40 or 50 items, no matter what the size of the population may be; and if they find no errors or very few errors, they can discontinue sampling. They can state that they have objective assurance that there are no more than x % of errors in the population at y % of assurance.

If errors persist in surfacing, they can switch to attributes sampling, having lost no time by the stop-or-go exercise. An example would be to seek adequate assurance that misfiled accounts payable vouchers are fewer than some acceptable percentage.

Judgement Sampling

Auditors often do not need objective, mathematical assurance of sample reliability. Indeed, a sample of a single item may satisfy an audit objective: If auditors wish assurance that a purported system is actually in effect, that all safeguards do in fact exist, they may conduct a "walk-through" of a selected item through the system to make sure that all the purported bases are there and that all were touched as the transaction flowed through the system.

On the other hand, one or two examples of misconduct may launch a "directed" sample search that pokes into suspected crannies and turns over specified rocks. No attempt will be made to attribute the sample results to the entire population. Therein lies the crux: does the auditor need to attribute sample results to the whole population? If he does not, judgement sampling, carried out in a reasonable fashion, may completely satisfy the audit objectives.

Acceptance Sampling

Acceptance sampling is widely used in industrial quality control work. It consists of selecting a sample from a given field. In practice, the selection is made from a lot of produced or purchased items in order to determine whether the lot contains more than a minimum number of unacceptable items. If the number of unacceptable items exceeds the minimum, the lot is rejected. If it does not, the lot is accepted. The method is largely numerical appraisal and does not provide for an estimate of the unacceptable items in the entire population. For that reason, acceptance sampling is not as useful as the methods previously mentioned. Nevertheless, internal auditors should be aware of acceptance sampling and the principles behind it so that they may evaluate the adequacy of the sampling systems used by quality control inspectors in their own tests.

Sample Selection

These six sampling plans tell internal auditors how many items they need, but they must use accepted sampling selection techniques to pick the sample items. Sample selection takes two forms; random and purposive.

Random sampling permits each item in a population to have an equal chance of being selected. It is completely unbiased; it is unaffected by personal preference. Purposive sampling, however, confirms a suspicion or probes a suspected area and is openly biased. Both techniques have their uses. For example, in an audit of accounts payable invoices, auditors may take a random sample for the purpose of attributing sample results to population values. Then, because they may be suspicious of the work of one accounts payable clerk, they may take a purposeful or directed sample of that clerk's work.

For random samples, the auditor has several choices.

- *Random-number tables* are tables of randomized digits used to provide sample-item numbers. Random-number samples are rigorous and demonstrate lack of subjectivity when properly used. They can be used when numbers are assigned to the individual items. They are burdensome to use.
- *Interval sampling* calls for the selection of every *n*th item after a random start. Interval sampling, or, as it is often called, systematic sampling, is usually easier to use than random-number tables. If the auditor is satisfied that no items are missing from the population being tested, it can provide adequate assurance of random selection.
- *Stratified sampling* helps divide the population into two or more strata or groups. Each group is then sampled or examined in its entirety. For example, accounts payable vouchers can be divided into two groups: high-value invoices and all others. The high-value invoices may then be examined completely, and the remainder may be randomly sampled. Stratification helps reduce the variability that so strongly affects the sample size needed to achieve the desired degree of sample reliability.
- *Cluster sampling* is used when the location or filing of documents makes random-number or interval sampling burdensome or excessively expensive. It involves selecting clusters of documents and then sampling from the clusters—multistage sampling—or examining all the items in the clusters selected. All selections must be made at random. The clusters may be all the items processed during certain days, items filed in file drawers, or documents bound in bundles. The reliability of cluster sampling is generally lower than that of random-number and interval sampling, and the auditor may have to examine larger samples to make up for the lost reliability.

Sampling Cautions

To the auditor, statistical sampling is like quantitative analysis to the manager: a tool. It does not take the place of audit judgement. It simply provides the internal auditor with more reliable information. What is done with the information and how it is used, spells the difference between superior internal auditing and number juggling. In the following paragraphs we shall discuss some of the matters the auditor must take into account in sampling.

Internal auditors must know and fully comprehend the principles of statistical sampling. They must understand them well enough to be able to put them to proper use or to defend their decision not to use rigorous quantitative techniques. Also, as we shall see later in this chapter, they must have enough command of the principles to point the finger at abortions of acceptable sampling techniques.

The evaluation of sample results calls for audit judgement, not sampling principles or computer technology. Carpenter's tools may be the same for two different people, but with them the tyro might build a lopsided table and a craftsman a masterpiece. Along with the numbers put together statistically, auditors must consider the system of internal control, the adequacy of management and supervision, and the quality of operating employees. They must analyze what happened, why it happened, and how the indicated conditions affect the organization. Finally, they must figure out what can be done to improve things if the sample indicates defects. They must be management-oriented first and statisticians second.

Internal auditors who are confident of a grasp of sampling principles will use random selection techniques when they are appropriate and employ directed, purposive sample selection when it best suits audit purposes. They will know, however, that the results of a directed sample are not representative of the entire population. The directed sample gives a biased picture, which makes wise managers wary when eager assistants present "evidence" of a widespread malaise. Managers expect more objectivity from internal auditors than deliberately plucked examples.

"Define your population" must be one of the cardinal rules of the auditor who embarks on a course of sampling. Will it be all the purchase orders for a year? Will it be just purchase orders valued over a given amount? Does the population exclude change orders? Does it exclude blanket orders stretching over several years? Does it exclude orders to foreign suppliers? Does it exclude subcontracts? Can the auditor be certain that no orders are missing from the population to be tested? In every sample selection the auditor must identify precisely what was tested, because only to that population may he project his sample results.

An attributes sampling plan requires the auditor to make certain assumptions that are implicit in the formulas and the table used to determine the sizes of the sample to be used:

1. Confidence level: the degree of assurance desired that the projection of sample results will lie within a certain range. Confidence level is expressed as a percentage—85, 95, 99% or some other degree of assurance.
2. Precision: the range within which the sample results will lie at the desired confidence level. It is expressed as plus or minus some number or percent such

as ±3%. Confidence level and precision are entwined. One cannot refer to one without mentioning the other.

3. Error rate: the estimated degree of error or other occurrence that exists in the population tested. The error rate is an estimate of variability in the population, and the greater the variability the larger the sample needed to provide representative results.

The auditor selects confidence level and precision to meet requirements of sample reliability. The higher the confidence level and the narrower the range of precision the larger the sample size needs to be. That is a determination that must be made to accomplish the audit objective.

Error rates, however, are conditions that auditors believe exist in the population to be tested. If they underestimate the error rate, the sample will be too small and might not give a reliable representation of the population. If they overestimate the error rate, they may select too large a sample and thereby waste precious hours. Making the appropriate estimate calls for audit judgement in terms of the population under review. One gauge of the maximum error rates to be expected would be the point at which alarms would go off if the particular error rate were exceeded. For example, the error rate in a payroll could not possibly be very high without alerting the treasurer, the employees being paid, or the budget people.

Similarly, the auditor should not set needlessly high reliability goals. A reliability goal of 99% confidence level and ±% precision calls for vastly greater sample size than for 90% confidence level and ±4% precision. For example, assuming a population of 10 000 and a 5% error rate, in the first instance the sample size would be 2 397; in the second it would be only 80. So the auditor will use judgement, and evaluate the system of internal control, the guidance and wisdom of the operating manager, the training and experience of the operating employees, and whatever fail-safe mechanisms management has constructed, and will then stipulate reliability levels that are reasonable in the circumstances and not unnecessarily rigorous.

Whenever internal auditors expect sample results to be considered representative of the entire population, they must let each item in that population have an equal chance of being selected. Otherwise, the sample may not be considered randomly selected and the rules of statistical sampling will not apply. The fact that an individual item is difficult to locate or time-consuming to examine is no excuse for rejecting it and selecting another. The rules of statistical sampling are rigorous, and the auditor who does not play the game according to the rules may not proclaim that results reasonably represent the population tested. Hence, neither personal bias nor population patterns must be permitted to violate the primary rule of statistical sampling: every item must have an equal opportunity of being chosen for the sample.

Ratio, Change, and Trend Analysis

Applications

Where should internal auditors put their powerful sampling tool to work? Like the managers, they must give priority to the areas of greatest hazard, but how are they to identify the areas? The long-range audit program will include the activities reasonably known to cause problems or those which, if uncontrolled, can result in serious losses. However, what of the incipient sores that are not yet bleeding? How to identify them before the entity's blood flows in earnest?

Diagnostic techniques are available to perhaps identify ailments before they get too serious. They call for the analysis of certain indicators that point the internal auditor's nose in the right direction. They provide information of an overall nature on trends of important functions. The internal auditor might observe and analyze those matters during an audit of an operation. However, audits are intermittent. What about changes that occur between audits? What about matters not detected by the ordinary system of internal control? What about changes in programs, the aberrant conditions not included in normal tests, and the effect of external factors that are not internally controlled?

The analysis of financial data concerned with ratios, changes, and trends can be like a microscope in the hands of the competent internal auditor. It is designed to highlight what is abnormal, what is changing, and what appear to be unexpected variations. It is performed by critically examining the relations that exist between sets of financial and operating data either over periods of time or against some expected standards.

The internal auditor is alerted by unusual variations in ratios, unexpected changes, and abnormal trends. A ratio measures the relative magnitude of two related factors inside or outside an entity. The changes that will interest the auditor are those that were not anticipated. Those indicators may help to recognize problems before they manifest themselves, are detected by management, or are evident through inflicted damage. Recognizing and analyzing a problem can go a long way toward solving it. There are three steps in the analysis:

1. Selecting appropriate data.
2. Measuring changes and interrelations.
3. Evaluating the changes and interrelations and learning why they happened.

Every entity of any size has a host of such relations. Usually it is not difficult to know what is considered normal or abnormal. That information can be obtained internally from past experience with the entity or externally by comparison with statistics available from various trade associations, the Small Business Administration, Dun and Bradstreet, Robert Morris Associates, and others. Useful internal data require just a little imagination to locate. For example, the use of packaging material should rise or fall in relation to the volume of shipments. When unusual variations occur, there may be a need to investigate

External data are equally useful because they supply objective standards not available internally. They are independent; and if they are current, they may indicate experience during comparable periods. Obviously, such information must be used with care. One must account for different methods of computation, the nature of the sources, varying policies, and the like. But when the differences are accounted for, comparison of elements on a per unit basis can be useful. For example, the entity's cost to produce a unit may be $5 for labor and $8 for material. Industry averages, however, may be $3 for labor and $6 for material. Such variances warrant close investigation.

Variations are significant indicators. For example:

- Relations between functions such as variances over time in the relation of net profits to net sales or of cost of sales to inventories.
- Lack of consistency between functions, such as increased scrap sales but decreased production.
- Differences in assumptions between management policy and actual practice, such as the amount of bonus payments for work at foreign locations versus management's understanding of the basis for such payments. For example, management may have been expecting reduced rates depending on the length of tour of duty whereas employees are paid continuing rates.
- Variations from such standards as budgets and standard costs.
- Changes over a series of periods in such ratios as net profits to net sales, miles traveled to fuel consumption, debt to interest expense, and sales to bad debt expense.

Comparisons can be made by relating elements to a totality or by company units.

Elements

The purpose here is to determine whether elements of some account or activity bear a reasonable relation to the totality. For example, each component of administrative expense must bear some reasonably consistent relation to the sum of all such expense. The auditor can measure current relations against past patterns and investigate significant differences.

Units

Unit costs can be useful in determining or establishing standards and analyzing variances. Some variances may be readily explained and may appear reasonable; others can point to problems. For example, changes in unit costs may be explained by material mix or by new methods of production. On the other hand, they may be caused by poorer material quality, increased rates of rejection, or inefficient production. Similarly, changes in labor unit cost may be caused by inefficiency, excessive machine downtime, or learning time.

Whatever variances are found, the internal auditor must analyze them. Certainly, if management has already provided for a system of detecting and analyzing variances, the auditor need not reinvent the wheel. But he can determine whether the data used are valid and whether abnormal conditions were acted on. If management has not developed such a system, the auditor should recommend the practice as a regular, continuing tool. How much more valuable for managers to monitor their activities constantly than for the internal auditor to do it intermittently. There is no substitute for self-control, and it is much more palatable than externally exercised control. The wise internal auditor will accompany a recommendation for a system of ratio, change, and trend analysis with a significant finding of such an analysis.

A great number of financial ratios are in common use; they include current ratios, current debt to net worth, working capital to sales, and cost of sales to inventory. Some that may be of particular use are:

- The *sales to inventory ratio* could point up too little inventory to support a given level of sales or increased inventory accompanied by reduced sales.
- The *average collection period* can be a good measure of the effectiveness of an entity's collection policy. The internal auditor can compare his findings with industry ratios to determine the reasonableness of collection policies and practices. A useful ratio can be computed by:
- Dividing net credit sales by 365 to obtain average daily credit sales.
- Dividing trade notes and accounts receivable, including those discounted, by the average daily credit sales.
- Comparing the two results.
- The *net income per unit of service ratio* offers a measure of profit per unit of available capacity: per room in hotels, per bed in hospitals, per ton-mile for trucks, per passenger mile for aircraft, per sales clerk in department stores, and per production worker in factories.
- The *commissions to sales ratio* is a measure of an important cost of distribution. In the Equity Funding case, such a measure might have shown a sharp increase in "sales" without a corresponding increase in salesmen's commission, since many of the "sales" were fictitious and did not involve the use of the sales force.
- The *bad debts to sales ratio* is a measure of how good a job the credit department is doing—whether it is constant, improving, or deteriorating.
- The *sales expenses to sales ratio* is a measure of the cost of the selling effort. It may point to an inefficient deployment of sales effort—continuing to cover areas or customers that produce too low a level of sales results.

Assisting the Executive

the Problem-solving Partner

The expansion in use of quantitative techniques has had its effect. Executives and managers with strong mathematical backgrounds take operations research problems in comparatively easy stride. They evaluate proposals based on quantitative techniques and can knowledgeably accept or reject them. Others are hoist on the horns of a dilemma: "I am faced by a technique that may well have great potential. It might save me money. But it's complicated and mathematical, and I don't understand it. Shall I reject it? I might lose out on something valuable. should I accept it without understanding its inner workings? That goes against my grain, and I might live to regret it!"

Knowledgeable internal auditors can be valued allies in such circumstances. Many a manager in circumstances of doubt has turned to the internal auditor for assistance in having doubts resolved.

The internal auditor can be a stout champion when the organization is under attack by other auditors. Two actual examples are illustrated. One involves statistical sampling, and the other involves ratio delay studies.

Statistical Sampling Study

Government auditors analyzed travel expenses of a company by means of statistical sampling. Travel vouchers were selected at random and examined. The differences between what had been recorded and what the government auditors considered allowable for the sample vouchers were then projected to the total population. The resulting extrapolation, reported as "overcharges," amounted to several hundred thousand dollars.

The government auditors issued a report to the company's financial officer setting forth the overcharges and asking for appropriate adjustments. The amounts involved were so large that the financial officer asked the company's internal auditors to review the statistical sampling methodology used.

The internal auditors met with the government auditors and were given an opportunity to review the working papers and the computer programs on which the requests for adjustment were based.

The internal auditor was able to point out some fatal defects in the sampling methods—violations of basic statistical sampling techniques. For example, the sample of travel vouchers were selected from those involving local travel only. Yet the extrapolation covered both local and foreign travel. The selection technique, therefore, did not permit each item an equal chance of selection. Other errors involved consistency of selection methods and were abundantly demonstrated. As a result, adjustments were made only for the expense vouchers actually examined and not for the amount originally claimed.

Ratio Delay Study

A team of government auditors performed a ratio delay study, also called work sampling, in five clerical departments of a company doing work for a government agency. Following a two-week study, the government auditors charged the company with significant "nonproductivity" in those departments. They projected the difference between observed activity and "acceptable" activity and computed estimated costs that could have been avoided for the year by less nonproductivity or idleness. The company's chief financial officer called upon the internal auditors for assistance in dealing with the government auditor's allegations.

Ratio delay studies employ a random sampling method of obtaining information about human and machine activities. They use random observations of individuals at work to determine the ratio of avoidable delays to total available working hours. The studies are based on the laws of probability and therefore rely on the principles of randomization and sampling reliability.

Reviews were made by two-person teams of observers entering the areas under examination at moments during the day that had been randomly selected. Also randomly selected were the names of the employees to be observed. Based solely on observation, the government auditors judged whether activity was (i) avoidably nonproductive (idleness), (ii) unavoidably nonproductive, or (iii) productive.

The observations for a two-week period were summarized and charted by the least-squares method. The charts displayed curves that rose sharply and then gradually leveled off. The charts portrayed early low points, (little or no nonproductivity) that indicated the workers were fully aware of the presence of the observers, and then the line would rise to indicate greater degrees of nonproductivity as the workers became accustomed and indifferent to the observers.

The curve would then approach a straight line, termed the asymptote, which was supposed to project from the findings the "normal" level of inactivity in the department being observed. The information was analyzed by computer program. Data points represented the number of observed nonproductive activities divided by the number of observation periods in the sample for a day. The software program takes a set of data points and determines by the least-squares method how well they can be described with six types of algebraic equations (curves). Above each curve, the straight-line asymptote represents the value that the equation (curve) would reach if the number of observations were infinite.

The government auditors, regarded the asymptote as representing the true level of nonproductivity. They had determined that 11% inactivity for the day was acceptable and that any amount over that point was not. After comparing the charts with the arbitrary 11% acceptable percentage of nonproductivity, the difference, considered avoidable, was extrapolated to a full year. An example of one of the curves is as shown in Figure 11.2. The asymptote to the curve is 23%—12% above the standard of 11%. The extrapolation, running about a half a million dollars for the five departments, sent a chill through the company's executives, as could well be expected. The failure to respond knowledgeably and convincingly to the charges could be a serious blow to the company's standing with government contract officers and adversely affect negotiations for future contracts.

The company's internal auditors reviewed the work performed by the government auditors and provided the information needed both to blunt the government's attack and to soften the government auditors' reports. Here are some of the arguments.

• The two-week sample was not representative of the one-year population of

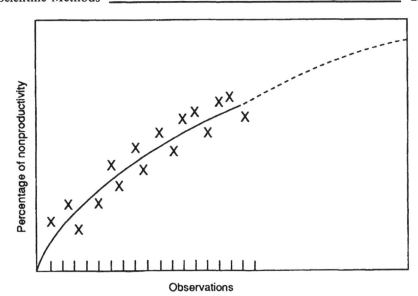

Figure 11.2 Projected Rate of Nonproductivity (asymptote = 23%)

activity. People tended to transfer frequently. Work tended to change. Seasonal cycles have a significant effect. Hence, every unit in such a shifting population does not have an equal chance of being selected.

- The government auditors subjectively selected one of the six CURFIT curves that they considered most appropriate to their contentions, not necessarily the one that was kindest to the company.
- There is a considerable body of scientific opinion to the effect that there is not necessarily a relation between the accuracy of a curve based on past observations and the reliability of the curve for purposes of forecasting.
- The standard of 11% selected by the government auditors was at variance with criteria shown in respected publications on the subject, which indicate that a level of 20% or less is acceptable.
- Insufficient observations had been made to produce reliable curves. Some of the rejected curves gyrated so wildly, because of too few observations, as to be meaningless. Those selected may have achieved their form by chance.
- The most serious indictment of the government report was the emphasis on numbers instead of activities. Ratio delay studies can be helpful when they point to specific defects in operations or supervision that management can deal with: people arriving late for work and leaving early, extended breaks, reading newspapers or magazines during working hours, lack of adequate facilities, and supervisors not knowing what their people are doing or where they are. The numbers alone—the percentages and the unsupportable extrapolations– give irritation without offering causes of corrective action. A manager can do something about identified conduct, but projections of hundreds of thousands of dollars are usually meaningless in terms of correcting conditions. Statistics merely indicate the potential existence of a problem; they do not define it. In the situation just illustrated, the internal auditor's analysis of the work sampling study resulted in a revised government report that was much less damaging.

The internal auditor can be a useful partner to managers in assessing and interpreting statistics. The statistical tool is powerful, but it is still only a tool. The hand that wields it must be skillful, and the mind behind the hand must provide understanding.

CONCLUSION

Quantitative analysis—operations research—can be extremely useful when the manager is fully aware of its benefits and shortcomings. The knowledge and skill of the mathematician can help the manager reach goals so long as the manager knows what the goals are and retains control over the scientific effort. Scientific method can test managers' assumptions, provide answers to what-if questions in mathematical terms, and present managers with alternatives. However, the managers must ask the right questions and ultimately make the decisions.

Probability theory and statistical sampling can be powerful instruments in the hands of knowledgeable internal auditors, but they are a means to an end and not the end itself. The internal auditor must understand the techniques, but is not obliged to use them exclusively. They can be formidable allies to managers who are faced with mathematical problems beyond their ken and they can provide a stout defense when the management sciences are improperly used against the manager.

REFERENCES

(1) *Sampling Manual for Auditors*, Table A.3, published by the Institute of Internal Auditors, Inc., with the permission of the copyright owner, Lockheed Aircraft Corporation.

Part III
The Process of
Management

12
Planning and Budgeting

PLANNING AND THE MANAGER

Nature of Planning

Definition and Purpose

Among the four functions of management, planning is primary. A manager cannot successfully organize or direct or control without careful planning. As the old carpenter said: measure twice and cut once.

Planning, like decision making, is the selection of a course of action from among various possible choices. The selection will be subject to certain premises that must be stated or predicted by the planner and to certain constraints that may be imposed by the environment. Hence, planning is future-oriented.

Logical as the need for it may be, planning is a comparatively modern development. Frederick Taylor laid great stress on it, but before World War II what planning was done was fragmented and poorly coordinated throughout the enterprise. Now many companies use comprehensive corporate planning and regularly create long-range as well as short-range plans.

A significant aspect of the revolution in management thinking is the increased interest in planning, the desire to bridge the gap between where we are and where we want to be. Many modern managers began deciding, well in advance of action, what to do, when to do it, how to do it, and who is to do it. They came to the realization that, with well-constructed plans, they could make things happen that might not otherwise happen or they could identify and forestall potential troubles. So the function partakes both of planning and controlling. When management sets forth desired ends, it uses the plans as a standard. When it uses the standards to ensure and measure accomplishment, it is controlling.

The future is ever uncertain, but managers must cope with uncertainties to achieve their ends. Plans therefore seek to minimize uncertainty and deal with the changes that the future is bound to bring. Planning focuses management's attention on objectives. Indeed, managers have no target to shoot at until they have decided on the objectives they must meet. Then by coordinating the objectives and plans of components within the organization, managers can gain more economical operations through the elimination of redundancies and overlaps.

Planning takes time. It is a difficult mental exercise, and many managers find the intellectual process frustrating and constricting. It is no panacea, because it cannot predict the future with certainty, but it has many more pluses than minuses. It forces managers to think through what they must do to reach their goals: try to resolve uncertainties, determine relations between themselves and others in the organization, allocate the ever-scarce resources available to them, set priorities, and, if nothing else, realize the need for lead time to gather together the means to get the job done.

At the higher levels of management, where overall strategy is framed, the planners must make the most important planning decision of all: what should our business be? Not what is it or what was it, but what must it be to survive? That kind of planning takes into account the one certainty: things will be different. Thus the central purpose of planning is to see that the mistakes of the past will not continue into the future. The uncertainties cannot be precisely predicted, but some of them can be reduced to alternative courses of action.

Advantages

Planning has the chief advantage of giving purpose and orderliness to an organization's activities.

A revealing study that validates the advantage of planning involved 36 firms representing 6 industrial groups. Of the 36 only 17 were found to have formal long-range plans. The results achieved by firms with formal plans were compared with the results of firms employing informal plans. In each case, the formal planners significantly outperformed the others in terms of earnings per share and earnings on total capital employed. Then to confirm the findings, comparisons were made in the planning companies between performance before and after each company began its formal long-range planning. The favorable comparisons for the firms which used formal planning held true.(1)

Whenever planners encourage advice from subordinates, they help both the subordinates and themselves. Cooperative planning motivates the subordinates to achieve by participating in and becoming committed to the plan. Also it is a self-imposed and valuable check on the wise executive. Individuals who hold the reins of power in any enterprise cannot trust themselves to be adequately self-critical. For those in power the danger of self-deception is very great, the danger of failing to see the problems or refusing to see them is ever-present. The only protection is to create an atmosphere in which anyone can speak up. Hence the need to countenance and institutionalize an element of internal whistleblowing.(2)

Among the less obvious advantages of planning is the process itself. It forces managers to look ahead and to seek out the need for change, to see more than one side by posing the what-if questions, to encourage achievement by setting goals, to encourage the broad view by seeking to fill the organization's needs, to balance the use of facilities by assigning priorities, and to help managers gain status by participating in an executive function.

Characteristics

Planning is not forecasting. Actually, it is simply because we are unable to forecast with sufficient reliability that planning is needed. Planning makes use of forecasts because the plans will be carried out in an uncertain future. However, despite the uncertainty some position about the future must be taken. That position is the forecast; it is not a plan.

A forecast is objective and passive; it describes anticipated conditions over which the manager has no control. Planning is subjective and active; it declares an intention to take steps to do something that is under management control. Forecasts are often taken from open, available information; plans are usually proprietary to the organization that makes them. The forecast rejects uncertainty by taking a definite position; plans accept uncertainty by taking a middle course of action and hedging against adverse conditions. A major difference is that forecasts are mechanically constructed from detail while plans are oriented toward a goal and the details are filled in afterward.

All planning can be characterized as strategic or tactical. The strategic plans are long-range. They are concerned with broad and fundamental issues; they peer beyond the horizon, and they pervade the entire organization. Tactical planning is short-range. It is primarily concerned with the most efficient use of available or allotted resources.

The longer the time element, the more strategic the plan. Usually, long-range plans are over 5 years; anything over 20 years is considered infinity. But that does not mean we cannot plan beyond that time. The tree that will not be cut for 90 years is part of a long-range planning program that starts today.

All plans, strategic and tactical, have common characteristics:

- The plan is not a mere wish; it is a specific course of action tied to identifiable products, organizations, and individuals.

  Example
  Specific people in the marketing department will mount an advertising campaign for product Y.

- A plan deals with action in the future on a decision made today. We will allocate $x of resources to the advertising program.
- Plans must be carried out in conditions of relative certainty or uncertainty.

Example
Production planning of specific products can be done with relative certainty. But the plan to increase the distribution of product Y by penetrating a new market is fraught with uncertainty.

- Planning is intellectual. It calls for imagination, thought, creativity, and foresight. Useful plans cannot be constructed solely from the debris of the past.

Example
Novel and innovative means will be needed to interest the public in product Y.

- Planning involves all managers, and it never ends. It permeates all levels of the organization, and it must go on all the time. Plans are future-oriented, so they are essentially tentative, because the conditions planned for may not come to pass. Hence the plans must be constantly monitored and reappraised.

Example
Marketing, sales, engineering, production, finance, accounting, and personnel are involved in the plans for product Y. The plans will be subject to change based on such factors as the public's acceptance or rejection of the marketing program and the availability of money, staff, and materials.

Strategic planning practice generally follows three different patterns:(3)

1. "Satisficing." Stay with the status quo. Don't break with the past. It is more important to survive than to grow.
2. "Optimizing." Do as well as possible. Optimum plans are not always carried out, but we can try to get close. Also the effort to achieve the best can yield valuable byproducts of information for future projects.
3. "Adaptivizing." Adapt operations to accommodate short- and long-range plans. For example, a company may have a cyclical demand that causes peaks and valleys of employment in the manufacture of its product. It might develop a long-range plan for another cyclical product whose valleys coincide with the first product's peaks.

Two other characteristics of strategic planning are flexibility and "suboptimization." Flexibility calls for plans that can change directions. The ability to switch must be built into the plan, and sometimes it can cost more in the short-range to achieve savings in the long-range. An example is spending more for movable partitions to cut the cost of relocating fixed partitions later.

Suboptimization requires trade-offs between competing groups. For example, sales and credit have different goals. Sales wants to sell all it can to whomever will buy. Credit will refuse to allow sales to marginal customers. Overall plans must coordinate the conflicting goals.

Steps in planning

The steps in planning approximate those in decision making, since both processes involve a selection from among alternatives. As in decision making, extended analyses for minor plans are not cost-effective. However, it is also not cost-effective to make sketchy analyses for plans involving heavy investments of staff, money, and materials. Here are some of the steps toward successful planning:

- *Resources.* Determine the resources available or attainable to carry out the plans: money, people, property, materials, equipment, and managers. When needed resources are neither on hand nor available, plans based on those resources are unachievable dreams.
- *Environment.* Determine the environments—external and internal—in which the plans must be implemented. If they are hostile to the plans and there is no way of making them friendly, the plans have no chance of being carried out.
- *Opportunities.* Evaluate resources and environment in relation to the opportunities available so as to produce the best fit of all three. At the same time, analyze problems that may affect plans to determine whether an apparently insurmountable difficulty can be an opportunity to produce an innovative, profitable result. For example, the need to reduce pollution can be transformed into an opportunity to reclaim chemicals whose value may exceed the cost of pollution reduction.
- *Objectives.* Determine the aims, purposes, and goals of the enterprise when setting all objectives, both long- and short-range. Objectives are the foundation stones on which all plans rest. The short-range plans must contribute to the long-range plans. Thus, subordinates who develop subsidiary plans must have a sound understanding of enterprise objectives. Executive management is charged with the responsibility for meshing long- and short-range objectives. Inconsistent objectives can be disastrous. After World War II, Montgomery Ward's long-range objective was to enhance profitability. But Sewell Avery's short-range decision to curtail expansion frustrated profit enhancement and put Montgomery Ward far behind its more adventuresome rival, Sears, Roebuck. Objectives will be discussed more fully later in this chapter.
- *Premises.* The premises are set at the highest level of management. They are the assumptions that form a framework around which estimated events that affect the plans are expected to take place. Everyone in the enterprise must use the same framework or the major and subsidiary plans may be uncoordinated. For example, if different units within an organization project widely varying inflation rates, the results may be a confused jumble of inconsistent plans. Premises also will be discussed later in this chapter.
- *Alternatives.* Search for alternative plans. Every plan has alternatives. Often the problem lies less in listing the alternatives than in reducing the number so that only the most promising alternatives will be analyzed. The obvious plan is not necessarily the one to select. Often the least obvious plan is the best.
- *Evaluation.* Weigh the various factors affecting each alternative. Each plan has its offsetting characteristics. An apparently profitable course may demand

large cash outlays and promise slow payback. Another may be less profitable but also less risky.

Important to the evaluation is the period of fullfilment. The plan must take into account the day of accomplishment. If a program of three years calls for plant facilities, the cost should be written off within that time. The plan is for the future, but the decision must be made now. So if fluctuations are anticipated, some flexibility will have to be incorporated into the long-range plan. A plant to produce a single product may have to be made capable of producing other products as well if it is possible that the first product may not meet public acceptance.

● *Selection.* After all reasonable evaluations have been made, the appropriate alternative must be selected. When the future holds threats, one or more of the discarded alternatives may have to be kept in inventory as a possible replacement.

● *Derivatives.* Once the major plan has been developed, lay subsidiary plans. The plan to go ahead with a new product calls for subsidiary plans to hire, transfer, and train employees, design tooling, procure materials, and market the finished product. Each department's derivative plans must be put under the microscope to see whether they contribute to the established objectives and are compatible with other plans. If ten departments intend to spend $5 million and only $3 million is available, some adjustments will have to be made.

● *Control.* Formulate the means of control, the reports, and the feedback needed to provide information on how well the plans are being carried out. Managers must be kept aware of progress, accomplishment, and roadblocks so as to receive current information on the progress of plans. Managers must be in a position to restructure plans that are not achieving the objectives.

● *Pretesting.* Past history is often wrong, inapplicable, or improperly interpreted, so the plan should be tested before it is put into operation. Simulation techniques have been successful for the purpose. Given a known result, determine how well the plan would handle the past situation.

By and large, the easiest part of the planning process is the selection from available alternatives. What is truly difficult, what requires the genius of a master planner, is the honing of objectives, the shrewd selection of premises, and the communication of both premises and objectives to the people in the organization who must carry out the plans.

Objectives

Purpose

The health and survival of a company or an industry can hang upon the objectives formulated by the leaders. Nothing is more important. In the 1960s Detroit saw the influx of small foreign cars, yet it failed to modify its objectives. An erosion of the American automobile market by a flood of small foreign cars was the result.

Objectives precede programs, policies, and all other management decisions. Thus they must be clear and they must make sense to the people in the enterprise. If they do not impel commitment, they may not be achieved. The student who is not truly committed to a college education may be sidetracked by a well-paying but dead-end job.

Objectives can motivate people. When they are moved by purposes that seize their imagination and understand their part in making the purposes come to pass, they become involved and committed. Their commitment to an objective can transcend their commitment to a job. A job is a means; the objectives set a goal. People often confuse the two; and when conditions change, they mindlessly keep following the book without knowing why it was written.

Similarly, many people follow the false grail of optimizing profits as the primary purpose of their business. There may be periods in an organization's existence when current profits must be subordinated to long-term aims. The major objectives of an organization are the fundamental standards by which the organization is judged. Optimizing profits is not a satisfactory constant. The true objective of the productive organization must take into account the employees and the social structure within which the organization functions. So the organization's three main objectives are:

1. To create something of economic value to a customer. No organization has a reason for being unless it can create customers and products of value for those customers.
2. To survive and to grow. Profits are needed to achieve the objectives; but the profits should be sufficient, not necessarily optimal.
3. To create values that are desired by the members of the organization. An organization is the sum total of its people, whose needs must be considered and satisfied if they are to make the organization grow.

Threading through the tapestry of key objectives is the central theme of what the business should be. The fundamental determination points the way to desirable objectives and the goals that must be set to meet them.

- Is the business of the university to educate or to perform research?
- Is the business of a prison confinement or rehabilitation?
- Is the business of a church religion or social relationships?
- Is the business of a medical school training medical students or carrying on basic research?

Development

The development of objectives and subobjectives (goals) calls for the following steps:

- To develop strategy—the purpose of the organization.
- To determine broad objectives.

- To set goals that are designed to meet the objectives and are measurable.
- To make the objectives and goals operative by communicating them to the people who will achieve them.

Goal setting is made difficult by conflicting demands upon the organization: the demands of stockholders, society, customers, employees, government, and financial institutions.

- The goal for higher wages for employees conflicts with the goal of higher return for stockholders.
- The goal of higher production may conflict with society's needs for less pollution.
- The commitment of more resources to research and development may paint a poorer picture to financial institutions.

An ever-present problem is to reconcile social demands, and profit needs. The social needs cannot be ignored. If they are, the business may be visited with hostile action from activist groups and from the government itself. Management's social responsibilities are being felt more keenly with the passing years. Enlightened, innovative management can answer the needs of both society and its stockholders. Dow Chemical spent millions on antipollution, but it was able to consider pollution to be a wasted resource. In some of its plants it was able to recover enough chemicals to balance the cost of pollution abatement.

Ethical questions influence objectives; management cannot turn its back on the spiritual values of the culture. Many companies live in a fishbowl under the penetrating searchlight of the press. They cannot afford to let the water get murky. As a result, codes of ethics have been established by some groups to offer guides for business behavior.

What evolves is that no system is completely rational. None is completely controllable or predictable. Every organization, in setting objectives and viewing interrelations, must recognize that it floats in a sea of constraints and limiting factors

Constraints

The US government imposes limitations on activities in restraint of trade through the Sherman Anti-Trust Act of 1890, which was followed by the Clayton Act of 1913, the creation of the Federal Trade Commission in 1914, and the Robinson-Patman Act of 1936. In the field of labor, constraints are imposed by the Wagner Act of 1935, the Fair Labor Standards Act of 1938, and the Taft-Hartley Act of 1947. In the field of commerce, constraints are imposed by the Securities and Exchange Commission, the Interstate Commerce Commission and the Federal Communications Commission.

Limiting factors within the organization can frustrate the setting or accomplishment of objectives. They are in a constant state of flux and can change as objectives are set and the planning process moves on. In 1945, the General

Electric Company mounted a large expansion program. Its primary objective related to such matters as organizational structure and production facilities. However, other factors, not immediately apparent, made themselves felt. GE's Ralph Cordiner said: "Not customers, not products, not money, but managers may be the limit on GE's growth."

The constraining interrelations and limiting factors, troublesome as they are, do not argue against planning and the setting of objectives. Rather, they show what the intelligent manager must consider. And they will affect management's commitments to its objectives.

Management commitments to objectives vary. Some may be deep-seated and thoroughly supported; others may be lip service. Management's dedication to its objectives can usually be discerned by its allocation of resources. If it puts its money where its mouth is, the objective is real. However if, for example, it vociferously espouses an expanded safety program but reduces its staff of safety engineers, the program and its safety-directed objectives can be considered suspect.

Premises

Purpose

A plan is as good as its premises. A meticulously well-thought-out plan for a picnic that fails to take into account a forecast that rain is a 95% probability is a futile exercise. Premises are predictions. The longer the plan the less certain the predictions, but premises must still be established. For example:

> In one case a company president, imbued with the spirit of cooperation, decided that planning must begin at the bottom. Accordingly, he asked his subordinates for budgets, but he provided them with no premises. Then when he received the departmental budgets, they were so inconsistent that it was impossible to put them together. Had he understood the importance of premises, he would not have asked for budgets without providing guidelines.

Executive management must describe its premises explicitly; it must state what conditions or predicted uncertainties will affect the plans to be established.

Types

Premises fall into three basic types:

- *Environmental.* These deal with the economy, society, and the government.
- *Competitive.* These are concerned with such matters as the enterprise's future, the plans of its competitors, its anticipated share of the market, its projected return on investment, its new products and patterns of marketing, and its dedication to research and development.
- *Internal.* These identify the organization's strengths and weaknesses, its resources, the cost of its information, its productivity, its manpower and management, and its standing with its customers and in the community.

Environmental factors, particularly public policy, strongly affect planning and the premises for plans. Questions on which positions must be taken include these:

• Will the government be friendly or unfriendly to the field in which the enterprise functions?
• Are prices likely to be controlled?
• What government agencies affect the enterprise's operations and which of their rulings impinge on the plans?
• How much has the government budgeted for products sold by the enterprise?
• What changes in fiscal and monetary policies are likely?
• What new tax legislation is in the offing?
• What sort of investment tax credit will be available?

No business can live as in a walled city, protected from the outside. The competitive factors have a strong impact on the positions that planners must take. For example:

• Are competitors coming out with an improved or new product?
• On the other hand, does competitive weakness provide opportunities that should be seized?
• What is the projected market for raw materials and labor?
• What is the trend in labor rates?
• What is the expected population trend or the shift from urban to suburban living?

Among internal premises, perhaps the most important is the sales forecast. It becomes the official position of the organization. It is the basis for all the other forecasts in the business; on it are built production schedules, inventory and purchasing plans, personnel requirements, additional production facilities, and financial requirements. Once the sales forecasts are disseminated as premises by executive management, then forecasts and estimates can be prepared by the people responsible for production planning, engineering, industrial relations, accounting, finance, and marketing.

Sales forecasting methods generally divide as follows:

• The jury of executive opinion—meetings and discussions at the top-management level; trading guesses about the future.
• The sales force composite—obtaining input from members of the sales force.
• Users' expectations—polling customers for their anticipated needs or unmet wants.
• Statistical methods—using such techniques as trend cycle analysis (projections from historical sales data), correlation analysis (relations between sales and other economic and noneconomic phenomena), and mathematical models.

The Subplans

Planning and plans are generally associated with broad objectives, programs, and projects. Also under the wide umbrella of plans are the various subplans that translate, dissect, and communicate the organization's major plans for its managers and employees. They are the guidelines that lead operating people toward the aims and purposes of the enterprise. They subdivide from the general and conceptual to the specific and concrete.

Policies are regarded as being the apex of the pyramid of subordinate plans and guidelines within an organization, but policies are most likely to endure if they resemble fundamental principles. Hence the hierarchy of subplans starts with principles and goes on from there to policies, procedures, rules, methods, standards, technofactors, and programs. Illustrations of how some of these subplans carry out a major plan are as follows:

- *Principle.* Ethical dealing with others is an obligation an organization owes to society.
- *Policy.* Our employees are not to be financially interested in our company's suppliers.
- *Program.* A conflict-of-interest program has been established to carry out this policy.
- *Procedure.* A specified series of steps are to be followed to provide information about dealings with suppliers and potential conflicts of interest.
- *Rule.* Any buyer who accepts a bribe or kickback from a supplier shall be summarily dismissed.
- *Method.* The facts about any employee reporting a potential conflict shall be reviewed by the employee's superior, reported to the legal department for recommendation, and ruled on by the executive committee.
- *Standard.* An employee shall not accept Christmas gifts from suppliers that exceed $25 in value.

Principles

Principles are general or fundamental truths. They are basic laws, doctrines, or assumptions on which other laws, doctrines, and assumptions are based or from which they are derived. They govern life and human behavior. When policies, procedures, and rules are based on accepted principles, they have a greater chance of being accepted by operating people. A policy based on the principle of fair dealing will receive better general acceptance than one based on chicanery. In formulating policy, therefore, the policy maker should state the policy in such a way that it accords with principles acceptable in the community.

Of course, policies may have to be set in areas where the fundamental truth is unknown and where a principle has not been enunciated, approved, and accepted. In such situations the policy maker must rely on business judgement and intuition. Policies still must be formulated to provide direction and achieve uniformity even though an underlying principle is absent.

Policies

A policy is a basic statement that serves to guide the action of people within an organization. It may or may not be in writing, but it establishes a position on a given set of circumstances. It avoids the need to make a new decision each time those circumstances arise. Yet it must allow latitude. An analogy is a freeway: drivers may not drive north on the southbound lanes, or vice versa. However, within the northbound lanes they may take whichever one will be help them reach their destination. Similarly, a policy permits initiative and discretion–but within limits.

Policies set out the area in which decisions may be made, but they do not make those decisions. To that extent they are a grant of authority. Enduring policies are likely to be broad enough to give room for individual judgement and yet not be so obscure or vague as to require complicated interpretations. Their purpose is to help achieve objectives; to be acceptable, policies should take into account the suggestions of those affected by them. Policies are the springboard for other, subordinate plans: procedures, rules, methods, standards, programs, budgets, and, a new breed, technofactors.

Policies should call for the exercise of judgement. Consistency is important but so is flexibility. The two may seem irreconcilable, but careful administration will adhere to the broad guidelines while making appropriate decisions within the guidelines. A policy to promote from within should permit the hiring from outside under special circumstances, but to fill higher positions from the outside more than 50% of the time would be a violation of the policy.

Broad policies are geared to broad objectives, hence the final arbiter of such policies must be top management. Lower management may propose. Indeed, in matters requiring special expertise, it should propose. A personnel policy should originate with the personnel department, but the signature at the bottom of the policy should be that of the highest responsible manager.

Organizations use three types of policies. Here are some illustrations:

- *Basic policies* affect the entire organization and are issued by top management.

  Example
  To sell a competitive product for every one sold by a competitor.

- *General policies* affect a large part, but not all, of the organization. They may be issued by top or middle management.

  Example
  To procure goods from the company's customers, all other things being equal.

- *Departmental policies* are relatively specific in nature and are usually issued by middle or lower management.

Example
Internal auditors making audits at suppliers' plants should call in every morning if that does not require a long-distance call.

Those who formulate policies should be aware of the standards for good policies. Some of them are as follows:

- Policies should be geared to and based on organizational objectives.
- Policies should be based on known principles; to run counter to accepted principles—technological or behavioral—is to invite violation.
- Subordinate policies should supplement superior policies and complement policies with which they must coordinate. Inconsistencies breed confusion.
- Policies should take a definite position, be understandable, and preferably be in writing.
- Policies should be stable and capable of standing the test of time. For the same reason, they should be flexible within reasonable ranges.
- Policies should be sufficiently comprehensive to cover most situations within their scope. The purpose is to avoid repetitive managerial decisions.

Some policies, as anyone who has worked in a large organization knows, exist by managerial acceptance. The formal policy, being repeatedly violated without challenge, is replaced by informal policy. The written personnel policy may restrict the lunch break to 30 minutes; but if employees take 45 minutes and are not corrected or disciplined, the informal policy will prevail.

Similarly, comparable policies may be inconsistent within an organization. A person moving from production planning to industrial engineering, for example, will have to learn the varying policies that must be observed in the new environment. The new policies will govern reward or punishment in the group, and they may be significantly different from what was experienced in the old group. For example, felicity of expression may not be important in production planning documents. In industrial engineering, where production regulations are spelled out, good writing may be strongly emphasized.

Policies may suffer from obsolescence as much as products do. Changes in objectives, strategies, competition and labor contracts can directly affect existing policies. Any enslavement by the status quo can be destructive. Safeway, as an example, had built its reputation on quality and resisted food discounting. It feared that its reputation would suffer if it cut prices to meet competition. Then as discounting spread, Safeway was forced to change its policy, and it moved aggressively into food discounting in 1970. Policies are often revised as a result of analyses of quantitative data:

One company was subject to marked sales fluctuations. This resulted in layoffs of as much as one-third of its people during slack months. A militant union objected violently. The company resisted until pressures caused it to embark on a feasibility study. The quantitative analysis showed that relatively stable production would result if off-season sales were discounted—transferring the inventory cost to retailers—and that a 15% reduction in labor costs could be achieved through reduction in overtime during busy periods. The result demonstrated that it was not only financially feasible but advantageous to all to change the company policy to stable production.

Procedures

When policies establish general guidelines, procedures specify a chronological series of tasks or steps to achieve an objective. When policies are guides to thinking, procedures are guides to action. They give in detail the exact manner in which activities will be accomplished. Policies grant vacations; procedures show how to apply for them. Obviously, therefore, procedures should be in accord with related policies.

Although they should be specific, procedures should also possess stability. They should therefore be structured with thought to take all normal circumstances into account and require new decisions as little as possible. Each step should be complementary to the steps before and after it. Each step should fulfill a definite need to move employees toward desired objectives.

Procedures, by and large, apply to repetitive work. They have little value if each task differs considerably from other tasks. In the typical large enterprise much work is repetitive, and procedures, once established, can be followed day in day out. The manager is freed from making the same decisions over and over.

Procedures must be reevaluated periodically. To that end there is a tendency, when some new application requires coverage, to tack it on to the old procedure. A complete revision can often be the most economical approach when significant changes are needed.

Rules

A rule is the simplest type of plan; it allows for no discretion. Rules may or may not be related to a procedure. The prohibition against drinking alcoholic beverages on the job is an unrelated rule. On the other hand, a rule that says all incoming letters requiring response shall be answered or acknowledged with 10 days is related to the procedure covering receipt of and response to written communications.

Methods

Methods specify in detail how one step in a procedure should be performed. The series of steps in an employment routine is a procedure; how to check employment references is a method. The specified method, if properly devised, sets forth the best way to perform a task. It accomplishes uniformity of product and service and thereby improves efficiency. Methods reduced to writing can be helpful in training new employees.

The Gilbreths, Frank B. and Lillian M., stressed the importance of methods in management and developed what we now call motion study. Employees relate to methods more than to any other form of plan because they are the easiest to understand, are tangible, and are intimately associated with the employee's work.

When methods, such as job instructions, carefully define the task, set forth specifically the steps to take, and show the time required to complete them, the greatest output can be achieved.

Standards

A standard, although used in the function of controlling, is developed in the function of planning. It is a yardstick against which products or processes are measured to determine their acceptability. To that extent all plans can be considered standards, but in common usage a standard is applied to performance results. Maintaining a tolerance of plus or minus .0017 inches for a production part and using no more automotive fuel than a gallon per 18 miles are examples of standards.

There are two types of standards:

1. Those specifying the end result of an activity. A blueprint that sets forth precise tolerances is a standard. So is a budget.
2. Those specifying the nature of the elements of an activity. The requirement that a buyer secure at least three written bids from qualified suppliers and award the order to the lowest bidder is a standard; it is assumed that the buyer who meets that standard is performing an acceptable buying job in seeking to obtain the best price.

Standards provide effective means of control. When clearly devised and accepted by those measured, they offer an incentive to meet established goals. Also, when all elements of a process are held uniform by standards, output tends to increase. On the other hand, standards do freeze conditions, and to that extent they may impede progress toward ultimate goals. Moreover, they rarely adjust to the differences in individuals. Hence, standards should be developed to take those opposing results into account. Clearly that is not easy, but the standard setter should be aware of the potential conflict.

Technofactors

Technofactors are technical approaches to planning; they supply assistance to managers that more conventional plans cannot. They apply chiefly to time, cost, or material flow. Among them are PERT, PERT-COST (see Chapter 11), and RAMP (Review Analysis of Multiple Projects). When PERT and PERT-COST are used on a single project, RAMP is used to control more than one ongoing program. For example, a contractor constructing several buildings concurrently can watch all the work as a unit through RAMP.

Rhochrematics is a technofactor used in the management of material flow and is helpful in automation studies. It seeks to integrate the flow of material from original source through production and processing to the final consumer. Its proponents claim improved customer service, lower costs, and better use of working capital. It depends heavily on good accounting data, mathematical techniques, and the use of the computer.

Programs

Because programs are designed to achieve some objective, they too are plans. A program is a combination of goals, policies, procedures, rules and the allocation of resources to carry out some course of action. It may be major or minor; it may involve the development and sale of a new commercial aircraft; or it may be a project developed to certify all weld operators.

Large programs may involve many subordinate plans, each important to carrying out the entire program. A major program may be successful only to the extent that all derivative plans work well. A single element or procedure may cause a huge program to stumble or fail.

Budgets

A budget, in terms of planning, is a statement of expected results expressed in numerical terms. Indeed, the financial operating budget is often called the profit plan. It can be expressed in any numerically measurable terms: dollars, work hours, machine-hours, or units of production.

A budget is also a control, but first it must be developed as a plan or standard against which accomplishment can be measured. We must plan before we can control. To that end budgets anticipate operating results over given future periods and provide a basis for appraising performance as plans become translated into results.

Budgets of varying complexity are developed in almost every ongoing enterprise. The principal benefit lies in forcing the manager to plan in precise terms the future of the organization. The requirement for concrete numbers prevents vague generalities. The numbers have other benefits as well:

- They emphasize the importance of careful planning; results inconsistent with the plans point up poorly constructed budgets.
- They force executives to establish measurable objectives. A budget is meaningless unless the manager knows what is being budgeted for.
- They increase participation in the planning process. Each lower-level budget is incorporated into the overall budget, which thereby embraces the plans of people at all levels of the enterprise.

- They supply objective standards to measure the efficiency of manager and worker alike. The numbered goal makes comparisons easy.
- They impel good planning. In effect, they are a facilitating technique and hence a result rather than the precursor of management planning.
- They help sharpen the organizational structure. Effective budgets are not possible if the organization is not sound. Thus the budget process points to defects in the structure.

The larger the organization, the more diversified the budgets needed to plan its course and control its activities. Over all, generally, is the planning or operating budget that establishes the relations between revenues and costs. It usually starts with a sales forecast; and after the forecast is officially approved, it becomes the sales budget.

As the chief source of information, the sales budget provides the data necessary to prepare the production budget. The latter sets forth in quantified terms the number of finished products that will meet the needs forecasted in the sales budget. The production budget is then used to prepare tooling, materials, purchase, and labor budgets.

The factory overhead budgets cover expenses not identifiable with finished products; they include rent, power, management salaries, and other indirect factory costs. Distribution budgets cover the cost of selling and delivering products. Administrative expense budgets cover general management functions at the headquarters office and the executive level. Cash budgets are designed to show the cash needed for operations and to prevent disastrous depletions; they are estimates of the cash receipts and disbursements during the budget period. Capital additions budgets detail expenditures for additional plant, machinery, and equipment, as well as improvements in existing facilities and replacements.

Some budgets are static; they remain the same during the entire budget period. But because budgets, like other plans, are future-oriented and because the future is uncertain, another form of budget is sometimes employed. When sales or production levels are unpredictable, a flexible or variable budget may be used. It provides for a range of volume levels and budgets that apply to the various levels within the range. Since budgets are also control devices, the variable budget permits more intelligent administration of activities based on varying levels actually encountered.

Behavioral Aspects of Budgeting

Budgets are absolutely essential to the functioning of the enterprise; their absence would probably mean chaos. Yet it is a rare organization in which budgets do not create a framework for conflict. Almost invariably the individual subject to a budget considers the budget unrealistic. The responses aroused are usually antagonistic and emotional. the staff people who develop the budgets are targets of dislike, and they become defensive themselves. Budget pressures evoke retaliation and devious means of producing inaccurate or self-serving results. The production supervisor with a tight weekly budget for manufactured items may hoard parts during a good week and release them during a bad one. The forces thus generated may in the long run diminish efficiency. That is not to say that budgets should be eliminated; for elimination would be completely destructive. It is to say that budgets involve more than numbers. They involve people as well, and the numbers can have repressive effects on the people.

The practices that management follows can go a long way toward minimizing if not eliminating budget problems. Management must recognize that some resistance to budgets is entirely normal and that some grousing does not necessarily mean an absence of cooperation. Virulent opposition may be minimized by a democratic style of leadership. The participative approach can have a salutary effect in bringing the maker and the subject of budgets together. However, the participation should be real and not window dressing.

Argyris tells of a study in which a controller boasted of participation in budget preparation.(4) He would convene a meeting of supervisors at which the budget for each supervisor was presented and discussed. Then each supervisor signed his budget. If he later complained when his realized production fell short of budgeted performance, he was shown his signature as evidence that he had "participated" in budget preparation. Actually, the meetings did not evoke frank discussions; there was a mere nodding of heads. What went on inside the heads remained hidden. Argyris points out that participation in the real sense involves group discussion in which people are comfortable enough to be spontaneous and feel free to accept or reject something new. Obviously, budgets cannot be set by mobocracy, but wise leadership can let participants feel they have had their day in court and have received a sympathetic hearing.

Participation in budgets also means providing supervisors or managers with the information they need to control themselves and learn why variances occur. Hence, an unfavorable variance need not be considered a dereliction of duty when circumstances forecasted did not come to pass and there is a valid reason for the variance.

Controversy will never be eliminated from the budget process, but it can be lessened by participative management.

PLANNING AND THE INTERNAL AUDITOR

Where the Internal Auditor Can Help

The internal auditor who spent all the time verifying completed transactions for accuracy and compliance with procedures was not noted for being forward-looking. The modern internal auditor, like the manager, looks over the horizon for what is beyond. This ability as an analyst and appraiser can be useful to management in the planning function.

It is not enough for the internal auditor to verify compliance with plans, policies, procedures, and budgets. Compliance may be meticulous; employees may be following the book to the letter; but the end results may not be meeting management's needs because the book needs a new edition to bring it up to date. So the internal auditor must not only verify compliance with the regulations, but must also determine that the regulations are in gear with the organization's objectives.

With that outlook, the internal auditor can assist management at all levels through planning-related audits. The assistance can be especially helpful in audits involving:

> The centralized planning functions of the enterprise
> The planning functions within operating organizations
> Compliance with procedures
> Methods improvement
> Budgets

Centralized Planning Function

Organizations have varied means of carrying out the long-range planning functions. Individual executives and managers must plan their own activities, of course, but some plans involve all or many of the groups within the organization. In such cases, central groups are usually assigned to develop drafts of policies, procedures, programs, charters, and the like. Often, by executive indifference, those groups are left to wield considerable power within the enterprise. Also, since they represent a staff function, there is a potential for animosity between them and the operating functions.

Internal auditors become involved with those staff functions either because they audit staff departments directly or because they appraise the policies and procedures during audits of operating functions and learn how well or how badly they are working. Here are some of the matters internal auditors should be concerned with in audits of planning functions as they question the workability of plans, policies, and procedures developed by the groups:

- Are the plans, including policies, procedures, and programs, compatible with the related objectives of the enterprise?
- Do the plans improve coordination of various objectives?
- Do plans anticipate problems?
- How reliable are the forecasting and data gathering?
- Is the subject matter of the plans important enough to warrant formal planning?
- Do the benefits exceed the cost of drawing up the plans?
- Will the plans capitalize on the abilities and ideas of individuals capable of

carrying them out?
- Do the plans help achieve uniformity of action among interfacing units?
- Do the plans allow for initiative?
- Are the plans properly communicated?
- Will the follow-up methods make it possible to measure the success of the plans?

Obviously, in such analyses, the internal auditor must have a sound understanding of company objectives. This will not happen if organizational status is low. Primary organizational objectives are promulgated at the highest levels in the enterprise, and the director of internal auditing must be able to convince executive management that performing a high-level function can only be achieved if the councils of executive management include the director of internal auditing. Privy to the minutes of the board of directors, and periodically meeting with the audit committee of the board and with top executives, the director of internal auditing will lay out the long-range audit program and inquire where the best service can be provided. A knowledge of top management's thinking improves the service the internal auditor can offer. It sharpens the ability to detect defects in the planning methods and the plans themselves. Here are some of the signs that may indicate defective planning mechanism.

- Insufficient top-management support. Is management really committed to and involved in planning?
- Inadequate line involvement. Is operating management sharing with the planning staff the development of plans for the operating units?
- Lack of relevance. Are plans attacking real problems, or are planners in ivory towers, out of touch with reality?
- Lack of use. Are plans being developed and then forgotten? An important service the internal auditor can supply is to inform the planner how plans are working.
- Lack of direction. Is top management communicating to line managers what the plans are supposed to be accomplishing?
- Lack of realism. Do plans take the politics of the organization into account? Do they suffer from weak analysis, inadequate forecasting, or insufficient information? The internal auditor is an experienced fact gatherer who can provide considerable assistance to the planner in devising significant plans.
- Inadequate thinking through. Are plans merely a simple projection of past experience? Do they take into account internal and external trends?
- Insufficient recognition of contingencies. Have the planners asked themselves the what-if questions? What can go wrong most likely will.
- Inadequate feedback and control. Are the plans moving the organization toward identified objectives, or are they merely workable mechanisms?
- Poor communication. Is there a clear three-way communication among top management, operating management, and the planning staff?

- Lack of integration. Are plans made up of uncoordinated parts? When planning is oriented toward goals, the sum of the parts is greater than the arithmetic total.
- Too much attention to detail. Nobody can predict the future precisely; predictions can be only general and within certain ranges. Is excessive detail obscuring the goals and handcuffing those who must carry out the plans?
- Undue rigidity. Is the breadth of long-range planning being confused with the narrower precision of budgeting? Excessive concentration on precise results undermines creativity.

The internal auditor can be especially helpful in bridging the gap between the planner and the doer. Internal auditors reviewing central planning activities can interview operating personnel to determine whether the plans are clear, understandable, and compatible with existing conditions.

It should be pointed out that the internal auditor's responsibilities do not include developing plans, programs, procedures, and rules for operating people. To include them would be to usurp a management function. Further, with respect to the plan developed and espoused, the internal auditor could no longer rely on objectivity in future audits of the planned activities. However, objectivity is not compromised when the internal auditor suggests control mechanisms for plans or reports on how well plans are functioning.

Planning Functions of Operating Activities

In every audit of a company, division, section, or group, internal auditors will be concerned with the planning performed by the unit's manager. They can provide an important service to the manager by taking a fresh look at the manager's planning function and pointing out areas for improvement. Also if internal auditors and managers work together as partners in making the evaluation, friction will be eliminated and improvement almost assured. Here are some of the matters they can consider:

- Determine the objective of the organization under review. Not until the auditor and the operating manager have agreed on an understanding of the objectives can they proceed with the next step.
- Identify the plans which have been devised to meet the objectives and relate specific policies and procedures to those plans. The analyses may reveal redundant, missing, or inconsistent instructions.
- Determine whether the objectives conceived at higher levels have been properly communicated downward and whether operating employees have been informed of the objectives and the related plans.
- Determine whether the organization of work, personnel, authority, and responsibility is adequate to facilitate meeting the objectives.
- Determine whether the plans provide for a feedback of information that

permits the manager to make periodic comparisons between plans and accomplishment.

A cooperative approach to the examination can be an education to both the manager and the internal auditor, and the education can continue with the appraisal of the objectives after the objectives have been identified. In the appraisal process, the internal auditor and the manager should probe into the adequacy of the objectives. It is a probe that the manager should have made but it is a rare manager who can be clinically dispassionate. It is difficult to be objective about our own creations. The internal auditor's presence and questions can improve the manager's objectivity if the internal auditor is careful not to arouse defensiveness. Here are some of the questions that should be answered:

- Are the objectives capable of being misunderstood or misconstrued?
- Are any significant areas not covered by objectives?
- Have the objectives failed to consider the company's responsibility to its shareholders, the government, the community, and its employees?
- Have people been made aware of the objectives?
- Is there any incompatibility between the objectives of the unit and those of the company? Between those of the unit and of complementary units?
- Does management just pay lip service to the objectives by not allocating resources to the accomplishment of objectives?
- Should existing objectives be divided or subdivided to make them usable, more clearly understood, and more easily met?
- Do existing controls provide for seeing that objectives will be met?
- Are objectives revised so frequently as to cause confusion and frustration?

Plans follow objectives, and plans also can benefit from analysis. For all significant plans and programs, the auditor should find out whether the manager considered such questions as these:

- Why must it be done? There should be a logical answer that meets the needs of the entire organization.
- What action is necessary to get it done? The action being taken may not be the logical one.
- Where will it take place? Is the location where the action is taking place the best location?
- When will it take place? Every plan must have a schedule and a due date. Long-range programs should have milestones of accomplishment.
- Who will do it? Responsibility must be laid on an identified individual or group of individuals.
- How will it be done? Have the procedures been clearly spelled out?

Internal audit appraisals involve the comparison of activities and functions with acceptable standards. The planning function is no exception. With the agreement of the manager, the application of standards can help sharpen the audit approach:

1. *Setting objectives*

   (i) Management should have a clear conception of the basic, long-term needs of the organization and should have those objectives reduced to writing.

   (ii) Annual objectives should be in writing, and the commitment made should be submitted to higher management. The objectives should contain provision for:
   - Improvements in the organization's operations.
   - Improvement of the organization's image.
   - Cost reduction.
   - Personal development of the manager and subordinates.

   (iii) Plans should be compatible with and improve coordination of company objectives.

   (iv) The manager should be able to identify specific, continuing major objectives of the organization, that is, those that should be met if there is to be no adverse effect on quality, cost, or schedule in significant areas of operation.

   (v) More stringent control should be provided over the accomplishment of objectives that are most likely not to be attained if neglected or poorly striven for and that are difficult and time-consuming to supervise, rather than over objectives of lesser importance.

2. *Assigning responsibility*

   (i) There should be a proper delegation of responsibility that provides for accountability to higher authority for the activities assigned and at the same time capitalizes on the ideas and abilities of individuals.

   (ii) Plans should provide goals that are subject to measurement and should provide reports on periodic measurement to insure the proper discharge of the responsibility assigned.

3. *Maintaining continuity*

   (i) Long-range plans should provide for continuity of effort on major programs; the short-range plans should be concentrated on achieving interim milestones or accomplishing less-extensive programs.

   (ii) Plans should be made for continuing companywide training programs.

   (iii) Plans should be made to establish a companywide personal development plan for each employee that encompasses not only company training programs but also outside study and development.

4. *Reappraising objectives*

   (i) The organization's plans, objectives, policies, procedures, and subplans must be reappraised periodically to make sure they remain consistent with the overall plans and objectives of the company, that they achieve uniformity among related organizations, and that their benefits outweigh their costs.

Reappraisals are often traumatic. Perhaps the most difficult task for the manager is to change thinking—both for the manager and staff. To many, change is fraught with peril. Better the devil we know than the devil we don't. Nevertheless, change feeds the muscle of every enterprise, and the internal auditor's stock in trade is change—to make better, to forsake the old ways that are not working. The internal auditor can help the manager achieve change by indicating that change is more acceptable to the manager's people when:

- It is understood by those affected.
- It does not threaten an individual's security.
- Those affected help create the change.
- It results from the application of established principles instead of from some personal order.
- It follows a series of successful changes, not a series of failures.
- It is inaugurated after prior related changes have been assimilated, not imposed during the confusion of other major changes.
- It has been planned and proved, and is not experimental.
- It affects people new on the job, not those old on the job.
- It affects people who share in the benefits of the change.
- The organization has been conditioned to accept change.

Planning decisions commit for the future. Goals may be well established; but roadblocks tend to arise unexpectedly. Managers must continually check on events to see whether changes in premises require changes in plans. The wise manager is aware of supervisory responsibilities, but may not have the time to check on events. The neophyte manager may not even be aware of the need for constant follow-up. On the other hand, the internal auditor, as the expert on control, must be abundantly aware of the need for monitoring plans, and can be of special assistance to managers in the audits of operating activities:

According to procedures developed in the sales department of a store, sales personnel were supposed to add the cost of outgoing parcel post and express shipments to the sales checks at the time of sale. That was the plan, but it was not working. The sales people did not take the time to consult the necessary manuals and rate charts to determine transportation costs, and supervisors were not monitoring the sales people to see if they were doing that job. When the internal auditors compared postage charged to customers with the actual cost of postage expense incurred, they found that the store was losing about $275 000 a year.

New systems were then installed. Scales were provided with direct dollar value readings from simplified shipping cost charts based on average rates. Determining shipping costs then became an instantaneous process which the sales people found simple to use. Annual shipping costs losses were sharply curtailed.

Internal auditors, like managers, must be profit planners. They must have the ability and authority to probe the economics, the operating methods, and all the other plans involved in making and selling the entity's product or service that may affect profit. Auditors are in a particularly advantageous position to make those probes. They can concentrate upon any of the organization's products or services and can cross traditionally functional boundaries of the enterprise to determine relations and decide on the needs of participating organizations. They can act as a catalyst to improve the planning practices of contributing groups:

> During an audit of a company's plant which produces farm implements, the internal auditor questioned the use of $\frac{3}{4}$-inch bolts and nuts on certain implements. He learned that the less costly $\frac{5}{8}$-inch bolts provided adequate strength. The internal auditor raised the question with all organizations involved in planning and production. An engineering study was undertaken as a result; and after a period of testing, the smaller bolts were prescribed. Savings ran $198 000 annually.

Compliance with Procedures

Since time immemorial, auditors have verified adherence to procedures. They compare operating actions with procedural requirements in all areas of the enterprise, point out deviations, and recommend corrective action.

The organization that develops the procedures, usually staff people, rarely has the authority to review operations, detect deviations, and require correction. That is the function of operating supervision, but operating supervisors are usually involved with the day-to-day problems of assembling parts, producing products, or providing services. The internal auditor can therefore help operating management by verifying compliance with procedures and reporting significant deviations together with recommendations for improvement:

> An integrated steel company operated coal mines located some distance from the steelworks. Coal was being brought from the coal mines to blend with the company's coal. Procedures laid down the specifications for the purchased coal. The internal auditor compared the specifications of the purchased coal with those prescribed by the companies. There was a considerable variance. Evidently communications had broken down between the various organizations in the company. One did not know what the other was doing. The internal auditor recommended closer cooperation and adherence to procedures. As a result a more economical blend of coal was used, saving about $200 000 a year. The internal auditor did not prescribe the blend or know how to go about creating it. That is a management function. However, the internal auditor had focused management thinking upon the problem; and that was enough.

Modern internal auditors go beyond reviews of compliance with existing policies and procedures? They question the policies and procedures themselves. As an internal auditor reviews an operation, the first concern is the objective. What is the operation supposed to achieve? The review will encompass the implementing procedures and seek to determine whether they assist or hinder the people who are performing the function.

Sometimes existing procedures may not achieve the needed goals, yet people are still following them because that is always the way things have been done. Now and again alert managers develop new procedures for their own group that can be more productive than those followed by the rest of the organization. The internal auditor, observing the breakthrough, can make it applicable to other groups as well, sometimes with substantial savings:

> In a branch audit, an internal auditor observed that the branch manager, instead of mailing all debtors' checks to the main office's central bank account for deposit, made a separate deposit by telegraphic transfer for large checks. When the internal auditor returned to the headquarters office, she analyzed the number of days between receipt of checks and deposits and found transit time ran from two to four days. She compared the cost of telegraphic transfer with savings of overdraft interest at 12% annually. At her suggestion procedures were changed throughout the enterprise to use telegraphic transfers for all deposits over $40 000. Savings ran between $300 000 and $400 000 annually.

Internal auditors can develop routine tests of procedures in all their audit tasks. By incorporating those tests in their audit programs and by routinely comparing procedures with the tests, they can provide a significant service to managers. Here are some of the standards:

- In every step of a procedure, there should be provision for accountability. A specific individual should be responsible for a specific step. Such clear-cut assignment helps reduce overlapping, redundancy, conflict, and loss of accountability. Procedures should designate not only what and how but who as well.
- Each step of the procedure should be supported by adequate manpower and equipment so that work will progress smoothly. Lack of balance among various steps can create bottlenecks.
- Each operating procedure should have a coordinate control procedure. Provision for doing a job should include provision for monitoring progress and accomplishment.
- Forms that initiate procedures should, as much as possible, be designed for use by all elements of the organization involved in the procedure. That eliminates the need for initiating new paperwork.

Analyzing procedures through flow-charting a process can graphically disclose failures to meet those standards. Also by explaining the standards to managers, the auditor can improve future procedure writing.

Methods Improvement

The Gilbreths, through time-and-motion study, were able to find better ways of performing work (see Chapter 4). Their efforts were generally related to factory work, but their methodology is applicable to all work within an enterprise. The internal auditor's analytical ability can be put to use in revising methods—the steps in a procedure—and searching for work simplification or improvement.

Work simplification, in essence, is the application of common sense. It seeks to find more economical uses of human efforts, materials, machines, time, and space. The steps the internal auditor can take in work simplification are essentially these:

1. Select for work simplification analysis the methods that appear to be bottlenecks or to be expensive or time-consuming.
2. By means of flow charts analyze each step of the process.
3. Ask why the task is performed, where, when, how, and by whom.
4. Seek improvement by:
   - Eliminating
   - Combining
   - Rearranging
   - Simplifying
   - Mechanizing
   - Reducing physical effort and fatigue
5. Put the simplified process into effect. All that went before is a futile exercise if the ideas are not carried out.

In the following example, an internal auditor achieved significant improvements and savings by having the work rearranged.

> An internal auditor observed that expensive assemblies were being scrapped in the last phases of production. As he dug deeper he found that in this critical phase of the process the company was using inexperienced people. At the internal auditor's recommendation, only experienced people were assigned to those stages of assembly where large man-hours had already been invested. Estimated savings totalled $400 000 in the first year and, because of increased production, $3.5 million over the next five years.

Budgets

In general, the internal auditor becomes involved with four different aspects of the budgeting process:

1. The establishing of budgets and updating the budgets as premises change.
2. The recording of actual costs.
3. The reporting of performance.
4. Management's use of performance reports.

The auditor's reviews of those aspects are performed both in the budget department and in the operating departments that are subject to budgets. In both areas the auditor can be of service to management. Here are some areas of concern in the budgeting department:

- The authority given to the department by top management to obtain information from operating organizations.
- The clarity and comprehensiveness of the instructions and premises issued within the department and to contributing operating organizations.
- The scheduling of steps in the budget development process.
- The coordination of the elements of the budget.
- The format dictated by the budget department to contributing organizations to obtain information that can be readily put together.
- The review process by which budgets are evaluated by top management.
- The types of reports used to evaluate budgetary performance.
- The manner of adjusting budgets when premises change.

In any review of an operating department, the internal auditor will be interested in the department's budget—the manner in which the budget was developed and how the budget is used as a management control device. Interest will center on:

- What support was developed for the budget proposals sent to the budget department?
- How does the operating department adjust operations to accord with budget changes?
- What variances are found between budgeted and actual costs? Are they properly explained and are appropriate steps taken to correct excessive variances?
- Are all people who are affected by budgets aware of the budgets?
- Does the department manager receive sufficient accounting information to enable tracking against the approved budget?
- What reviews are made of significant variances and what is done with the results?

Perhaps one of the more significant services the modern internal auditor can provide in connection with budgets is the effect the budgets have on people. Internal auditors who have had experience with budgets for their own audit projects are aware of the constraining effects budgets have. A budget can be likened to a belt on a loose pair of trousers. It constricts the wearer, but its absence brings total disarray. If the belt were imposed on the wearer by someone else, and if it were to be too short, the result would be resentment. If the donor were a person in authority, the resentment might not be exhibited, but it would still exist and fester. The wearer might try to obtain an extension to the short belt; if not, the resentment would increase.

Yet the belt is a necessity. The wearer must live with it. But the hostility toward those who imposed the galling restraint is ameliorated if the wearer had a voice in its design, if views on the size and shape were given a hearing, and if complaints on how it wears and irks are considered.

Internal auditors, in reviews of budgets and the difficulties in meeting them, can lend a sympathetic ear. They can determine whether the forms of budgeting are applicable to the budgeted activity. They can determine whether the particular conditions are considered in the imposition of the budgets. They can find whether the budgeted manager is receiving the kind of accounting information that will help him control activities. Many a manager has had to develop a jerry-built information system because needed data were not available in usable form.

The internal auditor cannot, of course, eliminate budgets for an operating manager, but can determine whether they are reasonable and sensible and whether they relate to the objectives of the activity and the enterprise. It is possible that suspenders could replace the belt and still do the job.

At another level, the internal auditor can glean, from a review of budgets, information that can be useful to management. Such broad-ranging activities can provide an overview than can be helpful in reducing costs:

> An internal auditor reviewed the capital appropriation budget of a multiple-plant company. He observed that acquisition of similar kinds of property—forklifts and over-the-road trucks—had been planned for several locations. The internal auditor asked if the acquisitions were coordinated to take advantage of group purchases. He found that communication between the outlying plants and the central office had broken down. Central purchasing said that it tries to take advantage of group purchases when matters are referred to them, but it seemed that such coordination was the exception, not the rule. The internal auditor suggested that the budget department furnish the purchasing department with a copy of the capital appropriation budget for all plants. There the budget could be reviewed for group purchase opportunities. The result was an immediate grouping of equipment under one order and a system for continuing the practice in the future.

In a 1976 survey by The Institute of Internal Auditors it was found that only 15% of over 100 large companies questioned used their internal auditors to perform audits of budgeting activities.(5) In surveys carried out by the US Institute of Internal Auditors in 1983 and the UK Institute in 1985 the figures had increased to 38% and 45% respectively, but this is still too low for such a core activity. It is unfortunate that executive management does not call upon internal auditors more often to review one of the most significant control measures in the enterprise. The budget process is no more difficult than any of the other complex activities the modern internal auditor appraises. The rewards accruing from an objective analysis and appraisal of the budgeting process can be significant.

CONCLUSION

Planning is the process of deciding where we want to be and what we want to do. Plans come in many shapes and sizes from designs for multibillion-dollar projects to simple job instructions. What characterizes any plan is a present decision to take future action. In that light, plans include programs, policies, procedures, rules, methods, standards, budgets, and technofactors. All plans must start with objectives. It is not reasonable to act without knowing the purpose of the action.

Also since plans are future-oriented, they must be premised on forecasts of what the future is likely to hold and on what constraints the future will impose. Plans work best when the people designated to carry them out participate in devising them. That is particularly true when the plans are constricting, such as budgets.

The internal auditor's appraisal techniques can be as useful in reviewing plans as in reviewing plan accomplishment. When reviewing compliance with plans—an established application of internal auditing—auditors should also be concerned with the propriety, applicability, and usefulness of the plan themselves. To that end they can serve management through methods improvement as they review the manner in which employees follow procedures. Many internal auditors do not audit the budget process. Executive managers and operating managers can benefit from an independent review of the budgeting activity both in the budgeting organization and in the units in which the budgets are imposed.

REFERENCES

(1) S. S. Thune and R. J. House, "Where Long-Range Planning Pays Off." *Business Horizons,* Vol. 13, No. 4, p.83.
(2) Gerald Vinten, "Whistleblowing Auditors: A Contradiction in Terms?" Chartered Association of Certified Accountants, London, 1992, Gerald Vinten, editor, *Whistleblowing—Subversion or Corporate Citizenship?* Paul Chapman, Publishers, London and St. Martin's Press, New York, 1994.
(3) R. L. Ackoff, *Creating the Corporate Future*, John Wiley & Sons, 1981, p. 63.
(4) Chris Argyris "Human Problems with Budgets," *Harvard Business Review,* Vol. 31, No. 1, p. 108.
(5) R. S. Savich, *Internal Audit of the Budget Process* (Orlando, Fla.: The Institute of Internal Auditors, 1976), p. 1.

13
Organizing

ORGANIZING AND THE MANAGER

Nature of Organizing

Definition and Purpose

To achieve its objectives and goals, the enterprise must bring people and processes together in logical groupings so that plans can be carried out efficiently and effectively. To be successful, organizing should establish appropriate relations among people to do two things: work together efficiently and gain personal satisfaction from assigned tasks.

Organizing is not a precise science. It has few if any principles inscribed on tablets of stone. It is affected by too many variables in terms of people and conditions to permit the organizer to develop groupings that will always insure best results. In the final analysis it can be judged only by the test of "Does it work?"

Importance of Organization

Good organization is no guarantee of best results. Bad organization, however, will almost surely guarantee bad performance because it is the breeding ground for employee conflict and frustration. The need for good organization is not always apparent, nor is good organization always high on the list of management priorities. The need can be obscured by good people working heroically to meet budget, schedule, and quality standards despite the inept way in which people and processes have been brought together. Whatever their efforts, however, an illogical organization creates waste and inefficiency because of friction among people and wheel spinning within the processes.

If good people perform well in a poor organizational environment, they might be able to perform magnificently in a good one. Good organization has a synergistic effect—the whole becomes greater than the sum of its parts. It improves both individual satisfaction and work productivity. The individual put in the wrong job cannot be easily moved to meet the goals expected.

Elements of Organization

Good organization should include these elements:

- Objectives and goals must be established because good organization has but one function: to carry out management's plans. Good organizing, therefore, derives from good planning, in which objectives and goals are developed.
- Components possessing the needed skills and abilities must be gathered, because the wrong people or resources will frustrate rather than facilitate the process.
- The components should be bound up in a system of relations that makes clear the responsibilities for given tasks and smooths the way for cooperation and coordination.
- The resulting framework must be compatible with the environment, that is, the existing technology, society, ethics, and politics.
- The final structure, with its inherent responsibilities, authority, and accountability, must be communicated graphically and unambiguously to those affected by it.

Over and above those essential elements, however, the organization that works best is one that permits managers to feel they are running their own businesses, meeting their own goals, and gaining personal satisfaction from the work they do, no matter how taxing the work may be. So each organization should provide room for discretion and for some freedom and self-determination. It should take advantage of whatever creativity resides in the members of the organization. Also it should take into account individual capacities, likes, and dislikes.

Designing the Organization

Designers of organization should not get intoxicated by the symmetry of their design. Organization is not an end in itself; it is a means to an end. It is the vehicle that helps bring people to performance and job satisfaction. That vehicle must be shaped to the purposes of the enterprise. Some of the shapes are as follows:

- *Skill.* The product moves to the skills available. In a factory, a piece of metal moves from the cutting department to the forming department to the heat-treating or anodizing departments and to the final assembly department. In a university, the students move from the history professor to the maths professor to the language professor.

• *Stage.* A housing development is constructed in stages: grading the land, laying out streets, building foundations, erecting frames, raising roofs, and completing the interior work. Ship building also is done in stages.

• *Team.* Different skills work on an assigned task. Teams are used in research projects, in hospital operating rooms, and in projects in industry.

• *Functional.* The functional type of organized work includes both stages and skills. It works well in the small companies for which Fayol designed the functional organization. It fits comfortably into mass production. Its benefits include clarity of assignments, because everybody knows exactly what they should be doing and so it provides stability to the organizational structure. Its drawbacks include resistance to innovativeness, so it does not build people. Contrast that with the team approach in which tasks change frequently and which calls for adaptability and inventiveness. In the team approach there is high freedom but no clarity of function. It is best for imaginative and managerial work. It works inefficiently in operating work.

The form of organization must fit the objectives of the enterprise—what the business is and what it should be. For example, America's Sears and England's Marks & Spencer are in the same business, but their concepts of what that business should be are quite different. Marks & Spencer sees itself as developing upper-class goods for the middle and working-class family. Sears views its business as being the buyer for the American family. Hence, in Marks & Spencer the research and development activity occupies a paramount organizational role. That is not true at Sears, where purchasing is paramount. In those similar companies, the organizational structures fit dissimilar objects.

Arranging the activities within the enterprise is a matter of relations. The best arrangement is to have as few relations as possible—all kept to a minimum, but each one working. In the Catholic Church, for example, one of the oldest organizations, there are only three levels of authority: the Pope, the bishops, and the parish priests.

Principles for organizing are not ironclad, but some specifications for good organization do exist. When they are violated, difficulties are invited. When they are followed, the resulting organization has at least an even chance of being productive. Drucker lists these specifications:(1)

• *Clarity.* People should know where they belong and where to go for information or instruction. Clarity does not necessarily mean simplicity. If nobody can get from here to there without a detailed map, there may be confusion and impediments instead of assistance toward performance.

- *Economy.* The structure should permit self-control as much as possible. The least number of people should be needed to keep the machinery of the organization going. The less input required to grease the organization wheels, the greater is the effort available for producing the end product.
- *Direction of vision.* Organization should direct people towards the right performance—the one that will meet organizational aims. It should concentrate on productivity rather than on effort. It should be a guide toward results rather than merely toward working.
- *Understanding.* All members of the organization should understand not only their own tasks but also the tasks of their subordinates, superiors and colleagues. Thus organizational structure should help rather than hamper communication and coordination.
- *Decision making.* An organizational structure cannot make decisions for managers, but it can improve or impede the process. Organization should therefore force decision making to the lowest level, depending on the circumstances and the significance of the decisions.
- *Stability and adaptability.* Each member of the organization needs a "home"; no one performs well on a street corner waiting for a bus. The feeling of stability is important to the individual. Yet people do move from one home to another, and so the organization should not be so rigid that the ability to adapt to change is inhibited.
- *Perpetuation and self-renewal.* The sands of time ever trickle away, and the mortal resources of the organization go with them. However, the organization itself must endure. Thus the form of organization and the number of levels should not prevent a young individual from reaching the top rungs while still young enough to be effective. That specification calls for provisions to develop and test each individual for the next rung of the ladder.

There is a fundamental logic to the steps in organizing. For example:

- Understand the objectives of the organization.
- Form derivative objectives, policies, and plans that flow naturally from the major objectives.
- Identify the activities needed to meet the objectives; they are the building blocks of the organization.
- Group the activities into practical, workable units. Base the groupings on similarity, importance, and the human and material resources available.
- Assign qualified people, or people who can be developed to perform successfully, to the groupings. Clearly set forth their responsibilities. Delegate to them the authority necessary to carry out their responsibilities.
- Bind the group together both horizontally and vertically through authority relations and systems of information.

There is much controversy about whether organizations should be built around functions or people. Perhaps the answer lies in the form of organization needed to carry out the activities designed to meet objectives. In a task-oriented organization, people are brought together to apply their skills to the tasks. The team approach is task-and people-oriented. Since the teams do not have to possess long-term stability, they should be built around the best people available for the particular job.

On the other hand, in an organization that relies heavily on stability, the structure should be built around functions. The organization might work for a while if it were built around people, but in time it might be difficult to manage and the replacement of managers might also be difficult. People's interests and abilities are often subject to change; functions are less likely to vary.

Centralization and Decentralization

Origins

In small businesses authority is usually centralized. The owner-manager retains authority and makes most decisions. Then as the business grows, the principle of span of management has its inexorable effect. The owner-manager no longer can effectively make all the decisions.

Henry Ford tried it. He insisted on keeping his finger on every activity. He had to fit every piece of the puzzle together. He delegated authority haphazardly and often reversed subordinates on decisions without consulting them. However, the business had grown too big for one-person domination, and its profits slid alarmingly. Not until Henry Ford II took over the company in 1944, brought in a management team, and delegated authority to those managers was the company saved from being a poor third in the automobile market.

Sears, on the other hand, followed the policy of decentralizing and allowing more decision making at lower levels. That forced managers to accept more responsibility, function autonomously—under central control—and perform more effectively.

Reasons for Decentralization

Decentralization, as we know it today, was born in 1920; Pierre S. du Pont sired it when he reorganized the family owned du Pont Company. Alfred P. Sloan, at General Motors, refined the process by providing decentralized operations with centralized policy control. The standard model of decentralized organization emerged later from the reorganization of the General Electric Company in 1950 to 1952.

The functional form of organization is best suited to decentralization, although it can also work effectively with teams. It can divide large complex organizations into a number of smaller businesses that are relatively compact and simple. It is therefore oriented toward results, and it works well with both operating and innovative activities.

Decentralization does not imply complete autonomy for the suborganizations. Strong control at the top is still needed to decide what activities to enter into or abandon, to allocate resources, and to decide what markets to pursue and what products to develop and produce. Top management cannot operate; but it must control. Philips of the Netherlands instituted decentralization with hundreds of subsidiary companies in 60 countries. It had a leadership role in a number of products from light bulbs to household appliances. Sales went up but profits went down. There was no control from the top. What happened was fragmentation instead of decentralization. Inventories were excessive and uncontrolled. Capital investment was unplanned. Overstaffing was the rule. Only when Philips installed centralized control, common measurement, and coordinated planning did profits improve.

Decentralization does not work for every company. Many factors determine its applicability in a particular organization. Some of them are discussed in the following paragraphs.

● *Costliness of decisions.* If the results of decisions may be costly—in terms of such matters as money, morale, reputation, and competitive position—authority tends to centralize. Top management will be afraid to delegate authority for such decisions. Moreover, when business is bad and economic conditions are at low ebb, there is a strong tendency to centralize rather than to decentralize.

● *Diversity of product line.* Centralization works more effectively when a large number of subunits produce or market similar products. However, if products are diversified and each subunit deals with a unique product, there may not be sufficient expertise about each product to permit effective centralization. Knowledgeable decisions can best be made by those closest to the product. That is one reason why large conglomerates must be organized along decentralized lines.

● *Uniformity of policy.* The philosophy of some companies calls for strict uniformity of credit, quality, service, delivery, and the like. Top management feels more comfortable with the same standards, accounting practices, financial records, and statistics for all. Decentralization would not find a welcome home with such managers.

● *Size.* the larger the enterprise, the greater the number of decisions that have to be made, the more levels between top and bottom, and the longer the time span between requesting and obtaining the needed decision. That does not mean that small organizations should not decentralize when the step is appropriate. It means that larger organizations are often forced into decentralization to achieve greater efficiency.

- *Geographic dispersion.* When facilities are geographically spread out, it may be difficult for top management to exercise control needed in centralized management. Decentralization beckons because of the distances from the top-level decision makers.
- *Nature of business.* Manufacturing companies, with their constant need to adjust to change, present more fertile fields for decentralization than centralization. Companies dealing in finance, however, find it easier to hold on to centralized authority despite size or geographic dispersion.
- *Desire for independence.* Individuals may become restive and frustrated when faced with delays in obtaining decisions from centralized authority. Besides, most people seek independence and freedom to make their own decisions. Centralized management, however, would be reluctant to permit local decision making if the people were not competent to exercise the authority.
- *Nature of growth.* Companies that grow from within find it difficult to decentralize; top management has always made the decisions and is reluctant to delegate decision making to others. Such a management philosophy, of course, tends to reject decentralization. If, on the other hand, the enterprise grew as a result of merger or acquisitions, and left the top managements of the acquired companies in power, decentralization comes naturally.
- *Ability to control* To delegate is not to abdicate. Top management must still remain responsible for the overall performance of the enterprise. Appropriate management controls must exist to permit decision making at the lower levels but also to provide accountability of subordinate decision makers.
- *External influences.* Increased government regulation may affect top management's decision to decentralize. Indeed, the need for uniform interpretations and application of government regulations may require a decentralized organization to recentralize, if only in certain parts of its operations.

Advantages of Centralization

Probably the most important advantage of centralization is that the chief executive officer has increased power and prestige, with the last word on more decisions. The psychology of top management can demand that. Such an executive may want to see strict uniformity of policies and practices continued. Specialists at headquarters are fully used and are close to the executive level. Besides, top-quality specialists can be hired because there is abundant work for them. Duplication is minimized, as is the danger of functions deviating from standards for long periods before the deviations are detected. To that end, elaborate control devices are not required because management is closer to the enterprise operations.

Advantages of Decentralization

Decentralization relieves the heavy load on top management. Delegation of some of the executive's load tends to develop generalists instead of specialists and eases the transition into general management positions. Greater responsibility at lower levels for the various "businesses" within the enterprise tends to develop closer personal relations in each business and to instill greater employee enthusiasm and loyalty. Each member of the "business" has a more intimate knowledge of the work. Trouble spots can be more readily located because responsible managers are closer to operations. In multiunit or multinational companies, the local managers have a closer contact with and understanding of local conditions. From the standpoint of top management, programs can be tested in one subunit without incurring risks in the remaining subunits. Indeed, risks of loss of resources can be spread out and thereby minimized.

More managerial talent can be developed because more managerial positions are available. Business can be run on a profit center principle because each unit is given freedom to improve the profits while being held accountable for results. Lower-level decisions may be more rational, since they take local problems into account. Products may be more readily diversified because a complete project can be developed to carry the product from conception to production and distribution.

The Choice Between Centralization and Decentralization

In the final analysis, the decision to decentralize or to recentralize and the extent of each depend on the individual circumstances. No two companies or chief executive officers are entirely alike. In the following example we shall look at the Whitbread company.

Whitbread is a long-established UK retail leisure company, dating back to 1742. It has major interests in beer, public houses, inns and restaurants, hotels and wine shops, and it owns the franchise for Pizza Hut, UK. It started as a family business with strong centralized control. Even as late as 1889 there were only nine clerks, and they kept accounts under the eyes of the managing partners. This had certainly changed by the 1990s, with a small supporting headquarters team, but the major emphasis on decentralized business segments requiring subtle differences in operating style and methods. Success has depended on the ability to recognize and exploit these differences, and yet gaining maximum benefit from the synergies which also exist. A number of formal and informal mechanisms ensure that Whitbread is greater than the sum of its parts.

Regular cross-business forums enable senior managers to spread best practice and to share market knowledge and new ideas. Managers have a great deal of freedom, but performance and ethical standards are high. This challenging environment generates great loyalty, and the informal networks which managers establish during the course of their careers are a major source of strength. Corporate-wide functions also contribute to the integration of the company. Slim and responsive, and including an active and effective operational auditing department, they are focused on achieving excellence in their fields, and providing leadership for their clients, the various Whitbread businesses.

In centralization versus decentralization, the law of the situation must apply, which is the same as contingency theory.

> In a little town in Louisiana a teacher had been hearing a class read a lesson about birds in a standard textbook. To drive home a point about the lesson, she asked one of the boys, "When do the robins come?"
>
> The boy promptly said, "In the fall."
>
> The teacher asked the boy to reread the text. Then the same question and the same answer. Infuriated, the teacher insisted on a rereading and then thundered the same question. In tears, the frightened boy finally gave the answer the teacher wanted: The robins come in the spring."
>
> And so they do—in Boston where the book was written. But in Louisiana, where the robins come to avoid the winter, they arrive in the fall. And the boy's knowledge of local conditions was superior to that of the text writer.

When decentralization is applicable and is practiced properly, it works well. General Motors has developed what many regard as excellent controls to measure the results of its decentralized operations. One is the costing system, which eliminates as much as possible such extraneous factors of cyclical fluctuations. Another is the rate of return on capital invested in each division. A third is an analysis of the competitive standing of the product of each division in the market. Divisions that sell principally to other GM divisions are measured by their ability to sell at lower prices than other suppliers. The impact of forces beyond a manager's control are eliminated as much as possible. At GM decentralization prevents infringement by top management on division decisions, yet fairly holds division managers accountable.

Mergers and Acquisitions—Departmentation

Departmentation designates a distinct area, division, or branch of an enterprise that is responsible for performance, has authority to carry out needed activities, and is accountable for results. Some companies have few levels in the hierarchy but many departments, all set horizontally and all reporting to a single superior. Such structures are said to be flat. Other companies have a large number of levels with relatively few departments reporting to a superior. Such structures are called tall. The flat structure calls for better people and greater responsibility because the broad span of control prevents close supervision. However, the flat structure has its drawbacks, because the fewer the strata the less opportunity for people to advance.

Tall structures provide closer control and greater opportunities for advancement; close supervision inhibits the development of self-reliant, innovative managers. Also, it results in greater costs, because there are additional managers and their staffs in the hierarchy. Finally, it complicates communication because of the filtration process that distorts messages as they are communicated from one level to another. The public sector, the armed forces and the police have tended to work on this basis.

Basis for Departmentation

Organizations may be departmented in various ways: by number of people, function, territory, product, customer, marketing channel, project and process of equipment. A brief discussion of each follows:(2)

• *Number.* The simplest form of departmentation is number. It is useful in the armed services, universities, collectors for community funds, and laborers. It has the benefits of rapid expansion or contraction. It is useful, however, only at lower levels of management.

• *Function.* The most common form is function; the basic enterprise functions in manufacturing, for example, are production, marketing, and finance. Function has the advantages that it is simple and logical, follows the basic principle of grouping specialists in a specific occupation, makes training easier, and provides tight control at the top over the subsidiary function. Its disadvantages are that responsibility for results is usually centered at the top. It narrows the viewpoints of the specialists. It does not tend to develop general managers, because the functional employee does not always see the business as a whole. It also reduces coordination between functions because each function is an island unto itself.

• *Territory.* Departmentation governed by geographical areas is used, obviously, in enterprises having a wide physical dispersion. All functions in an area are grouped under a territorial manager. That works best when it encourages local participation in decision making. The advantages, basically, are economical and may include lower freight rates, rent, travel costs, and labor. The disadvantages include the need for more and better managers (always in short supply) and duplication of such services as purchasing and accounting.

• *Product.* In large enterprises with many product lines, departmentation by product has gradually been evolving. It offers the advantages of growth and diversity of products and services, offers a good training ground for generalists, improves the coordination of functional activities, and provides for strict accountability for each product. As in territorial departmentation, however, it requires more and better managers and intensifies problems of top management control. It also results in duplication of some services that could be supplied more economically at a central location.

• *Customer.* In customer departmentation the customer is central to the way activities are grouped. Loan officers in a bank, for example, may deal with a restricted type of customer. Some departments of a company are concerned only with military products, others with civilian products. When it is appropriate, this form provides for greater customer satisfaction because particular customers or types of customers are dealing with specialists trained in their needs and activities. Yet problems of coordination can arise between the customer-oriented department and other departments organized in a different way. Also, facilities and manpower can be underemployed, particularly in periods of recession.

● *Market channel.* Some companies have expanded the product orientation to marketing channel departmentation. That can be brought about by the needs of varied markets. The Purex Corporation, for example, learned that neither product nor territorial departmentation would work for it. Purex found that buyers and ways of doing business were different in the supermarkets on the one hand and the drug chains on the other.

● *Processes and equipment.* In departmentation by processes and equipment, experts or machines in specific processes are grouped to perform special tasks. Electronic data processing departments that perform work for other organizations are prime examples. So are special heat-treating and anodizing groups in manufacturing companies.

Projects

The project concept is a violation of the principle of unity of command, yet it can and does work under certain circumstances and conditions. It is a form of staff with functional authority. It focuses on a large task; it is assembled for the task and is disbanded when the task is completed. It has been used largely in the aerospace industry, in which a contract is let for a specific piece of hardware or research.

Project managers are responsible for completing an end product by using people administratively responsible to other managers. They borrow talents from research, production, sales, finance, and other departments to carry out the task. They exercise more authority than is customarily assigned to a staff manager. Their people are, in effect, reporting to two masters. The administrative manager determines who will work on the project; the project manager tells those people what to do and is responsible for budget, quality, and schedule. The administrative manager is still responsible for ratings and raises for staff, but receives input on performance from the project manager. The disadvantage, of course, is the violation of unity of command; the advantage lies in permitting maximum use of specialization, which is focused on a task of great significance to the enterprise.

Project structures can and do work. But there must be full and free communication and a thorough understanding of tasks, functions, and responsibilities. Like all principles, unity of command can be successfully bent to specific uses if everyone understands the needs of the enterprise and of the people involved in and affected by the project.

Responsibility, Authority, and Accountability

Duties and rights determine what tasks a manager is to do and what powers there are to accomplish them.

Responsibilities

The duties are commonly referred to as responsibilities—the obligation of a person to carry out assigned activities. Responsibility flows down from superior to subordinate, and, although it can be assigned, it can never be relinquished. The superior, all the way up to the chief executive, still is charged with the responsibility to see that what is assigned to others gets done. The president who assigns the marketing vice president responsibility for a sales campaign is still responsible to the board of directors and the stockholders for the success of the campaign. It is not possible to say, if the campaign fails, "I gave the marketing person the responsibility and so the failure is not my fault."

Responsibility is a series of obligations that constitute a chain from superior to subordinate to subordinate. Responsibilities are a chain of relations established between organizational levels, and those relations create risks. The retention of final responsibility in the superior carries with it the fear that the subordinate will not perform as well as the superior. So many superiors fear to delegate some of their responsibilities to others. They make themselves indispensable; and they do not, therefore, build strong organizations or strong people.

Responsibility stems from function, and function stems from objectives. The clearer the understanding of all concerned as to what are the objectives, the functions, and the responsibilities, the more readily are people willing to accept and carry out responsibilities.

Unclear statements of responsibility result in job dissatisfaction. A study of 290 employees, including managers and technical people, measured role conflict and role ambiguity with varying levels of job satisfaction.(3) It was found that the classical theory of clear assignments and structure, standards and measurements, and emphasis on output reduced the conflicts and the ambiguities. People usually like to know what they're supposed to do and how much, but they function best when they have participated in delineating their tasks and responsibilities.

Assignments of responsibility can create problems when:

- There are gaps—when people are not sure who is to carry out a given task.
- There are overlaps—when two or more people are made equally responsible for given tasks.
- The assigned responsibility does not contribute to an accepted, understood objective—if the job has no meaning to the one responsible for it. That often occurs when the objectives change and the responsibilities remain the same.

Authority

Authority is a right to perform; it is a right to command; it is a right to enforce compliance. It comes into being from ownership, legal fiat, or status in an organization. New concepts about authority stress the "subordinate-acceptance approach." The manager must be accepted by subordinates; better performance is achieved by winning support, not by ordering it. Yet the ultimate authority must be there. In time of emergency the manager must have the "position authority" to command and to be obeyed. When fire erupts, there is no time for superior-subordinate debates.

Authority derives from responsibility. It is futile to grant authority when there has been no prior obligation—responsibility—to perform. Yet authority has certain limits. It is restricted by the technical expertise of subordinates and by objectives, plans, organization structure, statutes, agreements, and social pressures.

Like responsibilities, authority must be made specific if it is to have legitimacy. For example, a buyer may have the authority to issue purchase orders on her own signature for purchases under $500, but not if they are $500 or over. If the levels of authority are not clearly spelled out, confusion can result.

Top-management philosophy will dictate the extent of authority delegated. The more that centralization is required the less the authority granted. The greater the degree of centralization the greater the need for granted authority at the lower levels. In such circumstances there is less of a requirement for decisions to receive approvals, before and after, and managers are willing to risk the judgement of their subordinates and allow a certain amount of mistakes.

Of course, the law of the situation will affect the amount of authority granted. How large and complex is the organization? How competent are its people? How well have tasks been standardized and made repetitive? How geographically dispersed are the organization's activities? Most important, how effective is the system of communication? Is communication full and prompt, and is decision making aided by adequate, accurate data? In fact, the ubiquitous computer will probably put brakes on the trend toward decentralization and the increased delegation of authority.

Coequality

Authority and responsibility must be coequal. Logically, there can be no responsibility for a task if the authority to carry it out is lacking. So authority regulates the amount of responsibility that can be assigned. In fact, when authority is less than responsibility, the latter tends to fall to the level of the former.

Parity of responsibility and authority has long been held to be a truism, but, as McGregor says, it rarely obtains in practice.(4) No manager has complete control over activities. Uncontrollable factors such as illness of key employees, contract cancellations, government action, changes in customer preference, and unexpected vagaries in business cycles, all act as constraints, yet the manager is expected to carry out all responsibilities. Still, the superior who deliberately assigns responsibility and does not grant the concomitant authority is handcuffing the subordinate.

Accountability

Accountability derives from responsibility. Managers cannot hold subordinates accountable for tasks or people they have no responsibility for. On the other hand, whoever has been given responsibility and coequal authority can be asked to account for carrying out their responsibilities and for stewardship of the resources entrusted.

Single accountability implies one boss–one employee. It means that each person should be answerable to only one immediate supervisor. It is a part of the concept of unity of command. Unity of command may sometimes have to be violated to meet the laws of the situation, as in project organizations. As a continuing matter, it should be followed, since it is the only way the diverse and varied units of the enterprise can be logically organized.

Documentation

Subordinates will feel more comfortable when their responsibility, authority, and accountability are set forth clearly in organization charts, statements of responsibility, and job descriptions. These documents help establish and control relations among people and can also be useful in indoctrinating and educating new people.

Delegation

Nature

Delegation is the means by which responsibility is assigned, authority is granted, and accountability is exacted. It occurs, or should occur, when superiors or organizations have more work than they can handle.

Actually, without delegation, organization is impossible. There is a limit to close personal involvement in or supervision of tasks. When that limit is passed, the discretion and right to carry out tasks should be given to a subordinate by a superior. It is axiomatic, of course, that only that authority which the superior possesses legitimately can be delegated. Unfortunate indeed is the subordinate who is granted authority by a superior who never had it.

Failure to delegate can be disastrous. Safeway under Lingan A. Warren, the autocrat who made all the decisions, showed a poor profit picture. However, when stockbroker Robert Anderson Magowan took over, decisions were pushed down to the district level. Profits were lifted, and sales increased. Magowan knew little about the food business, but he fully understood organization and delegation. Ray Kroc of McDonald's dismissed one the best store managers after he found a hamburger wrapper in the parking lot. He did not even bother to seek an explanation. Fortunately the area manager saw to the reinstatement of the store manager.(5)

All involved in it must understand that the delegation process does not mean abdication. It implies granting authority; it does not imply divesting the superior of responsibility. Similarly, the sensible subordinate understands that no delegation is absolute. When the boss says, "Here's the job. Use your own judgement. Whatever you do is fine by me," this is not the real meaning. The subordinate had better follow the boss's policies and remain aware of the philosophies, or the authority will soon be withdrawn.

The boss who makes such a statement is not practicing the fine art of delegating. True, there may be receptiveness to new ideas from younger, innovative subordinates. There may be a willingness to let go some authority, or to trust subordinates to make some mistakes, but there must not be abdication of responsibility. To that end, each delegation must be accompanied by some sort of control, some form of feedback, so the superior still has arms around the organization, no matter how unobtrusively, and still has the means of knowing when to pull in the reins and take over.

The rule must be: delegate, but obtain feedback; follow up on what must be carried out; and don't be afflicted by unwelcome surprises because the reins were dropped completely.

Why Managers Don't Delegate

There are many reasons why managers don't delegate. First, of course, is their failure to assume the role of managership when they are promoted. There is the fear that, if they are not into everything with both hands and feet, they won't be justifying the trust placed in them by their own superiors.

Then too, their philosophy may militate against delegation. They may trust nobody but themselves. They may fear being exposed, because delegation opens up activities and may reveal shortcomings. They may, on the one hand, not trust their subordinates or, on the other hand, fear that subordinates may take over the managerial job. They may desire to dominate in all things, and part of that may be the unwillingness to accept the calculated risks that accompany delegation.

Studies of managerial failure put poor delegation at the top of the list of factors, which include psychological attitudes, lack of understanding of the principles of delegation, and failure to put known principles into effect. However, as in any other aspects of management, when the benefits and methods of delegation are understood, better management results.

Getting Managers to Delegate

The climate in the organization may have to be changed before managers become willing to delegate. When the fear syndrome permeates the organization, managers feel that they must be on top of every detail for which they are responsible. They feel that every question asked of them by a superior must be answered promptly and in specific detail. That reduces them to collectors and hoarders of information, both significant and trivial.

There should be no onus to saying, "I don't know the details, but I'll get them right away." So the first task for executive management that wishes to promote intelligent delegation is to make the delegator secure and to develop a climate that is free of fear of not having all the answers at the managerial fingertips. Managers should be taught by example that there is a need for delegation, that managers who can say "I'm the most expendable person in my organization" are highly prized.

Managers must be encouraged to believe in delegation, intelligent delegation, to understand that it does not exist in a vacuum, but must be granted to subordinates wisely and must include only those tasks the particular subordinate is competent to handle or can be taught to handle with reasonable success.

Also, managers must know that good delegation is made clearly. Guidelines are needed; parameters must be set; expectations should be spelled out. Some executives may boast that their delegations are deliberately vague to encourage innovativeness and provide flexibility. That may be true at the outset of a task involving many unknowns, but if the vagueness is permitted to continue, the dream of a happy innovative team gives way to the nightmare of a dissident group of frustrated people.

Principles of Delegation

A clear understanding of the principles of delegation improves the success of decentralized authority. Here are some principles:

- Clear definition of the job. The task, function, or activity should be defined, and the lines of communication for needed information should be thoroughly understood.
- Scalar principle and unity of command. Each delegate must know the delegator. The chain of command must be clearly delineated. It should be understood that the chain of command may be ignored at times—but only to obtain information, not decisions. Failure to observe unity of command may result in conflicting instructions.
- Retention of responsibility. Once delegates receive authority, they should be compelled to use it. Laziness that brings delegates constantly to the delegator for decisions they should be making on their own should not be tolerated. To that extent responsibility is absolute. Once subordinates accept responsibility, they

may not evade it. Then in turn the responsibility for the work of subordinates must be retained. They must also be taught that, when they encounter problems that are urgent and significant, they must promptly bring them to the attention of higher authority.

• Equality of responsibility and authority. When authority is granted, it should be keyed to the responsibility assigned. It should never be less or more than is needed to carry out the results expected.

• Splintered authority. Authority must be used intelligently. A manager should not have authority to make decisions involving the organization of a manager on the same level. Both managers should, when occasion warrants, be able to get together and work the problem out between them. Under the scalar principle, it is true, the decision should be referred to a common superior, but too many such referrals will swamp that superior. Although splintered authority cannot be avoided, too much may indicate the need for reorganization.

Spans of Management

The need for delegation harks back to the inability of human beings to be personally involved with too many diverse activities and too many subordinates. But how many is too much? Many studies have been made of spans of management or, as it is sometimes called, span of control. Some studies say the span should be 4 to 8 immediate subordinates at the upper levels. But in practice there are wide variances. The American Management Associations surveyed 100 large companies for information on the subject. It found from one to 24 executives reporting directly to a president. Only 26 presidents had 6 or fewer subordinates. The median number was 9.

But the numbers alone have little meaning. More important are such variables as subordinate training, good planning, number of changes, use of objective standards, and the excellence or poverty of communication. All those variables contribute to the appropriateness of tall or flat organizations. Tall organizations have narrow spans but many levels. Flat organizations have broad spans and fewer levels. The tall organizations have closer supervision but take a long time for decisions and communication to filter down. They make tight supervision easier, but they inhibit delegation. The flat organization sacrifices closer supervision for the development of more self-reliant subordinates.

Span of management increases geometrically with the addition of new people or units. More is involved than the added bodies; there are the added relations and intercommunications. If a manager has one subordinate, the number of relations is simply one: superior and subordinate, but add one more subordinate and what happens? The boss has two direct relations. Also, subordinate A relates to B and B to A: two more relations. Further, the boss now has relations with A and B as a group or B and A as a group. (Dealing with B while A is present is different from dealing with A while B is present).Thus, the number of relations jumps from one to six with the addition of one more subordinate.

V.A. Graicunas, a French consultant in management, developed a mathematical formula to calculate the rise in number of relations:

$$R = n(2^{n-1} + n - 1)$$

where R = relations
n = number of subordinates

By using that formula, a superior with five subordinates can be involved with 100 relations:

$$R = 5(2^4 + 4) = 5(16 + 4) = 100$$

What becomes important to the executive, therefore, is not only the addition of people to the organization but the geometrically increased demand on time because of the number of added relations. Then when the work is varied, the people inexperienced, and the delegation minimal, the demands on limited time can rise alarmingly.

Line and Staff

Nature

All people in an organization are connected by a line of command from the very top to the very bottom. A small organization has a straight line of authority from president to lowest worker; hence the term "line authority." That type of structure has much to commend it. It is simple; it can change direction; and it can make speedy decisions.

Large organizations are rarely simple. Retaining the direct-line concept increases levels and foregoes the use of specialists who can provide expertise the line managers to not possess. Hence the use of staff. A staff is a stick carried in the hand as an aid to walking or climbing. It performs as the climber uses or needs it. It does not perform by itself. It can be used or not as the climber wishes.

The concept of staff in organizations is as old as government and armies, in which it has been used since ancient times. More recently it has been used in business. The simple concept has now evolved into a relation that puzzles theorists and frustrates managers.

Definitions by the score have sprung up, but none has provided the ultimate, finite meaning. The reason lies in the many variations. For example, "line" has been defined as the function that contributes directly to the fulfillment of the economic objectives of the company. Hence many people think of line as primary and staff as secondary in importance. Do the accounting and tax departments contribute directly to the economic fulfillment of the company's objectives? Ask that question of the production manager, and the answer will be an emphatic *no.*

Departments have been identified as line and staff according to functions, but that identification is not wholly accurate. It depends more on objectives. A professor in a university is line, but if hired by a manufacturing department to carry out the same function—to teach people—he becomes staff. Office work may be line in an insurance company; it is staff in a manufacturing company. Even there the difference is not that clear. Between the director of office services and the lowliest clerk in that department there is a line relation. Line exists whenever a superior exercises direct supervision over a subordinate for the fulfillment of an objective.

The relationship becomes line-staff whenever one individual or group is responsible for meeting an objective and making the decision to that end and another is responsible for advising and assisting—usually on request. Hence a staff function may be characterized as one that is separated from the primary chain of command—the decision makers who deal directly with the organization's end products—to give specialized service and make the operation more economical and efficient. The specialists in large organizations are necessary, but they should be on tap, not on top.

There are different kinds of staff. The primary difference is between personal and specialist staff.

Personal

The personal staff have backgrounds similar to the background of the superior. They are the "assistants to" who take some of the load off the superior without having functional authority. They help plan, develop departmental budgets, obtain information, and make outside contacts to gain information, but never direct or order.

Assistants, however, as distinguished from "assistants to," share the line manager's authority. In relation to the president, however, an executive vice president is an assistant manager, not an assistant to the manager. There is definite line authority, although it may be subject to certain restrictions.

The general staff was initiated in the military to help a top manager handle enormous operations. In the US Army, it comprises G-1, Personnel; G-2, Intelligence; G-3, Operations; G-4, Supply; and G-5, Controller.

Specialist

The specialist staffs are broadly divided into advisory, service, control, and functional groups. Advisory staffs present opinions and recommendations on such matters as law, taxes, and insurance. Theirs should be completed staff work. The superior should not have to develop information, but should be able to merely agree or disagree with a proposal in terms of the entity's objectives.

- Service staff is designed to avoid duplication. Examples are central purchasing departments and data processing departments.
- Control staff restrains line authority and includes such functions as credit, security, auditing, and inspection.
- Functional staff supplies information on how and when to perform an activity. For example, the production control department represents functional staff in a manufacturing organization.

Because of their widespread use and because of some misconceptions about them, it may be useful to discuss further the service staff and the authority associated with functional staff.

Service Departments

Service departments differ from true staff functions. They produce a tangible end product. A typing pool turns out letters, and an EDP department turns out data and reports.

One purpose of the service department is to centralize activities to achieve economies; another may be to improve control. Examples of the latter are a central buying group and a central unit dealing with the administration of contracts.

Service departments may partake of both line and staff functions. When they act as line, they make all the decisions made by line people. However, when they act as staff, their decisions are restricted to research and advice; they provide line executives with the benefit of their staff expertise.

Sometimes service personnel are loaned to a line department or other staff department to provide more immediate service. Examples are cost accountants assigned to a manufacturing branch or a traffic expert assigned to a purchasing organization. By their very nature, those assignments, logical on their face, may lead to conflicts. The cost accountant may be asked to side with manufacturing in construing accounting department rules. The chief of accounting, it is true, gives the cost accountant raises and promotions, but the chief must rely on the manufacturing manager for input about the cost accountant's effectiveness.

Service departments exist because centralization is supposedly more economical than decentralization. However, that can be just theory, and most service departments are created on that theory. Rare indeed is the service department that is set up after the costs have been studied. Besides, there are other attributes than cost to be considered: the possibility of inadequate service, delays, poor communication, favoritism, and downright failure to act in emergencies. A careful analysis of individual situations may show that a line manager may get the job done better, with a precise knowledge of what is wanted and how it should be done. As an example, operating reports may be produced better, faster, and cheaper by people under the direct supervision of line management.

Functional Authority

Somewhere between line authority and staff authority is a blend called functional authority. It exists because it has to; in its absence the chief executive is flooded. It is actually a delegation to a staff organization of a slice of the chief executive's responsibility and authority.

Functional authority is the right to prescribe processes, methods, or policies to other line or service organizations. For example, the accounting branch has the authority to prescribe forms for the preparation of personnel time records. The chief of accounting's authority to that end extends throughout the enterprise. It supersedes the authority of any line manager to develop similar forms.

Functional authority is possessed by the personnel manager to prescribe grievance procedures, by the safety manager to shut down the plant if a hazard exists, and by the production scheduler in telling production when to process or construct its products. Obviously, functional authority should be resorted to as little as possible. Just as it is a slice of the chief executive, so it slices away the authority of the line manager. It encroaches on the unity of command. It is possible to find an operating manager having to bow to a half dozen functional bosses, and with arrogance so ready to surface in staff people, that can be frustrating and counterproductive.

Conflicts

Whenever one activity invades the domain of another, defenses rise and conflicts are spawned. It is a matter of authority. The staff officer has the authority of ideas. The line officer has the authority of command. Let the staff officer step over the line and try to command and the battle is joined. The line officer can benefit from the ideas of the specialist, but should not be asked to delegate the job to the specialist. That distinction is central to good working relations between line and staff. The specialist in efficient operations brought in to unearth waste and inefficiency must understand that, no matter how brilliant the suggestions may be, they will have to be sold, not told. If the line people are convinced that the suggestion was *their* idea, then this shows the true meaning of what staff has to offer: a staff for leaning, not leading, for assisting, not insisting.

The staff people must be guardians of the relations. Staff is the more expendable. If a hard conflict arises, executive management will most likely side with line, not staff. So staff should seek never to undermine line authority; it should be scrupulous in how it offers advice. To say, "Do this" infringes on line authority. Even to say, "Here's how I'd do it" can cause line to abdicate its own responsibility. If things go wrong, line can use the excuse "This is how staff said it should be done; don't blame me." How much better if staff asks "How do you think it should be done?" and then, when told, asks "Why?" and explores the reasons.

Staff can offer advantages to line: the actions of the line manager may become more scientific; the span of control may be lengthened; communication and coordination with peripheral organizations can be improved. At the same time, staff can increase the number and the complexity of organizational relations. Its people often tend to usurp line authority, even without setting out to do so, and the usurpation invites conflict. To avoid the evils of a redundancy of supervision, to preserve unity of command, and to hold line managers responsible for results, staff must be denied command authority.

Improving Staff-Line Relations

No sets of rules work for all people, but an understanding of what might work may dampen the antagonisms that threaten to ignite in any line-staff relationship.

Staff must understand, first of all, the basic authority relations in the organizing function. Those relations should be clarified through a clear identification of the particular staff's duties and responsibilities. Especially clear must be the limitations on staff authority. The staff people who are specialists must be just that: competent specialists in their field. They must be capable of earning the respect of the line people. They should, if at all possible, have some line experience so they will not be accused of being ivory tower theorists without the gut feeling of what it takes to make and implement line decisions. They should be kept aware of what goes on in the organization, lest the textbook proposals run aground on the rocky beach of existing limitations on what is practical.

They should be held accountable for their own performance. They too should be required to deal with budgets, schedule, and quality—standards that they impose on themselves or are imposed on them. They should not be given special treatment merely because they are staff. Their suggestions should be carefully thought out; they should not make suggestions they would not have made if they themselves were responsible for the line operation. Also, the suggestions should not be offhand comments that are left to the line to be put into usable shape.

The stress should be on interdependence and not on separation. Both staff and line should be evaluated on what they accomplish in concert rather than on how they perform individually. Good organizing fuses together all segments of the organization.

Line should be made fully aware of staff's contributions. It should be required to listen, not necessarily to accept, but line should understand that staff can make them look good. In General Motors, for example, the product division manager consults with the various staff divisions before proposing major programs or policies. Although there is no necessity to do so, with staff on your side proposals have a better chance of acceptance. From the standpoint of staff, if the advice is sound, valid, economical, and feasible, it will generally be accepted. Yet staff should be independent. It should feel sufficiently secure, because of expertise and status, to offer independent advice and not merely what line management wants to hear.

Informal Organizations

Nature

In every organization, like the double exposure on a negative, is the wraith of the informal organization. It is not readily defined, but it exists. It is pervasive; it is dynamic; and it must be considered. It cannot be incorporated into the formal organization nor can it be given formal status, because ordinarily it does not recognize the formal chain of command. However, the manager who ignores the informal organization may be courting trouble.

Informal organizations are composed of relations among its members that ignore the organization chart. A supervisor who has the authority, under the cloak of the formal organization, to issue direct orders to a subordinate may have an informal working relation that puts the two on a par.

Benefits and Drawbacks

That may not be all bad. The informal organization may benefit the formal one. It can fill gaps in the formal organization, and it can improve coordination among people. It can make the enterprise a more appealing place to work in. An offer of a more lucrative job may be ignored because the individual does not want to leave his or her "family." It provides a grapevine for information that does not come through the regular chain of command. Also it may very well make the manager more sensitive to his people and help him gain more cooperation and productivity.

On the other hand, the activities of the informal organization may run directly contrary to those of the formal one. The informal organization may impose limits on the decisions the manager feels are best for the organization as a whole, and because of its unstructured, fluid pattern it can create uncertainty. The wise manager will know who its leaders are and avoid antagonizing them.

Power, Politics, and Status

The informal organization is little affected by formal charts or statements of responsibility. Instead, it is guided and governed by such informal qualities as power, politics, and status. Power is the ability to apply pressures that are effective. There are many sources of power in the informal organization, but the most important is expertise.

Politics exists in every organization. It is a way of getting things done outside the formal network; it is also a way of advancing oneself in the formal organization. A five-year study was made of 149 managers in a large manufacturing company. The sample comprised the following groups:(6)

Promoted	47%
Lateral transfers	14
Remained on same job	22
Demoted	17
Total	100%

The characteristics in the promoted group were the ability to manoeuver and to get cooperation from the groups own level rather than from below and the ability to deal with confused and complex responsibilities. Those represent the sign of the good politician, the accommodator, and the compromiser. The study showed that people willing and able to engage in politics are more likely to be advanced in large organizations. Their characteristics are useful in achieving reconciliation and getting the job done. If improperly controlled, of course, doing manoeuvering can result in chaos. On the other hand, those who stick like a barnacle to the rule book will be personally safe, but will become known as brass-bound bureaucrats who are more concerned with being right within the letter of the law than in accomplishing objectives.

Status is rank. The informal organization has its pecking order that may be irrelevant and unrelated to the formal hierarchy. Management should disrupt that order as little as possible. Here is an example:

Employees riding to jobs in trucks had developed a pecking order based on seniority. The senior man rode in the cab. The crew sat in the truck in positions also dictated by seniority. The youngest sat next to the tailgate, and it was his menial task to open and close it. Ankle injuries resulting from jumping over the tailgate impelled management to require the man in the cab to open and close the gate. This created chaos. The *high-level man* doing a *low-status task!* Teams who solved the problem best were those whose supervisors let the informal organization work out the best way to follow the rule without disrupting the informal organization. In some cases the senior man was convinced that by undertaking to open the tailgate he was caring for *his* people.

Roles

Closely related to status in the enterprise is role: how a person is expected to behave in the position occupied in the enterprise. The formal job description sets forth the enterprise's expectations, but the informal organization has certain expectations of its own. If the two roles are incompatible, conflicts are almost certain to arise. The new supervisor who has to make demands upon former co-workers is in a role conflict. So is the foreman who has demands for productivity from the supervisor and conflicting demands for quality from inspectors.

Conflict also arises when there is disparity between the individual's personal needs and the needs of the organization, whether formal or informal: the ambitious worker whose co-workers warn against outputs above their norms, the young, eager college graduates given uninspiring jobs, the internal auditor asked by managers to overlook what is known to be wrong. All those situations create conflicts, and conflicts hamper performance. They are not matters that the manager or the internal auditor can quantify and draw inescapable conclusions from, but they exist and they are significant. Thus they must be weighed in determining causes of and means of correcting unwanted conditions.

Committees

Forms of Committees

A committee is a group of people who work together on some facet of a management function. There are hosts of committees in all forms of endeavour. Some are formal; some are informal. Some are permanent, some are temporary. Some are at low levels of management, some are at high levels. Indeed, at the highest level sits the board of directors. It will be discussed in Chapter 14. Be they high or low, formal or informal, committees have two things in common: they can often accomplish more than individuals working separately, and they can be a waste of time, money, and managerial talent.

Advantages

Committees can combine varied knowledge and experience. In doing so they can transmit knowledge among members, knowledge that otherwise would not be gained. The knowledge crosses organizational lines and can result in better coordination and cooperation. Varied groups that might not be represented in other ways may be heard from in committee deliberations.

Committees put together people of diverse talents, and through diversity they tend to overcome individual bias and prejudice. By being engaged in the deliberations, committee members become committed to carrying out the group decisions; and misunderstandings of what was intended can be dissipated.

Committees can be a good training ground for the newer members who are taught to speak before a group, engage in give and take around the table, and carry out assignments more willingly because they will be expected to report back on their accomplishments to their peers.

Disadvantages

Committees spend an inordinate amount of time on trivia; it seems that the more trivial the item on the agenda the more time spent on it. The reason may be that trivial items are more readily grasped, and so people can argue with confidence about them. The obscure and complex items are difficult to understand, and committee members are reluctant to show their ignorance before their peers.

Committees, if poorly organized or run, can be not only a waste of money but also unproductive. At Goodyear, the president called a meeting at short notice only to find that all those asked to attend were already at other meetings. So he asked for an analysis and received this information: more than 20% of attendants to meetings arrived late; only 85% took an active part; and 25% had no business there in the first place. The chairman was unprepared in 15% of the meetings, and more than 10% of the total meeting time was a complete loss because of late arrivals, interruptions from outside, and conversations not relevant to the meeting. Also those figures put the matter in its best light, because committee chairmen and members knew they were being observed.

Committees carry with them the dangers of compromise. A consensus, rather than a bold, innovative solution, usually results. Members may abandon what is new and different rather than fight for their ideas because of the pressures of other work or because they don't want to alienate colleagues. Then, too, committees are often chaired by superiors of the members, and the members may be reluctant to speak their minds to and disagree with their bosses.

It is easier to place responsibility on an individual than on a committee, but that problem can be alleviated to some extent by these two methods:

- Whoever is given committee advice must go on record as either accepting or rejecting it.
- Assignments for action should go to individuals who are responsible for carrying them out by agreed-upon dates and for reporting results back to committee members.

Making Committees More Effective

Committees cannot usually perform innovatively and with the dispatch of the individual, but some fairly simple rules may make them more effective:

- Make objectives and authority abundantly clear.
- Select a chair who is knowledgeable and who is blessed with traits that will provide reasonable assurance of a smooth operation: willingness to hear people out, but knowing when to step in and exercise authority to get things moving again. Define the duties of the chair, vice chair, and secretary.
- Limit members to those directly involved, those with a real need to serve and contribute. The average size is eight. Much over that and the committee becomes unwieldy; much fewer and the views may be too limited.
- Have a formal list of members to make sure all are notified and all receive committee reports.
- Prepare agendas and supply them to members along with the scheduled meeting dates.

- Record all committee proceedings, assignments, and results.
- Prepare summary reports to an appropriate executive. Set forth the number of meetings held, the people in attendance, the hours spent, the progress made, and the goals met.

Organization Charts

Organization charts are intended to show organizational relations. Some presidents are proud to say they don't need them, but the reasons against them are usually not valid. Like flow charts, they can graphically show up inconsistencies, gaps, and overlaps that need attention. However, they may reflect what should be instead of what is; they may display status, not describe authority relations. For example, the staff person reporting to the president may occupy a separate box on the chart that is higher than the one for a director who has much greater responsibility.

The activity chart is a more descriptive form of organization chart. Besides showing organizational relations, it shows the processes and responsibilities involved in achieving a particular objective. It displays:

- The actions, both major and minor, that must be taken to achieve the objective.
- The organizations involved in the actions and which organization is to take which action.
- The individuals in the organization who are responsible for the particular actions.

The procedural flow chart depicts each step in a function. The organization chart is tied in by broken lines to the pictured function: what each individual is to do and when, the documents involved in the process and where they are to go, and how the entire process ties together from beginning to end. One of the benefits of the procedural flowchart is to show management that a change in procedure may require a change in organization to accomplish needed results.

Organizational Change

No organization can stand still. Technology, ecology, needs of society, constraints of the government, products, and moves change. The enterprises affected must either change or regress, so an important part of the managerial function of organizing is to keep analyzing the key activities. Activities once thought essential and significant may have lost those qualities, but still occupy significant positions. Also, every time an activity changes, the organizational structure may also have to change.

The analyses sometimes come too late. The decrease in productivity is not analyzed for causes until disaster is imminent or erupts. Often the defect is the direct result of poor organization that makes production swim against a stubborn stream. General Motors and Westinghouse made marked strides after their reorganizations in the 1920s and the 1930s, respectively. Hence one of the jobs for the internal auditor is to see where poor organization inhibits productivity before the problem becomes too serious.

Change should not be made for the sake of change itself. Ideal changes are those that satisfy these three dimensions:

- Achieving organizational purposes; the organization should be able to accomplish its objectives more effectively.
- Achieving self-maintenance and growth; the change should have a positive effect on the individual's opportunities for growth and development.
- Achieving social satisfaction. Breaking up the social groups may bring about dissatisfactions and reduced productivity; on the other hand, building into the changed organization social and psychological factors can insure improved productivity.

Empire builders will, of course, always manipulate the organization to their benefit. The chief executive who is alert to incipient empire building can tell the would-be workers not to bother to extend their domains because plans for change and rotation will see to it that they won't have the same positions several years later. Organizations can pull themselves out of the past if certain considerations obtain:

- Accept criticism. Don't inhibit people from pointing out defects in the organization. Self-deception is a grave managerial illness.
- Recruit people with new ideas, and let them be heard.
- Question old methods. People become cocooned in their own red tape. Their vested interests and self-imposed procedures become more important to them than the needs and aims of the enterprise.
- Look toward what can be; not to what is or was. The practice of looking forward leads to new ideas and motivates people to climb out of their ruts.

Yet excessive change can be destructive. It keeps people off balance and frustrated. However, when change is necessary, it can be a positive rather than a negative force if those involved and affected are given their chance for expression, if their views are carefully considered, and if they know their well-being is taken into account.

Staffing

The Need

Some writers on management theory show staffing as a separate managerial function. For our purposes we show it as a part of the organizing function— supplying the organization with people who can operate the enterprise competently.

It includes recruiting, selecting, and developing people at all levels for all kinds of positions.

Qualified managers are in woefully short supply, and many who were good managers have lagged behind changing conditions and advanced managerial technology. "All managers are in a foot race between retirement and obsolescence; the best they can hope for is a photo finish."

It is puzzling that companies that plan sales and expansions so meticulously plan for recruitment and replacement of their most precious commodity haphazardly. Many executives and managers avoid thinking about the staffing aspect of their job because it must take into account the most variable and complex of resources: people. But plan they must lest they wake up one morning to find that their most needed people will soon reach retirement age. And lack of planning results in strategic and tactical errors that could be avoided, such as:

- Beginning the year with a major program that is suddenly terminated at the same time that professionals are laid off.
- Trying to hire really exceptional people at ridiculously low salaries.
- Hiring people with specific training who leave after a little while because there is no work for them in their field.

Some simple rules for management staff planning should be considered by all executives:

- Determine the number of managerial posts available. Establish the population of management positions.
- Obtain an estimate of turnover in managerial posts. The past five years is a reasonable period.
- Classify incumbents and potential managers according to:
  1. Those soon to retire.
  2. Those who will have to be replaced because they are not performing adequately.
  3. Those who are performing adequately but are not capable of handling a higher job.
  4. Those who are or soon will be ready for promotion.
- Consider the plans of the enterprise and allow both for expected changes in organization and for affirmative action requirements.
- Decide on the number of trainees that can be absorbed in the workforce or are needed to replace incumbents. Some companies use a 1 to 1 ratio; others go as high as 10 selections for each possible opening. The expected attrition rate will be a factor.
- Determine the sources for recruitment. Consider such matters as climate, distance, and family.

The Skills

The category of skills needed to be a good manager is difficult to develop. Any attempts made in that direction have been largely futile because the categories tend to delineate good people, not good managers. Certainly, one quality of the good executive must be to create a harmonious whole out of dissimilar disciplines. One approach to categorizing managerial quality is to examine three basic skills: technical, conceptual, and human.(7)

1. *Technical.* The manager need not have the technical skills possessed by subordinates, but should know enough about the disciplines managed to evaluate goals and objectives, adopt standards, and know whether the standards are being met. Furthermore, in making decisions related to the technical disciplines, it is necessary to know enough not to be led down the garden path by technicians.

2. *Conceptual.* Enterprise problems call for intellectual capacity to a high degree: the ability to ask the correct questions and evaluate the answers, the capability of keeping a number of concepts in mind and evaluating both them and the nature of the people advancing them, the intelligence to think problems through and come to a logical decision based on the matters presented in the light of enterprise objectives, and the ability to see patterns and relations.

3. *Human relations.* The manager must accomplish goals and objectives, and must meet standards through the work of others. The manager must, therefore, be skilled in understanding and motivating people, but that skill will not substitute for the other two skills. The manager's technical and conceptual skills combine in the process of making decisions; then the human relations skills take over to see that the decisions are implemented.

Many people who are placed in management fail because they lack certain qualities. They fail if they haven't the deep-seated desire to manage—to reach objectives through others and not solely through their own efforts. They fail if they haven't the intelligence to deal with the problems, concepts, decisions, and conflicts that attend any management position. They fail if they are unable to communicate with their peers, their subordinates and their superiors; for inability to communicate is an invitation to chaos and frustration. Finally, they fail if they do not have the integrity to reject the shoddy end product: to know what is good and insist on only that which is acceptable—both the standards and the products by which the standards are measured.

Generalists and Specialists

The field of management needs both generalists and specialists. Throughout the organization there is, by and large, a need for more specialists, but at some level generalists are needed to reconcile the differing and more parochial views of the specialists. The sales manager sees problems through the sales viewpoint. The purchasing manager sees them through another viewpoint. Perhaps neither will see them through the viewpoint of the entire enterprise, and that is where the generalist must have a leavening and catalytic effect.

Sources

Promotion from within is obviously favored by employees, but it can be incestuous, and it can breed a narrowness of view. Besides, many technically expert employees do not have the managerial bent. Open competition of recruits from both inside and outside the company calls for fair and objective evaluations by executives, and rarely will favoritism and politics be absent from such evaluations. Recruiting from the outside gives an infusion of new blood and new ideas, which often are desperately needed if the enterprise suffers from stagnation, but it does create problems of resentment among employees.

Scientific selection through tests is more of a hope than a reality. It has been tried, but there still is no sensational breakthrough in predicting success for managerial personnel. The ability to pick the winners remains a chancey thing. For that reason, it should be a firm rule that the manager to whom the successful candidate will report should have the authority to make the final selection. If the executive is to be given the responsibility for what happens in the department there should be the authority to determine the human resources needed.

When accountability for results is not clear-cut, committees may be used to make selections. That may be applicable to universities and to some government positions. Some of the items covered in an interview with an applicant are:

- Total number of dependents.
- Education.
- Plans for continuing education.
- Whether now employed.
- Length of last employment.
- Personal goals.
- Professional organization in which applicant was or is an active member.
- Offices held in the professional organization.
- Approximate net worth of the applicant.
- Minimum monthly living expenses.

Management Training

Both the organization and the manager have responsibility for continuing training. The universities cannot turn out the complete manager. They can provide an understanding of managerial functions and principles, but by and large these principles, without real-life illustrations, have little meaning to the student. Teachers who can coat the principles with the tangy taste of real experience are rare, because they must be both an academic and a businessman.

Seminars attended by working managers can be useful if the leaders have both knowledge and experience. Often, however, the seminar attendant may accept the principles of improved management but find them rejected by superiors when returning to the job. Education should therefore start at the top. Then too the experiences taught in seminars are general; they do not always come forward in a familiar frame of reference. They may just be a set of case studies and principles hanging on neat pegs, but they could be unrelated to the attendant's personal experiences or needs.

For that reason, a good working relation between the manager and the modern internal auditor can be rewarding. Internal auditors, coming upon a condition in the manager's shop, can analyze it and relate it to violations of management principles or good business practice. They can relate the principle to the condition and explain it in such a way that the manager sees the problem, the cause, and the solution in a sharply defined frame that portrays the real world in which the manager lives.

ORGANIZING AND THE INTERNAL AUDITOR

How the Internal Auditor Can Help

Internal auditing is a managerial control that functions by measuring and evaluating the effectiveness of other controls. Those are among the first words in the Statement of Responsibilities of Internal Auditors. The internal auditor is therefore involved in organization in almost every audit. There are two approaches. One approach is to examine causes of deficiencies and, if they related to defects in organization, suggest that management improve related organizational controls. That is the normal approach. The other approach is to direct the audit specifically to organizing and organizational control, that is, to:

- The design for carrying out particular activities to achieve enterprise goals.
- The means devised for reappraising the design in the light of changing goals.
- The means for modifying the design as needed.

The first method, the indirect approach, is the normal procedure. The second—specifically directed to the managerial function of organizing—is more rare. When executive management becomes disenchanted with the existing plan of organization, it usually turns to outside consultants. The consultants often do a creditable job because of their broad experience in the field, but they lack what the internal auditor has developed over the years: a personal knowledge of the enterprise objectives, goals, systems, and people. If internal auditors, management-oriented internal auditors, were to direct their efforts specifically toward the function of organizing, their assistance to management could become much more valuable. To that end they need the status and authority to carry out such audits.

Drucker tells us that there are certain activities within the enterprise that never should be subordinated to anything. They are what he calls the "conscience activities."(8) Among them are planning, setting standards, and auditing performance against the standards. Internal auditors, then, must report to persons who are in charge of the conscience activities so that they may measure and evaluate all activities within the entity, including the organization and the function of organizing.

Relating detected deficiencies to organizational deficiencies is useful, but greater managerial awareness of organizational matters carries the internal auditor to new and higher levels of sophistication and usefulness in the organization. We shall now explore the internal auditor's involvement with the aspects of organizing described earlier in this chapter.

Designing the Organization

It has been a precept in internal auditing that the internal auditor should never design the system to be audited. The reason is a reluctance to criticize our own creation. But that should not deter the internal auditor from reviewing proposed plans of organization or reorganization to determine whether they include the necessary checks and balances that provide a means of assuring executive management that activities will be carried out as intended. Indeed, the Statement of Responsibilities of the Internal Auditor addresses that very matter. It points out that auditors should not develop and install procedures, prepare records, or engage in any other activity that they would normally review and appraise and that could reasonably be construed to compromise their independence. However, the Statement goes on to say that "Objectivity need not be adversely affected, however, by determination and recommendation of the standards of control to be applied in the development of the systems and procedures under review."

Nowhere is that determination more significant than in the development of electronic data processing systems. Waiting on the sidelines to make post audits can prove disastrous. The internal auditor has too much to offer to hold back, or to be held back, during the early days when the system is being designed. The computer specialist is concerned with equipment, programs, and efficient computer performance, but within the frame of the large picture those concerns are parochial. The internal auditor, on the other hand, can offer a broad background that has concern for entity objectives and aims. The auditor can provide a stabilizing influence that embraces the needs of the entire entity, not just data processing.

Here is an example of the disastrous effect of noninvolvement by internal auditors in the design of an EDP system:

In one large railroad company, the internal auditors decided that it would be a good idea to have the computer reject inaccurate data—after the EDP system involving freight car records had been in effect for some time. The internal auditors worked up an audit test deck. Essential data were deliberately omitted. Incorrect data were deliberately added. For example, the test deck showed cars interchanged with the L&N when the railroad had no interchange with the L&N. The test deck showed interchanges with nonexistent railroads, with nonexistent car numbers, and in one instance a car interchanged on May *53rd*. Any self-respecting computer program with appropriate edit routines would have screamed TILT when the test deck was introduced. However, this program happily processed and printed out all invalid (among valid) transactions, including 22 days extra per diem for the car interchanged on May 53rd.

Management should therefore consider the internal auditor when new organizations and systems are in the design stage. The purpose is not to involve the internal auditor in the design itself. Instead, it is to make use of the auditor's knowledge of internal control to find out if any essential means of control are missing. That is their brand of expertise. As they audit a segment of an organization and review a system, the approach must be to ask themselves, "What is the objective of this operation?" "How does it mesh with entity objectives?" "What controls exist or *should* exist to see that the objectives will be met?"

In analyzing the design of a new organization or installation, the questions will be much the same. They are not always the questions asked by the designers of organizations, so that is why the managers should turn to the internal auditors early on.

Centralization and Decentralization

Decentralization may be essential because of the need to reduce spans of management, but it will not work without adequate control from the top. The internal auditor can be one of the means of control that keeps decentralization from becoming abdication. The internal auditor's services can be invaluable during the early stages when it is known that decentralization is inevitable.

In decentralization, conflict and frustration erupt unless the authority of the respective organizations and people is spelled out clearly. One of the steps the internal auditor should take is to develop a chart of management-approval authorizations. If the assignments of authorization are not specifically spelled out, the internal auditor should recommend a system of appropriate authority levels and leave to management the decision of just what the levels should be. If they are spelled out, the internal auditor should determine if they are being followed.

In employment, for example, personnel managers may process on their own authority the employment of all salaried people whose salaries are less than $2 000 a month. Hires between that amount and $3 000 must be approved by a vice president; between $3 000 and $5 000 a month by the president; over that by the board of directors. The dollar amounts will vary among companies, but the principle should be generally applicable

Internal auditors should be fully aware that decentralization does not imply complete autonomy. Attainment of common objectives, coordination of effort, and decisions on certain policy matters must be centrally controlled. It is their job, as they move through decentralized operations, to see that the principle is not being violated. The other side of the coin is that they must make sure that centralized control is not being duplicated. Here are two examples, the first example showing an internal auditor's finding that saved at least $3 million a year by eliminating duplication in a centralized operation:

> A business had some 250 retail outlets. Accounting was centralized. The outlets submitted weekly statements of sales and cash disbursements to the central office. They also sent invoices to headquarters for payment. Each outlet then received monthly statements of operations. The outlets were not, therefore, to maintain accounting records of their own.

> However, they did. The internal auditor found that each outlet had a clerk who kept an unofficial bookkeeping system so that questions could be answered when the monthly statements were received. The internal auditor found that those answers could be obtained for the managers of the outlets merely by expanding the income and expense codes of the chart of accounts. The monthly statement therefore was able to answer the detailed questions which the records of the unofficial bookkeepers were designed to answer. Now, instead of 250 bookkeepers, centralized machine accounting (equal to the compensation of only two clerks) provided the needed answers. Reducing the staff by 250 clerks saved about $3 million a year.

> In another company, a central purchasing unit was organized to process, companywide, certain materials that were used commonly by the many subdivisions of the company. Suppliers contracted to supply the materials at reduced prices because of the volume of business. However, in a companywide audit of purchasing procedures, the internal auditors found violations of the centralized purchasing system because buyers in the subdivisions had favorite suppliers whom they did not want to relinquish even though the prices were higher than those offered under the central contracts.

The internal audit, properly used, can provide one of the means of control that management must retain when it decentralizes its activities.

Mergers and Acquisitions—Departmentation

In companies that grow by merger, an internal audit team should review the organization and systems of the company to be taken over. When that company's systems of management are incompatible with those of the acquiring company, the auditor should report the facts and recommendations to executive management.

Departmentation, the grouping of activities to carry out objectives, is not often the concern of the internal auditor, but it should be. Too often the internal auditor accepts the department being audited just as it is and does not consider whether the activities are suitably arranged and whether the organization is most efficient in its present form.

The first task of the internal auditor should be to determine what activities are needed to carry out the department's objectives, whether they have been considered in designing the organization, and whether they are balanced in terms of departmental goals. One internal auditor found an element lacking in an organization, one that led to inefficient use of resources and excessive costs:

> The development of new products was the responsibility of the vice president, engineering. Three engineers reported to him:
>
> - A research and development engineer developed the new product.
> - A manufacturing engineer designed the production methods and determined what production equipment was needed.
> - An industrial engineer determined the most effective work methods, decided on the number of workers needed, and set production standards.
>
> Once developed, the product was transferred to the production area for manufacture. The products were then produced and delivered. However, the company was plagued by customer dissatisfaction and high scrap rates.
>
> It took a thorough, detailed analysis to determine the missing element in the organization. When a product was developed a prototype was built to make sure it would work, but the prototype, like most prototypes was relatively crude. Rarely is a prototype designed for mass production. Also products being developed had to be mass-produced. In this company, however, the item being mass-produced was the prototype model.
>
> So parts did not always fit. Subassemblies did not always mate. Costs were sky-high and so was the scrap rate. Then, since production units varied in quality, customer dissatisfaction was equally high.
>
> Mass production requires that the concepts of the research and development engineer be designed in greater detail and accuracy for production. Eliminate parts that might break. Stipulate parts and materials. Reduce the number of parts to simplify production. Restyle the product to appeal to the eye, and make sure dimensions are precise and mating points are exact.
>
> So that was what was lacking: a design department, or at least a design engineer. The analysis, in terms of what activities a department must include to meet an objective, disclosed improper departmentation.

The internal auditor must be concerned with the management controls that are violated through improper departmentation. Two illustrations, which are far from rarities, follow:

> In one instance, a quality control manager reported to a production manager. However, the objectives of the production manager are to turn out a volume of products on schedule and at lowest possible cost. The objective of the quality control manager is to make sure the products meet quality standards. Company objectives and customer satisfaction depend on all three of these attributes. When

costs rise and schedules are not being met, what would it avail the quality control manager to complain to the superior that quality standards are not being met and that work should be rejected or reworked?

In another case, a credit and collection manager reported to the sales manager. Their objectives conflicted. The credit manager was responsible for protecting the company from poor credit risks. The sales manager was responsible for high sales volume. Who wins out in borderline cases?

In both cases, the internal auditor should recommend that activities with potentially conflicting but with equally important objectives be given parity in the organization. Each should be in a department that has authority equal to that of the other. Otherwise, departmentation is not balanced, and that means that company objectives may not be met.

Departmentation should provide for cross-checks and should, by separation of duties, reduce the possibility of manipulation and embezzlement.(9)

In some companies, activities relating to record keeping, financial analysis, and custody of cash and securities are not properly grouped and separated. When internal auditors see the following organizational errors, they should recommend immediate separation of duties and activities:

- The person responsible for accounts receivable records is also receiving cash. This person could manipulate the records so that they would never reveal that cash had been converted to the person's own use.
- The person in charge of cash records is reconciling the bank account. Cash might be diverted and the bank records, under this person's control, would not send up flares to highlight the impropriety.
- Under a project organization designed to supervise the construction of facilities, the construction accountant reports directly to the engineering manager responsible for the construction. The special interests of the construction engineer may vary from those of the accountant. The accuracy and propriety of construction payments are likely to suffer.

In one case, an internal auditor observed that customer complaints were received by various departments in the company. The complaints were dealt with haphazardly and unsatisfactorily. The auditor recommended that a special unit be assigned the task of handling customer complaints in a timely manner and in accordance with clearly established company policies.

Responsibility and Authority

Early in an audit of an organization the internal auditor should review the statement of responsibilities for the organizational unit. The concern here is twofold: to determine whether responsibilities assigned are consonant with the unit's mission and to determine whether the statement bears evidence of review and approval and is up to date.

Executive management has a right to expect that the statement of responsibilities it prepared or approved describes accurately what the unit has undertaken or has been assigned to do. If a contract administration unit is responsible for seeing that certain government regulations are incorporated into subcontracts with suppliers, executive management should not have to check to see that the responsibility is being carried out. The internal auditor should determine whether that and all other assigned responsibilities are dealt with and are not left hanging in limbo. If an assigned responsibility is not being carried out by the audited unit, the internal auditor must determine whether there is a need for it to be carried out at all. If there is truly a need and the audited unit is not the place for the activity, it should be determined what other unit in the organization is or should be carrying it out.

The internal auditor should also look for divided responsibilities, which rarely work. Why, for example, a number of different people in different units are approving expense accounts, confusion will most certainly result. Different policies and standards may be applied. One approver may demand receipts for everything; another might be quite relaxed about the requirement. Employees submitting travel vouchers that are being subjected to differing policies might understandably be irked.

In some instances, the statement of responsibilities may be window dressing. The audited unit may have prepared and received approval for a statement that does not portray actual responsibilities. The statement may be a facade meant to impress superiors rather than express actual conditions. Since executive management rarely has the time to learn of those instances first hand, it assumes that the statement speaks the truth and that the unit is not burdened with responsibilities that in fact do not exist.

Sometimes responsibilities are undertaken to the detriment of the company. In one case of record a product manager extended responsibilities to include purchasing, receiving, and inventory storage. Attention was diverted from the basic mission. Just as bad, the company was being deprived of the checks and balances supplied by independent agencies responsible for those activities. The internal auditor analyzed the excessive centralization of responsibility and recommended realignment of the activities to restore the checks and balances.

The internal auditor should be concerned with the coequality of authority and responsibility. In one situation the internal auditor observed that the purchasing department was held responsible to commit company funds for the procurement of all supplies and services. In an audit of the marketing branch, it was observed that marketing personnel were making agreements with suppliers to obtain as sales aids valuable products used in merchandising and in advertising the company's goods. The marketing people would then ask purchasing to write confirming purchase orders to cover the transactions. Purchasing was frustrated. Under strict rules designed to maintain arms length, unbiased dealings with suppliers, it had the responsibility to make all commitments. Marketing had taken upon itself some of the purchasing authority without responsibility to abide by those rules. The internal audit report resulted in the return of authority to the purchasing department, where it belonged.

Delegation

Since delegation demands control, because responsibility cannot be relinquished, the internal auditor can become the delegator's best friend. Nowhere else in the organization can the delegator obtain objective, professional opinions on how the assigned tasks are being carried out. These are the questions in which the internal auditor wants specific answers about delegated authority:

- Does the delegate understand his or her responsibility?
- Is the authority commensurate with the responsibility?
- Is performance up to the delegator's standards?
- Have comparable responsibilities been assigned elsewhere; that is, is there an overlap in responsibilities?

In one situation the auditor was helpful in working out a particularly sensitive problem for the chief executive officer of a company. Because of a close relationship with the chief executive, the internal auditor was asked to inquire into an impasse between two senior vice presidents. The internal auditor, under the authority given by the chief executive, explored the problem in conversations with the vice presidents and their aides. The inquiry disclosed a lack of understanding of the precise delegation of responsibility to the vice presidents, and that resulted in an operational problem caused by the overlapping of responsibilities.

Spans of Management

The internal auditor, as the expert in internal control, should be well aware that knowledgeable supervision of subordinates is probably the best form of control yet devised. That form of control implies availability to solve problems. When the span of management is so broad that supervision is not performing its function, the internal auditor should make observations known. However, that is a matter that is difficult to quantify. It is not a fact that can be objectively supported and reported. Yet the internal auditor, as a professional observer of operations, obtains impressions during the audit of an activity that are as valuable as the data contained in his spread sheets crammed with tests of transactions.

Some auditing organizations approach formally the collection and communication of impressions on such nonquantifiable matters as supervision and morale. Those impressions are recorded in working papers and are then informally discussed with appropriate management people. Often the impressions serve to fortify vague feelings held by managers who are not closely tuned to ongoing operations, or at least not as closely tuned as is the auditor, who may have spent weeks in close contact with operations and the people carrying them out. The discussions can be as useful to managers as quantified deficiencies supported by reams of data.

Obviously, the discussions call for tact and discrimination. Let the auditor cry wolf once too often and credibility is lost. However, approached from the vantage point of management-level observations, the auditor's communication of his impressions can provide valuable input to executive management.

One organizational control problem was threatening to founder a company until the problem was solved.

> The president of a company manufacturing highly engineered, highly competitive consumer appliances was not an engineer himself. Nine people reported directly to him—not too wide a span, ordinarily. However in this company the span was too wide because the organizations represented by six of these people were highly technical: product development, manufacturing engineering, industrial engineering, quality control, production control, and production. The other three were personnel, finance, and marketing.

> The highly competitive nature of the products required the president to spend considerable portions of time on marketing. Yet the other activities kept calling for decisions; since the president was not schooled in those disciplines, the decisions were slow in coming and not always the best. New products took too long to develop, and manufacturing suffered from a high scrap rate. A competent, management-oriented internal auditor would have readily spotted the problem and suggested a solution: place the six technical activities under a vice president of operations, reporting to the president. This was the solution. The span of management was reduced to four, the technically trained vice president of operations tackled and solved the problem of scrap rates and manufacturing costs and the president took a long-deserved vacation.

Line and Staff

Internal auditors must always keep in mind this salient fact: they are staff and not line. They must sell, not tell. Let them seek to usurp a line manager's responsibilities and their usefulness and that of the line managers are seriously eroded.

Yet internal auditors, as one of the most significant monitors of a company's control system, have the responsibility for measuring and evaluating the enterprise's control system. When controls are weak, they must not relinquish their vigil until they have been strengthened. That would seem to be a contradiction, and many internal auditors have overstepped the bounds and incurred the enmity of line management by not knowing how to deal with the contradiction. On the one hand, internal auditors are told they must have sufficient status in the organization to have their recommendations considered; on the other hand, they are warned not to step over into line functions by issuing orders.

The solution lies not in what but in how. The internal auditor is responsible for reporting on what is wrong, on what conditions indicate weaknesses in control. The line manager is responsible for determining how the controls are to be strengthened. Obviously, the well-trained, experienced internal auditor will have ideas about how the condition may be corrected, and would be failing to function as a problem-solving partner if that information were withheld. However, never should the internal auditor say: "Correct the condition this way." Rather the internal auditor should say, "Here is the condition, here is the effect, and here are causes. This condition must be corrected. One of the corrective steps you may want to consider is this. But whatever steps you take, the condition must be corrected and we shall evaluate the adequacy and effectiveness of *your* corrective action." There is no stepping from staff to line in such an approach. There is only counseling and maintaining the staff function of guardian over the entity's controls.

Staff people—and this is particularly applicable to internal auditors—require the right temperament for the job, and people with that temperament are rare. They must want others to take the credit. They must help line people do the job of getting a defect corrected provided only that it is not immoral or insane. That requires a person who lets others take the bows for doing the job themselves rather than doing it for them and then pointing to themselves with pride.

Internal auditors often audit services used by the company: janitorial, legal, tax, maintenance, data processing, and advertising, among others. Some of those services may be rendered by company people; some may be obtained by purchase. The auditor can help executive management decide whether particular services should be purchased or performed in-house. Some of the matters of concern are:

- *Relative costs.* These include (i) waiting time for outside services, (ii) the frequency with which the services are needed, and (iii) the overhead expenses that would be incurred if the service were performed in-house.
- *Divided attention.* When services are purchased, it should be remembered that the supplier has other clients and that the auditor's company may be receiving a low priority.
- *What to ask for.* Sometimes managers dealing with outside services are not quite sure what they need. They may not know what to expect of outside legal counsel, for example. In-house counsel may be able to provide assistance in determining what is needed in a given circumstance.
- *Management of services.* The managers of the supplier's organization usually have the skill, experience, and background often lacking in managers hired for in-house services. That may be one of the greatest bars to performing some services in-house.

Each instance requires careful analysis that makes use of the internal auditor's ability to accumulate and array comparable costs and the line manager's determination of need for the services. Together, the internal auditor and the manager can compare both the measurable and the unmeasurable costs and benefits of the two alternatives.

The Informal Organization and Culture

The sensitive internal auditor working within an organization can soon discern the pattern of the informal organization that overlies the formal one. This is not only a matter of individuals but also a way of thinking that does not display itself in the formal organization charts. An entity or an organization within an entity moves forward if it has vitality, if it is able to generate and regenerate thoughts, ideas, and innovations. The absence of vitality makes itself evident in a number of ways:

- People cling to old ways even though the environment is changing.
- New goals have not been defined; the old goals are no longer challenging.
- Thinking relates to action on the day-to-day jobs; it is not reflected in looking forward.
- The company becomes institutionalized; it is different from the people who staff it.
- The organization has the reputation for stability and security, not for being venturesome.
- People rely on precedent instead of generating new ideas.
- Supervisors are intolerant of criticism; they discourage independent thought.

In addition to dealing with the informal organization, internal auditors who travel, particularly those who make audits in foreign countries, face dealing with the cultures of those countries.

Culture is cultivated behavior acquired through social learning, and it differs between New York and Texas as it differs between the United States and Japan. In the United States the internal auditor generally meets a philosophy that emphasizes the individual. In other countries, class distinctions may be more pronounced and there is a lack of the democratic atmosphere that characterizes the American economy. Auditors must take those differences into account and deal with them much as they deal with the chart of accounts or the organization chart.

In the United States promptness is a virtue, but in some countries it is customary to keep people waiting an hour or two before seeing them. Hours of work differ. In Greece, the workday is scheduled from 8:00 a.m. to 2:00 p.m. six days a week. In Latin America the midday siesta is a standard practice. Part of planning for an audit in a foreign country must include an understanding of that country's culture: what is accepted, what is taboo; how to work around the impediments raised by that culture to normal working methods. Knowing, for example, that in being kept waiting for appointments, we should stuff our briefcase with material that we can work on while cooling our heels.

In view of differing informal organizations, differing cultures, and the role that status plays in an enterprise, internal auditors must be careful how they make their recommendations. They must always be concerned with the needs of people. Those needs may not always square with the kind of mathematical logic that is the internal auditor's stock in trade. For example, a brilliant marketing executive whose efforts maintain the company's high share of the market may have a self-image of a ruler of all that is surveyed. A coterie of yes-people, who contribute little in terms of their own productivity, may do much in terms of the executive's productivity. The internal auditor who, with seeming logic, suggests the transfer of some of those people elsewhere—and has the suggestion adopted by the president—may find that the end result is the loss of an indispensable marketing director.

Committees

Committees are an important part of the functioning of a large organization, but their operations should not be beyond the sphere of the audit review. In fact, an internal auditor may sometimes be made a member of a committee to observe the committee's deliberations and point out committee decisions that may propose actions that run counter to the existing control system or do not provide for appropriate checks and balances. Questions the internal auditor will want answered include:

- Is the objective of the committee, its reason for being, made definite? Are there written specifications to guide committee members and keep the members from getting involved in matters outside their charter?
- Do members of the committee understand their roles? Are they a decision-making body? Or are they merely there to advise and counsel the chair?
- Are the duties of each member made clear? Serving on a committee is a job like any other job. People work best when they know what they are supposed to do.
- Is the committee too small to produce varied viewpoints or so big as to be unwieldy?
- Do members have equal status so none is dominated by another?
- Is an agenda prepared for each meeting?
- Are minutes prepared, and do they indicate that the purposes of the agenda have been carried out?
- Are assignments for action specific? Do they name individuals who are to perform the assignments. Are scheduled due dates set forth?
- Is there a means of following up on the assigned tasks?
- Does the committee report periodically to executive management on its activities and accomplishments? Are the reports supported by the committee minutes and other records?

- Do the committee's activities conflict with or overlap the activities of other committees?
- Is the committee still needed? Has it completed its mission without being disbanded?

With the right approach, the internal auditor can address those questions to the chair of the committee. That is the direct and most useful approach. If it turns out that many of the answers are in the negative, the very process of answering the questions may be an education to the chair.

Internal auditors can sometimes undertake a companywide appraisal of committees that deal with comparable subjects. They can prepare a large chart that permits the delineation of the key attributes of the various committees, as for example:

- Name of committee
- Meeting dates or frequency
- Chair
- Members
- Detailed functions and responsibilities
- Authority
- Implementing instructions

Such an analysis will highlight overlaps, gaps, and inconsistencies, and it can form the basis for questioning the continued need for one or more of the committees.

Organization charts

The absence of organization charts, statements of responsibility, and job descriptions is usually an indicator of inefficiency. Communication is difficult enough in relatively simple matters. When we consider the multiple relations in a fairly large organization, pictorial representation becomes all the more important. If organization charts are well prepared, everyone is looking at the same picture. True, two people may read different things into the same picture, but at least they are starting at the same point.

When organization charts are lacking, the internal auditor should prepare them and then ask appropriate managers whether they truly portray the organization as it is. The charts will often be the first picture taken of the organizational structure, and they could be a surprise to the executive.

When a president of a small industrial company asks "What is an organization chart?" we know without even entering the company doors there will be problems.

In this case, the president and an immediate subordinate prepared their first organization chart, and they did not need the consultant to make them realize that the organization was lopsided, that too many people reported directly to the president, and that the reason the president had to work 70 hours a week lay in malorganization. The president had no relief until the organization was restructured so that the president had a reasonable span of control and was able to delegate some duties to others.

In another case, an internal auditing organization was assigned by its company to review the organization and operation of the local YMCA. A review of the organization disclosed the need for changes at all levels from the board of directors down. The recommendations for improvement included a complete set of organization charts and supporting job descriptions. The audit resulted in a major improvement in the effectiveness of what had been a badly managed operation.

Change

As the robins herald spring, so the internal auditor heralds change. Yet organizational change is normally resisted by incumbents. For that reason, the internal auditor recommending change should gain the confidence of the auditee and make sure the recommendation is accepted before it ever appears in the audit report.

The internal auditor should also be concerned with the ripple effect of a single organizational change. No department in a company is a detached member; it is part of a complete body. A shift in one part is usually felt in other parts, particularly the peripheral or interfacing ones.

Then too, internal control includes the form of organization—the checks and balances provided by preventing an operation from being under the complete domination of one individual or one group. Hence whenever management proposes an organizational change, the proposal should be submitted to the internal auditing organization for views on whether the change will erode or weaken internal control.

The internal auditor is in a particularly good position to consider the effects of change. Over and above professional expertise in evaluating the adequacy and effectiveness of control lies knowledge of the interrelations of units and groups throughout the entire entity.

Staffing

Every entity and every unit within an entity takes on the color of the manager's thinking and philosophy. To identify that color should be the first task of an audit of operations. What is the manager like? What is the background? What is the management style?

The manager who has been trained in or has a natural bent for management and its rules and principles runs a far different operation than does the technician elevated to management position. The former's organization will most likely be designed to meet entity and unit objectives. Subordinates will know their place and their job and, equally important, they will know the jobs of those around them and the job of their superior.

The process of auditing such an organization is far easier than auditing an organization run by a technician unaccustomed to manage. There the internal auditor may have to show the usefulness of organization charts and job descriptions and how they are developed. Furthermore, in such an environment the auditor must be prepared, subtly, to teach and to counsel the manager on the principles of good administration.

The internal auditor can perform a useful service in certain aspects of staffing. A good management team must start with good hiring practices. The scoundrel on board was probably a scoundrel when working elsewhere, and one of the important means of restricting fraudulent acts is to restrict the hiring of those with a fraudulent bent. Yet often the personnel organization will hire people without even the flimsiest of background checks. When people are dismissed for improper behavior, the hiring process does not always provide for a means of preventing their rehire. Those are the sorts of controls the internal auditor is obligated to check in evaluating the adequacy and effectiveness of the entity's organizational controls.

The internal auditor should seek to determine whether each managerial position is defined specifically; without standards it is difficult to know what to hold the manager responsible for. In fact, recommending the establishment of job descriptions for managers forces the managers to think through what should be done and who is to do it. To set up the standards by which they can measure themselves can be an excellent device in training managers to function as true administrators.

Other matters the internal auditor should consider are:

- What was the basis on which the complement of people within the unit was established? Is it a sound one?
- Does the unit employ the right kind of talent? Is a clerk doing a job best handled by a technician? Or does an engineer do low-level administrative work?
- Do people have jobs that challenge their capacities and make them stretch? Can they see daylight ahead for themselves? if there is a high turnover rate, the challenge may not be there.

The internal auditor will, of course, be concerned with overstaffing. Executive management expects it, but it is hard to document and difficult to convince local management about. The proper audit approach, however, may pay big dividends for the organization. Here is an example:

An internal auditor, reviewing operations in an industry's distribution center, was certain the center was overstaffed. The auditor suggested, and the manager reluctantly agreed, that they cooperate in flow-charting the various processes in the center. The flow charts were developed in connection with extensive interviews of the personnel. When they were completed, the manager could see that:

- Procedures for processing orders could be simplified.
- A manually prepared stock card system duplicated an existing computer system

and could therefore be eliminated.
- A number of reports could be eliminated.
- A reshuffling of duties could cut down on errors and improve efficiency.

Faced with the uncompromising picture of what was and what could be, management agreed to changes which would eliminate duplication and unnecessary work and thereby cut the staff about 35%. Office costs were thus reduced by over $200 000 a years.

The Organizational Audit

The internal auditor schooled in principles of organization can approach the organizational audit with greater efficiency, less wasted effort, and can detect the telltale signs of organizational decay, such as:

- Failing to have a system of periodic self-assessment—not taking into account how future plans will affect the organizational structure.
- Lack of clear objectives.
- Failing to clarify relations among people and groups.
- Excessive spans of management. Failing to delegate authority and thus having everyone reporting directly to the boss.
- A multiplication of management levels so that communication and decisions take forever to filter down and each decision involves tortuous paper-pushing.
- Recurrence of problems that find their roots in malorganization.
- Errors in the process of delegating: delegating duties to people who are not knowledgeable; failing to balance delegation, that is, pushing authority down too far or not far enough.
- Inadequate communication—up and down or from interfacing organizations.
- Poor intradepartmental communication.
- Confused lines of authority; one subordinate reporting to two or more bosses.
- Authority without responsibility, and vice versa.
- Bottlenecks that prevent people from meeting schedules.
- Decisions that are in disagreement with company policies.
- Not using assigned functional authority.
- Staff-line conflicts.
- Executives who have reached their level of incompetence.
- Clashes between departments and people.
- An excessive number of committees. An inordinate amount of the executive's time spent on committees. Poor committee work. Too many people on committees.
- Lack of uniform policy on key issues.
- Putting the attention of key people on non-key issues and failing to set appropriate priorities.
- Overorganization—making organizational changes at the drop of a hat. Changes in organization are like surgery; they should not be lightly undertaken.

- Lack of checks and balances. Breakdowns in financial control.
- Failure to accomplish objectives.
- Lack of knowledge or skill at the management level.
- Too many coordinators and assistants. Their use may be the result of poor organization.
- Excessive tension or dissatisfaction on the part of managers.
- A great many specialists and no generalists or administrators.
- Lack of information about what is going on in the company; people find out what's happening in their own organization by reading the newspapers.

Internal auditors usually perform some form of audit of the elements of organizing each time they audit a department or operation. Rarely are they asked to perform an audit of organizational control for an entire entity. Yet such an audit or management study should be within the competence of the management-oriented internal auditor. The auditor should understand what questions to ask and what steps to take. Here are some of the questions that are pertinent to an audit of the organizing function:

- What are the provisions for preparing organization charts and statements of responsibility? How and how often are they updated? What provision is made to tie plans for the future into the organization chart?
- How is the development of the organization chart keyed to the objectives of the enterprise?
- What consideration is given to enterprise and unit objectives in developing statements of responsibility? To what extent do the objectives and statements agree? What gaps exist?
- What are the qualifications of managers to carry out their responsibilities?
- To what extent does the grouping of activities facilitate the meeting of objectives?
- What are the key activities of the organization? To which people has each of the activities been assigned?
- What is the authority of each manager? Was the authority placed close to the point at which action must be taken?
- How are managers made to understand their own work and that of others with whom they must interface?
- How is authority delegated? Are the delegates qualified to undertake their assignments?
- When delegations are made, what form of control is developed to provide feedback to the delegator from the delegate?
- How well are departments or units integrated? Which ones seem to operate without checks and balances?
- What consideration, if any, has been given to developing project organizations for major missions that are limited in their life span?
- What are the spans of control? Any area too broad or too narrow?
- What backup charts have been developed? How do they anticipate the need

for replacements for the next 5 to 10 years?
- What system does the company use to replace managers and develop new ones?
- What means are used to measure the progress and potential of managers?

There are undoubtedly many ways to make an audit of an entity's organization, but here are some of the steps to consider:

1. Accumulate all written materials relating to the organization structure.
   - Organization charts.
   - Statements of objectives and responsibilities.
   - Job descriptions.
   - Performance appraisals.
   - Qualifications for various jobs.

2. Review the materials to see if:
   - They relate to entity objectives.
   - They disclose gaps or overlaps.
3. Determine what is needed to do each job.
4. List the incumbent managers' qualifications in terms of education and experience.
5. Identify the requirements that were met and those that were not met; identify qualifications not needed in the present job and relate them to the requirements of other jobs; and indicate needed qualities that are not being met by the incumbent managers.
6. Suggest organization charts and job descriptions that might better fit the requirements and the existing personnel.
7. Suggest well-thought-out, detailed, changed procedures to replace those now in existence.

The scope and depth of such a study, the study's potential for major change, and the effect that drastic recommendations will have on operating personnel, together with the rule that internal auditors should not prepare procedures they themselves may later audit, call for two prerequisites for such a study:

1. Specific authority from a highly placed executive or from the audit committee of the board of directors to make such a study.
2. The inclusion on the audit team of a member of line management to insure balance and objectivity in the survey and the results and to write the changed procedures.

CONCLUSION

Organizing follows planning, and the form of organization must be keyed to the entity's plans and aims. Good organization is no guarantee of success, but poor organization will most certainly make goals much harder to achieve. There is a limit to what one human being can deal with personally; hence the need for decentralization. That calls for the delegation of some of the superior's authority; but the authority must be coequal with responsibility, and responsibility may never be relinquished. The reins may be long, but they must always be gripped firmly.

Large organizations cannot escape the use of staff people to help managers, but staff must know its place and have its authority clearly defined. Staff should be on tap and not on top. Each formal organization has an informal one, and managers must learn to deal with it; it won't go away. Committees are necessary, but they should not be a necessary evil if their charters are clear and if they are properly organized.

Organizational change is inevitable, but the trauma can be relieved if the changes are properly approached. There are too few good managers around. Those that were not born with the knack need training, and internal auditors can help. They should participate in the various phases of organizing, not to devise organizations, but to make sure they have appropriate checks and balances. Internal auditors are not often asked to perform comprehensive audits of the organizing function, but with proper techniques they should be able to inform executive management whether the organizational structure suits the purposes of the organization.

REFERENCES

(1) P. F. Drucker, *Management: Tasks, Responsibilities, Practices* (Oxford: Butterworth-Heinemann 1991), pp. 466–469.
(2) Harold Koontz and Heinz Weihrich, *Management* (New York: McGraw-Hill 1988), pp. 182–192.
(3) J. B. Rizzo, R. J. House and S. I. Lirtzman, "Role Conflict and Ambiguity in Complex Organizations," *Administrative Science Quarterly*, Vol. 15, No. 2, p. 161.
(4) Douglas McGregor, *The Human Side of Enterprise* (New York: McGraw-Hill, 1960), p. 158.
(5) R. L. Desatnick, *Managing to Keep the Customer*, Jossey-Bass, London and San Francisco, 1987, p. 113.
(6) F. H. Goldner, "Success vs. Failure: Prior Managerial Perspectives," *Industrial Relations*, Vol. 9, No. 4, p. 455.
(7) R. L. Katz, "Skills of an Effective Administrator," *Harvard Business Review*, Vol. 33, No. 1, pp.33–42
(8) Drucker, op.cit., p. 452.
(9) V. Z. Brink, "The Internal Auditor's Review of Organizational Control," *Research Committee Report 18*, (Orlando, Fla.: The Institute of Internal Auditors, 1972), pp. 38,39,45.

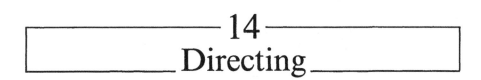

14
Directing

DIRECTING AND THE MANAGER

Nature of Directing

Definition and Purpose

Directing, sometimes referred to as actuating, is the function of moving resources toward a goal. It is largely interpersonal, and so it deals mainly with stimulating people to do what is necessary to meet enterprise objectives. At its best, it will succeed in making people want to meet those objectives because achievement will satisfy individual needs and help people meet their own goals. At its worst, it creates resentment, foot-dragging, and sabotage.

Directing is a complex combination of actions and concepts that include leadership, motivation, behavioral patterns, and communication. Because of their special importance to the organization, we have devoted separate chapters to behavioral patterns (Chapter 7) and communications (Chapter 9). In this chapter we shall be concerned chiefly with motivation and leadership. Some of the concepts in Chapters 7 and 9 will be reemphasized as needed for a rounded discussion.

Importance

Rare indeed is the person who worships at the shrine of work for work itself. Usually people work to exchange effort for some gain that makes the effort worthwhile to them. They will contribute only enough of themselves to continue the exchange. Yet buried beneath that minimal effort is a tremendous wellspring of potential that is rarely tapped. Indeed, few people use more than a small part of their capability, so a goal of successful management is to show people how their own needs can be integrated with those of the enterprise and make them want to reach down to those hidden resources.

In an age of extreme competition, when comparable companies have access to comparable technology and markets, the difference in growth and profit can often stem from the difference with which the members of competing companies contribute to organizational goals. Therefore, management must, in its directing process, create an environment in which people are willing to do twice as much as they think they can.

Some people are self-starters and need no urging; they know what is needed and will drive themselves toward it. Others are willing but need to be told where, how, and how much. The great majority, however, need to be stimulated to contribute willingly and enthusiastically. The manager who can inspire that enthusiasm, day after day and month after month, is worth more than rubies. This manager is the leader whom people will follow, the motivator who wakens drives and creativity, and is usually blessed with superiors who have developed a climate that encourages human growth.

Elements of Directing

Human complexity bedevils the function of directing. We hire more than the typist's fingers and the machinist's hands; we hire the whole typist and the entire machinist. With the people come their backgrounds, likes, antipathies, prejudices, abilities, disabilities, and vagaries.

Humans cannot be pinned down, dissected, and analyzed like a butterfly. Many behaviorists have tried, but no template for human beings has yet been cut. Nevertheless, the analyses have thrown some light on this complexity whose name is worker:(1)

- Not only complex, but variable from situation to situation, and from stimulation to stimulation.
- Comes to the job with certain fixed views; yet is capable of learning new motives through experiences in the organization and through the effect superiors and fellow workers have.
- Motives may change from organization to organization and from department to department within the same organization.
- May respond, and respond productively, to many different kinds of managerial strategies from the autocratic to the democratic.

It is true that the whole person is hired and brings along diverse needs. Yet the only human needs the manager will be interested in are those that can be satisfied within the confines of the organization. No manager has the time, energy, resources, or ability to satisfy all of the worker's human needs. The purpose of the organization is not to be a worker's psychiatrist. Rather, it should be to offer the right environment for the fulfillment of relevant needs: those that will be satisfied at the same time that organizational needs are met.

The directing process, then, is effective to the extent that subordinates contribute to organizational goals, to the extent they perceive a flowing together of their personal goals and those of the organization, to the extent they feel responsibility for contributing to the organizational goals, and to the extent they feel that their own efforts will achieve those goals. So the superior must know the goals and understand the people.

The aim of successful directing, then, is not to open doors, but to show where the key can be found . . . not so much to teach as to awaken desires to learn . . . not to pave the path, but to portray the rewards at the end of it . . . not to set the standards, but to show how the standards can be set . . . not to be the monitor, but to help each subordinate develop an inner monitor . . . not to give the answers, but to ask questions so that the subordinates are led toward finding answers . . . not to fulfill expectations but to paint a compelling picture of the satisfactions that come from self-fulfillment.

Motivating

Management's Responsibility

Every manager must motivate. Every manager must induce people to act in a certain way, and the *desideratum* of motivation is to inspire people to perform superlatively. That cannot be done either by simply getting out of the employee's way or by wielding a whip. The answer lies in reaching the motives within that will cause the individual to want to act in a desired manner. Hence managers are responsible for understanding employee attitudes—attitudes that have been acquired in myriad ways from a variety of sources. Chiefly, they result from past experience, from the groups with which the employee works, and from sources of authority.

Employee attitudes must first be understood and then be shaped if personal and organizational goals are to be met. For years managers operated on the principle that the only motivation worth considering was the financial reward. However, if that is the only reward, people will in time give of themselves only enough to get by. That is particularly true when jobs are uninspiring and unchallenging. There must be a personal incentive as well if the superior is to bring out the zeal and enthusiasm that are waiting to be mined.

The Motivators

Douglas McGregor said that the human being is a wanting animal.(2) Wants are endless; let one be satisfied and another springs up. What motivates a person to work are the things that are felt will satisfy these wants.

Different people, clearly, have different wants. Also any one individual will have wants that vary with the times, with the situation, and with the satisfactions achieved. The hierarchies of wants proposed by Maslow are as valid as the satisfiers and dissatisfiers proposed by Herzberg.(3)

Maslow's hierarchy demands satisfaction of physical needs before the social needs and relations with others emerge. Also the psychic needs, the needs for recognition and for self-fulfillment, will ordinarily not make themselves felt until the more basic needs are satisfied.

Herzberg's studies disclosed that certain benefits offered by the employer do not satisfy needs; all they do by their presence is avoid dissatisfaction. Hence, company policy, administration, salary, and fringe benefits—the so-called hygiene factors—do not of themselves satisfy other than the very basic needs. On the other hand, their absence will dissatisfy, and dissatisfaction results in absenteeism, labor turnover, and low morale. The factors that do satisfy are achievement, recognition, the work itself, responsibility, and advancement.

Both Maslow's and Herzberg's findings must be considered in relation to the situation and the type of individual involved. Among knowledge workers, achievement on the job is the key motivator. When such employees do not feel achievement, and when the hygiene factors are sufficiently attractive to keep them from leaving the organization, people will just go through the motions. They will not extend themselves.

Maslow's theory of the progressive satisfaction of human needs may not necessarily be applicable to managers; for such people may not need external stimuli to do a superb job. Contact with managers has demonstrated that, in many cases, all that managers need is the opportunity to perform and thereby satisfy both their own needs and those of the organization.

In a study of 82 scientists, the factors that satisfied the study's subjects had nothing to do with hygiene. What attracted and held them were interest in the work, the importance of the work, and projects that challenged them.(4)

The studies have resulted in no specific remedy for all the ills attributable to lack of motivation. However, the studies have pointed up the variability of employees, the heights to which motivated employees can rise, and the difficulty of the manager's job.

Indeed, the manager, who believes that job satisfaction will lead unquestionably to high job performance may be disappointed; studies have shown low correlation between the two.(5) Job satisfaction does not necessarily lead to high performance, but perhaps the correct conclusion is the reverse: high performance will lead to job satisfaction, and high performance will result from an appropriate system of rewards—not the hygiene rewards, but rewards that are directly linked to performance.

Obviously, all managers will try to move their subordinates toward some goals. The autocrat will do it with fear, punishment, and threats of dismissal.

That may work for a while, or it may work when jobs are scarce and the workers are striving to fill their basic physical needs. However, the autocratic style may not work when autocrats turn their backs or the job market benefits the worker.

The participative manager will try to offer rewards that fill the needs of the employee. Under proper conditions, production will be high if workers have a true expectancy that they will receive those rewards. Expectancy is based on three factors:

1. The physical and mental equipment to accomplish the task set.
2. If the job is done in accordance with or better than the standards set, there will be a reward.
3. The reward is equitable.

We have talked here of the tangible rewards, but many workers need more than that. Many jobs leave them with an unfilled need for "psychic income." That need can be satisfied if workers feel they have some effect on their destiny.

Various types of motivators have been tried and with varying success:

● *Authority.* The autocrat says: "Work or find other work." Authoritarian managers can obtain minimum performance with the whip, but the whip must be wielded constantly. It rarely motivates superb performance; and when it is set down, people slack off. In fact, strong unions and labor scarcity have largely caused managers to abandon it. They have begun to recognize that if the lashes are too severe, people will fight back, and in the long run flogging is destructive.

● *Competition.* Under the merit principle, people are stimulated to excel their peers to gain higher merit ratings and earn promotion. However, that form of motivation is notoriously difficult to administer, and objective measurements are almost impossible. The need for the individual to show superiority to associates can bring on resentment and adversely affect teamwork. In unionized plants merit has been superseded by seniority as a basis for advancement.

● *Zero defects.* A zero defects program, if carefully established, publicized, and administered, can move people to work together to meet and exceed qualitative goals. By doing things right the first time, the escalating costs of rework and correction can be brought down. A number of success stories have testified to the practical worth of a good zero defects program. In one sheet-metal shop it usually took 82 hours to correct errors committed during 13 800 production hours—a ratio of 168 to 1. After the ZD program was installed, it took only 16 hours to correct errors made in the same number of production hours—a ratio of 862 to 1.

● *Paternalism.* Paternalism is the approach of the benevolent despot. "If I'm good to my people and provide them with the benefits I think they should have, they'll be grateful and work hard." However, gratitude is a rare commodity. The benefits bestowed become benefits expected. They lose their gratitude-inducing appeal. They become just another hygiene factor whose presence does not satisfy and whose absence dissatisfies. Moreover, paternalism has one serious drawback in these more enlightened days: it assumes that the boss is superior to the workers and knows what is best for them. That may create more resentment than gratitude.

• *Implicit bargaining.* Bargaining that is implicit differs from union-type bargaining. A tacit understanding develops between superior and subordinate: live and let live. "You do your job, and I'll wink at the rules. You give me reasonable performance, and I'll see that you're protected." That may provide for country club living, but it does not stimulate superior performance.

Participation

Most people will extend themselves if they feel they are a part of the work they do, just as parents will usually dote on their own unlovely child and be indifferent to their neighbor's paragon. If the worker participates in developing and organizing the work, establishing standards, and setting goals, the job itself increases in stature and so do the worker and the manager. There is a challenge in clearing the high jump you have set.

Participation adds dignity to the job. It marks the worker as a part of the decision-making apparatus, and it can reduce employee resistance. However, management's offer of participation must be sincere. There are several approaches to participation:

• *Suggestion system.* A suggestion system can be useful, but it generally affects only a minority of the employees.
• *Multiple management.* In the multiple management arrangement, people participate in problem solving that goes beyond their normal assignments. For example, production committees made up of workers and managers might study ways and means of improving production efficiency and reducing production costs.
• *Consultative management.* In a consultative management arrangement, managers bring their people into the management process. Instead of making authoritarian, unilateral decisions, they ask their people to participate in the day-to-day administration of the job. But the final choice must still be that of the superior. People like to be heard, but they also respect a decisive superior.

Participation is not a panacea. It may work with some people and not with others. The subordinate must be capable of becoming involved in the participative process, but some workers may fear and be suspicious of it. The atmosphere of the organization must provide a climate that is kind to the participative approach, hence the wise manager moves slowly and carefully in involving staff.

Also, participation may hold dangers. Unions may be jealous of their workers' loyalties and regard participation as a management ploy to win people over to the company's side. Also, of course, emergent circumstances call for unilateral decisions. The worker expects strong leadership when danger threatens.

Criticism

Effective criticism can motivate people to improve; destructive criticism almost invariably accomplishes the reverse in the long run. For that reason criticism should be positive, and it will be more palatable if the evaluation process permits the subordinate to participate.

Rarely is criticism effective when it is approached in the white heat of passion. So the superior should avoid criticizing until sure of what needs to be accomplished. Having become satisfied that the goal is improvement rather than the temporary satisfaction of telling someone off, the problem should then be identified. Approaching the problem impersonally can avoid defensiveness and resentment. The proper approach is not "Here's what you did," but "Here's what happened."

So that the subordinate will not be kept worrying about the unknown, the introduction should be followed immediately with the negative things that must be said. The negative things should be objective and specific. Examples of unsatisfactory behavior are important. Questions of fact should be thoroughly resolved, and then the subordinate should be asked how unsatisfactory behavior can be improved. Seeking participation can relieve tensions. The superior should help by suggesting ways of working out the problems.

The session should be ended with a high note: point out the subordinate's good points and potentials. The session should not be ended until both supervisor and worker feel that the problem has been fully and fairly explored.

Creativity

Creativity is closely tied to motivation. Creativity needs the right environment. It cannot be forced, but it can grow if the climate is right. When people are told that creativity is welcome, they will regard their jobs and their environment differently. They will find that new life is brought into their work. They will start to observe the matters that may have formerly escaped their attention. They may start thinking; they may relate ideas and experiences they thought were long forgotten. They will start generating different and alternative courses of action. They will no longer be hemmed in by the forbidding walls of precedent. They will start drawing upon forces they did not know they had—emotional and preconscious forces. They will learn to be flexible.

From the standpoint of the manager, creativity as such is not enough. The manager is concerned with innovation. Creativity generates the ideas; innovation puts them to use. In results management, most managers and workers will be on the constant lookout for ways of achieving goals while making the job more rewarding.

Most importantly, the manager should recognize creativity for what it is: not necessarily the blinding flash of an Einstein's $e = mc^2$ but the developing of new ways of doing the same old things. More often, merely recognizing a problem and seeing the need for a better way is a creative act. Management is a creative and innovative pursuit. If managers provide the right environment, they can move their people to participate in a rewarding creativity.

Compensation

Motivator or Dissatisfier?

Compensation is the classic motivator, but managers find it difficult to make compensation more than a hygiene factor—one of Herzberg's dissatisfiers. As monetary needs are satisfied, they have less and less power to stimulate performance and more and more power to dissatisfy. If an executive in an organization is receiving a few hundred dollars less than a comparable executive, it is easy to lose sight of the fact that, after taxes, the difference in buying power is infinitesimal. Jealousy over the difference can lead to less effectiveness as an executive.

Economic benefits motivate when they satisfy pressing needs. When economic goals are not the most pressing ones, they will motivate only under the following circumstances:

- High compensation should be a goal that is important both to the individual and to the organization.
- The individual must feel confident that the exercise of energy and skill toward meeting organizational goals will result in greater compensation.
- The individual must be convinced of possessing the personal equipment to improve, that improvement is attainable.

Compensation comes in three different forms: (i) base pay or salary for the job, (ii) variable pay that is geared to the individual's productivity, and (iii) supplementary pay that is not geared to either the individual or the job (fringe benefits). Thus, total compensation includes both base pay and extra payments. The base pay is what is publicly known. It is the value of the position; and it is the basis for the amounts of such other benefits as life insurance, travel reimbursements, and bonuses.

This means of compensation should have relevance. They should be meaningful in terms of the situation. A salespersons contribution is readily measured objectively; compensation can be geared readily to performance that can be recognized by commissions. Conversely, the performance of a research scientist or a contract administrator cannot be measured readily, and hence it must be paid for through a straight salary.

Compensation plans may be what are termed shallow or steep. In an organization that is inherently conservative, one in which all managers follow the book and in which innovation and risk taking are not held in high esteem, compensation is shallow because variations in managerial ability are slight. On the other hand, when the organization wants and rewards aggressive leadership and vision, a great differential among managers may be both appropriate and necessary.

Incentive Compensation

Incentive plans include bonuses, commissions, profit sharing, and incentive pay. The organization has no obligation to pay bonuses. The bonus is based primarily on company profits and is granted on the basis of salary and performance. The individual should have a clear understanding of the basis for bonuses, and the basis should be consistently applied. One drawback associated with bonuses is the passage of time between performance and payment. Positive, instant reinforcement is usually lacking; the reward does not mesh with the deed.

The subject of profit sharing is broad and ramified. Profit sharing can be a powerful motivator to some, but people who feel they cannot directly influence profits through their own efforts may not find it an incentive. Also, morale may drop when profits turn to losses or when profit-sharing funds decline in value. Commissions, on the other hand, are directly and visibly related to performance, and so they can be strong motivators.

Incentive pay is usually based on time studies if it is to be objective. If the studies could be completely accurate and scientific, incentive pay would be relatively simple to administer, but they are complicated by trying to get the measure of the normal output of an average person expending average effort under average conditions. That is a chimera, and the workers are usually abundantly aware that it is. Since the employee's compensation will be governed by the studies, it is no wonder that war is declared as soon as the time-study engineers enter the door.

Deferred Compensation

Deferred compensation includes contractual payments, stock operations, and pensions. Contractual payments are agreements between employer and employee to defer payments of agreed-upon amounts until after retirement or after the term of employment. That form of deferred compensation can be mutually beneficial. The employer knows the amount committed. The employee can receive compensation at a time when the income tax bracket may be substantially lower. Both employer and employee should be aware, however, of the government regulations covering deferred compensation.

Stock options are rights to buy a corporation's common stock at a specified price within a stipulated period in the future. They can be highly motivating to some managers who can see their efforts resulting in higher profits to the company and increased prices for their stock.

Pension plans have proliferated in recent years. The trend appears to be toward the noncontributory plans—those in which the employee makes no contributions to the pension funds. Pension plans have both benefits and drawbacks. On the one hand, they provide a degree of economic security for employees. Younger employees can see daylight ahead for themselves as older employees retire at stipulated ages, and the deferred compensation is greater because of the employer's purchasing power, greater than the kind of insurance the employee could procure individually. On the other hand, employees are deterred from leaving the company because the longer their incumbency the better the benefits. Also, inflation can seriously erode real purchasing power.

Fringe Benefits

The list of fringe benefits keeps expanding. A partial catalog includes medical and dental care, counseling and legal aid, group insurance, paid vacation and sick leave, time at seminars and conferences, educational assistance, scholarships, and paid association memberships. Those benefits are undoubtedly socially desirable, but their ability to motivate is questionable. They are not affected by job performance. Most companies provide the same or similar benefits, so the benefits provide little competitive edge in vying for an employee's services.

Production Sharing

Individual incentives have rarely worked well, so there has been a trend toward plans that appeal to the group instead of to the individual. Probably the best known production-sharing plan is a system that Joseph N. Scanlon, a union official, developed in 1938.(6)

Scanlon's plan was more than a way to administer an incentive program; his purpose was to provide a new, cooperative way of business life. For instance, machinists were to communicate directly with staff engineers. The approach was one of problem solving instead of rancor and animosity. To be avoided were the pressures of incentive wages, crash production programs, and autocratic leadership. The aim was to convey to all workers of the company the idea that their opponents were not the company's management but rather the competing firms that were getting a larger share of the market or making a similar product better and at lower cost.

The Scanlon plan required a series of departmental committees made up of the foreman and a union representative. The committee purpose was to obtain and process suggestions for improvement. In addition, normal labor cost per unit of output, based on past experience, was determined.

If greater cooperation and efficiency reduced costs below the norm, the amounts saved would be divided among the workers. Sometimes the savings would be divided equally between the firm and the employee group. The employees' share would be allocated to the employees on the basis of base pay. Most important, reward was directly and instantly tied to productivity, since bonuses were distributed each month.

Some consider that workers' participation plans, such as Scanlon's, work only when the enterprise is doing well; that it works only in profitable businesses. Yet one of the first successful introductions of the plan was in a company that had its back to the wall; LaPointe Machine Tool Company in Hudson, Massachusetts. The workweek had been cut to four days, and the company was on the brink of bankruptcy. Part of the success of the plan there was attributable to a change in attitudes. Cooperation among all groups replaced backbiting and defensive self-protection.

At the Parker Pen Company, a unionized firm of 1 000 employees, incentive bonuses were paid in 142 of 168 months and ranged from 5.5% to 20% of payroll.(7) In a survey of 2 636 employees in 21 plants that adopted the Scanlon Plan, the employee role most emphasized was that of providing information through suggestions.(8) Under the plan, workers appear more interested in their company's health and seem to accept change more readily. Clearly, if employees make suggestions for improvement, they will embrace the change that brings it about. The greatest defect in the plan is reported to be the lack of effect it has on the individual's own job. That effect, evidently, can be had chiefly through job enrichment or job enlargement.

The plan will not work for everyone. It is of lower value to middle and top management. There improvement in leadership styles brings about greater participation. Among supervisors, who often lack participative skills, the establishment of formal committees that must be consulted provides reasonable assurance of employee participation. Since formal participation is tied directly to the reward of money, the incentive to participate is strong.

Probably the greatest contribution that Scanlon made was to show that management cannot consistently motivate people through gimmicks. Managers will motivate only when they create a climate that stimulates real cooperation throughout the entire organization.

One of the byproducts of a cooperative plan is improvement in morale. Morale was discussed in Chapter 7, Patterns of Behavior. Morale is not necessarily a satisfier. It may not increase production, but high morale has other benefits. Personnel turnover and absenteeism are lowered. Grievances and work stoppage are reduced in number. Recruitment is made easier and the task of the manager becomes less burdensome.

Leadership

Nature and Purpose

Management is responsible for giving direction to that which it manages. Resources available to the manager must be directed toward the greatest results, and the people must be led toward the greatest productivity and achievement. That is the function of leadership: to stimulate people to work with zeal and confidence. Zeal—intensity, ardor, and earnestness—is instilled by the inspiring leader. Confidence—technical ability—is evoked by the teacher who leads by setting good examples. The end result is getting ordinary people to do extraordinary things.

Leadership has three components: (i) those who lead, (ii) those who follow, and (iii) the situation that prevails. Always capable of making itself felt is a fourth component: irritation. People may not enjoy being told what to do, but many of them are not self-motivated and self-organized. They must be led and directed if enterprise goals are to be met. The leader may be liked or disliked, but must be respected. In times of stress and emergency people look to their leaders. To the ordinary individual, emergencies are to be feared; to the leader they are opportunities to display abilities.

We know more about leadership now than we ever did before, but there is still no comprehensive theory and understanding of the function. Leaders are a part of the group because they must pull their followers to heights they may not have believed attainable. Yet they are apart from the group because others, careers and futures are in their hands.

The wise leader uses whatever motivational system will get the job done. The fortunate leader is one who is blessed with a charismatic personality that inspires zeal in others. Above all, leadership is a process that is more emotional than intellectual or rational. Since people differ in what moves them, leaders must know their people and understand how to kindle their desires to achieve and how to keep the fires burning.

Thus the complex interaction of leader, led, and the situation will affect results. The same leadership behavior will not be effective in all situations. The leader who can assess the situation and adjust the style to meet it will have the better chance of meeting enterprise objectives.

It is a mistake, however, to assume that the happy employee is a productive one. A series of studies in a life insurance company, a railroad, and a group of factories manufacturing agricultural equipment encompassed the records of thousands of employees. The researchers found no correlation between job satisfaction and productivity.(9) Effective leaders are not people who create auras of happiness but they are people who can instill confidence in their own ability, who understand those being led, and who employ the motivational forces dictated by the law of the situation.

Characteristics

Executive ability cannot be cataloged or measured, but it can almost invariably be recognized wherever it exists. Many theorists have sought to identify the qualities that make for a successful leader, such as strong will, extroversion, power need, and achievement need, or intelligence, social maturity and breadth, inner motivation, and a human-relations-oriented attitude.

Although all leaders have their own personalities, traits, and ideas about how to lead, the way in which they behave will be affected by the group they lead. The quality of performance of the led will affect the behavior of the leader. A study was conducted of random assignments of leaders to high-performance groups and to low-performance groups. The study showed that leaders of high performance groups typically displayed more supportiveness of subordinates and that there was increased group cohesiveness and productivity. Leaders of equal ability were assigned to low-performance groups. They tended to manage autocratically, and the group produced unsatisfactorily as to quality and quantity of output. Leaders assigned to neutral control groups behaved in a manner somewhat between the two extremes.(10)

Many people who select and develop managers look for certain traits. That approach is open to criticism, since accomplishment, no matter how achieved, is more to be desired than particular traits. Nevertheless, the trait theory is as valid as any other theory. Here are some of the traits considered desirable in a leader:

- *Intelligence up to a point.* High intelligence is essential to deal with problems and make decisions. Beyond a certain point, however, the possessor may be impatient with people with lower intelligence or may prefer to be devoted to abstract ideas and research.
- *Emotional maturity that includes objectivity, dependability, and persistence.* The leader is energetic, willing to work long and hard, has drive, and is willing to give support and sustain others.
- *Initiative—being a self-starter and being able to see what escapes others.* This trait is predominant in executives; it is less often found at lower levels.
- *Communicative skills, including persuasiveness.* The leader is able to: speak and write forcefully; able to listen carefully and ask the right questions; able to convince people that they themselves want to accomplish what the leader wants accomplished.
- *Confidence.* The leader exudes self-assurance, and is sure that hurdles present opportunities to jump, not an excuse to balk.
- *Perceptiveness in appraising others.* The leader functions through others, so

must be able to understand the followers. Perceptiveness includes empathy: being able to put oneself in another's shoes and to see the situation as the other sees it. A leader knows people and is aware of their strengths and weaknesses.

● *Creativity and originality.* The leader must have the vision to find new ways and blaze new trails. Innovation is the sword that cuts the cobwebbed Gordian knot of custom and conformism.

Most managers master managerial skills more easily than leadership skills. Managerial skills are developed by following some basic principles of good administration. Leadership skills demand an understanding of human behavior and motivation, and that understanding is not vouchsafed to many. Few master leadership skills without trial and error and a good deal of heartache.

Leadership Style

Leadership style is a pattern of behavior that is designed to lead others, that is, to mesh the interests of the individual and the organization, so as to pursue some set goal. Lewin classifies the styles as autocratic, participative, and laissez-faire.(11) The autocratic leader can be coercive or benevolent. The former attribute is associated with fear, threats, and command; the latter with tact, praise, and bribery through fringe benefits. When the autocratic leader becomes aware of the importance of individual commitment to a cause or program, there is string-pulling and manipulation to convince subordinates that they are participating in decision making.

The participative leader has a higher regard for the capabilities of subordinates than the autocrat and asks for inputs from subordinates without relinquishing the seat at the head of the table. Subordinates honestly feel that they can influence the outcome of decisions. It is doubtful, however, that anyone contends that the participative style will work in all situations.

The laissez-faire leader is hardly a leader at all. Responsibility for decision making is passed on to the group. The leader looks for the consensus but often finds chaos.

As employees become more educated, as labor unions become more powerful, and as government makes itself more palpably felt, leadership styles will trend toward the participative. At present, the typical style of business leadership is one of benevolent autocracy.

For a while the behavioral scientists were vehemently antiauthoritarian. Their goal was to see participative leadership take over in all situations. However, they have begun to recognize that the manager, who is charged with achieving enterprise objectives, must use the style that is most effective in the particular situation.

Participative management does offer professional people and higher-management personnel some advantages. It is less advantageous at the lower levels, where careful communication from a competent decision maker who is reasonably consistent and has a good feeling for people will achieve higher productivity. Even at higher levels, a leadership style that skillfully blends the authoritative and the participative will promote an atmosphere of stability and an impetus toward achievement.

It is probably the rare supervisor who will have complete control over leadership style. Usually style is a reflection of the treatment received from the superior. Fleishman evaluated leadership courses attended by foremen at International Harvester. During the training session, the foremen appeared to recognize the benefits and embrace the concepts of employee-centered leadership. However, after they returned to their jobs, they reverted to former autocratic styles because they were unable to counteract the influences from higher up.(12)

Indeed, it seems that executives do not have the highest faith in the leadership abilities of their subordinate managers despite the fact that they feel their subordinates should be informed of what goes on in the company and should participate in decision making. "Democratic management" seems to be a matter of degree. It is just less autocratic than other styles.

Leadership Techniques

The study of leadership is meaningless without the study of followership. Most people want to be led. Most people want to feel they are being guided and moved by a person they can trust and be proud of. They want to be led by leaders who exhibit confidence, effectiveness, and a sense of purpose.

Leaders should act like leaders. Envy may make followers grumble about the aloofness of some leaders, but they would rather have aloofness than vacillation and excessive desire to be liked. Followers, deep down, want their leaders to be more knowledgeable than they are, to be more conservative, and to stand slightly aloof. The leader should be aware of that need in the followers. Even though that aspect may not be natural to them, they should seek to cultivate it—but with believability. The leader must always be aware of the effect of behavior on followers—the way the followers will interpret the unconsciously raised eyebrow, the secret smile, the careless word, the unmeant tone.

There is no magic potion that can create a leader; but if there were, confidence would be one of the chief ingredients. Confidence comes with experience and dedicated application, and it begets confidence. The leader who instills confidence in followers by effective training, teaching, delegating, and criticizing is creating morale. When morale is high, the leader can move mountains and do no wrong.

The need to develop leadership skills at all levels of management is urgent. Managers who were not born with the skills must cultivate them through:

• *Empathy*—putting yourself in another's place and actually tasting the other's emotions; truly understanding how others feel and what turns them on or turns them off. Empathy is hard to develop because managers are people too and have their own needs and desires. If they want to be leaders, they must learn and want to fulfill the needs of their followers.

● *Objectivity*—not taking action before analyzing the situation, not being moved to take irreversible steps before receiving input from those involved, not functioning by personal whim.

● *Self-knowledge*—learning how certain words and actions may affect others adversely and seeking to avoid those words and actions.

● *Legitimacy*—Knowing what you're doing and doing it well. Success inspires people; it becomes their own success as they bask in the reflected glory. The unsuccessful leader is soon left for the successful one.

Empathy, sympathy, and understanding will usually bring results, but the law of the situation will often have to prevail. Examples may have to be made, and sanctions may have to be exacted. Insubordination, by and large, cannot be tolerated. When people are permitted to break a rule with impunity, all the rules will soon be ignored. Sometimes sanctions may have to be imposed to reinforce the superior's authority, and sometimes an individual may deliberately have to be punished as an example to others. Often a little talk may do the job, but there are times when more serious steps must be taken. One drastic example is attributed to Frederick the Great, the successful Prussian military leader:

> He had issued a lights-out order and was making his rounds to see whether it was being obeyed. He saw a light coming from the tent of a captain. He entered the tent and saw the captain in the act of sealing a letter. The officer, terrified, dropped to his knees and begged forgiveness. Frederick asked him to resume his seat and add some words to the end of the letter. The officer obeyed and wrote as Frederick dictated: "Tomorrow I die on the scaffold." The next day he was executed. The example was harsh. But Frederick was concerned with the welfare of thousands of his soldiers whose security might have been compromised by an attack brought about by a careless light. The authority of the lights-out order as well as other orders was graphically if brutally reinforced.

When extreme measures are contemplated, the superior had better take into account how well liked the object of those measures is. When deciding to move rigorously, the superior should be able to justify actions.

Another successful technique of leadership is to keep in touch with reality, to go behind the top-level reports and documents and listen to the ordinary person. Here is an example:(13)

> Charles Kettering was primarily responsible for the diesel engine. Much trial and error led to the development of a large diesel-powered vessel. As Kettering wandered down to the ways to look at it before it was launched, he observed a watchman staring intently at the stern. "What are you looking at?" Kettering asked. "The propeller," answered the workman. "What about the propeller?" asked Kettering. "its size is off by at least an inch," said the man. "How do you know?" Kettering asked. "I know," said the workman. Kettering called on his

architects to compare the actual size of the propeller with the approved drawings. The propeller was indeed the wrong size and had to be rebuilt.

Leadership and Organizational Levels

The leaders in an organization can be divided roughly into three groups of managers: top (executive) managers, middle managers, and supervisors. All managers are responsible for planning, organizing, directing, and controlling. Similarly, all managers must have technical, conceptual and human skills, but at each of the three organizational levels the responsibilities and the skills are needed and used in different degrees.

1. *Top management.* The responsibilities exercised by top management relate chiefly to planning and organizing. Top managers make the basic plans and develop the broad organizational pattern. They formulate the decisions that have long-range effect. They defend the integrity of the enterprise. They reconcile the conflicts that constantly erupt within the organization, and they deal with the top level people in other organizations.

The conceptual skills are of special importance at the top levels: they constitute the ability to visualize what the future may hold and the ability to relate different ideas and see their relevance to a given situation. Top managers must be able to understand abstract ideas, be able to develop and visualize models and relations, and be blessed with the clarity of vision that guides them in anticipating the consequences of planned action. The human skills are not as essential to them on a day-to-day basis, but they create the climate within the company that blows the chill winds of fear, the warm sirocco of languor, or the brisk breeze of zeal and accomplishment. They move the middle managers to see that plans are carried out.

2. *Middle management.* "Middle management" is a general term applicable to all the levels of organization between the executives and the supervisors. In a flat organization there are few such levels; in a tall organization there are many. Middle managers have been referred to as the "fenders" because they are pelted by mud and muck from both sides. Their responsibility is to translate. They translate the abstract objectives and policies laid down by top management into the concrete goals and procedures to be met and followed by supervisors. They must also translate the concrete results their subordinate supervisors achieve into the general information that top management needs to make the executive decisions and hold the tiller of the enterprise.

Parsons suggests three levels of management function:(14)
(i) An inner technological core in which supervisors can be protected from uncertainty and achieve rationality.
(ii) A middle management that acts as the intermediary and speaks certainty to supervisors and uncertainty to executives.
(iii) An executive level that relates to the uncertainty of the environment.

Actually, middle managers deal less with subordinate managers and more with their peers. Sayles found that a great deal of the middle manager's time was spent in dealing with nonsubordinates—coordinating, keeping the work flow moving, advising, and staying abreast of what is occurring in the enterprise.(15)

3. *Supervisors.* Supervisors are the only managers in the organization who have managers above and nonmanagers below. They stand between the Scylla of middle managers who want higher efficiency, effectiveness, quantity, and quality and the Charybdis of the workers who want protection from on high while receiving more for less. To complicate further an already difficult job, they are often required to deal with the union steward—a force that strengthens with time.

Studies have produced five different viewpoints of the supervisor's function:

(i) The key person
(ii) The person in the middle
(iii) The marginal person
(iv) Another worker
(v) A human relations specialist.

The supervisor can be viewed as the key person because, to the worker, the supervisor is the personal representative of management, the one the workers deal with every day, and the face of management. On the other side, what management knows about its people is what is gained from the supervisors. That key position is as significant as the linchpin that keeps the plow hooked to the tractor.

For the same reason the supervisor can be regarded as the person in the middle. This position of strength makes for a key person; vulnerability makes for a person between opposing forces, caught between the expectations of the workers and the demands of middle management. Competing groups tug and pull, and it is impossible to fully satisfy either of the two groups and do an effective job.

Supervisors can find themselves in the position of marginal people standing forlornly on the side if neither their workers nor their manager accept them fully or confide in them completely. Sometimes managers deal with their staff specialists instead of their supervisors and the workers develop their informal organizations and stand behind the shields of their unions. Add to that the often infrequent dealings with fellow supervisors and we find an individual who sits on a lonely hummock.

For a while many supervisors saw themselves as other workers, and in the 1940s many supervisors tried to join labor unions or create foreperson unions. However, that was short-lived in the US because the Taft-Hartley Act of 1947 reaffirmed their status as members of management by forbidding them to join employee labor unions. Their legal status was changed, but their elevation from the ranks of workers often occurs without cutting the umbilical cord. As a result, many a supervisor has a self image as just another worker with little more money but a lot more headaches.

Finally, the supervisor can be viewed as a human relations specialist. With staff people taking over the problems of scheduling and quality, the most significant part of the job may be regarded as dealing in human relations.

The human relations aspect has been underscored in studies conducted by Likert and his colleagues in the Institute for Social Research at the University of Michigan.(16) The studies of supervisory practices covered public utilities, an insurance company, an automobile manufacturing company, a heavy-machinery factory, a railroad, an electrical appliance factory, and several government agencies. Two major criteria were used to evaluate supervisory effectiveness: (i) the productivity per hour or some similar measure of success in meeting production goals, and (ii) the satisfactions derived by employees. Likert found little relation between productivity and how employees regarded the company. Absenteeism and turnover may have been affected, but not productivity. In fact, management had commonly assumed that a favorable attitude toward the company would improve productivity, but the findings of the study did not support the assumption.

On the other hand, Likert did find a definite relation between the kind of supervision received on the one hand and both productivity and individual satisfaction on the other. The high-production groups generally had supervisors who were employee-centered. The supervisors who responded that they gave greatest emphasis to production were from sections with low productivity.

Low-production sections had supervisors who kept a close watch over their workers and supervised in terms of procedures instead of goals. High-production centers were in the charge of supervisors who supervised more generally and emphasized objectives instead of rules. To establish the cause-and-effect relation, supervisors were switched among sections. Their approaches did not change, but productivity did. The former low-productivity section improved under employee-centered supervision; the former high-productivity section slipped somewhat under production-centered supervision.

Likert found that the employee-centered approach—general goal-oriented supervision—did not imply a lack of concern with productivity. It meant merely that employee-centered supervisors knew they must achieve their productivity through people. They felt that applied pressure loses its force in time, whereas the goals stand as a grail, something to constantly reach for. He also found that high productivity did not mean low morale. Indeed, morale was highest in the section with employee-centered supervisors. So it would seem that today's supervisor should regard the elimination of some of the former jobs through increased technology and the computer as a signal to concentrate on the one factor with which neither technology nor the computer can deal: people.

Leadership and Orders

The order is the means by which people know what has to be done, and leaders should understand the techniques of giving orders so that their own orders will have a better chance of being followed. Managers should not make decisions calling for orders that will not be obeyed. If an order is refused or a decision challenged, the impasse may result in discharging an employee the executive very much wants to retain. The possible reaction of the employee should be taken into account, and a confrontation should be avoided by involving the employee in the decision making.

Orders should issue from the demands of the situation. They will be accepted with better grace if the source is attributed to the system. Indeed, if properly issued, the order can create a bond between supervisor and worker. The way the order is issued will have an important effect on how willingly it is carried out. It should be clear, so that it is understood. It should be concise, so that it is not beclouded by excessive detail and the employee can exercise some ingenuity. It should be consistent with the situation, with other orders, and with the worker's understanding of policies and procedures. Also the tone in which it is issued should not be officious; it should not convey the impression of a superior pushing an inferior around. It should imply a request for assistance. To that end, if at all possible, the reason for the order should be explained.

On the other hand, the superior should not be in such fear of giving orders so as to become excessively lenient. Leniency can be lunacy if it has no purpose. Indeed, the severe disciplinarian will be regarded as less severe than the lenient supervisor who suddenly becomes less lenient.

There is no perfect solution to problems of leading and exercising authority. The leader is contending with extremely complex relations between worker and superior, worker and colleagues, the worker and the union, and the worker and his or her upbringing. So the leader has less need of a set of rules than a method of analyzing the situation in order to act and obey the law of the situation.

Leadership and Change

Successful directing implies change. To lead a person in one direction often means that the person is being led away from another direction that was in mind. That involves dealing with an intricate set of psychological mechanisms.

Change can be imposed. The authority of the leader can be brought to bear and force can be applied: "Do it my way or else." That is rarely the best method, since the cost in human relations can be high. So an understanding of attitudes, of how a person tends to feel, see, or interpret a particular situation, is important. It is not change itself that is resisted; it is the methods used to require change.

Simple changes can be accomplished by straightforward discussions with individuals. The effort should be to point out the value of the changes to the individuals and subtly induce an adjustment of attitudes toward acceptance of the changes. Sweeping changes may need more planning and the laying of groundwork. The leader may have to take the heads of informal groups into confidence in order to pave the way. Even then the leader must move cautiously and must be able to assess the temper of the group itself, confident that, after conditioning the heads of the groups to change, the group does not reject the leader. Groups have resorted to the character assassination of heads who have not properly understood their needs and desires.

Change often requires an admission of having done something wrong; otherwise, why the need for change? If blame is not charged or implied, if both the leaders and the subordinates attack the situation and not the people, the possibility of successful change improves.

DIRECTING AND THE INTERNAL AUDITOR

The Internal Auditor's Involvement

When internal auditors deal with planning and organizing, appraisals can be completely objective. They can generally quantify findings and support conclusions with documented facts. Directing, however, is especially people-oriented; and except for certain hygiene factors, it often defies quantification. People do not fit into neat slots; they are not subject to simple addition and subtraction. Still, managers and leaders do need help and counsel in directing. That function provides management-oriented auditors with an unusual opportunity to move beyond the traditional role of evaluation by the numbers. They will have to tread more delicately than they do in traditional paths; but as managers, owners, and the members of boards of directors turn more and more to their unbiased counsel, they will be impelled to take a hard look at the directing process.

We have explored the internal auditor's role in behavioral patterns and communications in Chapters 7 and 9. In this chapter we will deal with his role in three other phases of directing.

1. *The Personnel Department.* The personnel department is normally responsible for determining the human needs of the enterprise—how people can be motivated and how their needs can be satisfied. Ordinarily, the department restricts its activities to the hygiene factors, to the factors whose absence breeds discontent. We shall concentrate on the auditor's review of those activities, but we shall also touch on appraisals of the satisfiers—the true motivators.

2. *Compensation.* Payments to employees take a large slice of the entity's dollar and deserve thorough audit attention.

3. *Leadership.* In terms of employee utilization, leadership is a fertile field for the internal auditor, but of increasing interest are the leadership qualities of the managers whose performance is being evaluated.

Personnel Department

Function

The personnel department is a staff function. It assists line managers in selecting, administering, developing, and rewarding people. At its best it brings to bear a technical expertise in human relations that is indispensable to the successful direction of human beings. At its worst it is a paper mill of policies and procedures, a deviser of gimmicks and pseudo motivators, and a mechanical administrator of fringe benefits. To carry out its true objectives, therefore, the personnel department needs to be staffed with people of judgement, wisdom, stature, and understanding. People with those qualities are rare indeed.

The personnel department deals with people at all levels: the hourly worker, usually unionized and generally in production areas; the salaried clerks, not invariably unionized and found all through the enterprise; and the management personnel, who include all salaried people other than clerks: technicians, professionals, and managers from supervisors to executives.

Audit Approach

Internal auditors can best help management if they approach the audit of personnel activities—as they approach any other operations—by first determining the operating objectives. Everything the department's manager does or seeks to accomplish should be keyed to those objectives.

Obviously, the temperament, needs, desires, and aims of the chief executive officer will affect the aims of the personnel manager. The internal auditor, in appraising departmental objectives, must do so in the context of the objectives set by the chief executive before being of any help to management. By and large, the objectives of the personnel function are:

- To identify staffing needs and availability and to train and develop manpower.
- To administer the various personnel programs and benefits.

Internal auditors should see how well those objectives are being met. When they are not being met, they should find out why and counsel managers on corrective action. Those matters will be explored in the following subsections.

Manpower Needs

The jobs to be filled need precise description; otherwise, how could the organization recruit and develop people needed to fill the jobs? Internal auditors should therefore be satisfied that Personnel has inventoried the needs of the entity and developed job descriptions that set forth the specifications for existing jobs and for jobs needed to carry out plans still on the drawing board. To look at the present alone is to permit the future to hold unpleasant surprises.

In making evaluations, internal auditors should review the entire system for an approach to analyzing jobs. They will want to know how the entire population of jobs—present and future—was determined. They will want to determine whether uniform criteria are used and, when necessary, whether reasonable weighting factors are employed to give appropriate significance to more demanding jobs. Also they will expect management to provide for periodic reevaluations to deal with changing conditions. The evaluators should also be kept informed of complaints and grievances so that inequities may be corrected.

The internal auditor should be satisfied that personnel does not inhabit an ivory tower. All department heads should be consulted on their needs and on the manpower peaks and valleys. The internal auditor must therefore determine how well current and future needs are or will be matched with the proper personnel.

All significant jobs should have backup people ready to step into the shoes of incumbents if need be, and each executive should know that an inventory of backup people is available. Personnel, as counselor on people matters, should see to it that an inventory is maintained. The experienced internal auditor knows how many managers avoid such housekeeping functions, so will expect a centralized agency, like Personnel, to assure reasonable, uniform backup inventories throughout the enterprise.

Staff Development

People recruited usually need orientation to fit them comfortably into their new jobs and training to improve their capabilities. Orientation is generally the function of the operating manager, but the process can vary from department to department. On the one hand, orientation can provide an inviting welcome mat; on the other, it can frustrate the newly hired employee. The personnel department that takes its responsibilities seriously will provide guidelines to operating managers on employee orientation. The specifics will be job-oriented, but the general guidelines should reflect an understanding of human behavior and the needs of people. Also people need to know how they can meet the particular needs of their employers.

The personnel department also has the responsibility for establishing programs, within available resources, to educate and train people to improve their capabilities. The internal auditor can evaluate those programs of orientation and training by measuring them against acceptable standards:

1. Orientation should include material that will inform the employee of rights and obligations. Internal auditors can review the materials given to all new hires to determine whether they are complete and understandable.
2. Steps in orientation should give the employee an understanding of what the company expects. Internal auditors can appraise the guidelines provided to operating managers and, on a test basis, determine whether the managers have

developed and are using programs to provide orientation. The auditor can examine exit interview records to determine whether inadequate orientation may have influenced employees to leave the organization.

3. Employees should be made receptive to additional training. Auditors can review the programs designed to inform employees of available training. Those programs should make the training attractive and capable of improving the employee's ability to better the position in the organization.

4. Training materials should be professional and should be tested for usefulness and relevance. The internal auditor can evaluate the process of selecting and developing the materials and review employees' evaluations of the training courses. Internal auditors can also interview operating managers to determine how useful they consider the training their employees receive.

5. Hazardous and very technical jobs should require special training and certification. Such jobs may include materials handling, explosives handling, welding, and working with chemicals or with electrical and electronic equipment. The internal auditor will want to know that records are maintained of all personnel engaged in such activities and that methods are in effect to insure certification and recertification.

How effectively employment and development activities are being carried out is difficult to appraise objectively; but when they are deficient, they are likely to be reflected in high absentee rates that, in turn, result in high turnover rates. Such rates can be determined by the following formulas:

Absentee rate:

$$\frac{\text{Total days lost}}{\text{Total days worked}} \times 100 = \text{absentee rate}$$

Turnover rate:

$$\frac{\text{Number of separations per month}}{\text{Average number on the payroll during the month}} \times 100 = \text{turnover rate}$$

A comparison of those rates with the rates in comparable industries or in other divisions of the company can furnish an index of employment and training effectiveness, provided due consideration is given to other variables.

One audit of a regional branch office included an analysis of sales personnel turnover. The analysis covered new hires and terminations during a 13-week period. The internal auditors observed that the largest percentage of terminations occurred after about 26 weeks of employment. Hence, the cost of training sales staff was not balanced by increased sales, since a large percentage of the sales staff left almost as soon as they had been trained.

Management had not been aware of the excessively high cost of training in relation to the benefits received. The audit report was a warning to management to review its employment, motivational, and compensation practices to reverse a costly trend.

Personnel Administration

Many internal auditors regard the payroll as the closest they should get to the personnel function, but internal auditors are not fulfilling their own responsibility if they do not review the operations of personnel administration. Those operations may not directly affect the earnings statement. Indirectly, however, the impact is enormous, because it is concerned with people. People, through their performance, affect earnings directly.

Because of the sensitivity and confidentiality of personnel administration activities, internal auditors would be well advised to avoid any adversary relation with personnel managers. Instead, they should seek to pursue a participative audit: agree upon the objectives of each function, determine the controls needed to see that the objectives are met, and identify the standards of good performance.

Each audit will call for individual programs that focus on the objectives, controls, and standards of the particular function. No canned checklist will help the internal auditor dissect the unique organism being examined, but here are some of the areas that will pay dividends for an in-depth study:

● *Personnel records.* Are the personnel records comprehensive; are they kept confidential and readily retrievable; and are they useful as histories of all employees? In one examination, the internal auditor found that personnel files charged out for updating were not controlled. As a result, there was no follow-up system to make sure that the histories of employees were being safeguarded.

● *Unemployment benefits.* Are records on terminated employees accurate and complete, and are protests lodged against improper claims by employees who left involuntarily without good cause or were discharged for misconduct? Is the company paying no more unemployment tax than the law requires? The following example illustrates the benefits of alertness to legal provisions:

> In one state, the employer's unemployment tax is based in part on these factors:
>
> 1. The percentage of decline between each year's gross wages paid over a 3-year period.
> 2. The percentage of decline between total quarterly wages paid during the 3-year period.
>
> When the ratio of decline is raised so are the rates. Two matters can adversely affect the ratio: a bonus paid in one quarter of a year. A seventh biweekly payroll, compared with six payrolls in the next quarter (usually occurring twice a year).
>
> The state law allowed the bonus and the biweekly payroll to be allocated over the year in which paid, thus eliminating the unnatural increase and decrease during the year. But the internal auditor found that the company was not taking advantage of these allocations. The recommendation was a recomputation of rates for the last two years, and as a result the company received a substantial refund.

● *Welfare and other services.* Included in welfare and other services are conflict-of-interest programs, credit unions, management clubs, social activities, employee purchases, suggestion systems, athletic programs, bonds, legal aid programs, and wage garnishment and credit letters. Those activities, like all other activities in the company, should be conducted in a businesslike fashion. Yet often, since they are people-related, those in charge of them may be pursuing objectives and following practices that are not in agreement with company policies. Audits should be made, therefore, to insure good administrative practices and adherence to the policies set forth by executive management. Here are some examples:

A company was receiving large discounts from local merchants. As a benefit to employees, the purchasing department accommodated them on purchases for such items as appliances. It issued purchase orders to the suppliers, paid the suppliers, and billed the employees. However, payments from employees were often slow, tying up company funds and calling for the assignment of one clerk to handle the record keeping. The purchasing department was reluctant to press for payment from fellow employees.

The internal auditor made a simple suggestion to correct the condition: For $16 the purchasing department bought a rubber stamp which said "This purchase must be paid for in cash at time of purchase." The employees then took the purchase orders to the merchants—who refused to give discounts without them—received the goods, and paid the lower prices. The results were gratifying:

1. Employees were still being accommodated.
2. No company funds were tied up in employee purchases.
3. Collection problems disappeared.
4. The need for the clerk was eliminated.
5. Local merchants were saved the expense of billing the company.

In an audit of a conflict-of-interest program administered by the personnel department, the internal auditor found:

1. The personnel department was not following up to see that all people required to sign declarations that they were not involved in conflict-of-interest situations had done so. Obviously, those from whom such declarations are not received may be the most suspect.
2. A number of employees who were newly hired, transferred between company divisions, or promoted to covered positions, had not signed the declarations, and there was no system to make sure such people did.

A company had organized a "recreation club" to promote employee welfare. An audit disclosed the following conditions requiring correction:

1. There were no alternates for executive committee members.
2. The blanket fidelity bond did not accurately indicate the people covered.
3. A resolution had been adopted to allow a welfare investigator to commit sums up to $200 per case in event of emergency, but the resolution had never been implemented. That caused undue hardship for employees in temporary need.
4. The recreation club's accounts, handled by one individual, had never been reviewed by the club's executive committee.

Compensation

Compensation administration puts a company in the middle of two opposing forces. One the one side is the need to offer compensation that will attract and hold competent people; on the other side is the need to remain competitive in the marketplace.

With those objectives in mind, the internal auditor perceives the need for certain control measures designed to see that the objectives will be met. Here are some examples of these measures:

- Means of classifying jobs in accordance with relevant and sensible criteria.
- Job compensation that is keyed to the particular classifications and at the same time is competitive with compensation for like jobs in other enterprises and departments within the auditor's enterprise.
- Employee evaluations made periodically to fit performance to compensation in the range within the employee's classification.
- Periodic reevaluation of all classifications and compensation to see whether adjustment to existing conditions is needed.

Internal auditors can determine the bases on which levels of compensation have been set. They can review the surveys made to determine whether they were thorough and whether conclusions drawn were based on sufficient and representative data. They can determine whether levels of compensation are reviewed and tested periodically. By analyzing records of grievances, they can find out whether employees feel that job analyses and compensation are fair. If the employees feel that they are unfair, they can find out why.

Leadership

Involvement

In terms of leadership, top managers can look to the internal auditor to assist them in providing information and counsel in answering, among others, these questions:

- Are the leaders at the middle-management level properly using the human resources subject to their stewardship?
- Are managers effectively carrying out their management functions?

The answer to the first question calls for relatively well-known auditing techniques. The answer to the second, however, goes beyond what is normally regarded as an internal audit responsibility and calls for tact, the development of standards, and a thoroughly professional approach. These issues were examined in Chapter 6.

Employee Utilization

The human resource is undoubtedly the entity's most important asset. The way it is used can mean the difference between the entity's success and failure. Yet internal auditing literature abounds with tales of employees wasting their time and managers being blissfully unaware of the waste. The internal auditor owes it to the organization to put the searchlight on such practices and to see that they are stopped. One approach auditors can take is:

- Analyze job classifications.
- For each job review data that show the levels of actual performance.
- Talk to both employees and their supervisors and observe on-the-job performance. Compare performance with what the job classification calls for.
- Evaluate performance to determine if the job is (i) carrying out company and departmental objectives and (ii) duplicating some other job.

Here are three examples of audit findings resulting from translating those general audit objectives to specific audit steps:

A message center was operating 24 hours a day to coordinate maintenance work on heavy machinery. The department manager wanted round-the-clock monitoring as a precautionary measure. The internal auditor found very low activity during swing, graveyard, and weekend shifts. It was therefore recommended alternate means of reporting maintenance requests, and three positions were dropped from the monitoring service.

Highly paid craftsmen were doing routine clerical work. The auditor compared job descriptions with work performance and substantiated his initial impressions. It seems that some organizational realignments had been made without considering the side effects. At the internal auditor's recommendation, the administrative work was transferred to existing clerical personnel and three craft positions were eliminated.

After a company reorganization, the internal auditor flow-charted certain processes and found that the realignment of duties created overlapping and duplication. Besides, certain supervisory positions had less supervisory responsibility after the reorganization. The internal auditor presented findings to management and thereby brought about the elimination of two administrative positions.

Those results were gained by (i) measuring work loads, (ii) determining what people were supposed to be doing, according to their work classifications, (iii) observing performance, (iv) interviewing people, (v) studying organization charts, and (vi) flow-charting processes.

In another situation a test of a payroll brought to light idle time that had never been identified as such and hence did not reach management's attention:

A statistical sample was taken from the 204 000 annual payroll payments. The test results showed that 10% of the employees paid in the sample had excessive idle time. These employees were charging their idle time to various indirect cost accounts.

The problem lay in the fact that management was not identifying idle time. For example, research had decreased. To keep the researchers on the payroll, their idle time was charged for extensive periods to indirect expense categories, inflating those accounts instead of disclosing the charges for what they were: idle time.

The internal auditors recommended reports to management which showed just how much idle time was being charged. Management could then make more knowledgeable decisions on workload scheduling, hiring and termination policies and pricing under varying conditions.

Internal auditors, as experts in internal control, should be concerned with overcontrol as well as with inadequate control and thereby help management make the directing process more efficient. Here is an example:

An internal auditor observed that a toolroom was attended full time by an employee whose wages plus benefits totalled $40 000 a year. The tools being safeguarded were worth about $8 000 and, besides, shop personnel usually entered the toolroom and helped themselves. At the internal auditor's recommendation the job of toolroom attendant was eliminated. Security guards at the gates represented sufficient deterrence to prevent employees from leaving the plant with those tools.

Evaluating Leadership

Asking internal auditors to evaluate leadership is like asking them to swim in shark-infested waters, yet deep-sea divers brave such waters when they believe the treasures awaiting them make the risk worthwhile. Experts in the field of human-resource accounting (HRA) believe the internal auditor has a function in that process just as in accounting for other assets. Here are some examples of the application of internal auditing techniques to protecting the resource that comprises the leaders within the organization.

- Report the failure to follow a promotion-from-within policy—a failure that could affect morale of employees and leaders alike.
- Prevent the luring away of leaders or potential leaders by appraising pension plans, fringe-benefit packages, or compensation plans and comparing them with industry standards.

Leaders in an organization may be torn between the organization goals of steady income and appreciation of market price of stock, on the one hand, and the improvement of their personal lifetime income, on the other. When the goals diverge, the divergence may be manifested by dysfunctional behavior on the part of the manager. Since a significant element of the directing process is people, should not then the internal auditor be concerned with the behavior of people during audit of that process? Mautz and Sharaf seem to think so when they say: "Unknown to the reviewer (audit function), the pressures which motivate the people in the 'system' may change sufficiently that they cease to act in an expected fashion, whereupon the internal control procedure loses its effectiveness."(17) Or more succinctly "Internal control is people." The Treadway Commission emphasized the same point when it stated that:

> "A strong corporate ethical climate at all levels is vital to the well-being of the corporation, all of its constituencies, and the public at large. Such a climate contributes importantly to the effectiveness of company policies and control systems, and helps influence behavior that is not subject to even the most elaborate system of controls."(18)

A later, related report has placed this aspect at the epicentre of its model of internal control:

> "The effectiveness of internal controls cannot rise above the integrity and ethical values of the people who create, administer and monitor them. Incompetent employees can render other internal control components inoperative. Integrity, ethical values and competence are critical to effective internal control, affecting the design, administration and monitoring of other components."(19)

The auditor's job, in the final analysis, is to measure; and to measure, we must have standards or at least questions to ask, questions that will elicit information about leadership style, the atmosphere in which the entity's systems function, and the use and maintenance of human resources.(20) Rensis Likert gives us some clues:(21)

- To what extent does the leader exhibit confidence in subordinates? Are their ideas sought? Are the ideas used?
- Do subordinates seem to be free to talk about their jobs to their superiors?
- To what extent does the leader make use of punishment, rewards, and employee participation?
- To what extent do subordinates feel committed to achieving organizational goals?
- In what way, if any, are subordinates made to feel a part of the drive toward meeting goals?
- How do subordinates report upward their accomplishments and problems?
- How is information on goal accomplishment communicated downward?
- How well do the leaders understand the problems, difficulties, and frustration felt by their subordinates?
- To what extent are subordinates involved in the decision-making process?
- From what sources are the bases and premises for decisions obtained—solely from the top or from subordinates as well?
- To what extent does the decision-making process motivate or disaffect subordinates?
- In what manner are goals established—by fiat or by group action?
- Is there evidence that the manner of goal establishment results in resistance to the goals by subordinates?
- Are review and control functions concentrated at the top, or are they fairly widely shared throughout the organization?

- Does the informal organization resist the formal one, or do both organizations seem to have the same goals?
- Are control systems used for policing or for self-improvement and decision making at the levels responsible for operations?

It may be some time before internal auditors routinely solicit answers to such questions and include the results in their formal audit reports. However, the information about subordinate managers is of vital importance to the chief executive officer or to executive or group vice presidents. If properly and confidentially carried out, the making of such inquiries and the confidential communication of the results can add another dimension to the internal auditor's usefulness.

On the surface there may seem to be an inconsistency in advocating, on the one hand, confidential information about operating managers and, on the other, a cooperative attitude in which manager and internal auditor work together in a problem-solving partnership. However, that is a fine line internal auditors have often had to walk. It harks back to the internal auditor's dual responsibilities: (i) To keep top management informed. Useful, objective, unbiased reports about middle managers constitute extremely important information to executive management; (ii) To leave every place a little better than the internal auditor found it. That calls for cooperation with operating managers. The line is fine, but the approach must suit the audit objective. That approach is far different in the detection of fraud than it is in recommending operating improvements. When the business community is made aware of the auditor's responsibilities, the apparent inconsistencies become understandable facets of a complex job.

Change

Perhaps more than any other function in the organization, internal auditing is concerned with change. In almost every audit assignment, the internal auditor is interested in seeing existing operations carried out more effectively, more economically, more efficiently, more safely, and with more concern for the environment. That calls for change. People fear change imposed by their own superiors; they fear it all the more if it is imposed by outsiders. The changes instituted as a result of an internal audit are feared all the more because they imply criticism that is brought to the attention of top management.

Hence the internal auditor of the classic stereotype, the cold, secretive, finger pointer, is rarely welcomed and recommendations for change are seldom embraced. However, the stereotype can be changed, and in many auditing organizations it has been changed. The reason for the change can be traced to the participative audit. In such an audit, the internal auditor changes approach from that of the policeman to that of the consultant—the problem-solving partner. The internal auditor, from the outset, takes operating management into confidence through open discussions about the preliminary survey, audit programs and audit findings.

The findings are not used as a reason to say, "Look what you did," but rather as an opportunity to explore a condition and determine, as partners, how to improve it. The audit report does not say to top management, "Look what I found and what I recommend," but rather, "A condition was observed and operating management promptly corrected it or took steps to correct it."

Until participative auditing becomes the preferred audit method, the fear of change and the resentment toward the recommender of change will remain. When operating managers and workers are brought within the circle that carries out the change, the moving force for change—internal auditors—will be more welcomed than feared, because "their" changes will become "our" changes.

CONCLUSION

Management performs through people. To the extent that people follow management's directions so will management achieve its objectives. People will be moved to perform with zeal and confidence only if their own objectives are congruent with management's and if they have been trained to perform competently. So the purpose of the function of directing is to arrange a marriage between the needs of the people and those of the organization. The motivator that probably has the strongest force and the longest duration is the charisma of a true leader coupled with the individual's strong positive feelings for the job. Other things, like compensation, fringe benefits, and a good environment, may keep staff on the job, but the great leader and the commitment to the job make them want to perform superbly.

The internal auditor can assist management by closely examining the "hygiene factors" or the compensation and fringe benefits. On the one hand, they should be competitive with those of other organizations. On the other, they should be reasonable, and they should not make an unnecessary drain on the organization's resources through waste, inefficiency, and ineffectiveness. In time, internal auditors will be asked to make reviews that many are now hesitant to carry out: reviews of the leadership capabilities of the managers whose work they now appraise. It is a thorn-imbedded road to travel, but the benefits to top management of an objective appraisal of those qualities may make the trek important and rewarding. The feasibility of such an approach is indicated in a collection of contributions on the topic of the strategic audit.

REFERENCES

(1) E.H. Schein, *Organizational Psychology*, (Englewood Cliffs, N.J.: Prentice-Hall, 1965), p.600.

(2) Douglas McGregor, *The Human Side of Enterprise* (New York:McGraw-Hill, 1960), pp. 36–39.

(3) A. H. Maslow, *Motivation and Personality* (New York: Harper & Row, 1954), pp. 43–46, and Frederick Herzberg, Bernard Mausner, and Barbara B. Snyderman, *The Motivation to Work* (New York: Wiley, 1959). pp. 59–63, 70–74, and 113–119.

(4) Frank Friedlander and Eugene Walton, "Positive and Negative Motivations Toward Work," *Administrative Science Quarterly*, Vol. 9, No. 2, pp.194–207.

(5) L. W. Porter and E. E. Lawler, "What Job Attitudes Tell About Motivation," *Harvard Business Review*, Vol. 46, No. 1, pp.118–126.

(6) F. G. Lesieur, ed., *The Scanlon Plan*, (New York: Wiley, 1958).

(7) F. G. Lesieur and E. S. Puckett, "The Scanlon Plan Has Proved Itself," *Harvard Business Review*, Vol. 47, No. 5, pp.113, 114.

(8) R. K. Goodman, J. H. Wakely and R. H. Ruh, "What Employees Think of the Scanlon Plan," *Personnel*, Vol, 49, No. 5, p. 28.

(9) R. L. Kahn, "Productivity and Job Satisfaction," *Personnel Psychology*, Vol. 13, No. 3, pp.275–287.

(10) G. F. Farris and F. G. Lim, Jr., "Effects of Performance on Leadership, Cohesiveness, Influence, Satisfaction, and Subsequent Performance," *Journal of Applied Psychology*, Vol. 53, No. 6, p. 496.

(11) Kurt Lewin, Ronald Lippitt, and R.K. White, "Patterns of Aggressive Behavior in Experimentally Created Social Climates," *Journal of Social Psychology*, Vol. 10, No. 2, and Ronald Lippitt, "An Experimental Study of Authoritarian and Democratic Group Atmospheres," *University of Iowa Studies in Child Welfare*, Vol. 16, No. 3.

(12) E. A. Fleishman, "Leadership Climate, Human Relations Training, and Supervisory Behavior," *Personnel Psychology*, Vol. 6, No. 2, pp. 205–222.

(13) Douglas McGregor, *Leadership and Motivation* (Cambridge, Mass.: The M.I.T. Press, 1966), pp. 118, 119.

(14) Talcott Parsons, *Structure and Process in Modern Societies*, (New York: The Free Press, 1960), chaps, 1 and 2.

(15) L. R. Sayles, *Managerial Behavior* (New York: McGraw-Hill, 1964), chaps. 5 and 6.

(16) Rensis Likert, *Motivation: The Core of Management*, AMA Personnel Series, No. 155, 1953; R. Likert and J. F. Likert, *New Ways of Managing Conflict*, McGraw-Hill, 1976.

(17) R. K. Mautz and H. A. Sharaf, *The Philosophy of Auditing* (Sarasota, Fla.: American Accounting Association, 1961), p. 145.

(18) Report of the National Commission on *Fraudulent Financial Reporting*, (Treadway Commission), American Institute of Certified Public Accountants, 1987, p. 35.

(19) *Internal Control—Integrated Framework*, Committee of Sponsoring Organizations of the Treadway Commission, New York, 1991, p. 59.

(20) Gerald Vinten, Editor, *The Strategic Audit*, MCB University Press, Bradford, England, 1991.

(21) Rensis Likert, *The Human Organization: Its Management and Value*, (New York: McGraw-Hill, 1967), pp.13–24.

15
Controlling

CONTROLLING AND THE MANAGER

Nature of Controlling

Definition and Purposes

Control is a guiding force; controls are the means of exerting that force. Control is exerted to correct deviations from the paths that lead to organizational objectives and goals and to remove from those paths whatever prevents efficient, economical, and effective performance. So the functions of planning and controlling are linked. Planning provides goals and standards. Controls measure performance to determine whether the goals have been reached and the standards have been met. The process of controlling is designed to correct any deviations and eliminate the roadblocks.

Everyone, from the chair of the board to the lowest supervisor, uses control to make sure that what is being done is what was intended, but the means used at the various levels of the organization vary. The control exercised at the executive levels differs from that exercised at the operating levels. The two kinds are similar in that they seek to insure the meeting of objectives. What differentiates the two is the nature of the objectives. The varied forms of control can therefore be defined as follows:

• *Executive control* is directed toward the achievement of an organization's broad objectives. It encompasses the employment of appropriate means by the policy-making officers of the organization to direct, restrain, govern, and check on the activities of the organization for the purpose of achieving these objectives. The means used include, but are not limited to, methods of assuring the achievement or compliance with long-range objectives and goals, budgets and forecasts, policy statements, organization charts, and statements of function and responsibility. The means also include an internal audit function.

- *Internal control* is directed toward the achievement of an organization's detailed objectives. It encompasses the employment of appropriate means at all levels of management to direct, restrain, govern, and check on those activities for which managers are responsible. Internal control comprises financial (or accounting) control and administrative (or operating) control.
- *Financial control* includes, but is not limited to, the use of budgets, systems and authorization and approval, systems of accounts and analyses, and separation of duties, particularly the separation of the duties for accounting and record keeping from duties concerned with operations and physical control over assets.
- *Administrative control* includes but is not limited to the use of production schedules, performance records, departmental budgets and forecasts, job assignment records, performance standards, logs, registers, forms, and check lists.

It seems obvious that, just as objectives may often overlap and coalesce, so will the various forms of control. It may often be difficult to tell when executive control becomes internal control and when financial control becomes administrative control. What is important is that control cannot exist in a vacuum. Its critical function is to see that some objective or goal will be met. Planning and controlling are therefore being treated, more and more, as integrated systems. One cannot work without the other.

Elements of Control

The essential elements of control are three:

1. Establishing standards that, when met, will provide assurance that relevant goals or objectives have been reached.
2. Comparing actual results with the standards.
3. Taking corrective action to return activities to the tracks leading to the desired goals or objectives.

Those elements have a quantitative thrust, yet controls are needed for both measurable and nonmeasurable events. The means used to retain good people are not measurable, yet they are significant because poor people do not an innovative, forward-looking organization make. Control is easy once one has the measure and the standard. Setting those standards is the most difficult task of management. Indeed, the more managers quantify that which is readily measurable, the less attention is directed toward the nonmeasurable, qualitative aspect of their resources—particularly people. So the manager who truly understands what the organization is to achieve must appraise the qualitative, not readily measurable, performance of staff. Reasonable criteria may need to be developed, and staff will need to be acquainted with those criteria. But what may seem completely unmeasurable at first blush may yield to quantification if the problem is thought through. For example:

> The Royal Canadian Mounted Police (RCMP) administers the Solicitor General's law enforcement program. It enforces federal statutes and executive orders, performs services in crime detection laboratories, police information centers, and identification centers.
>
> For many years now the RCMP has used performance indicators or standards against which to measure and evaluate police work. It weights outputs by staff hours taken to process the different types of cases. It then combines these weighted outputs to give a total output of the police operations. It shows efficiency of operations in terms of staff-hours per case. By providing standards and measurements in what might be considered nonmeasurable activities, it evaluates performance. But, more important, these methods have led to significant and worthwhile improvements, For example:
>
> - Shift scheduling helped the RCMP meet peak crime periods and reduce overtime costs.
> - Automation of the fingerprint system resulted in significant reductions of work hours. The measurements showed the need for automation.
> - A time-reporting system showed excessive police time used to transport prisoners by car. By using aircraft, police time was released for other duties.
> - Civilian personnel replaced police officers who were doing administrative work, thus permitting police officers to do the work they were trained for.

For a further discussion of nonmeasurable work, see Chapter 10, Measurement and Evaluation and Chapter 6, Systems and Chaos Theory, the Manager and the Auditor.

Attributes of Adequate Control Systems

Each system of control, each means of control, should be designed specifically for the objective it is intended to reach. To that end desirable controls should meet the following specifications:

- *Controls should be in tune with the needs and the nature of the activity controlled.* Controls suitable for a chief engineer will differ from those for a draftsman. The closer the plan is meshed with the goal to be gained, the more effective it will be.

- *Controls should be timely.* They should be synchronized with the events being measured. They should report events promptly when promptness is needed. However, when events must mature, real-time response may confuse more than enlighten. The results of the market testing of a new product may demand daily reports, but the progress of a research and development project may be controlled through monthly or even quarterly reports. The *desideratum* in a control system is to detect deviations when they impend rather than report them after they occur. The third element of control is to correct deviations, so the timely report will alert management before the event strays too far from the track. Controls should therefore be forward-looking; a cash budget can control cash needs more effectively than a bank statement reconciliation.

• *Controls should be economical.* They should never exceed the cost of that which is being controlled. Hence the manager should not seek to control the entire progress of every activity. Rather, the manager should focus and receive reports on the key points of key activities; the more the concentration on exceptions the more efficient the control. Control reports should provide the minimum information needed to alert a manager to action. The kind of information will vary, depending on the need. A warehouse manager needs daily information on inventory levels; a controller would be satisfied with that information every quarter.

• *Controls should be operational.* They should lead to corrective action; they should eschew that which is merely interesting and focus on that which needs a decision by the user. They must always be directed to that person who can take the needed action, not solely to the superior. A vast chasm stretches between control and the domination of others. Reports should be sent to the persons who need them to direct their efforts to the results they are in a position to control. So the controls could reflect the organization's pattern; they must focus on the place in the organization where action can most promptly and effectively be taken. Moreover, the person doing the controlling must be authorized to do it. As in the management function of organizing, the line-staff distinction must be maintained. Staff people should measure and compare; line people should take the corrective action.

• *Controls should be simple.* They must be understandable to those whose work is being controlled. Complicated controls confuse. They rarely work and they seldom survive. The manual that is simply stated and clearly illustrated will be used; the abstruse set of instructions will most likely be ignored. People who are a part of the control system should be told the objectives of their function so that they will recognize the significance.

• *Controls should be appropriate to what is controlled.* Information should be precise when precision is relevant and attainable; it should be approximate when that will suit the user's needs. There is a danger in false precision. It can mislead rather than inform. An approximation is not made more accurate by being carried out to four decimal places. It is significant for an executive to know that some event can be described only as an order of magnitude or within a range rather than be cozened into clutching to his bosom some meaningless number and then demanding that events correspond to it.

• *Controls should be objective.* Whenever possible, they should focus on events and not on people. The applicable standards may be quantitative, such as scheduled dates of delivery, or they may be qualitative, such as a training program to improve the quality of personnel. In each case, the standard should be determinable and capable of being measured against.

• *Standards should be flexible.* Flexibility should be built into the design of controls so that the controls will remain effective even though unforseen events come to pass or premises change. The flexible or variable budget is an example of a control that will be congruent with the event it is designed to measure. The philosophy of the organization should lean toward flexibility in controlling, have less emphasis on rigid compliance than on stimulating imagination, and promote understanding of what not to control and an appreciation that making mistakes is a part of the learning process.

• *Controls should be acceptable.* They should be agreed to by those whose work is being controlled so that people do not feel cribbed and confined. Those people should be asked to propose the means of control with which they would be most comfortable and which will accomplish the objectives of control.

Feedback

Feedback is implicit in the element of control that compares events with standards; it is performance information that is channeled back to management. That is the information that helps measure the adequacy and effectiveness of performance and triggers any needed action. A manager should have timely feedback, accurate feedback, useful feedback—the kind of information that will identify the problem and show where it is so that correction can be made.

In informal organizations, managers can accomplish feedback through personal observation. In formal ones they must rely on structured reports, including financial statements, statistical analyses, and other formal documents. Even in large, formal organizations managers should not lose touch with people. They cannot get the visceral feeling of what is happening by reading reports behind desks in mahogany row. The experienced manager can obtain a wealth of information by occasionally walking through the operating areas, observing what is taking place, and engaging in casual conversations with people.

Standards

Standards represent the translation of enterprise goals into specific, measurable outcomes; they become the benchmark for acceptable performance. Standards are applied in the measurement of various types of performance. Here are some:

• *Output.* Output standards specify quantitative performances such as machine-hours or staff hours per unit of output, units per day or week, or tons of steel produced per month.

• *Accuracy.* Standards on accuracy specify quality of performance, such as agreement with specifications, fastness of color, or number of rejections.

- *Expense.* The expense standards specify such things as material costs per unit, overhead per direct labor hour, or direct and indirect costs per unit of production.
- *Timeliness.* Standards related to timeliness may cover production schedules, project completion, or meeting customers' need dates.
- *Capital.* Standards concerning capital relate to the application of monetary units to physical items. They deal with capital invested, however, instead of operating costs. They relate more to the balance sheet than to the profit-and-loss statement. The standards include return on investment and such ratios as current assets to current liabilities, cash and receivables to payables, and turnover of inventory and notes or bonds to stock.
- *Revenue.* The revenue standards arise from the monetary values assigned to sales. They may include revenue per airplane passenger mile, dollars per ton of sheet steel sold, or average sale per customer.

Determining appropriate standards is essential to measuring performance, but standards will not be effective unless they are placed at strategic control points. The earlier the point, the greater the assurance that deviations will be anticipated or detected and hence will be corrected.

Factors to Be Controlled

The four factors most likely to be controlled are quantity, quality, schedule, and cost. Each of the factors needs some form of surveillance to see that the standards for that factor are being met. For example:

- *Production.* Is the factory meeting production quotas as desired specifications in time to meet sales commitments within established budgets?
- *Sales.* Are sales quotas being met; is there a proper balance among the company's products; are salesmen making their calls on schedule; and are advertising and promotion costs reasonable?
- *Personnel.* Is the workforce at reasonable levels; are the needed skills available and properly used; are work schedules met; and are wages competitive in the industry?

Certainly, management can set up strict and comprehensive controls and managers can sit on a network of feedback mechanisms over every function in the enterprise. However, that tends to dilute the energies of the executives, who spend so much time in controlling that they have no time for the other three functions of management: planning, organizing, and directing.

Executives must therefore focus on the major problem areas in the enterprise. Control systems should be set up in certain primary areas, as in:

1. Determining and improving the market standing of the organization.
2. Seeing that profitability meets forecasted needs.
3. Making sure materials are properly acquired and used.
4. Seeing that employees and managers meet established standards of performance, that their skills are being developed, and that their morale is satisfactory.
5. Providing assurance of adequate financial resources.
6. Maintaining needed productivity to remain competitive.
7. Assuring the acquisition and maintenance of physical resources.
8. Meeting the organization's responsibilities to society.

Accounting

Accounting is a well-known management control; indeed, organizations could not function without it. It is, in effect, a specialized language system that communicates information in numerical terms to executives and others. What must be remembered is that the language becomes merely noise unless it can serve to solve the organization's problems.

The significance of the numbers presented to managers can be determined only by understanding what lies behind the numbers. A manager may be told that net profits have declined over a period of time, but the information means little as a basis for decision making. The causes also must be understood. The reasons may be poor planning, need for tighter controls, or factors external to the organization that are attributable to neither planning nor control.

The manager must also be aware of the limitations on conventional financial statements. The changing value of the dollar blurs the apparent crisp accuracy of statements. When price levels escalate, the worth of assets is no longer realistic. To charge depreciation based on cost in such instances may drastically affect the ability to replace assets. The accountants must, of course, rely on and deal with historical costs primarily, but the manager must leaven the numbers with judgement of what goes on in the world.

Inventory valuation presents difficulties. The first-in first-out method (FIFO) treats inventory as though the first item purchased will be the first item sold or consumed. However, when that inventory was purchased at drastically different prices, the profits realized will not accord with reality. The manager will have to apply judgement to the inventory valuations.

Accounting information is purely numerical, but people are involved in all transactions. For example, an executive may compare two division managers on the basis of profit performance alone. The executive decision on rewards may be poorly founded if it is made without consideration of the fact that the lower profits in one of the divisions resulted from the death of a key executive, the unexpected introduction of innovative competitive products, or other factors completely beyond the control of that division manager.

Accounting information supplies information for control; it is not a control in itself. It may point to weaknesses, and only the manager can correct the weaknesses. Accounting is a powerful tool, and managers must understand the concepts and techniques associated with it. For example:

• *Responsibility accounting* seeks to so structure budgets and costs that they match the specific responsibilities of a segment or cost center of an organization. A manager or supervisor needs a report on costs only if some control over the costs can be exerted. That form of accounting provides better motivation to the operating manager, and it gives higher management a better basis for evaluating results.

• *Cost accounting systems* focus on the detailed costs of particular products. Cost accounting answers such a question as "How much did it cost to produce the products we sold last week, last month, or last year?" That simple question can require a complicated accounting system to answer it, yet cost accounting is a major element in the control of a business. It provides information to develop budgets, price products, and control costs.

• *Standard costs* describe what a particular product should cost to be produced. By measuring actual costs against standards, the levels of productivity and efficiency can be determined. Standard costs provide targets to shoot at, and when variances occur, they can call attention to possible deficiencies.

• *Direct costing,* sometimes described as variable costing, is a cost accounting system that provides for assigning to a product being manufactured only the costs that vary with the volume of production—usually direct materials and direct labor. Fixed factory and other fixed costs are treated as period costs. Since variable costs are controllable primarily by the people responsible for manufacturing the product, the use of direct costing (apart from its value as an aid in making production planning and pricing decisions) can serve as a useful means of controlling the volume and efficiency of production work.

Activity based costing

This is a relatively new approach to address the perennial problem of inequitable overhead cost absorption, and the consequential dangers of under- or over-pricing different product lines. It sees more validity in accumulating overheads, not on a departmental basis, but on an activity basis. Activities are regarded as incurring costs, and products as consuming those activities. So-called "cost drivers" need to be identified as the main determinants of the cost of activities. Activities will vary by type of organization, but could include the number of customer orders received, the number of production runs, the number of purchase orders placed, or the number of hospital X-rays ordered. The average cost per transaction is easily calculated as:

$$\frac{\text{Total cost of activity}}{\text{Number of transactions}}$$

This average cost is then used to charge each product line for the amount of service demanded from each activity center. Products now receive a more equitable share of the overheads they have required the firm to incur. Product costs and profitability will be more accurate than before, and this leads to improved management decisions about product offerings and acceptable prices.

Budgeting

Budgeting involves planning, decision making and controlling. We discussed some budgetary techniques and approaches in Chapter 12, Planning and Budgeting. As a decision of what will be expended, a budget is a plan: it is future-oriented. As a means of determining whether standards set are standards met, the budget is a means of control. Budgets have the significant benefit of forcing managers to plan and to control, to focus on measuring and appraising performance, but therein lies a weakness. Budgeting concentrates only on what can be quantified; it does not concentrate on quality.

The problem with budgets, and there are many problems, is not whether the controls they supply are necessary, but whether they are so used as to be effective. To develop budgets and to compare what is with what should be is salutary. However, not to analyze significant variances and determine why they happened is to miss the whole point of budgeting.

Rigid budgets also miss the point. What starts out as a means of controlling operations winds up as a means of frustrating people. Budgets must be seen for what they can do and what they cannot do. When they are properly used, their benefits are undeniable. They offer to everyone in the company the views of top management. They tend to direct the efforts of the organization to the most profitable channels. They emphasize the useful, time-saving principle of management by exception. They charge individuals with specific responsibilities. They promote considered actions and reduce the number of snap judgements on cost effectiveness. They help identify weaknesses in managerial ability. They minimize unnecessary and top-of-the-head spending.

When they are improperly employed, budgets are treated as omniscient pronouncements instead of mere tools that require judgement to achieve results. They do not insure results; they merely provide the means to point out deviations. They are only as good as the standards implicit in them, and good standards are not easy to develop. They are not graven on stone like God's commandments; they are based largely on forecasts and hence are marred by uncertainty. They provide numbers, not interpretations. They need to be communicated to all concerned, sometimes a difficult need to meet. Their use requires skill and experience, and those are often rare commodities. They may hide inefficiencies when they are based solely on precedent, since overestimating becomes a practice when budget paring is expected. They seem so precise and unassailable that they tend to replace common sense. They can be a straitjacket, as when a sales department desperately needs engineering information to consummate a large sale but the engineering department protests that it does not have the budget to supply it.

If budgets are to work, operating managers must participate in setting them and then accept them without mental reservations. Managers should have the latitude to shift funds under their control so long as total budget is met and significant matters are not hidden. Standards are needed to translate budgeted amounts into rational needs for the staff to show the resources needed to accomplish the budgeted work. Managers should not be subjected to across-the-board cuts, which are often evidence of inept planning and control.

Budgets are no better than the data, premises, and plans behind them. They have been cursed and criticized since they were first conceived, but their importance should not be underestimated. They are the only way by which an organization's goals and plans are translated into recognizable, unvarying units. They can be extremely useful guides for corrective action.

People

Managers have to face this hard fact: machines don't mind controls, but people resent them. Control procedures are instinctively disliked because they disrupt the image people have of themselves, and most controls highlight what is done poorly, not well. People will seek to the dark side of controls. They don't like the unpleasant criticisms controls may imply. They may refuse to see how their goals and the goals of the organization coincide. They may object to imposed standards of performance as being too high. Controls may be felt to be irrelevant; the sales person, for example, is intent on developing long-term goodwill while, at the same time, faced with current sales quotas. An outside group administering the controls becomes "the enemy."

Controls inevitably produce pressures, and pressures create conflict. When two groups are dependent on each other but perceive no compatibility in their goals, the resulting pressures bring animosity and ingenious ways of relieving the pressures while not actually meeting the goals.

Different managers use different ways to resolve conflicts brought about by reactions to controls. Some withdraw from the conflict; they retreat and engender contempt from the workers they seek to placate. Some try to play down the differences in order to smooth things over; they display insincerity in the process. Some try to bargain and compromise; they reach nobody's goals. Some impose their own values autocratically; they build up explosive pressure points. Still others resort to an open, frank confrontation and exchange of information and views, which usually is most effective.

By and large, the adverse effects of control can be minimized if managers practice:

• Participative management—encouraging employees to help develop controls.

- Setting standards that are reasonable and objective, that set a range of adequate performance, and that are acceptable to the people controlled.
- Developing general rather than detailed controls, so that employees can exercise judgement within broad parameters.
- Using controls as a means to achieve goals rather than imposing strict rules that bring automatic punishment for infraction instead of for failing to meet the goals.
- Keeping the goals simple, understandable, logical, legitimate, and keyed directly to what they are designed to achieve.

Management by Objectives

One form of control that still has abiding value is termed "management by objectives." The term was coined by Peter Drucker; the concept is excellent and has had much success.(1) It has also had disastrous results, and the reasons for the disasters may be attributable to the failure to remember Drucker's full title to his approach to management control: "Management by Objectives and Self-Control." Indeed, Drucker says that true management by objectives substitutes management by self control for management by domination.(2)

Management by objectives (MBO) seeks to integrate company and individual goals; the company to achieve profit and growth, the individual to develop by contributing to company goals. However, an MBO system requires prodigious effort to be successful, and there are enormous hurdles in its way:

- Many managers are functional experts. Their work is specialized and they enjoy their specialty. They would rather be concerned with their parochial goals than with the needs of the enterprise.
- Each level of management perceives the needs of the organization in different terms depending on the height of the level in the hierarchy. People at different levels may think they are talking about the same things when they speak of organizational objectives, but they are really speaking different languages. That is because, from different levels, one sees the same panorama in different detail. Methods of compensation among positions vary. The salaries of some people in the organization are fixed; the compensation of others is or may be tied to bonuses, commissions, or other factors that are based on performance.

Yet despite the hazards and roadblocks, MBO can make a big difference in the way people perceive their jobs and their commitment to their enterprise. That sharpened perception can lead to total commitment and improved performance. An effective MBO program, therefore, requires the following elements:

- Executive management must be sincerely committed to the program, must take an active lead in displaying that commitment, and must provide a climate in which the program can grow. Senior management must demonstrate its

commitment by taking the time to establish systems for MBO, developing overall realistic objectives for the program, communicating the objectives to subordinates effectively, and permitting participation by subordinates in goal setting.
- The objectives of all units within the organization must be synchronized with the aims of the organization.
- Goals must be quantitatively expressed. They should be measurable; they should be attainable; but they should make people stretch to reach them.
- The people being measured should be provided with information on their performance so that they can exercise self-control.
- The orientation throughout the organization should be participative to gain commitment from subordinates. To that end:
  (i)   Goals should be set mutually by superior and subordinate.
  (ii) The way subordinates perceive their own goals should be actively considered and merged with enterprise goals.
  (iii) Goals should not be so inflexible that they cannot be adjusted for unforeseen changes.
- The reviews of performance results should be used as a learning, and not a disciplinary, experience.

A good MBO program is pyramidal. Each level of the pyramid must be involved in the contribution individuals make to the unit of which they are a part. The objectives of a district sales manager's job should contribute to the performance of the sales department. The objective of the production manager's job is to improve the performance of the manufacturing branch. The objectives of an autonomous division are to improve the profitability and growth of the parent company.

Why then, do MBO programs so often go wrong? The answers are legion:

- Executive management decrees an MBO program and does not participate.
- The MBO program is not explained to its participants.
- Unit objectives are not thought through because goal-setting guidelines have not been provided to unit managers.
- Company objectives are not understood, are fuzzy, unrealistic, or inconsistent.
- Busyness is confused with performance. Instead of setting goals, management merely sets out work to be done.
- Goals are not measurable. Performance is therefore confused with traits or an appearance of hard work.
- Goals are short-term, sometimes at the expense of the long range.
- Goals are, on the one hand, continually being changed or, on the other, are so inflexible as to arouse frustration when basic premises or policies are changed.
- Unit managers are not provided with accurate, current information to help them manage themselves.

With all their problems and hazards, MBO programs have worked. The Purex Corporation installed an MBO program in 15 manufacturing plants. The individual managers set their goals; control reports were provided for self control; and the performance of the managers was periodically reviewed. The program resulted in substantial achievement, including individual plant productivity.

The Board of Directors

Decline as a Controlling Force

Peter Drucker has said that the decline of the board of directors as a controlling force in business is a universal phenomenon of this century. He says, with exaggeration perhaps spawned from frustration, that board have in common one thing: they do not function(3) The boards of Rolls-Royce Ltd and Maxwell Communications Corporation in England, Penn Central in the United States, and Montecatini in Italy were apparently the last to know of the disasters that were about to strike their companies.

The BarChris decision, however, brought US boards to a rude awakening. Many corporate directors were stunned by the judge's sharp attack on the lack of involvement in corporate reporting and the failure to ask questions about management's practices. The legacy of the Savings and Loans fiasco will remain for probably forty years in the US.(4) The Bank of Credit and Commerce International scandal had global impact.(5)

Audit Committees

The courts' concern with board involvement is becoming sharper and more specific. In April 1977, a United States district court judge handed down a final judgment and order in the case of the Securities and Exchange Commission (SEC) against Killearn Properties, Inc., a Florida corporation. The order required the company's board of directors to maintain an audit committee composed of at least three members of the board who should be outside directors—not part of Killearn's management. The court also set forth specific responsibilities for the audit committee of the board:

1. Review the engagement, scope of work, and audit procedures of external auditors.
2. Review, with appropriate people, the general policies and procedures the company uses with respect to internal auditing, accounting, and financial controls. Audit committee members should be generally familiar with the company's accounting and reporting principles and practices.
3. Review with the independent accountants, upon completion of their audit:
   (i)   Their proposed audit opinion.

(ii) Their perception of the company's financial and accounting personnel.

(iii) The cooperation they received in their audit.

(iv) How company resources can be used to minimize the time spent by outside auditors.

(v) Significant transactions not normally a part of the company's business.

(vi) Any changes in accounting principles.

(vii) Any recommendations for improving internal financial controls, choice of accounting principles, or management reporting systems.

4. Inquire of both company personnel and outside auditors about any deviations from established codes of conduct of the company, and periodically review those policies.

5. Meet with the company's financial staff at least twice a year to review the scope of internal accounting and auditing procedures in effect and the extent to which recommendations made by the internal staff or by the independent accounts have been implemented.

6. Recommend to the board the retention or discharge of independent accountants for the ensuing year.

7. Have the power to direct and supervise an investigation into any matter brought to its attention within the scope of its duties.

Some companies do not wait for the courts. For example, a special task force at Lockheed Aircraft Corporation, after completing a comprehensive review of the company's activities, recommended that:

1. The audit committee of the board be expanded from three to four and possibly five members, all of whom are "outside" directors.

2. The audit committee review the internal audit function, its status, its quality of work, and its relationships with and responsibilities to management, the audit committee, and the board as a whole.

3. The committee define the role of the corporation's independent auditors, including their relationship with and responsibilities to management, the audit committee, and the board as a whole.

4. The committee be informed of all questionable transactions.

5. The outside auditor's personnel be rotated in their assignments.

6. The independence of the internal auditors from the activities they audit be insured.

7. A broad policy statement be issued respecting standards of integrity and ethics to be followed by employees of the corporation, and compliance with these standards be confirmed by either the internal audit department or the corporation's independent auditors.

Demands for audit committees are rising. In January 1977, the New York Stock Exchange adopted an "Audit Committee Policy Statement." It required each domestic company with common stock listed on the Exchange, as a condition of listing and continued listing of its securities, to establish and maintain an audit committee made up solely of directors independent of management.

The Conference Board published in 1988 a survey of 692 companies, with questionnaires sent to members of the American Society of Corporate Secretaries.(6) This was an update of a previous survey of 1978, which was a landmark year, following the New York Stock Exchange requirement. Over these 10 years, audit committees have become more involved with internal auditing, with a 47% involvement compared with 25% in the previous survey. The internal auditor has now jumped into second place, behind the corporate secretary, as the person most often designated as secretary of the audit committee. As the person who determines the agenda, the head of internal auditing is now a close third to the chief financial officer, with the committee chair being the first place. Audit committees have been delegated increasingly broadened responsibilities, with support for an extension of this. Respondents also gave the audit committee high marks for having brought about improvements in traditional core areas—internal auditing, external auditing, financial controls and financial reporting. There has been improvement both in the full board's awareness and understanding of these matters, and also its effectiveness. It is gratifying to see the partnership between internal auditor and director operating so successfully.

A more recent study was of audit committees in large UK companies, surveying the Times top 250 industrial companies and 50 major financial institutions, achieving an 80% response rate.(7) Overall 53% of industrial companies and 88% of financial bodies had an audit committee, although the percentage among the subsidiaries of foreign banks was only 44. The main motive for having a committee was a desire to follow good corporate practice, but other important motives were to assist the directors in discharging their statutory financial reporting responsibilities, strengthening the role and effectiveness of non-executive directors, and enhancing the independence of internal and external auditors. The most important attributes of members of committees were personal qualities like sound judgement and independence from management, and a full understanding of the purposes and responsibilities of the committee. The availability of relevant information, like provision of an agenda and related material in advance of a meeting, and ready access to internal and external auditors, were significant effectiveness factors. Matters commonly discussed, which impacted on the internal auditor, included:

- The effectiveness of internal controls.
- Internal audit objectives and plans.
- Internal audit findings and reports.
- Whether proper action is taken on recommendations.
- The adequacy of resources devoted to internal audit.
- The organization of internal audit department, reporting lines and independence.
- Experiences and problems in carrying out audits.

- Relationships between internal and external audit, and coordination of their work.

Audit committees are increasingly the norm too in public sector and voluntary bodies.(8) Internal audit is more-and-more involved in the legal process in the US and this includes the audit committee, and both could be involved in litigation.(9) The more effective they can be shown to be performing, the more defense the organization will have in any legal action against it.

Responsibilities of Audit Committees

Different audit committees will undertake different roles and assume different responsibilities, but the basic role should be assuring stockholders and other directors that:

- Those responsible for auditing the affairs of the company have carried out their responsibilities.
- Both external and internal audit programs are appropriate.
- The reports of the external and internal auditors have been acted upon.
- The communications between the external and internal auditors are direct, uninhibited, and not subject to restraints by management.
- The auditors are receiving the full cooperation of top management.

The Mautz and Neumann report lists some of the practices that would contribute to the success of corporate audit committees, listed in the general order of importance according to the respondents to questionnaires.(10)

- The audit committee should have ready access to independent auditors.
- Independent auditors should brief the committee regularly.
- The committee should be provided promptly with relevant information.
- The independent auditors should notify the committee promptly about any problems encountered.
- Management should notify the committee promptly about problems.
- The internal auditors should have access to the committee.
- The committee should operate with an agenda and written statement of issues before its meetings.
- Audit committee members should visit company plants and offices.
- Internal auditors should promptly notify the committee of problems.
- Internal auditors should regularly brief the committee.
- The committee should have a written statement of its responsibilities.
- Management should regularly brief the committee.

The practices listed were the result of answers to questions asked of chief executive officers, nonofficer directors, internal auditors, and independent

CPA's. The nonofficer directors and the internal auditors agreed that ready access of the latter to the former was a most important practice. The chief executive officers placed it lower in the scale of importance.

The Foreign Corrupt Practices Act

Despite the fact that some views are reported as less important, continued pressures on companies and board of directors may make all these practices important and regular. For example, in the US the Foreign Corrupt Practices Act of 1977 amended the Securities Exchange Act of 1934 to add certain requirements that call for issuers (companies covered by the act) to maintain accurate records and to file certain reports.

The act calls for issuers to "make and keep books, records, and accounts which, in reasonable detail, accurately and fairly reflect the transactions and dispositions of the assets of the issuer." The law also requires issuers to "devise and maintain a system of internal accounting controls sufficient to provide reasonable assurances" about the execution and recording of transactions and the comparison of recorded assets with existing assets. The law forbids payments or gifts to foreign officials to influence their decisions.

Thus the problems of the directors mount, and the directors can get little comfort from expectations of insurance protection, with rising premiums and higher risks to be borne by the directors themselves.

Protection

Directors and officers have been held liable by courts for such vaguely defined acts as improvident investment of corporate funds, improper expenditure of corporate funds in a proxy fight, failure to obtain competitive bids for major purchases, and even failure to exercise "reasonable care" in the selection of a depositary bank that failed. New occupational health and safety laws as well as pollution and pension measures have also broadened personal liability.

Directors can obtain some measure of protection from audits made by external auditors, but many of the matters that place liabilities upon directors are generally outside the scope of the audits. Competitive bidding, safety and health measures, and pollution are cases in point.

A competent internal audit staff that is authorized to review all operations within an organization can provide an added measure of comfort to directors. They can do so by bringing to the directors' attention matters that present a hazard to the corporation. Reviewing company controls and practices concerned with competitive bidding, safety and health, and pollution is a part of many internal audit plans. As a result, it would seem fair to say that internal auditing, as it continues to expand its scope from financial auditing into audits of operations and is recognized as a strong deterrent force within a corporation, will have a beneficial effect in helping to obtain D&O coverage and perhaps even reducing policy premiums.

Sprinkler systems contribute to lower fire insurance premiums, Audit committees of boards are in desperate need of their own "sprinkler systems" to quench smoldering problems before the problems erupt into devastating flames. In the following section of this chapter, that aspect of the internal auditor's role will be explored further.

CONTROLLING AND THE INTERNAL AUDITOR

Nature of Controlling

Definition

The word "control" finds its roots in the process of auditing. It comes from the Latin *contrarotulus. Contra* means "against," and *rotulus* means a "roll." *Contrarotulus* was used in Roman times to describe the work done in the army to check accounts. One officer kept the roll of accounts. Another kept a duplicate roll so that one roll could be checked against the other. The current meaning is something that affords a standard of comparison or means of verification and also a restraining domination.

The skills of internal auditors grow as they depart from the ancient concept of *contrarotulus* to the modern one of standards of comparison. The ancient concept implies verification by comparing one document against another. The current definition invokes standards. The concept of standards implies a means of determining whether a goal or an objective has been achieved—far different from checking one number against another.

Controls and Objectives

The most important message this advanced concept has to offer is that control does not stand alone. Control must be considered in relation to the objectives management is trying to reach, and the internal auditor must therefore know the objectives before it is possible to properly evaluate the means of control.

Internal auditing is generally regarded as a "managerial control which functions by measuring and evaluating the effectiveness of other controls."(11) The internal auditor must know which means of control should apply to a given activity, and should be able to key the means of control required to what is perceived to be the principal objectives of the activity under review.

A system of control designed to achieve one objective may fail to achieve another, even though the activities involved are similar. For example, if the principal objective is speed of output, then the system of control needed will differ from that which would be required if the principal objective were accuracy. Daily performance reports must be issued promptly and estimates may suffice; the clock is in control. Financial statements must be precise; thorough verification is the control.

For the internal auditor to determine exactly what the objectives of an activity are may not be as simple as appears on the surface. On the one hand, management may not have issued a formal statement of functions and responsibilities for the organization or operation under review. Thus, the internal auditor may have no clue to the objectives that are sought to be achieved. On the other hand, detailed statements of functions and responsibilities in existence may be so comprehensive that they may well obscure rather than disclose the key objectives. If internal auditors let themselves be unduly influenced by such detailed statements, the auditors, instead of determining whether objectives are being reached, may merely be trying to see whether every single step prescribed has been taken. That misses the point of the management-oriented audit. Also, the audit may be needlessly expensive, since all objectives, not only the significant ones, might be analyzed in the same detail.

During the preliminary survey segment of the audit, therefore, the internal auditor should elicit from discussions with appropriate management personnel the major objectives and goals of the activity to be reviewed. Deciding what is major and what is minor is a matter of judgement based on the information gleaned by the internal auditor during the survey phase of the audit and a comparison of those objectives with what is known of the broad objectives of the entire enterprise.

Audits of Operating Controls

If internal auditors can determine significant areas of operations within the organization, identify their objectives, differentiate between major and minor objectives, determine whether the related systems of control are designed to see that the objectives will be met, and plan the audit accordingly, then they can feel that they are meeting their own objectives of giving management the greatest return for each audit dollar spent.

Two examples will illustrate the management- and objective-oriented audit of operations. The first is concerned with an operational audit of controls in an accounting function.

Objectives. The principal objectives of the accounts payable function may be regarded as authorizing payment for materials and services (i) actually ordered and received, (ii) at prices properly agreed upon, (iii) on the dates specified.
Controls. The system of control should include form of organization, procedures, instructions, methods, and devices. They would operate in the following way:

1. To make sure that payments are made only for materials and services actually ordered and received, control through the following form of organization should be established: The accounts payable function should be separate from

(i) stores, which issues requisitions for supplies, (ii) purchasing, which places the orders, (iii) receiving, which counts and verifies receipts, and (iv) cash disbursement, which pays the bills.

Control in the form of written procedures provides that accounts payable clerks are to receive and compare:
(i)   An approved copy of the purchase order for purchasing.
(ii) An original invoice on an imprinted billhead from the supplier.
(iii) An approved receiving report from receiving.
(iv) Executive certification of certain invoices to show receipt of services not covered by receiving reports or purchase orders.

2. To make sure that payments do not exceed prices previously agreed upon, control in the form of instructions should provide that the accounts payable clerks will compare invoiced prices with the prices shown on purchase orders and on approved change orders. Control in the form of methods and forms should be provided to obtain an authoritative decision when there is a disagreement among the prices, quantities, terms, or items shown on the related purchase order. In such circumstances, the accounts payable clerks will make use of an invoice discrepancy report to request instructions from the responsible purchasing agents as to whether payment may be made.
3. To see that invoices are mathematically and clerically correct, the clerks will check them for accuracy and will total and recompute them as necessary.
4. To see that payments are being made at the right time, suitable control devices could be installed. Each accounts payable clerk might be provided with a set of folders, numbered from 1 to 31, corresponding to the days of the month. Invoices could be filed on receipt in the folder whose number represents the discount due date. Invoices would be paid by that date and, to conserve funds, no earlier than that date.

Computers take the place of much of manual work, but the concepts are largely the same.

Tests. Having examined and appraised the system of control in the light of management's objectives, the internal auditor will then perform such tests as are considered necessary to determine whether (i) the system is working effectively and is achieving the principal objectives of the accounts payable function, (ii) the means of control are unnecessarily elaborate, or (iii) additional means of control are needed. The tests may include:

1. A sampling of paid invoices to see whether all necessary documentation has been received and considered prior to invoice payment, whether payments have been made at the appropriate dates, and whether invoices for services have been properly approved.
2. A review of appropriate approvals of invoice discrepancy reports and the basis on which those approvals were given.
3. A test of clerical and mathematical accuracy.
4. A sampling of folders to see whether the invoices have been properly filed, as well as an analysis of lost discounts.

Having tested the basic controls, the internal auditor might make certain additional tests to see whether the company's objectives are being met. For example:

1. Check to see whether purchasing is sending change orders to accounts payable promptly. Delays might result in improper payments and supplier dissatisfaction.

2. Determine whether executives approving invoices for services have satisfied themselves that services have indeed been received in the quantities billed. Some executives have the tendency to sign perfunctorily what is placed before them, particularly if the charge is not against their budget.
3. Analyze purchase orders to see whether they contain clear and explicit instructions regarding terms of payment. Accounts payable clerks often have to struggle with obscure provisions on the orders.

The second illustration deals with an actual audit of controls over the activities of a materials and processes engineering department. The department, in an aerospace engineering division, is made up of engineering specialists, usually with advanced degrees in their specialties, whose primary job is to appraise materials—as well as the processes the materials undergo—used in aircraft and missiles: aluminum, stainless steel, titanium, beryllium, molybdenum, exotic plastics, and the like. What follows summarizes some of the material taken from the internal auditor's working papers and report.

The internal auditor found, during his preliminary survey, that the engineers in the department were assigned certain materials to analyze, usually upon requests from other departments in the company. They studied the materials by reviewing the available literature and putting the materials and processes through laboratory tests. They combed the market for sources of the materials by talking to suppliers, studying brochures, and exploring any other avenues that were open to them.

Then they did several things. The one we are interested in here related to their responsibility for issuing formal reports on their analyses, showing the characteristics of the particular materials, and how they should be inspected when they come into the company's inspection department.

As the auditor saw them, the primary objectives of management in carrying out this responsibility were:

1. To obtain the best use of the efforts of the engineers. The engineers were high-priced specialists, and the inappropriate use of their talents could cost the company dearly.
2. To issue reports that were accurate and understandable. The reports included information on how to test the materials when they were received in the plant. The inspectors, who were not engineers, had to be able to understand the inspection criteria.

The forms of control that would be calculated to achieve those objectives, according to the auditor's research, might be as follows:

The Use of the Engineers

1. An organizational structure in which the engineers were directly responsible to a supervisor or manager who was also an accomplished materials and processes engineer.
2. A requirement that each request coming into the department for appraisal or test of materials or processes would be reviewed by the manager so that he could decide (i) whether the job should be done at all, (ii) how much time it would take

to complete, (iii) what priority to give it, and (iv) when it should be completed. Most of the jobs called for prompt action, usually within 60 days.
3. A simple job card showing the title of the job, the engineer to whom it was assigned, and the estimated man-days needed for completion.

Report System

1. A file of research materials behind each report so that someone—some other qualified engineer—could independently check on the accuracy of the report or that somebody else could continue with the preparation of the report if the engineer originally assigned to the job left the company or had to abandon the project in midstream.
2. The requirement that each draft of a report be reviewed by a supervisor, or some reviewer, for accuracy, clarity, support, reasonableness, compliance with procedures, inclusion of all relevant elements, and the like.
3. A standard format for the report, preferably with established headings or sections, so that the writer will not omit anything essential and users of the report can immediately find the section that they need.
4. A list of approved recipients of the report and a periodic—at least annual—inquiry of those persons to make sure they still need the report.

Unfortunately, the controls in effect did not measure up to those standards, and the tests the auditor made proved the defects in the system.

The auditor took the job cards to an adding machine and totaled the number of work-days assigned to jobs on hand. The total disclosed that if not another job was received in the department, the work already scheduled would take a full year to complete. Also new work was coming into the department each day.

Then the auditor discussed the reports with receiving inspectors, the people who had the greatest need for them. The auditor found that the inspectors were wasting a great deal of time trying to find the instructions they needed. The reports were voluminous and contained many sections; the inspection information was but one small part. Sometimes the instructions appeared in front of the report, sometimes in the back, and sometimes in between. Sometimes the instructions were headed Detailed Requirements, sometimes Sampling and Testing, sometimes Physical Properties, sometimes Test Procedures, and sometimes something else. When the manager of materials and processes was informed of the findings, he took the following corrective action on the two problems:

1. *Assignments.* The manager (i) developed backlog reports to show him the status of the workload, (ii) made a survey of all the jobs in the backlog to decide which ones would be eliminated, (iii) developed a new set of criteria for the kinds of jobs that would be accepted for investigation, and (iv) established a system of priorities for the work in process.
2. *Reports.* The manager agreed that the format of the reports needed some work. Accordingly, he established a standard layout for all the engineers' reports. The inspection section was clearly labelled and placed in the report so that it could readily be found.

As the engineering example indicates, the management-oriented internal auditor need not be a specialist. However, with an understanding of the relation between objectives and controls and being thoroughly indoctrinated in good business practice and in principles of management, it is possible to make a meaningful, effective audit in any area of the enterprise.

Internal Accounting Controls

External auditors also are turning to the objectives-oriented approach to studying and evaluating internal account controls. Internal auditors who wish to coordinate their work with the work of the external auditors should be aware of that approach. It identifies the specific objectives that should be achieved by the internal accounting controls exercised in a broad area of business.

Internal auditors can facilitate the work of the external auditors by studying an organization's control systems for, in conjunction with, or independently of, the entity's external auditors. Four cycles or activities of a business are:

1. *Treasury.* To receive capital funds from investors and creditors and to invest them as needed.
2. *Expenditures.* To acquire resources in exchange for the obligations to pay and to pay obligations to suppliers and employees.
3. *Conversion.* To hold, use, or transform assets.
4. *Revenue.* To distribute resources in exchange for current payments or promises of future payments.

A fifth cycle is concerned with financial reporting. Hence, almost every function involved in processing transactions or preparing financial statements can be keyed to one of the five cycles. The major exception is financial planning and control, which encompasses all of the five cycles.

Each cycle is made up of functions. A function is defined as a major processing task or part of a system that processes common transactions. Also, each cycle has specific control objectives. Those objectives relate to:

- *Authorization.* Compliance with established policies and standards.
- *Transaction processing.* Recognizing, processing, and reporting transactions and adjustments.
- *Classification.* Source, timeliness, and propriety of journal entries.
- *Substantiation and evaluation.* Periodic verification and evaluation of reported balances and the integrity of processing systems.
- *Physical safeguards.* Access to assets, records, critical forms, and processing areas.

To illustrate cycle objectives under the expenditure cycle for a purchasing operation, within the *Authorization* objectives, the following objective, among many others, is listed.

- Vendors should be authorized in accordance with management's criteria.

The standards to be met to achieve a particular objective, the risk if the objective is not met, and techniques used to achieve the objectives need to be identified. Some lists of the matters relating to vendor authorization are as follows:

Selection Criteria

- Current and potential ability and willingness to provide quality, quantity, timely delivery, and service.
- Price competitiveness, considering unit prices, volume discounts, transportation and credit terms.
- Policies regarding related-party transactions, conflicts of interest, sensitive payments, and the like.

Examples of Risks If Objectives are Not Achieved

- Payments made to suppliers not authorized to receive them.
- Late receipts, substandard materials, excessive prices.
- Purchases made from related parties without senior management's knowledge.

Examples of Techniques to Achieve Objectives

- Clear statements of criteria or acceptability of suppliers, and quality checks of suppliers by quality control inspectors.
- Requirements for competitive bids, subject to stipulated exceptions.
- Conflict-of-interest program calling for buying personnel to certify that they have not received gifts and that they are not affiliated with suppliers.

This is not a mere checklist, but instead provides the reasons for the controls and the risks to be anticipated if adequate and effective means of control are not installed. There are differences between the external auditor's and the internal auditor's use of the approach. External auditors may limit their reviews of internal controls to those on which they expect to rely. In some cases it may be more efficient to verify account balances directly than to rely on internal accounting controls. Also, the account balances may not be material to the overall financial statement.

Internal auditors, on the other hand, may evaluate controls to determine compliance with company policies and procedures or to identify control techniques that are ineffective or redundant.

The cycle approach to evaluating internal accounting controls has been adopted by other accounting organizations as well.

Budgeting

The internal auditor's interest in budgeting as a control device is to make sure that budgets are properly used to that end. For example, if a manager compares actual costs with budgeted costs and leaves it at that, then the entire point of the budgeting as a means of control has been missed.

The internal auditor, therefore, should be concerned not only with comparisons but also with whether significant deviations are being evaluated, the causes for the deviations are being determined, and the information is being put to use to prevent repetition or to provide new premises for future budgeting. When those steps are not being taken by the manager, the internal auditor should make the evaluations and explore the reasons. Aberrations disclosed by deviations can often lead to the discovery of serious operational defects—matters warranting the attention of senior management.

The internal auditor should also be concerned with their own budgets—the amount of time expended on audit assignments as compared with the time budgeted. The evaluation should take place after each assignment is concluded to determine whether:

- The original budget was appropriate.
- The variances can be explained by changes in the premises on which the budget was set.
- The auditor in charge had lost control of the project and of the assistants.
- Time was wasted on unprofitable sorties into irrelevant areas.
- Budgets for future audits of the same projects should be adjusted.

People

Relation to Internal Control

The knowledgeable internal auditor will base the audit program and the extent of tests on perception of the people involved in the system. Consider two departments performing comparable work. Each functions under similar systems of control, but the quality of personnel and supervision differs.

In department A, the manager is reaching retirement and finds that the most compelling focus of interest. Supervisors are busy putting out the fires that result from poor planning. They have little time to supervise or train their people. Personnel turnover is high, as is the rejection rate for the product that forms the department's output, and morale is low.

Department B is staffed by an alert, experienced manager who practices planning, organizing, directing, and controlling. New hires are put through a comprehensive training program. Supervisors review the ongoing process and periodically test transactions to determine whether they meet standards. Control reports from supervisors to the manager provide an excellent overview of backlogs, rejections, self-evaluations, and improvements. There is little employee turnover, and morale is high.

There can be little doubt as to which department is more likely to have the better overall system of control and in which department the internal auditor would feel comfortable about minimizing tests of transactions. Obviously, the internal auditor's study of an activity system of control must take people into account.

Relations to Objectives

The system of internal control will function effectively or poorly in direct relation to how well people understand the objectives of the system under which they are functioning. An example follows:

> In a manufacturing company, the scrap sales yard was several miles from the production plant. During production, large quantities of metals were cut, turned, or drilled and thereby generated substantial quantities of scrap. Some of the metals, such as stainless steel, copper, titanium, and beryllium, commanded relatively high prices in the scrap market. Periodically, the carts containing the generated scrap were hauled from the production plant to the scrap yard. Each cart was tagged; and as it left the production yard, the guard at the plant gate was to record the exact time of departure on the tag. A guard at the scrap yard was then to record on the tag the exact time the cart arrived there.

> An audit disclosed that the guard at the production plant was not recording the times the carts left the plant. When the internal auditor asked why, the guard grumbled that his chief was always coming up with rules that made no sense and that he didn't believe in wasting his valuable time on nonsensical rules.

> The internal auditor then explained to him the objective of the control: the value of the scrap metal was high. There had been instances when the driver, moving the scrap from one location to another, had left the assigned route to give the valuable scrap metals to unscrupulous scrap dealers in exchange for a few dollars. Recorded times were therefore essential control points. The exact time the trip between the two locations should take was known. If the difference between the times recorded by the two guards was exceeded by a predetermined percent, then the driven would be asked some hard questions and the scrap carts would be thoroughly checked. Once the guard understood the objective of the control system, he enthusiastically complied with the requirements he had previously considered nonsense.

Management by Objectives

The internal auditor's involvement in MBO programs has not been dealt with extensively in the literature. Certainly, there are aspects of the program that can be a part of the auditor's routine examinations. For example, internal auditors traditionally audit the timeliness, accuracy, and usefulness of management reports. Information to managers that helps the managers exercise self-control under an MBO program is little different.

Also, in any audit of an operation, activity, or department, the internal auditor is keenly interested in the objectives that have been established to determine whether they are congruent with those of the enterprise and whether reports of accomplishment are fairly stated and are not merely self-serving declarations.

But the comprehensive audit of an MBO system is probably a rarity. Functioning MBO systems that have top management support are most likely under close executive surveillance. Hence executive management may not see the need for an internal audit of them. Yet many MBO programs fail, and management may want to know why. Also, as audit committees of boards of directors learn to make use of the internal auditor's ability to analyze and appraise, they too may ask questions about ongoing MBO programs,

For those reasons, internal auditors should be prepared to embark on audits of all or part of an MBO program. As in any other management-oriented audit, the internal auditor should understand the objectives of such a program. Among the objectives are these:

- To provide a means of defining the results that executive managers can expect from operating managers.
- To assist managers in improving performance.
- To reward managers fairly for the results they achieve.
- To improve communication between the various management levels in the enterprise.
- To provide managers with the means of setting their own goals and controlling their own jobs.
- To develop managers for higher jobs and to have an objective means of determining when the managers are ready for those jobs.

To achieve the objectives, certain methods should be developed, and there would seem to be no reason why the internal auditor could not evaluate the adequacy and effectiveness of those methods. Here are some of the questions an internal auditor can ask about the system of devising and carrying out an MBO program listed under the four functions of management:

Planning

- How has top management demonstrated its support for the MBO program?
- Do MBO standards take into account certain basic premises such as:
  1. What is the company's business?
  2. What should it be?
  3. Should the company seek growth through internal expansion or through acquisition?
  4. Should the company take additional risks to stimulate growth?
  5. Should some product lines be abandoned?
  6. Should other product lines be acquired or developed?
- Are the objectives clear, specific, and measurable?
- Are the objectives attainable by some stretching?

- Is the range of objectives broad enough to include innovation, labor relations, and improvement of subordinates?
- Do the objectives take into account the organization's responsibility to society?
- To what extent do subordinates contribute to the formulation of objectives? Is participation genuine or just a manipulating device? How do operating managers regard it?
- Are the objectives within the resources of the organization?
- What provision is made to see that all those responsible for meeting objectives understand the objectives?
- Do the objectives seek to anticipate the unexpected? Do they have "what-ifs" built into them?
- What evidence is there that all concerned are committed to the objectives?
- Do the objectives merely define the normal responsibilities of the job—being solely a statement of functions and responsibilities—or do they go beyond them to establish mind-stretching goals?

Organizing

- Are objectives properly placed within the organizational structure?
- How is the work delegated to meet the objectives?
- Is there a clear distinction between staff and line responsibilities with respect to the objectives? Is there a distinct line between the doers and the advisers?
- Which functions of the organization are not covered by objectives?
- Does each person responsible for meeting objectives understand to whom he or she reports—is there unity of command?
- Do the objectives relate to many small jobs that do not force people to extend themselves?

Directing

- Is there a free flow of information up and down the line?
- How are policies relating to the objectives defined and interpreted?
- Are standards set as straitjackets or as a means of showing when objectives have been met?
- Does the system provide for good communication and liaison between departments to meet mutual objectives?
- Do people find superiors approachable for changes in objectives when premises change significantly?
- Are mistakes treated as crimes or as opportunities to learn?
- Are managers provided with training plans to help in their development?
- Are the training plans, or courses, relevant and useful?
- Is the information gained from training courses put to use in terms of setting and meeting objectives?
- Are rewards to managers fair in terms of their performance in meeting objectives?

Controlling

- Do managers receive information on how well or how poorly they are moving toward their objectives?
- Is the information adequate in terms of timeliness, relevance, simplicity, and usefulness?
- Is the management information system that produces the data adequate, and is it functioning effectively?
- Is the information excessive? Does it inundate the manager? Could it be made more useful through better summaries?
- Is the information too expensive in relation to the benefits obtained?
- Do the budgets related to the objectives seem reasonable? Are they excessive in terms of the importance of the objectives, or do they provide insufficient resources?
- How are the performance and the potentials of managers judged? Are there periodic reviews? What do the managers themselves think of the reviews?

Obviously, any comprehensive review of an MBO program would present some difficulties to an internal audit staff. With support from executive management or from the board of directors and with a knowledge of the standards to use in measuring the success or failure of the program, internal auditors could make a signal contribution to the MBO effort.

Some of the answers to the questions just listed may be difficult to support by reference to documentation, but it is well for the auditor to remember that the term "auditon" comes from the Latin *audire,* "to listen." Asking the right questions of managers and subordinates, listening patiently and sympathetically, and evaluating the answers intelligently can produce useful results. First, the very asking of a question can start the hearer thinking along lines of improving the program. Second, the appraisal of a large number of responses can sometimes provide overwhelming evidence of defects in the system.

For example, if all the subordinates of one executive declare that they have difficulty in meshing their objectives with company objectives and in understanding the basic premises for those objectives, there would seem to be a pretty serious problem in that MBO system. The problem is underscored if all the subordinates of another executive demonstrate that the company objectives and premises are abundantly clear to them. Obviously, one of the executives has not communicated adequately. Also, if 50% of the managers questioned complain that the information they are receiving to help them control themselves is late and useless, certainly the situation cries for improvement.

Auditors who understand their profession are always on the lookout for indicators that point to poor systems. Here are some indicators that relate to MBO programs:

- A history of objectives made but never met.
- An absence of understanding on the part of operating managers about the philosophy of an MBO system.
- Fuzzy or nonexistent goal-setting guidelines. If corporate goals are unrealistic, unclear, or inconsistent, the operating managers will have difficulty adjusting their own goals to company goals.
- Goals that are not made measurable. A manager should be able to know when his own goals and those of his subordinates have been met. That knowledge should come from objective sources, not subjective impressions.
- Goals that are all short run—never more than a year. That tends to produce management by drive rather than management by objectives.
- Using objectives as a punitive rather than a constructive force.

It could well be that MBO programs that failed might have survived and been successful if subjected to a competent, management-oriented internal audit.

The Board of directors

Relations with Internal Auditors

The internal auditor's involvement with the board of directors is most often through the audit committee of the board. That involvement is getting more prevalent as both the external and internal auditors educate audit committees about the importance of a competent, objective internal audit function as a means of information and control.

Audit committees themselves are beginning to see the need. The Securities and Exchange Commission (SEC) is now saying that anyone who was in a position to know what was going on in a corporation and could have done something about it would be held liable along with those who actually committed the offense. Accordingly, in the Penn Central case, the SEC included as defendants three outside directors of the company. Many directors are feeling their responsibility keenly. Former US Supreme Court Justice Arthur Goldberg is a case in point. His resignation from TWA's board of directors was prompted by his feeling that he was unable to fulfill his "legal and public" obligations as a member of the board. One of his proposals had been to engage an independent staff of technical specialists to assist outside members of the board.

Certainly, the audit committee can expect objective professional opinions from the external auditors on financial statements, but the review of internal controls and operating procedures is the full job of internal auditors. The internal auditors are intimately involved with the controls. They therefore have a great deal to offer an audit committee in appraising the company's operations. Thus, as audit committees mature, they have promoted the improved status and effectiveness of the internal audit function.

Obviously, for the internal audit department to provide assistance to audit committees, the internal auditors will require a high degree of independence.

That independence will be in direct relation to the status of the director of internal auditing in the enterprise and the charter the director is given by both management and the board. That is made clear in the 1978 *Standards for the Professional Practice of Internal Auditing* of the Institute of Internal Auditors Section 100, "Independence."

Internal auditors in different environments report organizationally to different levels within the enterprise. Some report directly to the board of directors. That is particularly true in the case of financial institutions.

In general, however, as indicated by the Institute's *Standards,* the *desideratum* is a "solid line" relation with an executive high enough in the management hierarchy to insure independence of the activities to be audited and a "dotted line" relation with the board of directors through the audit committee.

As stories of computer fraud become more common, audit committees are asking increasingly pointed questions about the adequacy of controls. The liability for material losses may well become the board's liability.

The responsibility for developing and maintaining systems of control to deter fraudulent practices is placed squarely upon the shoulders of management; it cannot be evaded. Management has line authority over its operations; it must therefore be accountable for whatever occurs within its operations. It is axiomatic that responsibility carries with it accountability. Certainly, management will look to the internal auditor for assistance, but it cannot thrust full responsibility for the prevention and detection of fraud upon the internal auditor.

It should be pointed out that section 280.03 of the *Standard*, calls upon the internal auditor, when suspecting wrongdoing, to notify "appropriate authorities within the organization." The Introduction to the *Standards* specifically states that the "organization . . . [includes] . . . management and the board of directors." Thus the internal auditor is not restricted to members of management in reporting suspicions.

This, then, raises a significant point: how should the internal auditor deal with management fraud? The specter of management fraud is pervasive, and the sins of the managers will be visited upon members of the board of directors. It is incumbent upon members of the board and upon internal auditors to be thoroughly aware of the many faces and methods of management fraud and how they can be protected against.

Nature of Management Fraud

Management fraud is not necessarily synonymous with fraud as defined by the courts. Management fraud, as considered here, embraces the deceptions managers practice to benefit themselves in any way, not solely by lining their pockets. In many cases management fraud is practiced just to make a manager look good—to make it appear that a unit, division, or company has met established goals when in fact it has not.

Management fraud is often practiced successfully because of the fiduciary status managers have in the organization. By reason of their position, managers command respect; their motives are rarely questioned by the external auditors; and their explanations are usually accepted.

In decentralized organizations particularly, division presidents, vice presidents, and general managers have almost complete authority. Corporate executives judge them on the basis of reported performance, and the reports can be made to tell stories that do not accord with the facts. Similarly, presidents of corporations can deceive the board of directors by concealing material facts, by duping the external auditors, and by either restricting the scope of internal auditors or dispensing with the internal audit function altogether.

Management fraud masquerades in a great many disguises. It has been found in overstatements of inventory, acceptance of inferior goods in collusion with suppliers, delays of key expenditures to show a healthy financial position, overstatements of receivables, records of fictitious sales, and understatements of liabilities. Here is one example:

A conglomerate, with about $1 billion in sales, arranged to divest itself of a profit center engaged in distributing rolls of sheet metal. The company acquiring the profit center asked for and received a certified statement of inventory on hand. The conglomerate's external auditors certified the statement, which reported $14 million of sheet stock.

However, the external auditors had been duped. Actually, there had been a huge inventory shortage. The accounting department manager had taken the inventory, had determined the exact amount of shortage, and had known how much of the records to falsify. His people had prepared inventory tags and delivered them to the external auditors. The auditors had verified the amount of the stock shown on those tags and had then deposited them in a box in the conference room they used during the audit. The manager added spurious tags to the box at night. Because there was little time to prepare the large number of tags needed to "build up" the inventory, some of them were made to show rolls of sheet stock weighing as much as 50 000 pounds. He also substituted new inventory reconciliation lists to tie in to the total tags, both valid and spurious.

When the sale of the division was consummated, the buyer took its own inventory and found it short by about $6 million. Understandably incensed, the buyer rescinded the sale. After the conglomerate took back the profit center, its chief executive officer sent for the consultants.

In their preliminary survey, these investigators converted $14 million of sheet stock into cubic feet. Then they compared that volume with the available space in the warehouse. They found that it could not have possibly held that volume of sheet; it was far too small. To confirm the lack of reasonableness of the inventory taking, the consultants scanned the inventory tags and found those with weights of up to 50 000 pounds. They then went to the warehouse and examined the forklift trucks employed to move the rolls of sheet stock. Not one of the trucks could possibly lift over 3 000 pounds. Rolls of stock, therefore, could not exceed 3 000 pounds.

The consultants verified purchases of the material reported in inventory and found that purchase orders supported an inventory of about 30 million pounds. Yet the reported inventory totalled about 50 million pounds. Obviously, the records had been falsified. Armed with these clues, the consultants started interrogating people and soon obtained a confession from the accounting manager.

He had puffed the value of the inventory to show exceptional performance. He felt compelled to do so in order to meet forecasts by a wildly optimistic profit center general manager. The consultants' findings resulted in a settlement of nearly $1 million from the external auditing firm, because its auditors failed to detect the spurious tags, and a claim of over $10 million under the fidelity bond.

Why Management Fraud Occurs

Managers are pushed into fraud by forces that can be external or internal. The pressures may come from superiors who set impossible goals. Since the goals cannot be met fairly, some managers falsify records and reports to make it appear that they have achieved them. Other managers may have an itch to outperform all others, to exceed past performance, to be given a coveted promotion, or to gain a better bonus. And if their reach exceeds their grasp, they resort to deception. Some of the reasons behind management fraud are as follows:

- Managers may make rash statements that paint them into a corner. A president may forecast unrealistically high profits to financial analysts. To make the forecast come true, the president may demand distortions in the financial statements that are made to sound plausible to the external auditors and are kept from the board of directors.
- Autonomous divisions may distort facts to hold off divestment. Their reports may show glowing performance not supported by the facts.
- Incompetent managers may deceive in order to survive. Good managers keep abreast of change; poor ones may have to distort reported facts to give the appearance of good performance.
- Managers may distort performance reports to receive larger bonuses. When the size of a reward is based on the size of reported numbers, managers may succumb to temptation if they feel they can escape detection.
- Ambition may force managers to show superior short-range performance with no concern for long-range growth. Good current returns may be shown by curtailing needed research, reducing maintenance of plant and equipment, and replacing good, well-paid people with poorly paid hacks. However, over the long term, the business may be ruined.
- Unscrupulous managers may serve conflicting interests, as when a president of a company owns a supplier organization from which she requires her buyers to purchase goods at inflated costs.

Each of those reasons exists in abundance in the business world, but like an ever-present virus, they multiply to cause serious illness when the body's guards are down. Corporate illness strikes when superiors do not insist on good business practices, do not know what is going on, and fail to see that reports are independently reviewed.

What to Do When Management Fraud Occurs

When management fraud is revealed, executive managers or boards of directors may take swift and drastic steps. The internal auditor who is called in to help determine the reasons for and the extent of the depredations should counsel against precipitant action. The board must initially regard the matter as a business problem, not a legal one. For example:

- Key personnel should not be dismissed before the problem is solved. First, there may be innocents among the guilty. Second, with the principals gone, it would be all the more difficult for investigators to obtain answers to their questions.
- Losses should be kept to a minimum so that the corporation can assure the bonding company that all appropriate steps were taken to prevent extension of losses and to mitigate damages.
- The corporation must look at the broader picture and not focus completely on the deception. It must be concerned with the organization's loss of credibility, with premiums on new fidelity insurance, and with the impact on new insurance coverage. Besides, the corporation should be able to point out to the insurance company that steps are being taken to see that there will be no recurrences.
- The corporation should be concerned with disruption to its business. When troops of auditors and investigators descend on a profit center, the effect may be devastating. An executive should be assigned to coordinate the efforts of all groups involved in the investigation. The groups would likely include:
  1. External auditors to perform so-called heavy reviews of financial reports.
  2. Internal auditors to analyze operating records and support in-house investigators or investigative consultants.
  3. Legal counsel to make sure of disclosures at appropriate times, to evaluate legal aspects of recoveries under any fidelity bonds, and to recommend legal action against the culpable parties.
  4. Investigative consultants to interrogate witnesses and to advise internal auditors which avenues to explore and what information to obtain and analyze.

Symptoms of Management Fraud

Internal auditors must expand the scope of their concern to protect the enterprise, to the extent they can, from the results of management fraud. They should be aware of the indicators of management fraud and know where to focus their attention when it occurs. When reasonable suspicions are aroused, they should report them to corporate executives if the fraud involves subordinates or to the audit committee of the board if the fraud involves senior management. Here are some of the indicators:

- *Consistently late reports.* Fraudulent reports are often delayed so that the deceiver will know which data should be manipulated.
- *Managers who regularly assume subordinates' duties.* The managers may be carrying out detailed work to hide their own depredations.
- *Noncompliance with corporate directives and procedures.* One financial officer of a subsidiary postponed the installation of a standard cost system because he wanted to hide his serious cost problems.
- *Managers dealing in matters outside the scope of the profit center.* One division manager acted as a broker on products outside his division's assigned responsibilities. He needed the cash to hide other manipulations.
- *Payments to creditors supported by copies instead of originals.* In one company the mixture of originals and duplicates hid duplicate payments and kickbacks. The artful mixture fooled the external auditors. The company employed no internal auditors.
- *Negative debit memos.* At one profit center, credit memos were generated by the computer. When the financial officer wished to write off a credit memo, she issued a negative debit memo. The external auditors were dutifully provided with all the credit memos. They were not made aware of the debit memos. There was no internal audit organization.

The control of management fraud begins with an environment and control system created by the top people in the enterprise: senior management and the board of directors. The control system should include a qualified internal auditing organization with a broad charter and a comprehensive audit program. In a proper environment, competent internal auditors can take steps to see that appropriate systems of control have been installed and to alert senior management and the board whenever the controls are not adequate or are not functioning as intended. Internal auditors should be concerned with the following matters:

- Established standards, both budgetary and statistical, and the investigation and reporting of all significant deviations.
- The use of quantitative and analytical techniques (times series analyses, regression and correlation analyses, and random sampling) to highlight aberrant behavior.
- Comparison of industry norms against company performance.
- Identification of critical process indicators: melt loss in smelting, death loss in feed lots, rework in manufacturing and assembly, and gross profit tests in buy-sell or retail operations.

- Analysis of operations that look too good as well as performance that does not meet standards.

Internal auditors will have to educate audit committees of the board on the protection the committees can obtain from competent internal audit service. Some members of boards of directors have little inkling of what the modern internal auditor can accomplish in the evaluation of control systems and the appraisal of the company performance. Many internal auditing departments have developed sophisticated programs to educate audit committees about their accomplishments and their potentials. They have enlisted the aid of the external auditors to help in the education process. Many successful audit committees have matured as a result of the team effort by the board, the internal auditors, and the external auditors.

The aroused interest in the internal auditing function will have significant benefits and will also carry heavier responsibilities. For the external auditor, a strong internal audit function will permit increased reliance on the systems of internal control—their adequacy and effectiveness. For audit committees the internal audit function will create a new window to the organization's operations to provide the committee with current information on the company's systems and problems and to offer it a source of special studies whenever needed. For the internal auditors the relationship will permit a broadened audit scope and opportunities for improved service to the organization, both management and the board.

However, with the opportunities will come weightier obligations. Internal auditors will have to rise to the occasion. They will have to develop their understanding of the management process and their ability to make meaningful analyses in all areas of the organization and to provide management-oriented recommendations to improve operations and profitability. The internal auditing profession as a whole will have to elevate the quality of its practitioners by promoting special courses and programs in the universities that will turn out modern internal auditors who will be equipped to take their places as respected problem-solving partners to those who guide the destinies of their organizations. The growth of masters degrees in the subject is heartening, with South Bank University in London being the latest and third institution in England to offer such a qualification in partnership with Luton University.

ETHICAL AND ENVIRONMENTAL AUDITING

The business ethics and environmental audit has the potential to become an important aspect of internal control as well as of corporate communications, with the internal auditor being a significant element. A working definition is: a review to ensure that an organization gives due consideration to its wider social, ethical and environmental responsibilities to those both directly and indirectly affected by its decisions, and that a balance is achieved in its corporate planning between these aspects and the more traditional business-related objectives.

We now have the 5Es of audit: economy, efficiency, effectiveness, environment and ethics. The ethical audit has tended to be an activity carried out by pressure groups external to organizations. With an increasing emphasis on the wider corporate and social responsibilities of organizations, this external only approach is less than adequate. Organizations which take their stakeholders for granted and abuse their wider responsibilities, including the environment, may find that their continued viability is in doubt. Ethical and environmental audit is, after all, merely an extension of existing legal and regulatory requirements. This provides internal auditors with a justification for an involvement in business ethics, thus enlarging the scope of internal audit to its farthest vistas.

Audit activity has not traditionally been regarded as a significant part of corporate communication. With increasing demands being placed on corporations by a wide range of stakeholders, and a skepticism about business ethical standards, the traditions of independence and objectivity of an audit has attraction to corporation and stakeholder alike for those corporations which want to be, as well as be seen to be, ethical. Unlike most internal audits, this one is likely to be greeted with a glare of publicity, as the organization proves to the world its ethical stance.

The ethical organization (company, central or local government department, voluntary body or whatever) is the only viable form of organization in the longer term. Any organization that wishes to survive and flourish needs to be in constant and dynamic interaction with the wider environment. Customers, investors, employees and the community at large (which always includes potential customers, investors and employees) all need to be considered. An organization that constantly creates a negative ethical impact may find the withdrawal of public approval and of the market for its product or services. This is, therefore, an area of control that can be vital to the survival of the organization, especially where environmental pollution or health and safety is involved, as a company like Union Carbide is well aware.

EPILOGUE

Controlling is not a discrete function of management. It is directly related to the planning function, because nothing can be intelligently controlled until the objectives of the operation to be controlled are understood. Determining objectives is a planning function. That concept is significant for both managers and internal auditors.

Management by objectives is a control concept that has always had great promise. It is often improperly implemented, however, because those who seek to install it in an organization forget that the original concept was "management by objectives and self-control." The concept implies that those whose work is to be controlled should participate in setting the objectives and be given the means needed to control themselves. Although internal auditors have not often been involved in comprehensive audits of MBO programs, there is no reason that they cannot successfully carry them out.

Boards of directors have been placed under mounting pressure by the courts, the SEC, and the New York Stock Exchange to install audit committees made up of outside directors. Those pressures have created an increased awareness of the assistance internal auditors can give the boards of directors. To provide management-oriented assistance,however, the status of many internal auditors in organizations will have to be elevated and the scope of the audits broadened. As primary monitors of the organization's internal control systems, the internal auditors will be relied upon more and more by both the external auditors and the audit committees of boards of directors.

Although responsibility for the prevention and detection of fraud is limited to due professional care, the internal auditor can be useful to executive management and to the board by being alert to the symptoms of fraud—both employee and management fraud—and by assisting professional investigators in determining the extent of any fraud that has been detected

The sharpened focus on internal auditing is providing greater opportunities for internal audit staff, but it is also placing greater responsibilities upon them and heightening the demands of professionalism in the internal auditing function. As the governance of corporations, the public sector and charities comes under the microscope, following the world-wide consequences of lack of control, all eyes are on the internal auditor as a major tactical and strategic response. The Israeli Banking and Insurance Acts now require internal audit, and in the Netherlands there is a requirement, where internal audit exists, for it to comment on the statutory accounts. Following problems in the Australian public sector, such as in the Queensland police force, there has been a renewed emphasis on an effective internal audit service.

The Treadway Commission in America is paralleled in the United Kingdom by Sir Adrian Cadbury's committee on corporate governance, which reported in 1992 with strong recommendations on audit committees and independent appraisals of companies. In similar vein were committees in Australia in the Republic of Ireland, and elsewhere.(12)(13) Global issues call for global solutions. The world-wide community of internal auditors is ready to meet the organizational needs and demands of the 21st century. In such partnership it is possible to continually strive to move auditing towards excellence and to produce a world that is economically viable and sustainable. Internal audit can then truly demonstrate its dual serving of both the needs of the organizations in which it is placed, and the wider needs of society.

REFERENCES

(1) Peter Drucker, *The Practice of Management* (New York: Harper and Row, 1954).

(2) Peter Drucker, *Management* (Oxford: Butterworth-Heinemann, 1991), pp. 336, 348.

(3) Ibid, p. 536.

(4) S. Pizzo, M. Fricker and P. Muolo, *Inside Job. The Looting of America's Savings and Loans*, (New York: McGraw-Hill, 1989).

(5) Gerald Vinten, "Internal Auditing after Maxwell and BCCI," *Managerial Auditing Journal*, Vol. 7, No. 4, 1992, pp. 3–5.

(6) Jeremy Bacon, *the Audit Committee: a Broader Mandate* (New York: Conference Board, 1988).

(7) Paul Collier, *Audit Committees in Large UK Companies*, Research Board (London: Institute of chartered Accountants in England and Wales, 1992).

(8) Andrew Chambers, Georges Selim and Gerald Vinten, *Internal Auditing* (Chicago: Commercial Clearing House; London: Pitman, 1987), pp. 277–290.

(9) James Fargason, *Law and the Internal Auditing Profession* (Florida: Institute of Internal Auditors, 1992). pp. 35–37.

(10) R. K. Mautz and F. L. Neumann, *Corporate Audit Committees: Policies and Practices* (Florida: Institute of Internal Auditors, 1977), pp. 68, 69.

(11) *Statement of Responsibilities of Internal Auditing* (Florida: Institute of Internal Auditors, 1991).

(12) Henry Bosch, Chair, Corporate Practices and Conduct Committee (Sydney: Australian Securities Commission).

(13) The Financial Reporting Commission, *Report of the Commission of Inquiry into the Expectations of Users of Published Financial Statements* (Dublin: Institute of Chartered Accountants in Ireland, 1992).

APPENDIX A
Statement of Responsibilities of Internal Auditing

The purpose of this statement is to provide in summary form a general understanding of the responsibilities of internal auditing. For more specific guidance, readers should refer to the *Standards for the Professional Practice of Internal Auditing*

OBJECTIVE AND SCOPE

Internal auditing is an independent appraisal function established within an organization to examine and evaluate its activities as a service to the organization. The objective of internal auditing is to assist members of the organization in the effective discharge of their responsibilities. To this end, internal auditing furnishes them with analyses, appraisals, recommendations, counsel, and information concerning the activities reviewed. The audit objective includes promoting effective control at reasonable cost. The members of the organization assisted by internal auditing include those in management and the board of directors.

The scope of internal auditing should encompass the examination and evaluation of the adequacy and effectiveness of the organization's system of internal control and the quality of performance in carrying out assigned responsibilities. Internal auditors should:

- Review the reliability and integrity of financial and operating information and the means used to identify, measure, classify, and report such information.
- Review the systems established to ensure compliance with those policies, plans, procedures, laws, and regulations which could have a significant impact on operations and reports, and should determine whether the organization is in compliance.

- Review the means of safeguarding assets and, as appropriate, verify the existence of such assets.
- Appraise the economy and efficiency with which resources are employed.
- Review operations or programs to ascertain whether results are consistent with established objectives and goals and whether the operations or programs are being carried out as planned.

RESPONSIBILITY AND AUTHORITY

The internal auditing department is an integral part of the organization and functions under the policies established by senior management and the board. The purpose, authority and responsibility of the internal auditing department should be defined in a formal written document (charter). The director of internal auditing should seek approval of the charter by senior management as well as acceptance by the board. The charter should make clear the purposes of the internal auditing department, specify the unrestricted scope of its work, and declare that auditors are to have no authority or responsibility for the activities they audit.

Throughout the world internal auditing is performed in diverse environments and within organizations which vary in purpose, size, and structure. In addition, the laws and customs within various countries differ from one another. These differences may affect the practice of internal auditing in each environment. The implementation of the *Standards for the Professional Practice of Internal Auditing,* therefore, will be governed by the environment in which the internal auditing department carries out its assigned responsibilities. Compliance with the concepts enunciated by the *Standards for the Professional Practice of Internal Auditing* is essential before the responsibilities of internal auditors can be met. As stated in the *Code of Ethics,* members of The Institute of Internal Auditors, Inc. and Certified Internal Auditors shall adopt suitable means to comply with the *Standards for the Professional Practice of Internal Auditing.*

INDEPENDENCE

Internal auditors should be independent of the activities they audit. Internal auditors are independent when they can carry out their work freely and objectively. Independence permits internal auditors to render the impartial and unbiased judgements essential to the proper conduct of audits. It is achieved through organizational status and objectivity.

The organizational status of the internal auditing department should be sufficient to permit the accomplishment of its audit responsibilities. The director of the internal auditing department should be responsible to an individual in the organization with sufficient authority to promote independence and to ensure a broad audit coverage, adequate consideration of audit reports, and appropriate action on audit recommendations.

Objectivity is an independent mental attitude which internal auditors should maintain in performing audits. Internal auditors are not to subordinate their judgement on audit matters to that of others. Designing, installing, and operating systems are not audit functions. Also, the drafting of procedures for systems is not an audit function. Performing such activities is presumed to impair audit objectivity.

The *Statement of Responsibilities of Internal Auditing* was originally issued by the Institute of Internal Auditors in 1947. The current *Statement,* revised in 1990, embodies the concepts previously established and includes such changes as are deemed advisable in the light of the present status of the profession.

APPENDIX B
The Institute of Internal Auditors Code of Ethics

PURPOSE: A distinguishing mark of a profession is acceptance by its members of responsibility to the interests of those it serves. Members of the Institute of Internal Auditors (Members) and Certified Internal Auditors (CIAs) must maintain high standards of conduct in order to effectively discharge this responsibility. The Institute of Internal Auditors (Institute) adopts this *Code of Ethics* for Members and CIAs.

APPLICABILITY: This *Code of Ethics* is applicable to all Members and CIAs. Membership in The Institute and acceptance of the " Certified Internal Auditor" designation are voluntary actions. By acceptance, Members and CIAs assume an obligation of self-discipline above and beyond the requirements of laws and regulations.

The standards of conduct set forth in this *Code of Ethics* provide basic principles in the practice of internal auditing. Members and CIAs should realize that their individual judgement is required in the application of these principles.

CIAs shall use the "Certified Internal Auditor" designation with discretion and in a dignified manner, fully aware of what the designation denotes. The designation shall also be used in a manner consistent with all statutory requirements.

Members who are judged by the Board of Directors of The Institute to be in violation of the standards of conduct of the *Code of Ethics* shall be subject to forfeiture of their membership in The Institute. CIAs who are similarly judged also shall be subject to forfeiture of the "Certified Internal Auditor" designation.

STANDARDS OF CONDUCT

I. Members and CIAs shall exercise honesty, objectivity, and diligence in the performance of their duties and responsibilities.

II. Members and CIAs shall exhibit loyalty in all matters pertaining to the affairs of their organization or to whomever they may be rendering a service. However, Members and CIAs shall not knowingly be a party to any illegal or improper activity.

III. Members and CIAs shall not knowingly engage in acts or activities which are discreditable to the profession of internal auditing or to their organization.

IV. Members and CIAs shall refrain from entering into any activity which may be in conflict with the interest of their organization or which would prejudice their ability to carry out objectively their duties and responsibilities.

V. Members and CIAs shall not accept anything of value from an employee, client, customer, supplier, or business associate of their organization which would impair or be presumed to impair their professional judgement.

VI. Members and CIAs shall undertake only those services which they can reasonably expect to complete with professional competence.

VII. Members and CIAs shall adopt suitable means to comply with the *Standards for the Professional Practice of Internal Auditing*.

VIII. Members and CIAs shall be prudent in the use of information acquired in the course of their duties. They shall not use confidential information for any personal gain nor in any manner which would be contrary to law or detrimental to the welfare of their organization.

IX. Members and CIAs, when reporting on the results of their work, shall reveal all material facts known to them which, if not revealed, could either distort reports of operations under review or conceal unlawful practices.

X. Members and CIAs shall continually strive for improvement in their proficiency, and in the effectiveness and quality of their service.

XI. Members and CIAs, in the practice of their profession, shall be ever mindful of their obligation to maintain the high standards of competence, morality, and dignity promulgated by the Institute. Members shall abide by the *Bylaws* and uphold the objectives of The Institute.

Adopted by Board of Directors, July 1988.

APPENDIX C
Summary of General and Specific Standards for the Professional Practice of Internal Auditing

100 **INDEPENDENCE—INTERNAL AUDITORS SHOULD BE INDE-PENDENT OF THE ACTIVITIES THEY AUDIT.**

    110 **Organizational Status**—The organizational status of the internal auditing department should be sufficient to permit the accomplishment of its audit responsibilities.

    120 **Objectivity**—Internal auditors should be objective in performing audits.

200 **PROFESSIONAL PROFICIENCY—INTERNAL AUDITS SHOULD BE PERFORMED WITH PROFICIENCY AND DUE PROFESSIONAL CARE.**

    The Internal Auditing Department

    210 **Staffing**—the internal auditing department should provide assurance that the technical proficiency and educational background of internal auditors are appropriate for the audits to be performed.

    220 **Knowledge, Skills, and Disciplines**—the internal auditing department should possess or should obtain the knowledge, skills, and disciplines needed to carry out its audit responsibilities.

    230 **Supervision**—The internal auditing department should provide assurance that internal audits are properly supervised.

    The Internal Auditor

    240 **Compliance with Standards of Conduct**—Internal auditors should comply with professional standards of conduct.

250 **Knowledge, Skills and Disciplines**—Internal auditors should possess the knowledge, skills, and disciplines essential to the performance of internal audits.

260 **Human Relations and Communications**—Internal auditors should be skilled in dealing with people and in communicating effectively.

270 **Continuing Education**—Internal auditors should maintain their technical competence through continuing education.

280 **Due Professional Care**—Internal auditors should exercise due professional care in performing internal audits.

300 **SCOPE OF WORK**—THE SCOPE OF THE INTERNAL AUDIT SHOULD ENCOMPASS THE EXAMINATION AND EVALUATION OF THE ADEQUACY AND EFFECTIVENESS OF THE ORGANIZ-ATION'S SYSTEM OF INTERNAL CONTROL AND THE QUALITY OF PERFORMANCE IN CARRYING OUT ASSIGNED RESPONSI-BILITIES.

310 **Reliability and Integrity of Information**—Internal auditors should review the reliability and integrity of financial and operating information and the means used to identify, measure, classify, and report such information.

320 **Compliance with Policies, Plans, Procedures, Laws, and Regulations**—Internal auditors should review the systems established to ensure compliance with those policies, plans, procedures, laws, and regulations which could have a significant impact on operations and reports and should determine whether the organization is in compliance.

330 **Safeguarding of Assets**—Internal auditors should review the means of safeguarding assets and, as appropriate, verify the existence of such assets.

340 **Economical and Efficient Use of Resources**—Internal auditors should appraise the economy and efficiency with which resources are employed.

350 **Accomplishment of Established Objectives and Goals for Operations or Programs**—Internal auditors should review operations or pro-grammes to ascertain whether results are consistent with established objectives and goals and whether the operations or programmes are being carried out as planned.

400 **PERFORMANCE OF AUDIT WORK**—AUDIT WORK SHOULD INCLUDE PLANNING THE AUDIT, EXAMINING AND EVALU-ATING INFORMATION, COMMUNICATING RESULTS, AND FOL-LOWING UP.

410 **Planning the Audit**—Internal auditors should plan each audit.

420 **Examining and Evaluating Information**—Internal auditors should collect, analyze, interpret, and document information to support audit results.

430 **Communicating Results**—Internal auditors should report the results of their audit work.

440 **Following Up**—Internal auditors should follow up to ascertain that appropriate action is taken on reported audit findings.

500 **MANAGEMENT OF THE INTERNAL AUDITING DEPARTMENT— THE CHIEF INTERNAL AUDITOR SHOULD PROPERLY MANAGE THE INTERNAL AUDITING DEPARTMENT.**

510 **Purpose, Authority, and Responsibility**—The chief internal auditor should have a statement of purpose, authority, and responsibility for the internal auditing department.

520 **Planning**—The chief internal auditor should establish plans to carry out the responsibilities of the internal auditing department.

530 **Policies and Procedures**—The chief internal auditor should provide written policies and procedures to guide the audit staff.

540 **Personnel Management and Development**—The chief internal auditor should establish a program for selecting and developing the staff of the internal auditing department.

550 **External Auditors**—The chief internal auditor should ensure that internal and external audit efforts are properly co-ordinated.

560 **Quality Assurance**—The chief internal auditor should establish and maintain a quality assurance programme to evaluate the operations of the internal auditing department.

Index

Printed and bound by CPI Group (UK) Ltd, Croydon, CR0 4YY

23/04/2025

14660955-0002